CURRICULUM DEVELOPMENT

PROBLEMS, PROCESSES, AND PROGRESS

by

Glenys G. Unruh

and

Adolph Unruh

•

McCutchan Publishing Corporation
2526 Grove Street
Berkeley, California 94704

ISBN 0-8211-2003-4
Library of Congress Catalog Card Number 82-62032

Printed in the United States of America

Cover design by Terry Down, Griffin Graphics
Typesetting composition by Delmas

Contents

Preface

Ideas that are potentially powerful for progress in curriculum development and instruction are woven into the major themes of this book. It provides frameworks for curriculum development that will aid in analysis, revision and growth, will respond to new knowledge, and will relate complex decisions to one another and to forces acting on the schools.

Problems are recognized as opportunities for positive action. *Processes* essential to effective curriculum planning are discussed throughout the book. *Progress* in various related areas of research and action are reviewed and stressed as resources for advancement and quality.

Curriculum Development: Problems, Processes, and Progress can be contrasted to Glenys Unruh's prior book, *Responsive Curriculum Development: Theory and Action.* This new book includes several more areas of increasing significance in curriculum development than were apparent a few years ago. It explores a wider range of the aspects of curriculum development than are usually included in a single book by contemporary authors in the field.

This book and the prior one both emphasize the historical background of curriculum development for insights into present issues and the need for a theoretical base to avoid shallow approaches devised to react to passing pressures. While the previous book devoted more space to the elements of a theory, this book presents theory construction in one chapter as an example that can be adapted and applied in diverse local situations.

Curriculum Development: Problems, Processes, and Progress is aimed at contemporary circumstances and future projections. It provides numerous examples and alternatives for action that can inspire further ideas and adaptations, not just the abstractions that so often dominate curriculum writing. In addition to historical perspectives and theoretical assumptions, new features include the many ramifications of leadership, new roles for principals, the planning process, proposals of new reformers, the politics of curriculum decision making, extensive examples of goal setting ranging from classroom to global levels, as well as effective ways to assess needs beyond test scores. A distinct feature is the chapter on status, trends, and recommendations in six major subject fields. This area is often ignored in curriculum development books, although it is certainly the bottom line for planners and implementers. Problems in curriculum implementation are recognized and in-service education is discussed in practical terms.

We include a section on supervision, another area not usually discussed in curriculum books, along with clarification of its role. Up-to-date professional thinking and methodologies for evaluation of programs and curriculum are thoroughly presented. Rapid technological and societal changes and their effects on schooling and curriculum development are brought to the attention of planners as inevitable challenges and problems to be faced in the immediate and foreseeable future.

This book is directed to students engaged in the professional study of curriculum development, university professors, and curriculum leaders in the elementary and secondary schools. The text recognizes that the authority and responsibility for curriculum leadership in the public schools has shifted to persons not usually trained for it: principals and other administrators. The book's appeal is to serious professional educators who wish to examine a comprehensive treatment of the problems, issues, and fundamental considerations underlying different points of view, to those who want to formulate their own thoughtful conception of the curriculum field. It is a consistent approach to the many facets of curriculum development. Historic perspectives are included throughout to assist in preventing repetition of past mistakes and can point up past achievements, which can in turn reveal solutions to current problems and suggest positive actions for the future. Included are extensive references for further investigations of each major topic.

Curriculum is defined as a plan concerned with the purpose and content of what is to be learned. It anticipates the results of instruction. Instruction is the process of teaching, delivering the curriculum, and providing learning environments for students. Curriculum development is a planning process of assessing needs, identifying goals and objectives, preparing for instruction, and meeting the cultural, social, and personal requirements that the curriculum is to serve. Evaluation leads to constant revision and improvement of the curriculum. Curriculum planning must analyze the likely consequences of various approaches before instruction takes place. It must be a process of developing an overarching mission based on values; developing policies; setting goals, objectives, and standards; choosing learning activities; assuring proper implementation; and being ready when things go wrong to revise and renew. In times of austerity—scarceness of money, personnel, or time—objectives must be reconciled with limited resources.

Our emphasis throughout the book is on the network of decisions that must be made in curriculum planning, the hard choices among goals and values, and the influences of a complicated society that must be faced in curriculum development. New demands on leadership are cited and the qualities of effective leadership are stressed.

Chapter One, "Meeting Curriculum Issues," addresses the imperative need to meet current concerns about the school's curriculum with constructive action for improvement. The issues of today are shown in the light of a historical perspective that encompasses recurring movements and reforms in curriculum development. We advocate a comprehensive view of the curriculum to avoid the piecemeal approaches that continue to characterize some of the suggested reforms. New priorities for curriculum development are outlined, including excellence, competence, equity, diversity, and the ethics of democracy and citizenship.

Chapter Two, "Effective Leadership," is a strong statement about the status of educational leadership and the urgent need for effective leaders, particularly in curriculum and instruction. Signs of ill feelings towards the schools are evident in the public press, and criticisms are aimed at many levels of education. The principal has been identified as the key to instructional improvement at the school level, but leaders are needed at all levels who can articulate a sense of direction for schooling and who have skills for working with the public in collaborative ways to achieve school improvement. We discuss styles of leadership, describe effective schools, and detail planning skills. The qualities and characteristics of effective leaders in curriculum and instruction are emphasized.

Chapter Three, "Influences on Curriculum Decisions," illuminates the political context in which important educational decisions are made and describes conflict-versus-consensus models. The impact of legislation and court decisions on curriculum development are placed into perspective, and examples of mandated changes are given. We discuss their potential effects on curriculum, both positive and negative, as well. The possible impact of pressures from extremist groups, book censors, and other special interests is described. Community power and the varied viewpoints of the school's many constituents are discussed as are the appropriate roles of lay citizens, boards of education, administrators, curriculum specialists, teachers, and students as participants in curriculum development. We review the proposals of the new reform advocates.

Chapter Four, "Theoretical Assumptions," emphasizes the necessity for curriculum development to be built from a theoretical base that has been carefully conceptualized and interpreted to all those affected so that piecemeal reforms, curriculum imbalance, and short-lived innovations will be avoided. The interactions of the elements that comprise the total curriculum are set forth. Principles from various conceptions of the curriculum are presented with interpretations of conflicting points of view. In this chapter, a matrix is provided with theoretical propositions placed on axes of determinants and results, which provide a means for studying relationships at each intersection and at combinations of intersections. These form constructs that provide possibilities for generating new knowledge, hypotheses, and suggestions for curriculum improvement. With new insights, the curriculum developer can make better choices among alternatives in building a framework of basic assumptions for curriculum to meet the needs of a particular school, school district, or other organizational unit.

Chapter Five, "Goals and Objectives," underscores the power of purpose in curriculum development. Purpose translates into a plan for action based on estimated consequences; it sets directions and provides the driving force towards accomplishment. The place of each level of purpose—mission statement, general goals, and specific objectives—is clarified. The involvement of those affected by the curriculum in determining its goals and to what degree is discussed, as is the importance of familiarity with the local setting and the needs and desires of the people. Many examples of goal statements are given, both classic and contemporary, for use by local school planners in seeking reasonable expectations. The interrelationships of major goals are diagrammed and interpreted. We provide samples of classroom level objectives for several grades.

Chapter Six, "Assessing the Needs," views both educational and psychological needs as essential considerations in the curriculum planning process. The development of the need concept over several decades is reviewed, including its recent emphasis in federal reform efforts for curriculum improvement. Need is seen as a discrepancy between present circumstances and desired or ideal circumstances. The place of needs assessment in the curriculum development cycle is clarified, and methodologies including the Delphi method are described. Advantages and disadvantages of various procedures are reviewed. Asking the right questions is seen as an important part of the process, as are certain cautions to be observed. Several examples of needs assessments are provided. We identify the significance of human needs and powers and discuss emerging trends.

Chapter Seven, "Examining the Content Areas," reviews six major subject areas of the curriculum: English and its branches of reading, writing, spelling, and listening; mathematics; science; social studies;

foreign languages; and the arts. Current status, issues, concerns, trends, and recommendations for strengthening each subject field are presented. The basics are discussed in perspective as part of a total curriculum. Inquiry methods, cognition, and motivation of students are given importance. Information on types of materials, possibilities of overreliance on textbooks, and suggestions for the classroom setting are included.

Chapter Eight, "Implementing Curriculum Plans," is directed towards the reality that curriculum lacks meaning until teachers and students bring it to life in the classroom. Several major surveys have found that the curriculum reforms of the past twenty years or so have failed to be implemented in the classroom to a large extent. Consequently, research centers and professional organizations have studied the problems of curriculum implementation in depth. This chapter reviews their findings. The complex nature of curriculum implementation is revealed in the analysis of factors affecting the process, levels or degrees of use, and the many dimensions of implementation that reach beyond just familiarity with the subject matter. Success in implementation is broken down into its components, and applications in the classroom are described. The qualities needed by the supervisor in the process of implementation are highlighted, as are examples of various supervisory approaches.

Chapter Nine, "Curriculum Evaluation," explores the changing concepts of program evaluation. As pressures for improvement built up during the recent federal reform era, more and more attention was given to evaluation of the curriculum, including both qualitative and quantitative data. The significance of evaluation in curriculum development and the relationships between decision making and evaluation are emphasized. A distinction is made between research studies and evaluation studies and between formative and summative evaluation. The contextual domains of curriculum evaluation are identified. Models and procedures are described in some detail including: goal attainment models and ways of measuring; judgmental models, such as accountability and adversary models; decision-facilitative models, including CIPP, CSE, discrepancy, and accreditation. We also discuss descriptive case studies; responsive, goal-free, and artistic models; and various assessments such as those at the local level of multicultural curricula or the hidden curriculum and those of national and international significance. Standards for program evaluation as determined by a joint committee of notable educators are recognized, and criteria are arranged in a checklist.

Chapter Ten, "Future Awareness," speaks to the rapid rate of change in society which demands that curriculum developers become aware of the necessity to study new conditions and trends in technological, social, economic, and environmental developments and their potential effects on curriculum and instruction. We review several major studies that vividly describe predictable problems with tremendous potential either for despair or the zest of greater and greater challenges. The advent of a new age of technology opens vast possibilities for advancement in many areas including new approaches to curriculum and instruction. The forecasts, awesome in their capacity for either the decline or progress of civilization, point up the need for awareness and constructive planning. We present a range of ideas for exploring the future in the classroom.

1

Meeting Curriculum Issues

Issues centering around the school curriculum are featured almost daily in the news media, where constant information is provided on the perceived shortcomings of the public schools. Curriculum leaders frequently feel that they are under seige, and the responses of curriculum specialists are usually reactive, taken in the interests of immediacy. Consequently they achieve only short-lived "solutions," when they work at all.

"Reforms" of some sort then sweep over the schools, and observers have noted that curriculum development is like a swinging pendulum or a cycle-recycle process. This shallow view of curriculum development can largely be attributed to the ahistorical posture of many curriculum specialists. Few doctoral programs in curriculum require a study of the history of the field; thus, succeeding generations, knowing little of past experiences and mistakes, tend to repeat them. Herbert Kliebard has observed:

Generally speaking, the foremost scholars in other fields continually engage in a kind of dialogue with their ancestral counterparts—rejecting, revising, or refining the early formulations and concepts. No such cumulative approach to the content of the curriculum field has yet emerged, and this has had the telling effect on the relative permanence of curriculum thinking. Issues tend to rise *de novo*, usually in the form of a bandwagon and then quickly disappear in a cloud of dust. Sometimes these issues have their counterparts in an earlier period, but this is rarely recognized. The field in general is characterized by an uncritical propensity for novelty and change rather than funded knowledge or dialogue across generations (1975, p. 41).

Furthermore educators have not recognized or have not publicized data-based research on the successes of the public schools. Harold Hodgkinson (1979) has pointed out that American public schools are now preparing

1

half of the school population for college as well as they once did for just the top 10 percent. Research has shown that knowledge is presently available in what correlates with learning. Data gathered over several years reveal the positive impact of early education, even *in utero* influences. Primary children are reading better. The impact on earning capacity of blacks can be directly attributed to improvements in quality education and increased length of schooling. Access to college has increased markedly in the past decade for women and minorities. Nevertheless, much remains to be done. Tests show needs in reading comprehension, writing, mathematical reasoning, and other higher cognitive skills. Meanwhile, the voices of critics seem to predominate.

Today, as in the past, critics seem to focus on an element or elements they perceive to be missing in the curriculum and instructional processes. Most frequently they dwell on the shoulds or should nots, without providing much assistance to curriculum developers on the whys (comprehensive theoretical concepts) or the hows (ways to achieve desired results in curriculum development).

Historical accounts of public education reaching back into the nineteenth century reveal successive polarizations of viewpoints, limited approaches to curriculum development, and periodic upsurges of dissatisfaction with school offerings. A pattern of recurring themes in the proposals for reform over a hundred-year period in America has emerged, according to a study by Thomas James and David Tyack (1983). In conservative times—the 1890s, 1950s, and 1980s, for example—the focus has typically been on more attention to academics, the basics, discipline, curriculum coherence, and the special needs of talented students. In more liberal times—the 1930s, 1960s, and early 1970s—attention transferred to social issues, personal development, and other nonacademic functions of schooling.

Pressures from influential sources that constantly shift from one concern to another have resulted in an apparent lack of rigorous, systematic thinking about curriculum development and its theoretical bases. Without a comprehensive theory of curriculum development and effective means of implementation, society-centered, subject-centered, efficiency-centered, and other limited approaches will continue to compete with each other as exclusive routes to curriculum planning.

CONTEMPORARY DISSATISFACTIONS

Active critics and reformers perceive a variety of faults in the contemporary educational scene. The leading edge of concern is for excellence, quality, stiffer requirements for graduation, higher standards for curriculum and instruction, and the teaching of thinking, reasoning, and analytical skills. More efforts to attract and keep talented teachers have been demanded, and numerous state and national groups began studies of the schools in the early 1980s. (The reforms promoted by these groups are described in Chapter Three.)

A recent Gallup Poll (1983) provides ample evidence that the American people consider education to be very important, particularly for their own children, and place a high value on public education. However, the poll continues to find lack of discipline a major concern about public schools. Some observers attribute discipline problems to the child-centered orientations of educators that can be traced back to the ideas of Comenius, Rousseau, and Pestalozzi or to mininterpretations of John Dewey's philosophy (1916). Dewey, however, in his later years sharply criticized educators who disregarded organized subject matter in favor of mere activity on the part of students (1949).

J.T. Sewall (1981) places the blame for undisciplined students on the "open education" concepts of the late 1960s and early 1970s. These were educational innovations designed for self-actualization of the student and for free expression of student rights and interests. During that era, teachers and other adults seemed to be filled with doubts about themselves as authority figures. Thus, according to Sewall, the child is free today; modernism has emancipated him and her from restrictive puritanical ethics. "It has rendered virtually all aspects of juvenile life, including effort, voluntary. It has left many young people dangerously isolated, with little control over themselves or allegiance to their communities." He observes that underachievement has become a student "right," and since fewer adults are willing to intervene in the affairs of the young, marginal students can readily slide toward apathy or delinquency. Students seem to be divided into strivers and nonstrivers, he said, with the gap between widening.

Right-wing organizations have attacked public education in recent years with accusations that schools teach atheism and that textbooks should be narrowly censored (see Chapter Three). The stresses of social and economic problems in today's society make for the predictable growth of organizations seeking simplistic answers. A major campaign against public schools by ultraconservative groups, however, could imperil the future of democracy in the classroom, pluralism in society, and the maintenance of inquiry in public education.

Others have been disillusioned with the individualizing techniques advocated by reorganizers of the 1970s who sought to solve educational problems through various organizational innovations such as team teaching, multimedia emphasis, and unique school designs known as pods or open space schools. A three-year study by the American Institutes for Research found that these educational innovations did not demonstrate a substantially positive impact on achievement. Indeed, the degree of organizational innovation designed for individualization was negatively related to growth in reading and arithmetic as measured by standardized achievement tests (1977).

Coming from a different direction are critics from among the curriculum theorists who are known as reconceptualists. In their view, schooling is dominated by a technological or technocratic mode of thought that is inadequate for dealing with the social, moral, and political complexities of educational concerns. The technocratic mode, in its emphasis on scientific management and preconceived objectives, can provide an instrument of social control that perpetuates inequities, as discussed by Michael Apple (1974, p. 6).

Some of the leading writers in the area are James Macdonald, William Pinar, Dwayne Huebner, Michael Apple, and Maxine Greene. The work of these and others is reviewed and critiqued by Karen Mazza (1982), who also provides extensive references for those who would investigate reconceptualization in depth. She notes that this approach is both an attempt to renew curriculum theory and to raise questions about the present state of schooling. She identifies as the greatest strengths of reconceptual inquiry its questioning of mainstream curriculum theory, challenging taken-for-granted patterns of instruction, and stimulating imagination of new possibilities. In addition to exposing the influence of technocratic models on the curriculum field, the reconceptualists have challenged the dominance of behavioral objectives and predetermined learnings as central categories in curriculum, raised the issue of valuing educational experience in other ways, and focused attention on the dehumanizing effects of schooling on the development of the self. The strongest theme is that of sociopolitical critique. Many of the reconceptualist writers have stressed the importance of developing alternative theories and practices that are guided by values of social justice. Mazza notes that missing from their inquiry are designs and practices that can contribute to the desired transformation of the curriculum field and schooling. The relationship of reconceptual theory to practice has not yet been set forth. Nevertheless, they have raised questions of quality that can contribute to more effective curriculum planning. (Reconceptualization is discussed in Chapter Four in connection with other notions of the curriculum.)

Above all, schools have taken a beating from the critics in the battle for literacy. Highly publicized reports of declining scores on the College Boards and other standardized tests sounded the alarm. High schools have been charged with graduating many functionally illiterate students, and from industry and labor pressed for trade, commercial, and agricultural instruction in the schools. Public school officials began to be more aware of immigrant education problems, and political, economic, and social changes foreshadowed new demands on the schools.

Among the efforts to "Americanize" immigrants was the settlement house idea, an attempt to bring about social improvement through family and community education, which was increasingly foisted on the schools. This meant that schools would be ultimately concerned with the total lives of individuals rather than restrictively or even primarily with things intellectual. This notion was expressed later in the "whole child" concept.

Democracy and Education

In the early 1900s, political reformers also looked to the schools. Problems of exploitation of resources and labor for personal gain, unequal distribution of wealth, personal misery brought about by industrialization, and corruption in politics all came in for sharp criticism by crusading humanitarians, resulting in reform legislation. The exhortations of Jane Addams, Jacob Riis, William Jennings Bryan, and Theodore Roosevelt spurred the concept of progressivism in social and political life, and progressivism in education as well emerged.

Francis W. Parker had proclaimed in 1894 the theme of democracy in education: that every school should be an embryonic democracy protecting children's rights, preserving their freedoms, and building on their natural gifts. John Dewey's classic, *Democracy and Education*, appeared in 1916. Dewey carefully analyzed the fundamental conditions of democracy and sought educational arrangements to nurture and support these conditions.

Harry Broudy's review of the status of democratic processes in education (1971) notes that Dewey cast the problem of democracy in education in fundamental terms and provided an internally consistent set of conceptual tools for dealing with it. The Dewey concept emphasized shareability—that the sense of community is constantly deepened by the sharing of pooled resources and communication that applies methods of intelligence to new problems. Dewey elevated the scientific method to humanistic levels and spelled out steps in thinking and problem solving. He viewed group inquiry as suited to a range of abilities and as the answer to elitism in education.

Although educators viewed the Dewey concept as desirable, they disagreed on how to carry it out in practice. To some it meant a school without structure or predetermined objectives and content. Harold Rugg viewed such superficial interpretations with alarm in 1926 and urged educators to realize that curriculum making is a complex, highly specialized task that must be the cooperative endeavor of many minds.

Despite its varied interpretations, the Dewey concept brought an upsurge of curriculum development in the 1920s and 1930s that moved away from traditional classicism and toward emphasis on the needs of the individual and of society.

New currents of educational thought were reflected in the report, *Cardinal Principles of Secondary Education*, released in 1918 by the Commission on the Reorganization of Secondary Education, which had been appointed by the National Education Association five years earlier. The report manifested a shift in the conception of the high school from an institution for the few to an institution for all. It favored the comprehensive high school, embracing both vocational and academic curricula in one unified organization. Seven primary educational objectives were recommended as central aims of education at the elementary, secondary, and higher education levels. These were: health, command of fundamental processes, worthy home membership, vocation, citizenship, worthy use of leisure, and ethical character. The specific task of the secondary school was to realize these objectives in the lives of *all* children from about twelve to eighteen years of age. For the next forty years or so the cardinal principles provided the orientation and terminology for the development of secondary education.

Progressive Education

The Progressive Education Association, formed in 1919, was another significant influence on curriculum development. What had been a loosely formed movement against the mental discipline approach and formalism in education became an organized movement. Through the decade of the 1920s, the association emphasized progressivism in *elementary* education; in the 1930s, it shifted to secondary education with its sponsorship of an eight-year study by the Commission on the Relation of School and College.

Conflicting schools of thought within the Progressive Education Association led to internal strife. Lawrence Cremin (1962) identified these as scientism, sentimentalism, and radicalism. The trend of scientism is illustrated by those who took the testing and measurement boom stimulated by Edward L. Thorndike's mental testing during the military recruitment drives of World War I and applied it to the labeling of children. In many schools, this led to prejudgment of children and assignment to curriculum tracks for their supposed levels in life. Sentimentalism encompassed the rhetoric of child-centered curricula, which led to some bizarre applications in a few schools, such as planless classes engaged in chaotic self-expression. Radicalism included the social reform movement led by George Counts (1952), who charged the schools with responsibility for changing the social order. Counts called for recognition of a world society and for bringing progressive education to all social classes, not just the upper middle class.

William Van Til (1974) in an essay originally published in 1962, reminds us that basic questions raised by the leaders of the progressive education movement of the 1920s and 1930s—John Dewey, William Heard Kilpatrick, George Counts, and Boyd H. Bode—have not yet been answered: What are the aims of education? On what foundations should the curriculum be built? Given such aims and foundations, what should the schools teach?

Kilpatrick's mark on curriculum development was his faith in the potential of the learner when that potential is cultivated by skillful and sensitive teachers. Bode saw the method of intelligence in human affairs to be the road out of the value confusion between democratic and authoritarian influences. Each of these—Bode, Counts, and Kilpatrick—touched on a part of the whole. Dewey visualized reconciliation of the individual, society, and philosopical foundations, but he did not achieve translation of his ideas into a new curriculum.

Hilda Taba (1962), too, recognized the conflicts within the progressive education movement and the opposition from without, but she emphasized that the underlying concepts and the experimentation and research of the day contained the essential elements of a renaissance in a theory of curriculum building. Unfortunately this did not come about; however, several important principles began to emerge.

In a review of progress in curriculum development Robert Schaefer (1971) identifies elements of curricular and pedagogical theory on which there was relative consensus by the 1920s. These are:

1. Education must take account of the developmental needs of children.
2. Learning cannot be externally imposed but rather must involve activity of the mind of the learner.
3. Knowledge is gained through participation in social life.
4. Curricular decisions may be improved by application of the scientific method.
5. Curriculum and instruction must take account of individual differences in learners.
6. Curriculum and instruction must take account of the needs of society.
7. Schools in a democracy should maximize development of the individual.

The shortcomings of the progressive education movement are also identified by Schaefer (1971). He sees the ultimate failure of the work of the Progressive Education Association (which terminated in 1955) as its failure to comprehend the fundamental forces that move American education and to involve appropriate groups in decision making and curriculum planning. Lay power to sustain the movement was missing. The movement centered in the upper middle class and seemed to ignore the great transformation of society that was taking place because of the rise of industrialism. Fewer and fewer persons like Jacob Riis, Jane Addams, Woodrow Wilson, and Theodore Roosevelt concerned themselves with educational reform, as educators isolated themselves from community and culture.

The field of education also became isolated from the university as a whole. Teachers' colleges and schools of education came into control of curriculum planning, and the split between "scholars" and "educationists" began. The experimental schools of the 1920s and 1930s were not conceived as laboratories in inquiry but as prescriptive exemplars. Teachers did not become students of society, of the child, or of curriculum. There was little or no attempt to develop or evaluate theories of curriculum. The exhilaration of the revolt from formalism brought a reaction of zeal and enthusiasm on the part of teachers rather than disciplined inquiry and testing of hypotheses. At the same time, the entire responsibility to learn how to cope with all conditions seemed to be placed on the teacher in the classroom. No supportive technology was offered by the universities for the teacher's use in the workaday world.

Nevertheless, concepts from the progressive education movement can be found in practice in the 1980s. And the movement produced a study that continues to provoke questions and stimulate thinking about curriculum and evaluation.

The Eight Year Study

Significant to the field of curriculum development is the Eight Year Study, a longitudinal study covering the period from 1932 to 1940 (Aiken 1942). Sponsored by the Commission on the Relation of School and College of the Progressive Education Association, the study was designed to explore possibilities for allowing secondary schools freedom to attempt fundamental reconstruction. Thirty public and private high schools were invited to participate, and more than three hundred colleges and universities agreed to allow these schools to ignore the usual college entrance requirements. Each school planned its own program within general frameworks that were variously designated "broad fields," "problem approach," "experience curriculum," and similar terms. General purposes of the study were to achieve greater mastery and continuity of learning, clearer understanding of the problems of civilization, increased social responsibility, release of creative energies, greater freedom for students and teachers, and greater emphasis on guidance and counseling. Wilford M. Aiken, chairman of the commission, wrote in 1942, "We are trying to develop students who regard education as an enduring quest for meanings rather than credit accumulation."

Evaluation of the Eight Year Study was done under the direction of Ralph W. Tyler of the University of Chicago. The evaluation procedure was to match each of 1,475 graduates of the experimental schools who entered college with graduates of other secondary schools who were also in college. The pairs were matched for similarities in socioeconomic background, aptitude, interests, age, race, sex, and other variables. Uncontrolled variables included teacher competence and financial expenditures of the schools. Results of the study showed that graduates of the experimental schools attained higher levels of performance in several important areas, including problem-solving, intellectual curiosity and drive, and resourcefulness in meeting new situations. Only a slightly higher total grade average was achieved by the experimental group, but it had higher grade averages in all subject fields except foreign languages. Aiken's general conclusion was that success in college was not predicated on completion of traditional units of college preparatory subjects.

Tyler has identified some conclusions of the Eight Year Study that are related to curriculum development (1971, pp. 42–43):

1. Although a number of state and regional studies drew upon the experience of the Eight Year Study and developed curriculum materials, units, and ideas, teachers and students made little use of the products of commissions unless they were deeply involved themselves in developing, modifying, and trying out curriculum plans.
2. Summer workshops, in which teachers and consultants worked together in drawing upon materials developed by distant commissions, enabled teachers to adapt and use units built by others.
3. Pupil-teacher planning in the summer workshops was found to be a useful means of developing and selecting learning activities consonant with the purposes and interests of the students and at the same time devising learning experiences appropriate for the larger educational objectives.
4. The importance of evaluation as an essential part of curriculum making was established. As new courses were formed and resource units developed, the evaluation staff of the Eight Year Study was helping teachers and specialists clarify their objectives, define them in terms of behavior, and identify situations in which students' behavior could be appraised.

progressive educators and life-adjustment curricula had fooled the American people into thinking that all was well with the schools. American social hysteria increased, and zeal mounted for increasing the academic rigor of the separate subject fields.

Inspired by fears for national defense, the federal government and private foundations poured funds into "curriculum reform" projects. From initial efforts in mathematics and science, the reform movement spread into other subject fields. Curricular redesign in the 1950s was essentially directed at the elite students—college-bound youngsters whose ambitious parents and teachers were most likely to be found in the resource-rich suburban communities.

Again, a single principle was the basis for curriculum development. The work of Jerome Bruner (1960) and others emphasized the "structure of the disciplines" as a basis for curriculum design. Bruner called attention to the general usefulness of structure within a discipline as an organizing principle, but he did not set forth a comprehensive curriculum development theory. Hilda Taba (1962) noted that the either-or practice still prevailed and that while in the 1930s the cry was for attention to the child, in the 1950s the battle was to reintroduce disciplined content, with the problem of balance still unresolved.

James Macdonald (1971) observed that the "curriculum reform movement" of the 1950s and 1960s was in no real sense a *movement* because its separate parts were never really related or coordinated. Rather, it was a historical accident—a combination of Sputnik, McCarthyism, interested professors, federal money, and the ambitions of commercial publishers.

Curriculum Projects

In the late 1950s and into the 1960s, large sums of money were granted by the federal government and private foundations for curriculum development projects. In 1959 the Woods Hole Conference was called, and psychologists ranging from Freudian to behaviorist in approach engaged with representatives of the various curriculum projects in an examination of the learning process, motivation, and the nature of intelligence as these related to problems of curriculum content. Bruner's 1960 report of the Woods Hole Conference, *The Process of Education*, seemed to fuse nineteenth-century subject matter emphases with elements of progressive education.

In the early 1960s, a pattern of characteristics began to emerge in curriculum projects:

1. The emphasis was on discrete academic disciplines such as biology, chemistry, physics, economics, geography, literature, and grammar.

2. Curriculum content was built around concepts, key ideas, and principles, even though in some cases these were devised after the selection of new content and not as prior direction to the selection process.
3. Modes of inquiry, inductive thinking, and ways to lead the student to discover for himself were built into the curriculum plans.
4. The projects employed a wide variety of materials, such as books, films, and laboratory equipment.

Although schools were slow to adopt the new curriculum programs in the early 1960s, there was a movement toward clarification and redefinition of the goals of education, a movement away from such limited objectives as "covering" a body of factual information, and a movement toward educating students in modes of inquiry.

Contributions of the 1960s

An important contribution of the 1960s to curriculum development was the wider collaboration of scholars and a few selected teachers in the creation of curriculum guides and materials that offered new patterns to replace mediocre approaches to curriculum development. Although curriculum committees in local school systems had been writing numerous curriculum guides, these were for the most part outlines of content and activities lifted from several textbooks. The textbook publishers in turn had customarily collected curriculum guides and published more textbooks, setting up a cycle of limited content and ideas. Collaborative efforts in the 1960s led to wider involvement by many groups in curriculum making during the 1970s.

The stress on "inquiry" in the curriculum developments of the 1960s continues to affect curriculum and instruction. Teachers feel uncomfortable if they find themselves merely "covering" a body of factual information in their instructional approaches without engaging the students in problem formulation and introducing higher thought processes.

The curriculum projects, although widely diverse in subject matter, methods, and materials, shared a common commitment to teaching students how to learn, encouraging them to acquire skills and insights as well as information, and leading them to discover ideas and arrive at general principles and concepts. Students were not expected to rediscover all knowledge but rather to learn the use of knowledge and facts for finding connections between ideas and to develop solutions to problems.

Another major contribution of the curriculum development decade was its emphasis on variety and alternatives in materials and procedures. A rich array of materials and media began to be available to curriculum developers. Pamphlets, source books, readings, and original documents began to compete with traditional textbooks. Multimedia kits, audiovisual resources, simulations, models, and nonverbal games became widely known. In the science laboratories, students approached unknowns through original experimentation rather than being confined to repetitive laboratory exercises, although both had a rightful place in maintaining the balance between the known and the unknown. Technical equipment invaded the libraries and caused a welcome upheaval in the role of the librarian.

In all, the combined effects of wider involvement in curriculum making, emphasis on inquiry and thought processes, fresh content, and growing variety in curriculum materials and resources have produced lasting gains. However, shortcomings must also be noted.

Shortcomings of the Curriculum Projects

As the new curriculum developments came, subject by subject, into the schools, there was a tendency toward separation of and competition among subject field interests. Little attention was paid to design of the curriculum as a whole.

The new curriculum developments emerged from the separate disciplines; therefore, the division of knowledge and skills into various subjects was maintained, and reading, mathematics, social studies, science, music, and art each emphasized the known fundamentals. Little attention was given to the more integrative qualities of knowledge—appreciations, understandings, and insights that are frequently, although not exclusively, triggered by interrelated and interdisciplinary approaches to learning.

During the curriculum development decade, students seemed to be the participants who were least consulted in curriculum planning, and they reacted in many cases with either extreme apathy or extreme activism. In the inner cities, a barren environment and human indifference had reduced schools to barely endurable custodial institutions. In the suburbs, more affluent students began to resent the adult pressures for college acceptance and social conformity that seemed to be blighting their growing-up years.

Preoccupation of the curriculum developers with curriculum structure and new teaching styles left them somewhat unprepared for the shock of the "crisis" that gained national attention in the late 1960s. American education seemed to have failed to respond to changing social needs.

Calls for Relevance

Belatedly, the special needs of large segments of the population attracted the attention of courts and legislators. The 1954 Supreme Court decision in

Brown v. Board of Education outlawing segregated education initiated the civil rights movement, which forced public attention on the problems of blacks and other minority groups. The mass media of the nation now turned from demanding curriculum reform in the teaching of mathematics, science, and other subjects, to a new focus on the plight of urban and rural disadvantaged children. Schools were forced to heed the urgent cry of minority citizens.

At the same time further charges of school inadequacies came from another quarter. From education's New Left came forth a flow of exciting and also disquieting publications about the nature of schooling. Kozol's *Death at an Early Age* (1967), Holt's *How Children Fail* (1964), Dennison's *Lives of Children* (1967), and others of a similar tone captured wide audiences, both lay and professional. Their concern was for relevance, individuality, freedom, autonomy, responsive environments, cultural pride, honesty, value clarification, meaningful communication, and ethical growth. Disenchanted students from affluent suburban schools joined militant blacks in challenging the curricular and instructional offerings of the schools.

Congress entered more heavily into the education arena in the 1960s, and from 1963 to 1968, enacted twenty-four major pieces of educational legislation. The new laws touched every aspect of education from preschool to postdoctoral. Funds were poured into early childhood and compensatory education, and other programs designed to reach the handicapped and disadvantaged.

Bruner (1971) looked back over the curriculum-reform movement of the early 1960s and concluded that the revisions of curriculum made then were insufficient to meet society's problems. Vietnam, urban ghettos, poverty, and racism had brought disillusionment with the idealistic vision of the American way of life. In a revolt against the establishment, Ivan Illich (1971) and others called for new forms of schooling. Bruner found that American education had entered a state of crisis. He concluded that the educational system was, in effect, a way of maintaining a class system—a group at the bottom.

That the curriculum lacked relevance for many students became a general assumption. The unresponsiveness of the schools to the changing culture, social issues, and the needs of youths was dramatized in the 1960s and early 1970s by student disruptions in numerous high schools. The implications of these student uprisings for curriculum development seemed clear. *Toward a More Relevant Curriculum,* a 1970 report of a national seminar, emphasized that the most important single change needed in the schools was development of responsiveness in curriculum. Responsiveness and relevance began to be manifested in various ways in the schools of the country.

One answer was the rise of the "free-school" movement, which entered the public school scene in the form of alternative schools in the early 1960s and grew steadily through the following decade. A survey reported in *Changing Schools* (1973) identified more than 600 alternative public schools in 1973. Various types and combinations were manifested which could be roughly classified as follows:

Open schools were elementary schools inspired by the British integrated-day concept of open education, in which learning activities were individualized and organized around interest centers within the classroom or building.

Schools-without-walls provided learning activities in nonschool facilities throughout the community such as storefronts, business establishments, museum facilities, and other locations beyond the traditional school building.

Continuation schools included inner-city street academies, dropout centers, reentry programs, evening high schools, and other arrangements for assisting students to complete a high school education who would not otherwise have done so.

Schools-within-schools included minischools and satellite schools, usually within the traditional school building. These maintained fairly strong administrative ties to their parent schools while emphasizing a more informal learning program than the traditional school offering.

Magnet schools or learning centers were organized around themes and concentrated learning resources in one location available to all students in the community. These included the arts, career education, science and technology, cultural pluralism and awareness, and other interests. Magnet schools have continued their popularity, particularly in desegregation plans for urban centers.

Advocates of the early alternatives in public education were characterized by their zeal and enthusiasm for educational reform. Some writers compared the movement favorably with the positive aspects of the progressive education movement of earlier years. Lawrence Cremin, however, noted several important differences between the progressive education movement and the alternative school movement:

What is most striking, perhaps, in any comparison of the two movements is the notoriously a-theoretical, a-historical character of the free school movement in our time. The present movement has been far less profound in the questions it has raised about the nature and character of education and in the debate it has pursued around those questions.... It has been far less willing to look to history for ideas.... Further, the movement has had immense difficulty going from protest to reform, to the kinds of detailed alternative strategies that will give us better educational programs than we now have.... Where they have failed, it seems to me, is at the point of theory: th~y have not asked the right questions insistently enough, and as a result they have tended to come up with superficial and shop-worn answers (1973, p. 3).

Cremin also spoke to the paucity of substance in the early alternative schools—those born from the humanism of the 1960s that were expressions of frustration and reactions to the irrelevant establishment, to the Vietnam war, and to the materialism of America. Many of the alternatives that were simply antiestablishment have vanished. Their organizers seemed to know what they were against but not what they were for. In their place have risen new alternatives whose goals are directed toward more substantial education. In 1981, Mary Anne Raywid found that public alternative schools had grown to more than ten thousand. Alternatives were found in 80 percent of the nation's larger school districts and also appeared in the smallest districts, according to Raywid's study, with an estimated three million youngsters enrolled in alternative programs in the United States.

The element of choice is still a powerful motivator for the establishment of new and different schools. The current magnet schools exemplify this principle. Students and teachers feel better about attending a school that they have chosen. The idea of choice in public schooling received a boost with the appearance of David Tyack's *The One Best System* (1974) as well as Mario Fantini's earlier book, *Public Schools of Choice* (1973). Today's alternatives, particularly magnet schools, are frequently organized around traditional themes such as citizenship or the basics. Magnet schools for the performing arts continue to be popular, and others emphasize mathematics and science, career exploration, Montessori methods, mass media, classical education, and business or economics. Even military academies can be found within the public school offerings.

An analysis by Barbara Case (1981) done on the success of alternative schools identified five basic factors that appear to have contributed to the survival of established alternative programs: a given program must be attractive to students and parents, have clear goals, legitimacy in the education community, a positive school climate, and have reliable sources of funding. The latter supports Fantini's contention that alternatives or magnets must become a part of the public school system if they are to survive.

In the chronology of curriculum development, however, the transition from free schools to today's magnet schools was not smooth. The earlier free-school movement not only produced the early alternatives that largely failed to survive but also is perceived to have permeated the traditional schools with permissiveness. Discipline problems and declining standardized test scores subsequently precipitated the accountability movement of the 1970s and back-to-basics slogans, mandated competency testing, and new regulations requiring excessive recording and reporting of information of the early 1980s.

ACCOUNTABILITY

Accountability as a broad societal concept is highly acceptable. Watergate inquiries, Ralph Nader's investigations on behalf of consumer interests, the work of environmentalists, attention to population growth in relation to poverty and starvation, cost accounting in the schools—all of these reflect the responsible concern of individuals and institutions for the consequences of their decisions and actions.

In the realm of education, however, "accountability" can develop into a narrow definition focused on student acquisition of basic skills in reading and arithmetic as measured by standardized tests. Carried to extremes, accountability could include the factoring of per student allocations of state funds into some kind of fixed equation with student achievement scores. The question of accountability related to money has been raised by taxpayers who want to know what they are getting for their education tax dollar.

Emphasis on curriculum accountability has also created new zeal for traditional forms of curriculum. The three Rs, calls for high standards, and homework all have received new impetus. By 1982 every state had either enacted competency-testing legislation or was considering it (Odden and Dougherty 1982). In addition, several states were contemplating competency tests for teachers. Competency testing, which grew out of the movement to assign accountability for student achievement to the schools, has become for legislators an obvious solution to the monumental task of monitoring educational policy and practice in the local schools. (See Chapter Three for discussion of the political context of curriculum development.)

Thus the accountability crusade of the 1970s, admirable though its purposes may have been at the outset, is in danger of becoming one more in a long series of narrowly interpreted approaches to curriculum development. Arthur Combs (1972) sounded an early warning about the hazards of accountability programs that focus almost exclusively on test scores for detailed behavioral objectives. A truly comprehensive approach to accountability, he said, must consider at least five major problems related to curriculum and instruction:

1. *Basic skills.* Specific, atomistic behavioral objectives can be applied successfully only to simple skills and problems for which they are appropriate and must be constantly updated. The information explosion and rapidity of change make "right" behaviors rapidly obsolete.
2. *Intelligence and holistic behavior.* Accountability must contribute maximally to intelligent behavior and problem-solving action directed toward fulfillment of the individual's and society's needs.
3. *The nature of learning and the causes of behavior.* Attention should be concentrated on the causes of behavior rather than on behavior itself. Personal meanings are the causes of behavior, and these are formed through two aspects of learning: the provision of new information or experience, and the discovery by the learner of its personal meaning.
4. *Humanistic goals of education.* Developing humane qualities, self-actualization of the individual, good citizenship, learning to care for others, and working together are all aspects of humanism for which schools must be accountable. "We can live with a bad reader," says Combs, "but a bigot is a danger to everyone."
5. *Professional accountability.* Teachers can and should be held accountable for professional behavior—being informed in subject matter, being concerned about the welfare of students, being knowledgeable about their behavior, and understanding human behavior in general. Professional educators may be held professionally responsible for the purposes they seek to carry out and the methods they use.

Accountability in a comprehensive context, as Combs has recommended, has important implications for curriculum development. Interpretations that confine accountability to the "basics" would narrow the responsibilities of curriculum leaders to an unacceptable position.

QUALITY EDUCATION

A demanding array of tasks faces the public schools. Priority is urged for quality, competence, and excellence. Schools are expected to set higher standards, offer effective instruction, recognize the implications of high technology, and meet society's needs for new skills in new fields.

The revival of public interest in education is a positive indication that schools are on the threshold of an era of new attention and possibly new resources. The mission of education as the avenue for opportunity in American democracy remains unchanged. What has changed is the awareness of new demands made on the schools. Without strong public schools to perpetuate democracy, it could die in one generation.

REFERENCES

Aiken, Wilford M. *The Story of the Eight Year Study.* New York: Harper and Row, 1942.

American Institutes for Research in the Behavioral Sciences. *Impact of Educational Innovation on Student Performance: Project Methods and Findings for Three Cohorts,* vol. 1. Arlington, Va.: ERIC Document Reproduction Service, 1977. ED 132 177. Also *Executive Summary,* ED 132 177.

Apple, Michael. "The Adequacy of Systems Management Procedures in Education and Alternatives." In *Perspectives on Management Systems Approaches in Education,* edited by Albert H. Yee. Englewood Cliffs, N.J.: Educational Technology Publications, 1973.

Bestor, Arthur. *Educational Wastelands.* Urbana, Ill: University of Illinois Press, 1953.

Broudy, Harry S. "Democratic Values and Educational Goals." In *The Curriculum: Retrospect and Prospect,* part I, pp. 113-52. Seventieth Yearbook of the National Society for the Study of Education. Chicago: University of Chicago Press, 1971.

Bruner, Jerome S. "The Process of Education Reconsidered." In *Dare to Care, Dare to Act,* edited by Robert R. Leeper, pp. 19-32. Alexandria, Va.: Association for Supervision and Curriculum Development, 1971.

Bruner, Jerome S. *The Process of Education.* Cambridge: Harvard University Press, 1960.

Case, Barbara J. "Listing Alternatives: A Lesson in Survival." *Phi Delta Kappan* 62 (April 1981): 554-57.

Changing Schools, nos. 001, 008 (1972, 1973). Newsletter published by the Educational Alternatives Project of Indiana University.

Combs, Arthur W. *Educational Accountability.* Alexandria, Va.: Association for Supervision and Curriculum Development, 1972.

Commission on Reorganization of Secondary Education. *Cardinal Principles of Secondary Education.* Washington, D.C.: National Education Association, 1918.

Counts, George S. *Education and American Civilization.* New York: Bureau of Publications, Teachers College, Columbia University, 1952.

Cremin, Lawrence A. "The Free School Movement: A Perspective." *Notes on Education,* October 1973, p. 3. Newsletter published by Teachers College, Columbia University.

Cremin, Lawrence A. *The Transformation of the School.* New York: Alfred A. Knopf, 1962.

Dennison, George. *The Lives of Children.* New York: Random House, 1967.

Dewey, John. *The School and Society.* Chicago: The University of Chicago Press, 1949.

Dewey, John. *Democracy and Education.* New York: Macmillan Co., 1916.

Fantini, Mario D. *Public Schools of Choice: A Plan for the Reform of American Education*, New York: Simon & Schuster, 1973.

Gallup, George H. "The 15th Annual Gallup Poll of the Public's Attitude Toward the Public Schools." *Phi Delta Kappan* 65 (September 1983): 26-47.

Hodgkinson, Harold. "What's Right with Education." *Phi Delta Kappan* 61 (November 1979): 159-62.

Holt, John. *How Children Fail.* New York: Pitman, 1964.

Hulburd, David. *This Happened in Pasadena.* New York: Macmillan Co., 1951.

Illich, Ivan. *Deschooling Society.* New York: Harper & Row, 1971.

James, Thomas, and Tyack, David. "Learning from Past Efforts to Reform the High School." *Phi Delta Kappan* 64 (February 1983): 400-06.

Kliebard, Herbert M. "Persistent Curriculum Issues." In *Curriculum Theorizing: The Reconceptualists*, edited by William F. Pinar, p. 41. Berkeley: McCutchan, 1975.

Kozol, Jonathan, *Death at an Early Age.* Boston: Houghton Mifflin, 1967.

Macdonald, James B. "Curriculum Development in Relation to Social and Intellectual Systems." In *The Curriculum: Retrospect and Prospect*, part I, pp. 97-112. Seventieth Yearbook of the National Society for the Study of Education. Chicago: Univeristy of Chicago Press, 1971.

Mazza, Karen A. "Reconceptual Inquiry as an Alternative Mode of Curriculum Theory and Practice." *The Journal of Curriculum Theorizing* 4 (Summer 1982): 5-89.

National Assessment of Educational Progress. *Reading, Thinking, and Writing: Results from the 1979-80 National Assessment of Reading and Literature.* Denver: NAEP, 1981.

Odden, Allan, and Dougherty, Van. *State Programs of School Improvement: A 50-State Survey.* Denver: Education Commission of the States, 1982.

Parker, Francis W. *Talks on Pedagogics.* New York: John Day Co., 1894.

Porter, E.F. Jr. "Why Johnny Still Can't Add." *St. Louis Post Dispatch* November 29, 1981.

Raywid, Mary Anne. "The First Decade of Public School Alternatives." *Phi Delta Kappan* 62 (April 1981): 551-54.

Rickover, Hyman G. *Education and Freedom.* New York: E.P. Dutton, 1959.

Rugg, Harold, ed. "Curriculum-making: Points of Emphasis." In *The Foundations and Technique of Curriculum-making*, part I. Twenty-sixth Yearbook of the National Society for the Study of Education. Bloomington, Ill.: Public School Publishing, 1926.

Schaefer, Robert J. "Retrospect and Prospect." In *The Curriculum: Retrospect and Prospect*, part I, pp. 3-25. Seventieth Yearbook of the National Society for the Study of Education. Chicago: University of Chicago Press, 1971.

Sewall, G.T. "Victims of Freedom and the Failure of Adult Will." *Education Week* (November 16, 1981): 17.

Smith, Mortimer. *The Diminished Mind.* Westport, Conn.: Greenwood Press, 1954.

Taba, Hilda. *Curriculum Development: Theory and Practice.* New York: Harcourt, Brace and World, 1962.

"Toward a More Relevant Curriculum." Report of a national seminar. Published by the Institute for Development of Educational Activities, Melbourne, Fla., 1970.

Tyack, David B. *The One Best System.* Cambridge: Harvard University Press, 1974.

Tyler, Ralph W. "Curriculum Development in the Twenties and Thirties." In *The Curriculum: Retrospect and Prospect,* part I, pp. 26–44. Seventieth Yearbook of the National Society for the Study of Education. Chicago: University of Chicago Press, 1971.

U.S. Office of Education. *Life Adjustment for Every Youth.* Washington, D.C.: USOE, 1945.

Van Til, William. "Prologue: Is Progressive Education Obsolete?" In *Curriculum: Quest for Relevance,* 2d ed., edited by William Van Til, pp. 9–17. Boston: Houghton Mifflin, 1974.

Wilson, L. Craig. *The Open Access Curriculum.* Boston: Allyn and Bacon, 1971.

ADDITIONAL READINGS

Barr, Robert D. "Alternatives for the Eighties: A Second Decade of Development." *Phi Delta Kappan* 62 (April 1981) 570–73.

Callahan, Raymond. *Education and the Cult of Efficiency.* Chicago: University of Chicago Press, 1962.

The College Board. *Academic Preparation for College: What Students Need to Know and Be Able to Do.* New York: The College Board, 1983.

Cremin, Lawrence A. "The Problem of Curriculum Making: An Historical Perspective." In *What Shall the High Schools Teach?*, pp. 6–26. Yearbook of the Association for Supervision and Curriculum Development. Alexandria, Va.: ASCD, 1956.

Davis, O. L. Jr., ed. *Perspectives on Curriculum Development 1776–1976.* Yearbook of the Association for Supervision and Curriculum Development. Alexandria, Va.: ASCD, 1976.

DeNovellis, Richard L., and Lewis, Arthur J. *Schools Become Accountable.* Alexandria, Va.: Association for Supervision and Curriculum Development, 1974.

Dropkin, Stan; Full, Harold; and Schwartz, Ernest, eds. *Contemporary American Education: An Anthology of Issues, Problems, Challenges.* New York: Macmillan Co., 1965.

Eisner, Elliot W., and Vallance, Elizabeth, eds. *Conflicting Conceptions of Curriculum.* Berkeley: McCutchan, 1974.

Elam, Stanley M. "Holding the Accountability Movement Accountable." *Phi Delta Kappan* 55 (June 1974): 657, 674.

English, Fenwick W. "Contemporary Curriculum Circumstances." In *Fundamental Curriculum Decisions,* pp. 1–17. Yearbook of the Association for Supervision and Curriculum Development. Alexandria, Va.: ASCD, 1983.

Frazier, Alexander. *Open Schools for Children.* Alexandria, Va.: Association for Supervision and Curriculum Development, 1972.

Friedenberg, Edgar Z. "New Value Conflicts in American Education." *School Review* 74 (Spring 1966): 66-94.

Goodman, Paul. *Growing Up Absurd.* New York: Random House, 1966.

Gorton, Richard A. *Conflict, Controversy, and Crisis in School Administration: Issues, Cases, and Concepts for the '70s.* Dubuque, Iowa: William C. Brown, 1972.

Katz, Michael B., ed. *School Reform: Past and Present.* Boston: Little, Brown & Co., 1971.

Kimball, Solon, and McClellan, James. *Education and the New America.* New York: Random House, 1962.

Kohlberg, Lawrence. *Collected Papers on Moral Development and Moral Education,* Vol. 2. Cambridge: Center for Moral Education, Harvard University, 1975.

Kohberg, Lawrence. "Moral Education in the School: A Developmental Vice." *School Review* 74 (Spring 1966): pp. 1-30.

Krug, Edward A. *The Shaping of the American High School.* New York: Harper & Row, 1964.

Popham, W. James, and Rankin, Stuart C. "Minimum Competency Tests Spur Instructional Improvement." *Phi Delta Kappan* 62 (May 1981): 637-39.

Pullin, Diana. "Minimum Competency Testing and the Demand for Accountability." *Phi Delta Kappan* 63 (September 1981): 20-22.

Saxe, Richard W., ed. *Opening the Schools: Alternative Ways of Learning.* Berkeley: McCutchan, 1972.

Schrag, Peter. *Village School Downtown: Politics and Education.* Boston: Beacon Press, 1967.

Silberman, Charles E. *Crisis in the Classroom.* New York: Random House, 1970.

Smith, Gerald R.; Gregory, Thomas B.; and Pugh, Richard C. "Meeting Student Needs: Evidence for the Superiority of Alternative Schools." *Phi Delta Kappan* 62 (April 1981): 561-64.

Squire, James R. *A New Look at Progressive Education.* Yearbook of the Association for Supervision and Curriculum Development. Alexandria, Va.: ASCD, 1972.

Tyack, David. *Turning Points in American Educational History.* Waltham, Mass.: Blaisdell, 1967.

Unruh, Glenys G., and Alexander, William M. *Innovations in Secondary Education.* 2d ed. New York: Holt, Rinehart, and Winston, 1974.

2

Effective Leadership

Signs are abundant that effective leadership is needed for public education. Leaders—policy makers, educators, parents, and students—are needed to work creatively on all fronts. Signs of credibility loss show up at various levels and even signs of outright animosity toward schools in some quarters. Schools have experienced a bad press; citizens are told that they ought to be dissatisfied with their schools. In response to allegations that too many students cannot read, write, or add, state governments have expressed lack of confidence in local schools to manage their own affairs. They have done this by mandating standards and minimum competency requirements. Citizens have resisted tax levies for schools, and many parents have transferred their children from public to private schools.

Educators are said to disagree among themselves about goals and methods. Teachers—once viewed as dedicated persons with a missionary spirit for educating the young—now go on strike and constantly demand more money and benefits. School principals frequently appear to be unsure of their roles; they tend to resort to coping behavior or simply keep a low profile.

Leaders are needed who can come forward with serious proposals and the energy needed to reestablish confidence in public education. There is a need to articulate a sense of direction for schooling, a need to let the public know the goals and ambitions of the leaders.

The marketing skills of public school officials seem weak, and not enough publicity is given to information on what is right with education. The fact that the United States has one of the most accessible and comprehensive public school systems in the world seems to go unnoticed by the media and unappreciated by the public. The United States has steadily increased the percentage of citizens who complete high school, according to Harold Hodgkinson (1979). Thousands of communities have desegregated their schools peacefully without either violence or decline in student performance. Also, an immense body of research is now widely available for those who seek information on what correlates with learning, how to reduce learning problems, how to develop the higher cognitive functions.

The power is there, if it can be used effectively. Legislators are interested, boards are more sophisticated, large numbers of parents are ready to join educators for better schools. The knowledge and talents of people are available. In the past, public education has been able to recognize its shortcomings and do something about them; with competent leadership it can do so again.

NEW DEMANDS ON LEADERSHIP

The challenge to leaders in education is enormous. Promising examples of progress in curriculum development and instruction are often uncoordinated, and the entire society itself is unsettled, with its economic problems, new views on family life, and a trend away from traditional values. Cultural pluralism—an admirable concept—has not yet invoked a unifying principle. Schools are being pressured by many publics, each demanding a louder voice in school decisions, a greater share of the power, and special programs for its own interest group. The curriculum fluctuates in response, trying to meet many concerns.

Leaders in the schools are required to learn new ways of managing and leading, to learn to work with diversity in a changing society, and to learn how to achieve consensus out of conflict. Effective leadership skills are needed, not just a thin veneer with no real change that is called *conflict resolution, stress management,* or *coping skills.* Needed are dialogue and collaboration with other public and private educational organizations, more civic involvement in the needs of the schools, retraining and staff development, and meaningful student participation in citizenship roles. Planning skills, discussed later in this chapter, are an essential need.

New demands on leadership, summarized by Rosabeth Moss Kanter (1981), include conditions and dilemmas that many of today's school administrators seem unprepared for. Restoring faith in public education poses a particular challenge in a time when public opinion polls show an increasing distrust of all large institutions in our society. This requires educators to demonstrate by example and appropriate decisions that schools are trustworthy and are pursuing high-quality standards and values.

Leaders are also subject to greater risks because of the public's growing awareness of rights for public review and legal action, whether in the courts or in due-process proceedings in the institutions. Leaders are expected to inspire rather than order people to use their strengths and abilities. Today followers require a greater voice in decisions, and more responsive structures are needed for people to participate in at relatively low levels in the hierarchy. More time is needed, too, for gathering and analyzing data from many sources before acting. Simple answers do not fit complex situations.

All of these emerging demands must be met at a time of slow growth or decline in resources, often in the face of school closings and decisions about terminating personnel. As stated, many of today's educators were trained for growth rather than decline, and they lack the skills essential for these new tasks. Changing social conditions, emphasizes Kanter, are requiring schools to search for leadership in new and even unexpected places, to encourage the leadership talent of people at all levels of organizations including women and minorities, and to create new images of leaders—not just to rework the old stereotypes.

Minimum qualifications for today's and tomorrow's leaders, described by Allen Berger (1982), include imagination, intelligence, scholarship, compassion, honesty, courage, business and legal acumen, health, a sense of humor, and magnanimity. All these are in addition to the usual requirements for administrative competence.

INSTRUCTIONAL LEADERSHIP

Instructional leaders include superintendents and boards, both state and local, who set policy and announce the mission or broad goals of the public schools. However, this chapter is largely directed toward the leadership qualities, characteristics, and tasks that come into play at the scene of action in curriculum development and implementation. The term *instructional leaders* as used here refers to those in supervisory roles: assistant superintendents, curriculum directors and specialists, instructional supervisors, master teachers, and particularly principals.

New roles have emerged for principals and other supervisory personnel with the new demands for leadership. The traditional supervisor's role has frequently been drastically changed by the paperwork requirements of accountability mandates, or else it has been eliminated. Principals find themselves the target of numerous recent studies that have identified them as the key to school improvement. If the demonstration of leadership is a command performance, how does one meet the challenge once the administrative position has been accepted? We describe the many facets of leadership in the following sections.

MANAGERS OR LEADERS?

Pressures for a management approach to the administration of schools may have—if not well understood—reduced the image of many principals and instructional "leaders" to that of persons in pursuit of trivia. Efforts for efficiency through management by objectives, criterion-referenced testing, and emphasis on short-range planning may have limited the leader's role in some instances to paper supervision—records and reports.

Effective leadership for school improvement goes well beyond such a simplistic view. Good leadership requires a viable mix of management functions, leader behavior, and instructional leadership skills. Management functions include skills in planning, organizing, and directing. Leader behavior implies far more: motivating others toward the attainment of goals, building consensus, developing the talents of others. Instructional leadership requires both management and leadership skills in the processes of curriculum development, supervision, staff development, and evaluation.

James MacGregor Burns (1978) designates the managerial function as custodial, competent but uninspired. He views leadership as more lofty: an attempt to unite people in pursuit of higher goals. In hard times, according to Burns, managers will focus on placating separate interests, while leaders will set in motion processes for achieving fundamental changes.

Quality in leadership, according to Thomas Sergiovanni (1982), requires competence, but competence is not enough; quality means excellence. Competence and excellence are different in his analysis. Competence is a *prerequisite* to excellence and includes such skills as team management principles, contingency management tactics, shared decision-making models, and group process techniques. These are the tactical requirements shown in Figure 1 from Sergiovanni, and they refer to the necessary but short-range competencies. These are specifics that are easy to teach and learn, readily packaged for workshops, and generally accessible.

Excellence is much harder to achieve. It is the leadership component that goes beyond management and includes the strategic requirements shown in Figure 1. Excellence refers to the ability of the leader to differentiate between the strategic (long-range) and the tactical (short-range) requirements and to know how these interrelate. Excellence includes the principles that give integrity and meaning to leadership, as well as the ability to move principles into effective action. The ability to influence groups and individuals toward attaining desired goals is another component of excellence. These qualities are more intangible than competence; they go beyond competence and make the difference in the quality of leadership.

Figure 1.   Strategic and Tactical Requirements of Leadership

Tactical Requirements	Strategic Requirements
Ask, what should be done now to achieve objectives? An atomistic or task-specific view is important.	Ask, what is good in the long haul? A holistic view is important.
Develop a contingency perspective to supervision, management, and organization that permits altering arrangements to suit unique short-term circumstances.	Develop an enduring philosophy of supervision, management, and organization to ensure consistency and to give proper purpose and meaning to events.
Emphasize leadership styles that are carefully and skillfully matched to task requirements.	Emphasize leadership qualities that reflect and nurture this philosophy.
Develop operating structures, procedures, and schedules for implementing purposes.	Develop an overall plan or image that provides a frame for implementing purposes.
Decisions should be governed by stated objectives.	Decisions should be governed by purpose and philosophy.
The outputs to be achieved are important. Be concerned with structures and results.	The meaning of events to people is important. Be concerned with processes and substance.
The development and articulation of sound techniques are a key to success.	Sensitivity to and involvement of people are a key to success.
Quality control is a result of careful planning and organizing the work to be done and of continuous evaluation.	Quality control is a state of mind that comes from loyal and committed people who believe in what they are doing.
Evaluation should be short term to determine if specific objectives are being met and to enable the provision of systematic and continuous feedback.	Evaluation should be long term to more adequately determine the quality of life in the school and to assess effectiveness more holistically.

A basic corollary: Strategic requirements should never be sacrificed in favor of tactical.

From Thomas L. Sergiovanni, "Ten Principles of Quality Leadership," *Educational Leadership* 39 (February), p. 331.

LEADERSHIP STYLES

Styles of leadership are also important. If the leader is flexible and perceptive, these will vary appropriately to fit differing situations in the complex life of the instructional leader. Emerging concepts of instructional leadership advocate skillful use of both task-oriented and human-relations oriented behavior. Favorable leadership situations for instructional leaders are those in which the task is clearly structured, and relationships between the leader and the group are warm and friendly. Unfavorable situations would be those in which the task is unclear, the leader is merely permissive, and relationships are unproductive.

Leadership as a concept is easily tossed about but not easily defined, although many writers have tried. Some exploration of the concept is needed before it is applied to curriculum development. One of the most comprehensive descriptions was written by Ralph Stogdill (1974) who found several types of leadership, which indicates the difficulty of describing "a" leader.

Leadership Types

authoritative	(dominator)
persuader	(crowd arouser)
democratic	(group developer)
intellectual	(eminent person)
executive	(administrator)
representative	(spokesperson)
permissive	(laissez faire)
situational	(socially determined)

It is likely that the good leader will utilize many of these types, if not all, according to circumstances that come up (situationally determined). Experience has shown that a more democratic type of leadership behavior produces better and longer-lasting results. What this calls for is helping the members in the group to identify their objectives and needs and to relate these to the goals of the institution. Then the leader works to get the group started and motivated to move ahead with interest and drive.

This discussion can be simplified by referring to leaders as organization oriented or as people oriented. The organization-oriented leader is a driver, task minded and production oriented, so much so that people matter less than the work. This leader runs what some call a "tight ship." This leader is quick to make appointments, give directions, organize committees, and assign tasks. The structure is set up in no time at all, and personnel are quickly assigned roles and functions. The people-oriented leader wants a happy and friendly group and shows concern for feelings and sentiments. To this leader, people—the workers—are the most important consideration. The leader helps teachers attain a feeling of security in the job and satisfaction in their work. Leaders of this kind encourage staff development, and they provide personal and professional support. The former type is referred to frequently as having the ability to initiate structure—groups, procedures, and schedules. In the latter, the consideration trait is very strong.

When there is too much consideration for people, a country club climate may come into existence, and production is likely to suffer. On the other hand, when the leader is too production oriented, morale problems surface. When people are too unhappy with their work loads, one finds evidence of waste, slowing down, and absenteeism. Between these extremes there is an area in which various leadership styles can function effectively.

Figure 2 illustrates a modification of the Blake and Mouton grid (1964) for use in discussing leadership types. The vertical axis represents degrees of the trait of consideration and people orientation. The horizontal axis represents the emphasis placed on production, the trait of structure initiation. Since different people need different kinds of leadership and different situations demand differentiation, the curriculum leader will find room in the territory bounded by the angle ACD to act appropriately. It would be very difficult indeed for a leader to draw a line from A to B (high-production, high-people consideration) and hold to it.

The leadership style of a person is the behavior pattern that person presents when trying to influence others—as perceived by the others. Leadership types, as noted above, can be gauged in several ways ranging from authoritative to laissez faire, with numerous other terms used to describe variations. The most commonly used terms in educational language are the contrasting ones of authoritarian and democratic leadership. Neither is entirely adequate for the contemporary scene, according to Raphael Nystrand (1981), who reviewed several widely noted leadership theories. The authoritarian model emphasizes management links in a clearly defined chain of command, decisiveness by administrators, task orientation, and assent by subordinates. The democratic model stresses participatory decision making, informality, good human relations, and colleagueship. The authoritarian model focuses on task completion, while democratic models temper task completion targets with consideration for the feelings of those affected by the decisions. Democratic leadership is generally advocated for schools, and not only teachers but also students and community members frequently argue that they should be involved in even minor decisions. (The pros and cons of committee structure are discussed later in this chapter.)

Figure 2.   Leadership Grid

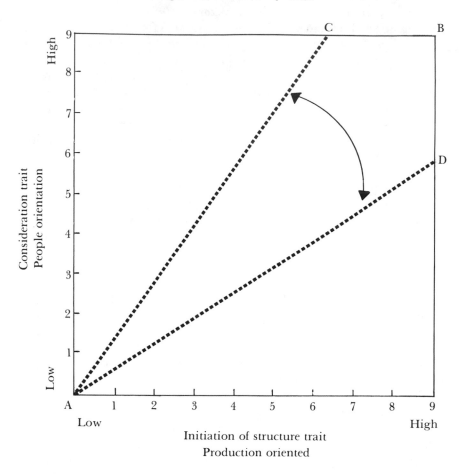

While decision-making modes could vary from one-person unilateral decisions to skillful use of consultation with others to achieve consensus and delegate tasks, the effective leader will be guided by the conditions of a particular situation. The best leadership is situationally appropriate to the problem at hand. There is no single best way for leaders to behave at all times, concludes Nystrand, but it is important for leaders to understand their subordinates' needs for affiliation, social approval, achievement, intrinsic rewards, and self-perceived ability to carry out tasks. It is also important for the leader to understand the immediate environment: the nature of the task, the primary work group, and how it all fits into the formal authority system.

Paul Hersey and Kenneth Blanchard (1982) emphasize that leaders differ in their abilities to use varied styles in different situations. Some persons seem limited to one basic style, a rigidity that could be effective only in a situation compatible with their style. Other leaders are able to modify their behavior according to the situation and the maturity of a group. For example, with a group of low-maturity (insecure or unwilling) persons, it is necessary to provide specific instructions and to closely supervise performance. For persons of moderate maturity (willing but unable), the leader needs to explain decisions and provide clarification. Persons of moderately high maturity (able but insecure) have reached the participatory level, according to Hersey and Blanchard, and the leader here should use a style that encourages idea sharing and facilitates decision making. When working with persons of high maturity levels (able, willing, and competent), the appropriate leadership style is that of delegating responsibility for decisions and implementation (pp. 154–61). (See Chapter Eight for discussion of maturity levels in staff development.)

THEORY Z AND QUALITY CIRCLES

Theory Z is a term advanced by William Ouchi (1981) to identify a Japanese management style that not only yields greater productivity but also higher degrees of worker satisfaction, loyalty, and performance. Introduced in Japan as early as 1949 by American management theorists in the form of quality-control techniques, the ideas were later expanded and implemented there as well as in several American companies. Theory Z has applications to instructional leadership. One of the chief features of Theory Z is its use of groups called *quality circles*. These units share management responsibilities with workers in order to more effectively locate and solve problems.

To understand Theory Z, it is helpful to first review Douglas McGregor's Theory X and Theory Y (1960), which have been widely quoted in school administration studies. *Theory X* is the traditional view of management as direction and control. It is based on assumptions that people characteristically dislike work and must be coerced, controlled, directed, even threatened with punishment to get them to work toward achievement of organizational objectives. This view assumes that people prefer to be told what to do and want security above all. *Theory Y* is based on far different beliefs. It assumes that people find work a source of satisfaction, that they will exercise self-direction and self-control, that they will accept responsibilities and gladly undertake activities which increase their knowledge. Theory Y also assumes that the intellectual potentialities of the average person are not fully utilized in our society.

Theory Z is primarily an application of McGregor's Theory Y at the organizational level. Four highly interdependent characteristics form the basis for Theory Z, according to James O'Hanlon (1983). These are a commitment to an overall philosophy that guides all decisions and actions; emphasis on the long-term view even though results may not show for years; trust, demonstrated through widespread sharing of information, frequent joint involvement of workers and managers on projects, delegation of responsibilities with managerial support; lifetime employment; and participative decision making, which is said to yield more creative decisions and more effective implementation.

The organizational characteristics of American school staffs do not parallel Japanese business organizations, and a number of changes would be required for school management to be conducted in a Z manner, according to O'Hanlon's assessment of differences. Such American characteristics as segmented rather than holistic concern for schools, lack of collective decision making and responsibility, short-term employment, and explicit control mechanisms might tend to hinder or inhibit implementation of Theory Z. Nonetheless O'Hanlon suggests steps for implementation, which include the chief administrator as the key to success.

Quality circles, a major feature of Theory Z, are being adapted in one form or another by an estimated four thousand organizations in the United States other than schools, observed by Larry Chase (1983). Such groups include banks, hospitals, government organizations, service agencies, and several corporations. Schools have been slower to adapt the concept, but interest is growing. Techniques, check sheets, resources, typical problems for quality circle consideration, and a discussion of the politics of implementation in schools are detailed by Chase (pp. 18–25). The circles typically consist of two to ten employees who meet regularly to examine work-related problems. They decide on the specific problems to study, launch experimental projects directed toward solutions, and follow up with suggestions to management. Plans drafted at the circle level are moved upward in the organization and modified along the way with feedback to those involved at each level. Ouchi notes that consensus building is slow, but commitment and support are strong once a decision is reached and approved at the top level.

PARTICIPATORY LEADERSHIP

Advocacy of participatory or democratic leadership is embedded in the literature of educational administration and supervision, frequently without enlightenment about its dilemmas and problems. Willis Harman

(1981) finds an inherent conflict involved in participatory management. One premise it is based on is the need persons have for opportunities to learn, for self-fulfillment, and for personal growth. The conflicting premise is that it is the function of management to contribute to the goals of the organization and to seek efficiency, organizational growth, and productivity. But what if person-centered goals are self-chosen and fulfilling in ways that have a negative impact on the achievement of the organization's goals? Then it is likely that organizational goals will take precedence over humanistic goals, and conflict is inevitable.

Other dilemmas of participatory leadership are noted by Kanter (1981). The leadership style might smack of paternalism or maternalism, which the group may resent. The manager may be fearful of losing power. Decision making requires time, a scarce commodity in many staff settings. Once they have power, group members do not always know how to use it or organize well for results. Social and emotional problems may be generated. Some members may expect too much to happen too soon; problems do not magically disappear and, indeed, new ones are likely to develop.

Participation—when properly orchestrated, however—tends to raise morale, increase the sense of involvement with meaningful activities, improve the productivity of the organization, and encourage a sense of social responsibility. Harman sees another dimension of participatory leadership beyond the logic of strategic and tactical skills. He describes this as the creative-intuitive dimension in which the individual's consciousness is in touch with the others of the group and with the best interests of the organization. Then all are working together in harmony with a deep and satisfying sense of ethical values and human goals. Harman refers to the perennial wisdom that has been around for thousands of years and suggests that today's leaders try harder to find the goodness that exists in each and all human beings.

Committees

Which matters should be referred to committees and which should be managed in the office? James Enochs asserts that one of the reasons people have lost confidence in their schools is that the people heading them are constantly asking everyone else what should be done (1981). Institutional impotence should not be substituted for leadership, he states; he suggests that leaders are appointed because they are believed to have some measure of better judgment, some uncommon and desirable abilities that others do not have. If this leader then refers important matters to committees, which subsequently try to please every interest, the results will likely move down to the lowest common denominator with little or no progress made.

Thus, active leadership implies setting standards, using judgment, and exercising quality in establishing techniques for committee work. Some types of decisions should not be unloaded on curriculum and instruction committees. Among these are the management of details, schedules, and obvious one-person decisions. Policy decisions that emanate from or eventuate in board of education actions are not in the domain of curriculum committees. Also the final decision on the mission of the school does not rest with a staff group, although committees should have input.

Leaders in curriculum development should provide training for faculty and others in group process techniques and theory. They should build the climate in which participatory leadership can flourish and the objectives for curriculum improvement can be pursued. The professional maturity of the faculty makes a difference in how much autonomy the group can manage or how much direction it needs. Deciding which problems should be referred to the faculty include the following criteria, which are guidelines for participation in decision making:

1. The decision will significantly affect the members.
2. A group decision is likely to be better.
3. The group will share in the outcome and have a responsibility for it.
4. Cooperative execution is required.
5. It is necessary to exhaust all possible alternatives.
6. The decision will need group support.
7. The impact of the decision on others (students, parents, and so on) needs to be predicted and evaluated.
8. The talents and expertise of others are needed.

Emerging Leaders

For its success, committee work frequently depends on emerging leadership. We will briefly examine contrasts between emerging leaders and status leaders. Status leaders, who have their positions by virtue of appointment, include principals, superintendents, directors, and so forth. Status leaders come into the power and authority they have by virtue of their office. Emerging leaders are often recognized by groups that elect them to chair committees or that appeal to them informally to lead the group. It is easy to see how jealousy or friction might arise between the principal (status leader) and the faculty spokesperson (emerging leader). But if the two can work together and if emerging leaders can be educated, persuaded, and involved in the activities necessary to bring off a curriculum development or implementation project, considerable energy and talent can be released.

Emerging leaders can generate many new ideas, and often inspire extraordinary productivity. Emerging leaders are sometimes critical of the status quo, which the less secure status leader may perceive as a personal attack. But it is from emerging leaders especially, though from others as well, that alternatives to proposed decisions or actions are raised which are opportunities for improving those initial choices. To silence these sources of ideas by such means as personnel transfer or something else is to move the quality of decisions back to a socially accepted norm and mediocrity. In this case, no one will take risks; teachers will settle back into old routines, and curriculum bulletins will continue to be generated but not read.

The instructional leader will find reflective leadership—the ability to develop perspective—helpful. This means taking the time to step back from the scene of action; playing the role of a disinterested observer; visualizing the committees, the leaders, the personalities at work; and evaluating the quality of one's own leadership. Being as completely detached as possible from all that goes on—what does the status leader see? What was the long-term plan, and does it still appear reasonable now? Were all the resources—human, material, and financial—made available? Was some critical factor withheld? Was all the information available, or was some retained in the files of the central office so that emerging leaders would have to seek it out? Rigorously evaluating the ongoing committee work and the leader's role may help avoid pitfalls and stymied progress.

SCHOOL EFFECTIVENESS

Prior to the mid seventies few analytical studies were done on the factors that contribute to school effectiveness. This might be attributed to disbelief that schools can make a difference, stemming from James Coleman's report, *Equality of Educational Opportunity* (1966). This document conveyed the conclusion that home environment variables were most important in explaining variance in achievement levels for all racial and regional groups and that school facilities and curriculum were the least important variables. Although the findings were intended as a spur to remediation measures, the perception took hold that principals and teachers could not do much for children who came from disadvantaged homes. In the early seventies and continuing through the decade, however, studies began to appear that counteracted the Coleman report, particularly in reference to the urban poor.

Basing their measures of success on standardized achievement test scores, study after study produced evidence that certain characteristics are present in effective schools: see, for example, Wilbur Brookover and Lawrence Lezotte (1977), George Weber (1971), and Ronald Edmonds (1979). Reviews of these and other studies of urban schools and other elementary and secondary schools by James Sweeney (1982) and Joan Shoemaker and

Hugh Fraser (1981) concluded that three consistent findings characterize effective schools: the leadership of the principal, an orderly school climate, and high expectations. It was also evident in the effective schools that there was common agreement on the mission of the school, use of instructional objectives to guide the learning activities, and evaluation used as feedback for improvement.

The Principal

That the principal is the key to an effective school is not a new concept. Ellwood P. Cubberley (1923), a highly esteemed author and pioneer in professional education, wrote, "As the principal, so the school." John Goodlad (1979), drawing from the Study of Schooling, a long-term, comprehensive, firsthand examination of public schooling in America, stated, "The principal is central to the attainment of the kind of school implied. She or he, far more than any other person, shapes and articulates the prevailing ambience and creates a sense of mission" (p. 346).

In contrasting the principals' roles in improving and declining schools, Ronald Edmonds concluded from his analysis (1979) that there was a clear difference. In the improving urban schools, the principal was more likely to be an instructional leader, more assertive as a leader, more of a disciplinarian, and someone who took responsibility for the evaluation of the achievement of basic objectives. In the declining schools, the principal appeared to be permissive, to emphasize informal relationships with teachers, and to be less interested in the evaluation of the school's effectiveness on student achievement (pp. 19–20).

Speaking to a principals' group in October 1981, Edmonds said, "Nothing will happen unless the principal presides. No program will go forward, no material will be used, no strategy will be implemented unless the principal knows, approves, and about which the principal is able to say 'this fits into our program, our purposes, our mission, and it is an integral part of our activities'" (p. 8).

Research on effective schools, summarized by James Sweeney (1982), pinpoints the behaviors a principal needs to follow if he or she is to be the instructional leader of an effective school: emphasize achievement and give high priority to activities, instruction, and materials that foster academic success; take part and accept responsibility in decision making about methods, materials, and evaluation procedures; ensure a school climate that is conducive to learning; set high expectations for the entire school and evaluate progress frequently; coordinate instructional programs for a total effect on the school's goals; and support teachers and communicate with them about goals and procedures.

A study sponsored by the Assessment Center of the National Association of Secondary School Principals identified twelve skill dimensions that most characterize successful principals. As reported by Paul Hersey, these qualities are: problem analysis, good judgment, organizational ability, decisiveness, leadership, sensitivity, stress tolerance, oral communication, written communication, a range of interests, personal motivation, and high educational values. For many principals these skills and attributes are as yet latent, awaiting development, according to Hersey (1982).

A number of principals take their cues on what is important in their districts from the central office and from minutes of the board meetings. This trait adds to the problem of curriculum development because most school boards are management oriented. Many members of boards are from the business world, and the literature circulated by the state and national school board associations is management oriented.

Curriculum development requires leadership that goes beyond management. Curriculum leaders must know how children learn, how they can be motivated to grow in their educational experiences, and how to select content that will expand knowledge. The content of the curriculum results from many hours of hard study and thought, the application of clear educational values, and a deep knowledge of the disciplines that comprise subject matter. It is not an assortment of scattered ideas. Boards of education need and want to understand curriculum matters, but not enough school administrators have been trained to help educate board members about curriculum theory, the history of curriculum development, or necessary steps to take in curriculum planning. It is possible, then, that many school administrators place curriculum matters on an emergency-only basis.

That curriculum development and the improvement of instruction have not historically rated a high priority among matters for school board consideration was borne out in a study by Jack Bronson (1975). He inspected the minutes of two nonmetropolitan school boards and two suburban school boards over a five-year period to see how often and how much discussion on curriculum and instruction he would find as entries. Curriculum and instruction ranked sixth on a ten-item list in the minutes of the suburban districts and seventh in the nonmetropolitan districts. The entries ranking first for both kinds of school districts were employment and personnel. Except in instances of serious problems, most of the personnel examples could have been managed in appropriate offices of the central administration.

But a school board's neglect of program improvement matters does not offer a valid excuse for the lack of instructional leadership by principals. Admittedly, principals cannot solve all the problems of education, but they can exemplify the changing concepts of leadership that can give the impetus to school improvement on a building-by-building basis. This requires more than just being busy. The necessity for principals to keep abreast of legal mandates, legal rights, and liabilities has caused many principals to let go unnoticed the impressive accumulation of educational research findings from the past decade.

How sixty carefully selected, efficient principals chosen from across the United States spend their time was the subject of a survey of Richard Gorton and Kenneth McIntyre (1978). Personnel concerns were most important, followed by school management, with curriculum and instruction in third place. When asked what type of in-service programs they needed, principals placed low priorities on program evaluation, curriculum development, school and community communications, teacher in-service education, and time management. Curriculum development did not rate as a need for their own retraining, in the principals' views, yet curriculum has become the focus of widespread dissatisfaction.

In a similar study by Joseph Rogus et al. (1980), only about 40 percent of junior and senior high principals of the sample surveyed felt that they already had strengths in tasks related to curriculum development: for example, providing curriculum leadership, communicating with the community on questions of school goals, and utilizing outside resources to improve curriculum. These studies and others point up a serious national need for strengthening the preparation and in-service programs for principals.

In-service training for principals has tended to dwell on personal growth or organizational development asserts James Olivero, and the training programs have overlooked areas they need the most (1982). He identifies these from a survey of California principals as:

1. School climate—the ability to analyze the relationship of school morale, climate, and policies and to actively work toward the development of a positive school climate.
2. Personnel evaluation—the ability to provide leadership in the development of teaching performance standards and to evaluate teaching performance.
3. Communications—the ability to establish an effective two-way communication system using a variety of procedures that allow for clarification and facilitation of communication among staff members, students, community members, and district personnel.
4. Supervision—the ability to use an effective planning model for developing and implementing curriculum designed to improve and maintain a high quality instructional program.

These topics and others related to leadership are treated in more depth in other sections of this volume.

The school principal will have to give serious attention to professional growth for improving leadership skills in curriculum and instruction. This need can readily be seen from sociopolitical, economic, and educational trends that are clearly discernible. There is mounting pressure for greater excellence and higher quality in school programs. At the same time, declining enrollments and financial problems are causing cuts in curriculum support staff and faculty. More and more districts and their committees are looking to principals and other school administrators for curriculum leadership, an invigorating and positive school climate, higher expectations, and skill in planning.

School Climate

An effective school climate is an educational environment—school or classroom—that is permeated by an atmosphere of learning. Curriculum materials, classroom structures, faculty lounge conversations, everything going on in the school contributes to purposeful activity.

Arthur Combs et al. made these observations of a desirable school climate. The goals are clearly defined, and the structure is understood and accepted by the group. Within appropriate limits, students are given responsibility and freedom to work. There is a balance of common tasks and individual responsibility for specific tasks, which are unique and not shared. Motivation for learning is high and seems inner directed. There is less teacher talk and more teacher listening to students when ideas are explored, and there is an honest respect for solid information. Evaluation is a shared process and includes more than measures of academic achievement (1962, p. 237).

Beginning with the school facilities, they should be orderly and inviting. Each classroom and corridor and the building and grounds should speak of an exciting learning environment. Adolph Unruh and Harold Turner (1970) wrote:

An exciting climate is based on three imperatives: (1) Broaden the stage for learning; bring the world into the classroom. Introduce students to the multisensory classroom with powers to create interest. (2) Develop the environment to feed young people's curiosity and interest. Provide much to see, to feel, to operate, and to hear—an environment that simply cries out, "touch me!" or "lift me and examine!" and "try me out—turn me on—push the button!" (3) Make learning itself exciting and satisfying. Encourage students to engage in processes because they want to know (p. 127).

As an overall guideline, processes have more transfer ability than do isolated bits of knowledge. When emphasis is placed on processes, the environment builds in motivation for learning. The climate of the school should include but go far beyond the drill needed for acquiring basic learning tools. Some of the processes students can use in an exciting learning environment are:

1. Selecting the events or phenomena to be explained, materials to be used, tools needed, and perhaps partners for the task.
2. Gathering and collecting data according to a plan or design.
3. Observing the phenomena, reading about them, inventing instruments and situations to make closer observation possible.
4. Measuring, weighing answers, scaling responses for statistical treatment, and recording measurements accurately.
5. Analyzing the data, the process itself and the results such as form, style, and plot in literature; structure of experiments and insights into knowledge.
6. Classifying and developing order among ideas, data, and relationships.
7. Generalizing, arriving at conclusions, and justifying conclusions on the basis of evidence.
8. Interpreting results (scientific, social, artistic), extrapolating and interpolating when these processes are indicated.

These are among the attributes of an effective school climate, a climate that principals and teachers can create.

Expectations

The most consistent finding in the majority of studies done on school effectiveness is the crucial connection between expectations and achievement. Study after study in Shoemaker's and Fraser's review of the "effects" literature emphasized that students and teachers tend to live up to their leader's expectations of them (1981, p. 181). Sparked by the publication of Robert Rosenthal's and Lenore Jacobson's *Pygmalion in the Classroom*, in 1968, researchers have long been interested in the effects of teacher and/or principal expectations on student achievement. Findings have upheld common sense knowledge: when parents, teachers, principals, or other role models expect poor achievement or behavior of a child, that is what results. Conversely, high expectations normally produce favorable results.

It is frequently hard to deal with negative expectations because adults usually believe quite firmly that they are treating all students fairly; they are apparently unaware of the differences in the signals they give low- versus high-achieving students regarding expectations. Current research, summarized by Thomas McDaniel (1982), suggests that teachers communicate lower expectations, less tolerance, even less affection for slower or unattractive students than for their opposites. Teachers tend to seat low-ability students farther away from them, call on them less often, give them less time to answer questions, provide fewer clues and follow-up questions in problem situations, criticize their wrong answers more often, praise correct answers less often, provide less feedback, and interrupt the performance of low-ability students more often than those of high ability (p. 467).

As a direct and understandable consequence, slower or unattractive students tend to volunteer less, seek teacher help less, and take fewer risks. These behaviors all in turn confirm their teachers' expectations. Some students become passive, bored, and uninvolved in learning activities; others become disruptive, defensive, and display aggressive behavior.

What is the principal's role in setting high expectations? The principal or other instructional leader can sensitize teachers to their differential expectations by effective use of supervisory techniques (see Chapter Eight). Principals and other leaders can promote the value and approach that all students *can* learn and that teachers *can* teach them.

High expectations should permeate the school: for the leaders themselves, for teachers and other employees, and for students. Expectations related to student and teacher performance, the cooperative development and maintenance of high standards, and courtesy and respect for everyone should be lived and felt in the school. The following is a profile of behavior for all school participants:

1. Every student and adult has intrinsic worth.
2. Every human being, student or adult, has a need to achieve and to be recognized.
3. Every student and adult should have opportunities for growth and self-improvement.
4. Every student and adult has the need to belong, to be a member of the group, to be an "insider."
5. Every student needs many opportunities to contribute to the lessons, to the discussion, to the progress of the group. Every teacher needs opportunities to be involved in curriculum planning, strategy development, evaluations, and follow-up action.
6. Every person in the school should have the right to know whether he or she is progressing and to what degree.
7. Every student and adult should be regarded as a unique combination of attitudes, abilities, skills, intelligence, understandings, insights,

stamina, perceptions, and motivations; and special abilities and interests should be utilized in the pursuit of effective learning.

8. Every honest inquiry merits attention, and every student's question should be given honest attention. Every teacher who comes to the supervisor or principal with a problem should receive considerate assistance and not be penalized with a critical note in his or her personnel file.

According to Hersey and Blanchard (1982), the feeling of competence is closely related to the concept of expectations. The relative sense of competence persons have depends on their successes and failures in the past. If their successes overshadow their failures, they will tend to feel competent. They will have a positive outlook toward life, seeing almost every new situation as an interesting challenge that they can meet successfully. If, however, their failures predominate, their outlook will be more negative. Since expectations tend to influence motives, people with low feelings of competence will often be motivated to avoid new challenges, new learnings, or risk taking (p. 37).

THE PLANNING PROCESS

Planning for change has never been easy, and the dynamics of social and technological change in contemporary society make planning even harder. However, unplanned change in education cannot bring about the major improvements needed. Planning is the process of coordinating the appropriate contributions, needs, and interests toward procedures for formulating policies, goals, and a program of action. This section explores the elements and complexities of the planning process.

Historical Phases of Planning

Karl Mannheim's studies of humanity and society (1961) trace the stages of planning back to primitive people, relate growth in thinking to growth in planning, and indicate the significance of planning in advancing societies. The first traces of thinking were characterized by chance discoveries preceded by trial and error. Mannheim identifies a second phase in the history of thought as inventing: people have somewhat limited and immediate goals and set themselves tasks to reach these goals, but they depend on natural selection and social processes to do this. In the stage of inventing, people rationalize and suppress according to both individual and societal necessities and adaptations.

Mannheim advocates advancement to another stage, that of planning or planned thinking, in which the individual and society move toward intelligent mastery of the relationships of a multidimensional environment. An essential element in the planning stage is that the person not only thinks out individual aims but also attempts to grasp a whole complex of events and guide the cycle of events. Planning avoids the problem of static structures by continuously accommodating to change. Mannheim continues:

Discovery and invention by no means lose their function on the emergence of planning. But problems in thinking which can be solved only by planning cannot be left to discovery just as, on the other hand, planning always must build upon the stages of discovery and invention. In the same way, thinking in terms of interdependence (which is one aspect of planning) does not supersede abstraction with its separation of spheres. But one must know precisely how each stage of thought is related to the others and how they supplement one another (p. 38).

Bringing together knowledge and action is the crux of the problem. Planned change involves mutual goal setting and a conscious deliberative and collaborative effort to apply knowledge systematically so that successful procedures can be designed.

Curriculum Planning for a Free Society

Ronald Lippitt (1965) relates planned change to curriculum-related needs, and he emphasizes the complex nature of the processes of change. Individuals and groups must be helped to see their particular area of involvement and responsibility and to collaborate in action research that discovers common interests among conflicting interests. They can be aided in drawing on the best available knowledge related to the established mutual goals, understanding the social forces and other factors bearing on the situation, and reviewing the likely consequences of alternative actions. Leadership involvement requires not only seeking knowledge and viewpoints from various sources but also skills in creating and supporting a problem-solving approach.

John Dewey's philosophy was consistent with that of contemporary advocates of planning. He rejected routine plans and programs handed down from the past, but he stressed that education is not a matter of planless improvisation: "the central problem of education is to select the kind of present experiences that live fruitfully and creatively in subsequent experiences," and "growth is not enough; we must also specify the direction in which growth takes place, the end toward which it tends" (1938, pp. 28, 36).

Planning involves creativity and leadership; it recognizes polarizations; and it recognizes and attempts to bridge such either-or viewpoints as sameness versus diversity, the interests of the small unit as opposed to those of the whole, simple or complex problems, and order versus confusion. Planning leads to action, and action is effective when the essence of a need is found, when goals are valid, and when detailed, open, and observable planning takes place.

Planning for change in a free society demands a commitment to a system of values that will serve as criteria. Warren Bennis's studies of organizational behavior (1969) reveal that any change program involves a set of core values. These values emphasize the human being as a proactive, growth-seeking, inquiring, confronting person. In addition, the value system features an influence process that is transactional, meaning that the influence is a two-way process and that, regardless of status differences, there must be reciprocity if the final decision is to be "owned" by all parties concerned.

Bennis states that value power is the strongest of the possible sources of power. Values based on concern for other persons, experimentalism, openness and honesty, flexibility, cooperation, and democracy are the underlying values of planned change in the concept he advocates. Other sources of power, says Bennis, are relatively weak in comparison. Coercive power, which depends on rewards and punishment, is less durable, except under conditions of vigilant surveillance. Power stemming from the authority and credibility of experts and specialists advising a given group is transient and tends to weaken rapidly with the passage of time. The values that work toward liberating the spirit and realizing the potential of people are the values that provide the driving force for excellent planned change.

Bennis (1969, p. 573) notes a series of growing fundamental changes that seem to gradually be taking place in the basic philosophy underlying managerial behavior in educational planning as well as in business and industry. These changes are:

1. A new concept of the person, based on increased knowledge of complex and shifting needs, which replaces the oversimplified innocent push-button idea of a person.
2. A new concept of power, based on collaboration and reason, which replaces a model of power based on coercion and fear.
3. A new concept of organizational values, based on humane democratic ideals, which replaces the depersonalized mechanistic value system of bureaucracy.

These transformations are not unanimously accepted or even understood, Bennis cautions, to say nothing of being widely implemented in day-to-day affairs. However, his studies indicate that they have gained wide intellectual acceptance in enlightened quarters. They have stimulated rethinking and consideration for the persons involved and are being used as a basis for policy formulation by many large-scale organizations.

Interdependence in Curriculum Planning

Planning decisions in curriculum development relate to various kinds of problems at many policy and operational levels, and all of these are highly interdependent. Four major divisions of educational planning, identified by Marvin Alkin and James Bruno (1970) are: (1) economic planning, dealing with the allocation of resources to education; (2) educational policy planning, dealing with choices among broad educational goals; (3) internal educational planning, dealing with choices among methods, media, and technologies; and (4) operational planning, dealing with choices among methods of implementation and methods of monitoring success and failure.

Effective curriculum development assumes a high degree of interdependence of elements and persons and an orderly approach to planned change. The elements of responsive change—humane values; democratic processes, goals, needs, objectives, policies, action programs, and evaluative processes; and interrelationships among the groups concerned with curriculum development—are all required if the changes are to endure. Changes brought about because of a selfish interest, an emergency, pressure from one group or another, or merely the charismatic quality of a leader may soon fade if procedures to ensure coordination in the planning process have not been carefully worked out.

Vast networks currently exemplify many types of interdependence. Technological media for instantaneous worldwide mass communication, global transportation, multinational corporations, and international political and economic arrangements are all indicative of a changing world view. Future-oriented curriculum development necessarily commits itself more and more to the idea of planning. The planning process, by involving the human quest for self-awareness and by using reason to achieve and stretch human potential and possibilities, can open organizational operations to self-inquiry and analysis. Useful strategies for effecting change and new methods of planning are emerging that have applications to curriculum development.

STRATEGIES FOR EFFECTIVE CHANGE

Three general types or groups of strategies for change identified by Robert Chin and Kenneth Benne (1969) are useful in analyzing techniques for planned change in curriculum development. These are designated in this discussion as enlightenment, reeducative, and coercive strategies.

Enlightenment strategies assume that people will follow rational interests once these are revealed to them. In this category, some person or group who knows of a situation proposes a change that is desirable, effective, and in line with the interests of those who will be affected by the change. This strategy depends on building knowledge, diffusing the results of research, using experts as consultants, and clarifying definitions in order to communicate better and to reason more effectively so that a realistic common basis can be established for acting and changing. A utopian ideal is emphasized as a goal. Difficulties in getting new knowledge into practice are frequently attributed to the unsuitability of the supervisor.

School administrators sometimes feel they have fulfilled their duties for improving instruction by employing a speaker and arranging for a two-day workshop for teachers. At the workshop, new curriculum guides prepared elsewhere or record keeping forms for a new and complex approach to instructional management may be distributed, for example. After the event, the guides and forms are sometimes promptly filed in desk drawers, and classroom practice continues as before. The superintendent may attribute the new practice's lack of implementation to the principal, supervisor, curriculum coordinator, or person whose responsibility it is to improve instruction. The next move is to replace the supervisory person and look to the next one to "make" the teachers follow through. Thus, there is considerable emphasis on personnel selection and replacement.

The enlightenment strategy, as noted by Chin and Benne, has been highly successful in technologies related to things, scientific research, and engineering problems. This kind of strategy has been less successful in areas that demand attention to people's attitudes and values and to considerations of social and cultural diversity.

Reeducative strategies are in the attitudinal realm—ways of working with people and values—while enlightenment strategies rely more on directives, memoranda, and efficiency-oriented measures. Reeducative strategies are committed to releasing and fostering growth in the persons who make up the system to be changed. This approach emphasizes that persons are capable of self-respect and respect for each other in their responses, choices, and actions. Improving the problem-solving capabilities of the group is a major objective in the reeducative family of strategies, and the persons involved are as committed to reeducation of the participants as they are to effecting change in the system. Emphasis is on norms of open communication and trust between persons, on lowering status barriers between system participants, and on assuming mutual responsibilities for planning change. It is believed that creative adaptations to changing conditions may arise from within the group that is planning for change and do not necessarily have to be imported from outside. Effective conflict management is a part of the reeducative process.

Intelligence in action—Dewey's conception—is basic to this strategy. Dewey believed that our best hope for progress was for people to learn to use a broadened and humane scientific method in facing problem situations. Chin and Benne note the contribution to reeducative strategies of Kurt

Lewin (1954), who emphasized the interrelationships among research, training, and action in the solution of problems, the identification of needs for change, and the use of improved patterns of action in meeting these needs. The reeducative process would draw on research and knowledge, particularly through collaborative relationships among people.

Coercive strategies depend on the influence of one person or group on another. In the recent history of curriculum development, federal appropriations have exercised a coercive influence over the decisions of local school officials concerning various emphases in the school curriculum. Other examples of coercive power affecting curriculum development are judicial decisions supporting civil rights, legislative rulings regarding high school graduation requirements, and other administrative rulings on courses and programs to be offered and competencies acquired. The coercive strategies depend on the management of power or the recomposition of a power group for change.

Whether influenced by coercive strategies or by enlightenment strategies, curriculum workers still have considerable latitude for introducing democratic, reeducative methods of change. While curriculum developers must take account of actual concentrations of power wherever they work, reeducative strategies can find an appropriate place somewhere in the organizational arrangement.

Bennis (1969) emphasizes that curriculum leaders need more than energy and ambition. They must also have a professional attitude; be engaged in a self-education process; be concerned with improvement, development, and measurement of organizational effectiveness; be highly interested in people and the process of human interaction; and be interested in changing the relationships, perceptions, and values of existing personnel rather than replacing personnel as an expedient measure if problems arise. The curriculum leader is confronted by a wide range of human problems that must be considered in planning for change: problems of compatibility between individual needs and institutional goals, problems related to the distribution of power, problems related to managing and resolving conflicts, problems of responding appropriately to changes in the societal environment, and problems posed by future thinking versus status quo thinking.

Major, long-term challenges facing our society generally, with special reference to education, include the need for leadership, according to Samuel Halperin (1981). Educational leaders are needed who can accommodate greater diversity, plan educational goals and standards in the face of uncertainties regarding available economic resources and society's shifting values and expectations for the schools. Another challenge associated with rapid changes in technologies and tasks is to bring about the self-renewal of an aging work force in the schools; to create ways to help people gain new insights, skills, and knowledge. Halperin sees the training and nurturance of effective leaders as crucial to the future of schooling.

EFFECTIVE LEADERSHIP FOR CURRICULUM DEVELOPMENT AND CURRICULUM IMPLEMENTATION

In summary, instructional leadership is not for the weak hearted, single minded, or incompetent. Effective leaders are badly needed in all aspects of the educational enterprise and critically needed at the grass roots level. Yet effectiveness will be tested by a whole array of complexities: turbulent societal conditions, new demands on schools, and internal struggles within the schools. New leadership competencies are called for, yet competence is not enough; excellence is needed if schools are to regain public confidence. Managerial skills are a first requirement, but leadership means more—it implies vision, a deep sense of what American education is all about, and what it will take to reach its goals. Curriculum leadership is critically important for the future of schooling. Succeeding chapters speak to political influences, theoretical assumptions, goals, needs, content, implementation, evaluation, and future awareness—all components of curriculum development and implementation. (Supervision, which is a function of leadership, is discussed in Chapter Eight.)

REFERENCES

Alkin, Marvin C., and Bruno, James E. "System Approaches to Educational Planning." In *Social and Technological Change: Implications for Education*, edited by Phillip K. Piele, Terry L. Eidell, and Stuart C. Smith, pp. 189-244. Eugene, Ore.: Center for the Advanced Study of Educational Administration, University of Oregon, 1970.

Bennis, Warren G. "Changing Organizations." In *The Planning of Change*, 2d ed., edited by Warren G. Bennis, Kenneth D. Benne, and Robert Chin, pp. 568-79. New York: Holt, Rinehart, and Winston, 1969.

Berger, Allen. "Old Questions Will Produce Old Answers to the Problems of Education Leadership." *Education Week* 2 (October 13, 1982): 24.

Blake, Robert R., and Mouton, Jane. *The Managerial Grid*. Houston: Gulf Publishing Co., 1964.

Bronson, Jack Dodge. *Board of Education Exposure to Curriculum and Instruction in Selected School Districts*. Dissertation, Saint Louis University, 1975.

Brookover, Wilbur B., and Lezotte, Lawrence W. *Changes in School Characteristics Coincident with Changes in Student Achievement*. East Lansing, Mich.: College of Urban Development, Michigan State University, 1977.

Burns, James MacGregor. *Leadership*. New York: Harper & Row, 1978.

Chase, Larry. "Quality Circles." *Educational Leadership* 40 (February 1983): 18-25.

Chin, Robert, and Benne, Kenneth D. "General Strategies for Effecting Changes in Human Systems." In *The Planning of Change*, 2d ed., edited by Warren G. Bennis, Kenneth D. Benne, and Robert Chin, pp. 357-70. New York: Holt, Rinehart, and Winston, 1969.

Coleman, James S., et al. *Equality of Educational Opportunity*. Washington, D.C.: U.S. Government Printing Office, 1966.

Combs, Arthur W.; Kelly, Earl C.; Rogers, Carl R.; and Maslow, Abraham H. *Perceiving, Behaving, Becoming*. Yearbook of the Association for Supervision and Curriculum Development. Alexandria, Va.: ASCD, 1962.

Cubberley, Ellwood P. *The Principal and His School*. Boston: Houghton Mifflin, 1923.

Dewey, John. *Experience and Education*. New York: Collier Books, 1938.

Edmonds, Ronald. "An Interview with One of the Leaders in the Search for Effective Schools." *Missouri Schools* 47 (October 1981): 4-8.

Edmonds, Ronald. "Effective Schools for the Urban Poor." *Educational Leadership* 37 (October 1979): 15-24.

Enochs, James C. "Up from Management." *Phi Delta Kappan* 63 (November 1981): 175-78.

Goodlad, John I. "Can Our Schools Get Better?" *Phi Delta Kappan* 60 (January 1979): 342-47.

Gorton, Richard A., and McIntyre, Kenneth E. *The Senior High School Principalship*, Vol. II. Reston, Va.: National Association of Secondary School Principals, 1978.

Halperin, Samuel. "The Future of Educational Governance: Prospects and Possibilities." In *How Can the U.S. Elementary and Secondary Education Systems Best Be Improved?*, pp. 75-84. Compiled by the Congressional Research Service, Library of Congress. Washington, D.C.: U.S. Government Printing Office, 1981.

Harman, Willis W. "Two Contrasting Concepts of Participatory Leadership." *Theory into Practice* 20 (Autumn 1981): 225-28.

Hersey, Paul W. "The NASSP Assessment Center Develops Leadership Talent." *Educational Leadership* 39 (February 1982): 370-71.

Hersey, Paul W., and Blanchard, Kenneth H. *Management of Organizational Behavior: Utilizing Human Resources*. Englewood Cliffs, N.J.: Prentice-Hall, 1982.

Hodgkinson, Harold. "What's Right With Education." *Phi Delta Kappan* 61 (November 1979): 159-62.

Kanter, Rosabeth Moss. "Power, Leadership, and Participatory Management." *Theory into Practice* 20 (Autumn 1981): 219-24.

Lewin, Kurt. *Field Theory in Social Science*. New York: Harper & Row, 1954.

Lippitt, Ronald. "Roles and Processes in Curriculum Development and Change." In *Strategy for Curriculum Change*, pp. 11-28. Alexandria, Va.: Association for Supervision and Curriculum Development, 1965.

McDaniel, Thomas R. "What's Your Principal Quotient?" *Phi Delta Kappan* 63 (March 1982): 464-68.

McGregor, Douglas. *The Human Side of Enterprise*. New York: McGraw-Hill, 1960.

Mannheim, Karl. "From Trial and Error to Planning." In *The Planning of Change*, edited by Warren G. Bennis, Kenneth D. Benne, and Robert Chin, pp. 34–37. New York: Holt, Rinehart, and Winston, 1961.

Nystrand, Raphael O. "Leadership Theories for Principals." *Theory into Practice* 20 (Autumn 1981): 260–63.

O'Hanlon, James. "Theory Z in School Administration." *Educational Leadership* 40 (February 1983): 16–26.

Olivero, James L. "Principals and Their Inservice Needs." *Educational Leadership* 39 (February 1982): 340–44.

Ouchi, William G. *Theory Z*. New York: Avon Books, 1981.

Rogus, Joseph S.; Poppenhagen, Brent W.; and Mingus, Julian. "As Secondary Principals View Themselves: Implications for Principal Preparation." *The High School Journal* 63 (January 1980): 167–72.

Rosenthal, Robert, and Jacobson, Lenore. *Pygmalion in the Classroom*. New York: Holt, Rinehart, and Winston, 1968.

Sergiovanni, Thomas J. "Ten Principles of Quality Leadership." *Educational Leadership* 39 (February 1982): 330–36.

Shoemaker, Joan, and Fraser, Hugh W. "What Principals Can Do: Some Implications from Effective Schooling." *Phi Delta Kappan* 63 (November 1981): 178–82.

Stogdill, Ralph M. *Handbook of Leadership. A Survey of Theory and Research*. New York: The Free Press, 1974.

Sweeney, James. "Research Synthesis on Effective School Leadership." *Educational Leadership* 39 (February 1982): 346–52.

Unruh, Adolph, and Turner, Harold E. *Supervison for Change and Innovation*. Boston: Houghton Mifflin, 1970.

Weber, George. *Inner City Children Can Be Taught to Read: Four Successful Schools*. Washington, D.C.: Council for Basic Education, 1971.

ADDITIONAL READINGS

Argyris, Chris. *Management and Organizational Development: The Path from XA to YB*. New York: McGraw-Hill, 1971.

Baldridge, J. Victor, and Deal, Terrence, eds. *The Dynamics of Organizational Change in Education*. Berkeley: McCutchan, 1983.

Bennis, Warren G. *Beyond Bureaucracy: Essays on the Development and Evolution of Human Organizations*. New York: McGraw-Hill, 1973.

Corbett, H. Dickson. "Principals' Contributions to Maintaining Change." *Phi Delta Kappan* 64 (November 1982): 190–92.

"Effective Schools." Issue. *Educational Leadership* 40 (December 1982): 4–69.

Fantini, Mario D. "Anticipatory Leadership and Resource Management in the Future." *Theory into Practice*. 20 (Autumn, 1981): 214–18.

Joyce, Bruce. *The Structure of Educational Change*. New York: Longman, 1983.

Lezotte, Lawrence W. "Climate Characteristics in Instructionally Effective Schools." *Impact on Instructional Improvement* 16 (Summer 1981): 26–31.

Sergiovanni, Thomas, J. *Supervision of Teaching.* Yearbook of the Association for Supervision and Curriculum Development. Alexandria, Va.: ASCD, 1982.
Torrance, E. Paul. "Education for Quality Circles in Japanese Schools." *Journal of Research and Development in Education* 15 (Winter 1982): 11-15.

3

Influences on Curriculum Decisions

Curriculum development is a complex activity that takes place within a complex political milieu. It requires special expertise, political awareness, and a continuing dialogue among the decision makers for clarification of purposes and resolution of value conflicts.

Who decides what will be taught in schools? What are the influences on curriculum development? Classroom teachers surveyed by the Institute for Research on Teaching readily responded that the curriculum is influenced by parents, upper-level teachers, the principal, district instructional objectives, textbooks, and standardized test results (1981, p. 2). When federal and state mandates, court decisions, pressures for excellence, and the activities of special interest groups are added to the list, the enormity of the task facing curriculum specialists and local curriculum committees seems almost overwhelming.

THE NEW POLITICS OF EDUCATION

Further complicating the scene is the jolting realization by school administrators that conflict has replaced consensus as the political model for many school districts. Historically, education evolved from a society that fit the consensus model. The power arrangement was monolithic, as Dan Dodson has observed, and was seldom challenged. The myths and values of the "American way" were accepted; minorities, women, and others who sought to rise in status, simply disciplined themselves to the ethos of the power group and strove to be recognized on its terms (1974).

Today, the consensus era is passing. Society and schools are coping with conflict. School districts have attracted the news media and gained publicity as arenas of conflict involving community groups, teachers' unions, school boards, school administrators, and at times, state governments and federal courts. Reform commissions are issuing reports and recommendations. Protest groups of many kinds have made demands on the schools. The emotional issues include curriculum and standards along with busing, school closings, financial problems, and other concerns.

Elements of the new political model—for which many administrators are unprepared—include: attempting to distinguish between proper and improper demands; reconciling differences of goals and values; mediating, bargaining, seeking compromises, building consensus; and providing new services wanted by constituents.

Only the most naïve person in a decision-making role would today attempt to insulate the process of curriculum planning from public scrutiny and discussion. Such a closed approach could introduce serious biases into the curriculum and result in dissension in the community and notoriety in the press.

Conflict Versus Consensus

From a study of conflict and consensus in six school districts, Samuel Bacharach and Stephen Mitchell (1981) concluded that there are both negative and positive aspects to consensus. Some dissent is crucial to change toward improvement. Total consensus would indicate a lack of ability to adapt well; given the turbulent nature of the contemporary educational environment, the ability to adapt is crucial to survival.

Bacharach and Mitchell identified several important factors in forming a consensus and maintaining it at a constructive level. In their focus, consensus was on agreement about the roles of the administration, the teachers, the school board, and the community. *Roles* referred to responsibility (authority and influence) and practices (mechanisms to carry out the responsibilities). An assumption was made that the administration's expertise was its primary resource; legitimacy, the school board's primary resource; classroom expertise, the teacher's primary resource; and mobilization, the community's primary resource. Disagreement on roles produced conflict when decisions on issues were to be made, as each group would approach a decision with a different view and different goals.

In this study, administrators were found to be particularly defensive about curriculum issues, obviously because their expertise was questioned. Thus, it seems befitting for administrators and other leaders in curriculum development to be aware of the complexities of the new politics of education and to become competent in building consensus when working with diverse points of view.

Critical Variables

Critical variables, identified by Bacharach and Mitchell, include: the administrator's awareness of potential unrest and impending mobilization of special interest groups, the school board's ability to constructively represent widely differing political and social viewpoints, and the strategies employed by the superintendent to form and maintain consensus. Successful strategies used by superintendents to dampen disruptive criticism before it surfaced in the decision arena were in the general areas of (1) the rational use of knowledge in supplying the proper information and (2) consistent emphasis on the board's responsibility as the active, legitimate, and responsible agent in district affairs.

In successful examples of forming and maintaining consensus, superintendents made use of staff-community committees to gather data and information for background in preparing recommendations to the board. Also a good working relationship existed between principals and their faculties within these districts, with teachers having input into school matters.

Over time, the stability of a given district in the face of potential conflict seemed highly related to the administrator's leadership in attending to matters demanding immediate attention and at the same time adapting a long-term perspective. Each action taken was considered in terms of its long-range consequences for the district. Bacharach and Mitchell concluded that the wise use of information and the wise involvement of participants are crucial factors in today's politics of education.

The Context of Curriculum Decisions

Emphasizing political sophistication for curriculum leaders does not imply partisan politics à la Republican, Democratic, or any other political party. The politics of curriculum development refers to the influence professional educators, governmental agencies, educational agencies, and pressure groups or individuals have on the process of making curriculum decisions based on the allocation of values in education. Sides in local education-related conflicts are seldom drawn on political lines. Rather people divide themselves on the pros and cons of a given issue.

Community Power. From his studies of community power in the fifties and early sixties, Ralph Kimbrough (1964) warned educators of their need for enlightenment about the potential of community power and the need to recognize the significance of political influence in educational decision making. Kimbrough deplored the administrative style then prevalent of the self-made genius at the helm of a school district who had little or no use for shared decision making to enhance his or her expertise. Kimbrough advocated cooperative development of curriculum improvement decisions and programs with those to be affected by the consequences.

Sensational accounts of school districts embroiled in community disputes over school programs were published in the ensuing years, and educators began to recognize the impact that the politics of education can have on school programs (Bendiner 1969, Masotti 1967, Meranto 1970). As a result, comprehensive overviews and guides to policy making and professional action in the face of political turbulence are available to the educator today. Representative writings are *Schools in Conflict* by Frederick Wirt and Michael Kirst (1982) and the National Society for the Study of Education's *The Politics of Education* (Scribner 1977).

Opposing Beliefs. In regard to curriculum development, political power gains strength from differences in fundamental beliefs about curriculum. Should the curriculum center on the minimums of basics or the development of the intellect? Should it include efforts to solve social problems, allow for diversity, or eliminate all save the academic subjects? From consensus on basic assumptions, knowledge and decision-making processes can be used for rationality in curriculum planning. (Conflicting conceptions of the curriculum as well as ways to establish a theoretical base responsive to the time, place, and people of its locale are explored in Chapter Four.)

It is important for curriculum developers to be aware of the probable consequences of either-or approaches to curriculum development. For example, a single-interest adoption of a back-to-basics approach that neglects attention to citizenship, development of reasoning and creativity, or the great ideas of the past, present, and predictable future would hardly be adequate in contemporary America. Similarly, any one of these examples could be carried to extremes to the exclusion of other important learnings and content. However, if a curriculum leader attempts a constantly shifting approach that makes use of whatever politics or procedures seem to fit a given occasion, he or she can be accused of developing curriculum by default and of indicating that curriculum development does not need any special expertise of its own to develop a theoretical base.

The Background

Curriculum development must involve practical decisons based on judgments about facts; it must include a study of wants and values. Curriculum development can indeed become a coherent field of study that follows a belief in rational inquiry. To accomplish this, Decker Walker says that curriculum developers must take into account:

All those activities and enterprises in which curricula are planned, created, adopted, presented, experienced, criticized, attacked, defended and evaluated, as well as the objects which may be part of a curriculum, such as textbooks, apparatus and equipment, schedules, teacher guides, and so on...[also] the plans, intentions, hopes, fears, dreams and the likes of agents such as teachers, students, and curriculum developers or policy makers (1973, p. 59).

Thus, not only must the curriculum developer recognize the conceptual and theoretical issues permeating the field, but this person must deal with the question of *who* should be permitted to plan curriculum. Who are the decision makers: federal agencies, educational laboratories, reform commissions, state boards and legislators, publishers, local boards, administrators, teachers, parents, other citizens, students? Each plays a role and each is critical of the others. Cynicism about the schools has come about as greater and greater hopes and expectations have been pinned on education and as more people are being affected by the educational process.

More people are working to become actors in the decision-making process. The desire to participate in decision making is inherent in the American tradition. In a survey by the National Institute of Education's Curriculum Development Task Force (1976), one of the main conclusions was that the classic curriculum questions of what shall be taught and how shall educational programs be organized were overshadowed by the desire to be involved. This desire was accompanied or perhaps motivated by a feeling of impotence and by the view that "someone else" was in control.

Involvement of the participants is one critical factor in curriculum planning; consensus on basic theoretical assumptions is another. Add to these the complexity of the milieu within which curriculum development must take place, and the magnitude of its importance becomes evident. Various surveys have pointed to major problems and issues facing the schools and consequently bearing on curriculum development. Trend analysts view the educational system as avoiding its responsibilities in helping find solutions for world scarcities and limits. Richard Lamm (1980) and others have identified major problems that may have disastrous effects on our planet's future including pollution, resource shortages, unwise use of land, toxic and hazardous wastes, and geometrical population growth. (Future awareness and relationships to curriculum are the subject of Chapter Ten.)

Schools are not only expected to address living in an interdependent world of limits but also to assist students in moving out on the leading edge of technology and adapting to a shifting economy and job market, and to seek new learnings continually. At the same time, schools are held accountable to the taxpayers for their money's worth in schooling; schools must adhere to mandates of the legislatures and be involved with the courts in assuring equality of access to education. In the thirty-year period just past, curriculum leaders became more and more conscious of multiple influences on curriculum as pressures shifted.

Curriculum-related pressures of the 1950s were for revision of subject matter and academic excellence. This was followed by the social reform era of the 1960s. Demands for attention to disadvantaged minorities reached a crescendo in the 1970s, with new attention to racial minorities, handicapped children, non-English-speaking students, and feminist interests. Expectancies for beneficial results became public concerns. This brought about legislative action resulting in numerous federal and state laws that impinged on or, indeed, frequently controlled much of what was included in the school's curriculum. Legislators at federal and state levels concerned themselves not only with educational achievement, desegregation, affirmative action, due process standards, and equal opportunity for all, but they also became involved with single-interest advocacy groups interested in school prayer, creationism, sex education, and textbooks. Then on the heels of the social reform movement came renewed pressures for excellence and quality. We will discuss spheres of power and the roles of participants in the schools next.

SPHERES OF POWER

Federal Government

The role of the federal government in education reached its zenith in the 1970s, when education attained cabinet status. The courts also became more and more involved in school issues. State governments increased their efforts to influence the curriculum, and local districts lost some of their autonomy. However, with the turn to a conservative national administration and withdrawal of federal funds for certain projects and programs, federal influence began to recede. Nevertheless, it has had a lasting impact on the curriculum of the schools.

Although the United States Constitution has not given Congress any explicit authority to control the school program, Congress found a way to do this by taxing and spending on behalf of education and then attaching conditions to grants that schools must meet if they are to receive federal money. Given this approach, several federal programs had an unusually strong impact on the schools. Federal regulations that prohibit discrimination on the basis of race or sex forced far-ranging changes in school organization and policy. This was achieved through regulations and guidelines for local districts that were developed by the Office of Civil

Rights and the previous Department of Health, Education and Welfare. Schools that failed to observe these regulations were threatened with the loss of all financial assistance from the federal government, a loss they could ill afford once the programs had been developed and installed.

Programs for Educationally Deprived Children. The most significant amounts of money provided by the federal government have been allocated to programs for educationally deprived children through Title I of the Elementary and Secondary Education Act (ESEA) of 1965 and its successor, Chapter I of the Educational Consolidation and Improvement Act (ECIA) of 1982. The intent of Chapter I is to serve educationally deprived children of school age in low-income attendance areas of the public schools. It is hoped that with special funding and special programs the cycle of deprivation can be broken so that another generation will not repeat the pattern of low achievement. Schools are required to develop intensive curriculum programs, seriously evaluate them, and use the data annually for upgrading and improving the conditions for learning. Title I and Chapter I produced a management style that was foreign to most school programs of the past, including objectives-based instruction, explicit record keeping, and a prescribed norm-referenced testing and reporting model.

Education for Handicapped Children. The passage of Public Law 94-142, the Handicapped Children Act of 1975, has had a dramatic impact on the operation and administration of public schools. Curriculum and services must now be provided for children with severe or profound handicaps as well as for those with mild disabilities. These are children who until recently were almost never found in the public schools. New resources, including qualified teachers, support personnel and services, facilities, and materials, are required by P.L. 94-142. The first step for schools has been to locate these children, not an easy task as many parents prefer to keep severely impaired children hidden from society.

Schools are required to place all handicapped children in the least restrictive environment, which means that many are now put in the mainstream, that is, in the regular classroom. This has precipitated staff development in programming for individual children. An individualized educational plan (IEP) must be formulated for each handicapped child. This is a written statement developed in a planning conference involving a person in authority plus the teacher, specialists, the parents or guardian, and, if appropriate, the child. The IEP includes a description of the present levels of educational performance with long-term and short-term objectives and a statement of specific educational services to be provided, including student participation in regular educational programs to the greatest possible extent. Schedules to determine progress and effective criteria for evaluation must be included. Written IEPs provide for accountability by the school and often require unique types of curriculum materials and methods.

A further requirement of the instructional leader of the building, usually the principal, is to plan the total schedules of children who have one or more special programs so that "pull-outs" do not counteract one another or prevent coherence in these children's school experiences. A study by the Rand Corporation (1981) of twenty-four elementary schools that operated four or more programs (Title I, bilingual, and so on) showed that some children, particularly Hispanics, may be pulled out of class so frequently for special instruction that they still have not had classes in science or social studies as late as grade five.

Bilingual Requirements. Bilingual education created major issues in some localities, stemming from Section 601 of Title VI of the Civil Rights Act of 1964 which provides in part (quoted by Zirkel 1978, p. 98):

No person in the United States shall, on he ground of race, color, or national origin, be excluded from participation in, be denied the benefits of, or be subjected to discrimination under any program or activity receiving financial assistance.

The Supreme Court eventually played a role in enforcing this Act. From the *Lau* v. *Nichols* decision and the laws behind it, the newly organized Federal Department of Education (ED) set additional regulations for bilingual education. Schools were to be required to provide not only an intensive English program, but also other course instruction in both the student's primary language and English. In districts that enroll students from many countries, qualified teachers in several languages would have been needed. With the Reagan administration in Washington, however, the bilingual education regulations were set aside, and the education of children who do not speak English was left to local authorities.

The issue was whether basic educational policies should be controlled by Washington or by each local school board. In this instance, local autonomy won out in part because of the current administration's focus. Inevitably, if some of the responsibilities for equal rights, equal opportunities, and improving education for children with special problems are abandoned by the federal government, then state and local educational agencies must take on more responsibility.

Research and Development. Throughout the years of federal grants for education, various types of curriculum materials and teaching aids and strategies were developed by educational laboratories and research and development centers. These included projects in science, mathematics, reading, environmental education, ethnic studies, career education, and consumer education. Grants were also made to improve education for gifted students and to expand school libraries.

The programs and materials stemming from the curriculum improvement projects financed by the federal government differed substantially from the previous textbook materials used in schools, particularly in science and mathematics. The new science programs were organized around basic structural concepts, threads, themes, and the like. A typical example of the change in approach was cited by Glenys Unruh and William Alexander (1970), who compared a biology textbook of 1948 with the 1968 editions of the Biological Sciences Curriculum Study (BSCS) versions, a program sponsored by the National Science Foundation and the American Institute of Biological Sciences:

In the older textbook, unit topics included the cold-blooded vertebrates, the warm-blooded vertebrates, animal communities, the plant groups, and springtime biology. The BSCS program is centered around nine unifying themes of biology: evolution, diversity, genetic continuity, complementarity of organism and environment, biological roots of behavior, complementarity of structure and function, regulation and homeostasis, science as inquiry, and the history of biological conceptions (p. 60).

The Physical Science Study Committee (PSSC), a physics program sponsored by the National Science Foundation and private foundations, built its curriculum structure around four parts: the universe, optics and waves, mechanics, and electricity and modern physics. A chemistry program, also sponsored by the National Science Foundation, called the Chemical Bond Approach emphasized the electrical nature of matter, chemical bonds in terms of limiting models, energy changes accompanying chemical changes, and atomic and nuclear structure including atomic size, nuclear charge, ionization potential, electro-negativity, and atomic orbital assignments (Blackwood 1963).

A unified science curriculum was recommended for elementary and junior high schools rather than separate science disciplines. The American Association for the Advancement of Science and other groups of science educators advocated sequences to teach the processes of science: observation, communication, measurement, classification, space and time relationships, inference, and numbers. All of the new science programs of that period stressed inquiry and discovery methods—helping students learn the processes of investigation through classroom work. Laboratory work was a central part of the curriculum, and it was expected that students would have opportunities at times to approach frontiers of science, to investigate unknowns.

The new math emphasized mathematical principles and abstract thinking. The subject matter was built around a reorganized structure and pervasive concepts like symbolism, number, relation, function, field, measurement, and proof. Applications of algebraic and geometric concepts were introduced in the early grades, and elementary children learned of bases other than ten. The ability to discover patterns in abstract materials was a major component of mathematical thought (Davis 1965, pp. 46-50). Emphasis on drill or arithmetic computation, however, seemed to be reduced, which brought criticism from some quarters. These new approaches to curriculum reform, on the other hand, received considerable praise and enthusiasm from participating school districts, as well as research and development centers and regional laboratories that created, disseminated, and assisted in implementing the new curriculum products and techniques.

The movement for academic curriculum reform in the 1960s eventually faded away except for some adaptations of teaching materials produced by commercial publishers. Specialists hoping for significant improvement in teachers' capabilities and teaching styles, substantial increases of students entering the scientific and technical professions, and better understanding of modern scientific principles and interrelationships among the disciplines were often disappointed. Goodlad's conclusions (1970), substantiated by findings of the Rand study (Berman and McLaughlin 1976) were that nonimplementation was common and that, at best, a limited number of teachers had made adaptations and modifications of the new curricula.

With the new concern and vigor that has been directed toward improved teaching and learning in science and mathematics in particular and other major areas of the curriculum in general, the knowledge gained through research and development over recent years may yet come to fruition in the schools. The message here for curriculum leaders seems obvious. Instead of viewing curriculum revisions created by educational laboratories and research and development centers as peripheral to the "real" curriculum, why not draw on the best thinking available?

The Courts

At the same time that the federal government increased its regulations for local school systems, the courts became more and more involved in school issues. Although claiming no special expertise in professional education, lawyers and courts have been called on to resolve school problems. Generally, these problems relate to basic rights set forth in the First and Fourteenth Amendments to the United States Constitution and similar provisions in state constitutions. These problem areas can be roughly classified as matters pertaining to separation of church and state, race, distribution of wealth to schools, and individual freedoms.

Church-State Issues. Religion in the schools is an issue that has come before the courts on numerous occasions. The basic principle on which decisions have rested is that public schools may neither advance nor inhibit religion. On this basis, the Supreme Court struck down school ceremonies that involve reading from the Bible and recitation of prayers, even though these may be nondenominational prayers and even though students who object may be excused from participation. But just as the courts have barred instruction in what is called religion, the Supreme Court has said that the schools may not establish a creed of atheism (van Geel 1979, p. 29).

In regard to the issue of creationism versus evolution, court decisions have declared that requirements to include the Genesis account of creation in science textbooks and curricula are in conflict with the First Amendment of the Constitution (Skoog 1980). Nevertheless, bills are constantly being introduced in state legislatures seeking to include creationism or prayer in school programs and so circumvent previous court rulings.

Tuition tax credits, proposed for legislative action at the national level, would permit parents to take a credit on their income tax for each child in a private nonprofit elementary or secondary school. Under a similar proposal, parents could receive allocations of money, known as vouchers, to apply on children's tuition at the schools of their choice.

New private schools have appeared in all parts of the United States in recent years, usually organized by small groups of parents who want a particular feature emphasized by the school and narrowly defined. Admission is usually restricted through certain requirements that reflect the theme of the school. Many of the new private schools have been organized by religious groups of fundamental persuasion. Parents of long-standing private schools, particularly those organized by well-established churches, as well as the parents of the new private schools, have supported public funds for private schools in the form of tax credits or vouchers. Currently it is estimated that 11 percent of the nation's 45 million elementary and secondary students attend private schools.

The United States Supreme Court has approved a state tax deduction plan for education (a Minnesota law upheld in *Mueller* v. *Allen*), which includes not only private school tuition but also certain expenses for public school education such as summer school tuition, private tutoring services, education for the handicapped, required items of clothing for physical education, and materials for art classes. However, at the federal level, proposed legislation, accompanied by political party pressures, remains a controversial issue.

Civil Rights Issues. The main interest of the courts has been to enforce minimum constitutional requirements and assure at least a minimally adequate public school program for all students. Thus constitutionally required school programs influencing several areas are emerging from the courts. Certainly the federal courts have directed major efforts toward increasing the integration of minority students. Almost every school in the country with a racially heterogeneous student body has developed an integration plan, and many school districts have been involved in litigation over racial integration. In the decades following *Brown* v. *Board of Education*, Topeka 1954, many school districts revised their curricula to include multicultural studies and eliminated textbooks that seemed biased toward middle-class whites. Busing and antibusing advocates sharpened controversy in all parts of the country. Although not quite as volatile as the integration-busing issue, sex discrimination under Title IX caused almost every school district in the country to revise its policies toward affirmative action.

Several effects of court actions on the schools include the creation of explicit guidelines and more formalized procedures in the schools by administrators and teachers, certain limits on the options of teachers and administrators, and more attention to the rights of students and teachers. Changes toward racial integration in the organization and administration of many schools have produced programs to establish equal opportunities for students. As a result, some educators, though accepting the principle of equity and justice in education, seem to expect the legal system to do their work for them. Leadership in curriculum development demands that the responsibilities of educators not be shifted to the courts. Educators should not be tempted to evade or rescind laws simply because new demands are made by another group. Instead of complaining about procedural details, curriculum leaders should keep firmly in mind that the laws are intended to extend the franchise of the people—especially the poor and minorities but not just them—allowing all to share equally in the benefits of a democratic society.

State Legislatures

The growing influence of the federal courts and Congress has been paralleled by an increasing influence on the school by state legislatures. State legislatures seem to be writing more and more legislation to deal with the day-to-day operations of the schools. Bills are being introduced to deal with aspects of due process, equal educational opportunity, the rights of minorities and women, collective bargaining, school finances, and the special interests of pressure groups.

Mandates. The most spectacular efforts of state legislatures have been in the development of competency-based tests and instructional management plans for elementary and secondary students. Nearly every state has either enacted some form of competency-testing legislation or is considering it. A few states are proposing competency tests for teachers, particularly those entering the profession, to ensure that they have the "minimum competencies," too, along with their potential students.

Competency testing grew from the movement to assign accountability for student achievement to the schools. Legislators view competency testing as an obvious solution to the monumental task of monitoring educational policy and practice in the local schools.

This new development signifies a drastic change in understanding who is in charge. Historically, the Tenth Amendment left legal authority over the school program entirely to the state. The state legislatures and state boards of education have had more authority than they have used; in practice they did not exercise their full power. Traditionally, state legislatures have adopted statutes that specify what should be taught in the public schools, but these usually provided only the barest directives, seldom going beyond listing broad subject areas.

Legislatures have usually required that schools offer and students take certain courses in United States history, English, mathematics, the United States and State constitutions. Some states have added other requirements such as courses in driver education, drug abuse, consumer education, career education, and the contributions of minority populations. A few states have legislated a study of free enterprise and the evils of communism. A survey of state curriculum mandates for the American Bar Association by Joel Henning and others (1979, pp. 104–123) provides a summary.

Recent legislative activity by state legislatures and state boards of education has increased the effects of influence at the state level. In addition to requirements for statewide pupil testing programs, some states have imposed new kinds of graduation requirements. An example is the requirement of the New York Board of Regents that no student may graduate from high school, starting in 1979, without being able to read at a ninth-grade level.

Mandatory statewide testing has been instituted primarily to call attention to the vast majority of low-achieving schools that are composed of lower-class white, black, and Hispanic students. The demand that schools be held accountable for the achievement outcomes for all children has raised the difficult question of what the outcomes should be. The focus has been on the "basics," but definitions of *basic* have been made at the state level; local schools have had little voice in the decisions about testing.

Although many educators deplore mandatory testing programs, schools have generally fallen in line, and some gains have been reported. The National Assessment of Educational Progress (1981) noted a rise in test scores among black children, and certain disadvantaged schools reported in Chapter Two (under "Effective Schools") have had similar gains. However, the data suggest that gains have been made in the mechanics of reading more than in analytical skills or indicators of increased comprehension.

Several state departments of education have issued favorable reports from mandated programs. Florida's competency program, for example, has survived opposition. The unusual gains are credited to higher expectations, as predicted by State Commissioner Ralph Turlington in 1979 (p. 650). Florida's victory in the competency battle was a precedent-setting decision by a federal district judge that upheld the right of the State of Florida to withhold diplomas from seniors beginning in 1983 who did not pass the state's functional literacy test (Klein 1983, pp. 1, 17). Instead of diplomas, the youngsters receive certificates of completion, indicating that they have finished twelve years of schooling.

The decision in the case of *Debra P. v. Turlington*, which was brought by a group of black plaintiffs, is expected to influence other states to require high school students to pass a mandated test before receiving a graduation diploma. The judge who wrote the decision ruled that seniors who have attended integrated schools since first grade have had equal educational opportunities in the constitutional sense (same textbooks, curricula, libraries, attendance requirements) and five opportunities to pass the test between tenth and twelfth grades, with remedial help offered if they failed. The decision, supported by the U.S. Court of Appeals, seemed to say that a mandated testing program, matched to curriculum objectives, is a legitimate educational tool for states or local districts to use. (Caldwell and Walton 1983, pp. 1, 16-17).

As federal influence in education has waned, state governments have realized that they have powers not formerly exercised. Further, with public interest in education at a high level, there can be political advantages associated with legislation about schooling. Preoccupation with test scores and the rudiments of education will not be enough, however. State curriculum leaders and other professional educators also have influence through their hands-on knowledge about the complexities involved in providing high quality programs, and their voices should be heard.

Local Boards of Education

Local school boards frequently find that they are being hemmed into a narrow decision zone in some matters as a result of legislated mandates, court decisions, and the requirements of various governmental agencies, as well as pressures implicit in the data released by testing agencies. These external pressures cannot be charged to governmental "centralization" because no single control point exists. Rather there are multifaceted centers of power. Local school boards find themselves dealing simultaneously with a range of requirements and problems coming at them from many sources.

Local school board meetings today can be opportunities for indignant citizens to express themselves, and they range from orderly town meetings or forums to shouting matches that can end in pandemonium. School closings, busing, and money matters can be volatile issues, and these all appear on the agendas. Moreover, teachers' unions are becoming highly expert in bargaining for their interests, especially in the areas of salary and working conditions, with curriculum on the horizon.

School board members must increasingly enlist expertise on their side, particularly legal counsel. They must depend more and more on the superintendent and the superintendent's staff for gathering relevant information. School boards must also be able to reach higher levels of government through lobbyists and politicians.

The role of the local school board in curriculum development lies in the realms of policy development, goal setting, and dialogue with those affected by the school's curriculum. Board members have access to information that can increase their understanding of governmental mandates, students' needs, and diverse views of community members. Boards can employ administrators, teachers, and other staff to support the goals of the school district. It is the board's responsibility to make sure that the district's goals are appropriate and that curriculum and instruction are planned to meet those goals. Maintaining constant and open communication with the community is a necessary duty of school boards in order to interpret school policy and represent constituents. Working out rational approaches to the demands of extremists is another duty, sometimes an unpleasant one.

The New Right

Pressures on American schools are coming from ultraconservative groups that are antievolution, antiseparation of church and state, against "secular humanism," and against sex education. A well-funded movement is supported by various groups and individuals who have expertise in gaining access to the news media. The developing coalition, often known as the New Right, utilizes computers containing the names and addresses of an estimated 25 million supporters of various right-wing causes. Other branches of the movement include the Moral Majority and the Educational Research Analysts in Texas, a group organized for the purpose of censoring textbooks. Educational implications of the New Right activities are described by Charles Park (1980) and Ben Brodinsky (1982) in journals that also provided space for responses by advocates of New Right beliefs.

Brodinsky sees the New Right as an aberrant conservative movement, a movement that includes parents concerned about the public schools (angry, alienated, or disappointed), but is led by zealots and extremists who want to remake the public schools in the New Right image or else destroy them. Potent and sophisticated tools are used for propaganda, promotion, fund raising, and proselytizing. The work of the New Right proceeds on many fronts and through many types of organizations. Influence is directed toward parents and other taxpayers, school boards, administrators, teachers, state and national lawmakers, and even the president of the United States. Attacks on the public schools have come at a time when they are beset by many problems, most beyond their control.

Some of the more disturbing aspects of the New Right approaches are their efforts to limit and control the learning materials in public school classrooms and libraries through censorship and their efforts to search out and destroy elements within the public schools that promote the education of free, inquiring minds. "Secular humanism" is a term created by the New Right as an all-purpose charge to cover any element of the curriculum that might open vistas to students that are not approved by the New Right's very narrow rules. Curriculum leaders find themselves defending humanism, a philosophy that emphasizes commitment to the improvement or enlightenment of the human condition through the imparting of knowledge.

Censors. Professional educational associations are warning their members that extremists are seeking to limit inquiry by students and limit their reading materials to a particular ultraconservative point of view. A study sponsored by several educational associations and published by the Association of American Publishers (1981) reveals that activities of the textbook censors are being felt in the publishing industry. It is well known that the publishing industry wields considerable power in curriculum decisions, and that teachers rely heavily on textbooks for instruction. Therefore, the matter of censorship becomes significant in curriculum development.

Statewide adoptions of textbooks in twenty-two of the fifty states not only directly affect the kinds of educational materials used in those states, but also influence materials available in the other states. Publishers tend to meet the preferences of the largest states, Texas and California. In Texas, New Right advocates have been influential; they have tirelessly campaigned there and elsewhere against the materials they have selected for censorship.

Topics listed as targets for censors, compiled by Greg Birchall (1981) include materials with "life education" components: those that attempt to teach students about sex, drugs, alcohol, values, careers, consumer issues, and interpersonal relations. No retrospective criticism of historical figures would be permitted. Ethnic studies, global studies, and women's studies are frowned on as they are associated by the New Right with the "Communist conspiracy." These extremist groups are opposed to a concept of intellectual freedom that says the school and library should provide a forum of ideas for students to question and examine.

If educators are to successfully withstand these challenges to curriculum content and methods, they must develop the ability to work closely with parents and other members of the community in all matters relating to the school program. Involving the community in preparing a policy for selecting materials as well as a clearly defined method for dealing with complaints will be the best support system if an organized group or concerned individual challenges the school's curriculum, textbooks, or library materials. Sample procedures for inclusion in a policy statement on reconsideration of library and instructional materials have been compiled by Robert Foley (1983).

Professional Reform Advocates

Unrelated to the New Right are several professional proposals for educational reform presented by recognized experts and officially commissioned groups. As in the past, a synthesis of the current recommended reforms will emerge, and the impact will affect curriculum and instruction throughout the United States.

Common themes characterize the recommendations of the various commissions: (1) strong emphasis on academic goals with considerable attention to mathematics, science, computer fluency, and communication skills; (2) advice on the education, professional training, evaluation, tenure, and incentive pay for teachers, all directed toward strengthening the quality of teaching; and (3) a general concern for better preparation for life after high school graduation based on an apparent assumption that nearly every student will eventually require postsecondary education of some sort to acquire needed job skills.

Major differences of method show up in the work of the reform groups varying from "think tanks" to a comprehensive study based on visits to hundreds of classrooms. Most groups relied heavily on national testing data as well as interviews, hearings, conferences, and research papers. All are deliberative, judgmental, and prescriptive; that is, strong recommendations are being put forward by each group as its report becomes public. All are deeply concerned about the quality of American pubic education. The National Commission on Excellence in Education (1983) warns of "a rising tide of mediocrity" in the schools. The Twentieth Century Fund (1983) report declares that "the nation's public schools are in trouble," and a task force from the Education Commission of the States (1983) observes that the schools are in need of "deep and lasting change." John Goodlad, drawing from the conclusions of the Study of Schooling (1983c) said that "it will take enormous expenditures of energy to make our schools vital places of learning." Several projects intent on reforming the American high school are underway (Gray 1982), and all indications are that their recommendations will be in tune with those of other reform groups. The Chief State School Officers organization has issued statements addressed to the "crisis of quality" in the teaching profession as well as endorsing a strengthened academic curriculum (Ranbom 1983, Smith 1982). Although the proposals have come at a time when school finances are in trouble and many schools and teacher education institutions are short-staffed, the school reform offensive has captured the attention of the person-on-the-street and political leaders as well as educators. The advocacy of corporate executives, university presidents, academicians, and school administrators and the connections made from education to economic health and national security have stimulated more openness to the proposals. Following in capsule form are reports of the methods used, findings, and recommendations of prominent reform groups.

National Commission on Excellence in Education. Strong statements characterize the well-publicized report of this commission (1983). Appointed by the secretary of education, Terrel H. Bell, in 1981, a bipartisan panel of eighteen members including university presidents, professors of science, public school administrators and a teacher, a corporation executive, a governor, and two representatives of foundations or consulting firms were directed to examine the quality of education in the United States and report within eighteen months. The charge to the commission included assessing the quality of teaching and learning in the public and private schools, colleges and universities of the nation and making comparisons with those of other nations; studying the relationship between college admission requirements and achievement of high school students; assessing the impact of a quarter century of social and educational changes on student achievement; identifying notable programs that have led to student success in college; and defining problems to be faced and overcome in pursuing excellence in education.

The commission relied on five main sources of information: (1) more than forty papers commissioned from experts on a variety of educational issues (now available in the ERIC system); (2) testimony of more than two hundred persons with expertise related to matters under discussion at eight meetings of the full commission, six public hearings, two panel discussions, a symposium, and a series of meetings around the country; (3) existing analyses of data including those showing decline in the Scholastic Aptitude Tests, the National Assessment of Educational Progress in science achievement, other standardized tests, and unfavorable comparisons with student achievement in other countries on international competitions; (4) letters from concerned citizens and educators; and (5) descriptions of promising programs and approaches in education. The opening assertions of the commission's report convey its tone:

Our nation is at risk. Our once unchallenged preeminence in commerce, industry, science, and technological innovation is being overtaken by competitors throughout the world. . . . Our society and its educational institutions seem to have lost sight of the basic purpose of schooling, and of the high expectations and disciplined effort needed to attain them. . . . That we have compromised this commitment is hardly surprising, given the multitude of often conflicting demands we have placed on our nation's schools and colleges. They are routinely called on to provide solutions to personal, social, and political problems that the home and other institutions either will not or cannot resolve. We must understand that these demands on our schools and colleges often exact an educational cost as well as a financial one.

Recommendations of the commission relate to content of the curriculum, standards, time on task, teaching, leadership, and fiscal support. In brief, it is recommended that:

A. State and local high school graduation requirements be strengthened. To receive a diploma the student would be required to take four years of English, three years of mathematics, three years of science, three years of social studies, and one-half year of computer science. If college bound, two years of foreign language are added.

B. Schools, colleges, and universities adopt more rigorous and measurable standards and higher expectations for academic performance and student conduct. Four-year colleges and universities would raise their requirements for admission.

C. More time be devoted to learning. This would require more effective use of the school day, a longer school day, or a lengthened school year. More attention would be given to gifted and talented students as well as slow learners. More homework and stiffer discipline control were advised.

D. The preparation of teachers be improved and steps be taken to make teaching a more respected and rewarding profession. Persons preparing to teach would meet higher standards for admission to college and university teacher-preparation programs. Salaries for teachers would be competitive, market-sensitive, and performance-based. Excellent teachers would be rewarded, average ones encouraged, and poor ones dismissed.

E. Educators and elected officials be held responsible by citizens across the nation for providing the leadership necessary to achieve these reforms, and citizens provide the fiscal support and stability needed.

Critics point out that the report's suggested improvements would cost far more money than is presently available for education. Moreover, the federal government shows no inclination to assist but would leave fiscal matters to local and state resources. It has also been noted that reports by prestigious groups, valuable as they are, do not always recognize the many subtle and complex factors affecting student achievement in the schools. Others support the work of this commission and point out that some of its recommendations could be achieved with present finances by making more efficient use of the school day, adjusting requirements and standards, and strengthening curriculum content.

Task Force of the Twentieth Century Fund. Released almost simultaneously with the report of the Commission on Excellence and covering the same time schedule of work, this study underlined the commission's laments about poor school performance, but it took a stand for strong leadership and fiscal support by the federal government to dramatize the importance of the national interest in educational excellence. Sponsored by the Twentieth Century Fund, an independent research foundation that conducts policy studies of economic, political, and social issues, the task force was charged with examining the effects of federal funding on education in the past, both its strengths and weaknesses, and making recommendations for or against future federal involvement. The twelve-member task force, comprised of university and public school representatives, held eleven sessions, examined federal educational policy in elementary and secondary education, and studied reports of various effects in the schools.

Recommendations for the federal government include a point of view about leadership in education as well as fiscal support for specified responsibilities. The report emphasized that state and local governments should continue to bear the major responsibility for providing educational services, but it is increasingly important that the federal government emphasize the pressing need for a high quality system of education for all young Americans and exert leadership in fostering excellence in education. The task force rejected the principle of tuition tax credit or voucher plans. It went on record against collective bargaining by teachers and pointed to the process as having a negative effect on the quality of teaching. The task force called on schools to renew their emphasis on the primacy of literacy in the English language and would use current funding for bilingual education to teach English to non-English-speaking students. Proficiency in a second language was encouraged for all students. Federal expenditures for education would avoid peripheral topics, fruitless quests for "quick fixes" or projects that cater to special interest groups. Counterproductive types of federal intervention would also be avoided, such as excessive paper work and mandated programs that require local and state school offices to employ additional personnel and reallocate substantial amounts of scarce revenues to meet federal requirements. Recommendations include federal monetary support of advanced training in science and mathematics for secondary students, incentives for master teachers, and local programs to help failing students. Federal aid would be extended to programs for poor, handicapped, and immigrant students. Research in education would focus on the learning process, information about the educational performance of students and teachers across the nation, and rigorous evaluation of federally sponsored educational programs.

National Task Force on Education for Economic Growth. Echoing concerns of other panels about America's public schools, this task force sponsored by the Education Commission of the States (1983) concluded that students are not being adequately prepared for the demands of an internationally competitive, technology-based economy. The forty-one members of the task force were mostly from outside professional education: thirteen governors, fifteen executives or board chair holders of leading corporations, three state senators or representatives, and ten with university or school leadership backgrounds. The goals of the task force were to (1) create national understanding of the need for a well-educated work force and the changing work skills needed for economic growth; (2) promote policies and programs to improve education, both public and private; and (3) establish partnerships among community, business, labor, government, and education leaders to improve education leading to economic growth. Two meetings of the full group and five subgroup meetings were held. Data for consideration were largely drawn from existing studies. Emphasis was placed on the inadequate preparation of applicants and employees for today's jobs and the fact that millions of dollars must be spent by corporations on remedial programs in basic skills such as reading and mathematics.

The report of the task force stressed the nation's economic interests and called for deep and lasting change in the schools. Included are recommendations for state action plans covering kindergarten through twelfth grade; better use of existing resources; school and business partnerships; longer school days and school year; more demanding requirements in discipline, attendance, grading systems, and homework; and concentration by principals on instructional leadership with administrative tasks assigned elsewhere.

Study of Schooling. By far the most comprehensive of recent studies of schools in terms of scope and firsthand observations in classrooms is the in-depth study by John Goodlad and his colleagues. Extending over nearly a decade, the Study of Schooling has yielded a wealth of reports and information about American schools. *A Place Called School* (1983a) fully treats the major themes of the findings, and summations and recommendations are readily available as well (1983 b,c). The purposes of the study were to describe in detail representative samples of schools; examine teaching practices, subject matter, use of time, and instructional materials; and generate some hypotheses to guide further research and efforts to improve schools.

Thirteen clusters of schools were studied, each including an elementary, junior high, and senior high school. They were widely diverse in regard to location, size, family income, and racial composition of the student body. Data collection teams of twenty persons spent approximately a month in each cluster of schools and its community. All principals were queried as were 1,350 teachers, 8,624 parents, and 17,163 students. The functioning of 1,016 classrooms was intensively observed. Documents detailing goals and curricula from fifty states were examined as were extensive samples of textbooks and other instructional materials.

One overriding generalization from analysis of data is that a sameness in curriculum and instructional methods prevails whether the school is large or small, urban or rural, serves affluent or poor people. As additional schools increased the data bank, this observation held true.

Although schools have lofty goals, Goodlad concluded, teaching and curriculum are geared to a low common denominator. The curriculum was prescribed by the topics and content of textbooks, and emphasis was on factual recall rather than problem solving or exploratory thinking. Opportunities to conceptualize the broad structures of knowledge were sacrificed on behalf of narrower or shallower segments of learning that became the objectives of instruction. The range of teaching procedures appeared to be limited almost entirely to explaining, lecturing, monitoring seatwork, and testing. Teacher talk was by far the dominant classroom activity. Of 150 minutes of instruction time in secondary schools, only 7 minutes were initiated by students; the rest by teachers. Talking that required organization of thought was seldom available to students. Writing, another activity conducive to the development of thinking skills, was also shortchanged, as most writing required only short responses to teachers' questions.

A matter of major concern emerging from the Study of Schooling is the misuse of student energy. The classroom observers were particularly impressed with the prevalence of student apathy. Even more disturbing is the observation that students seemed to enjoy passive listening because the demands on them were light and their minds were free to dwell on other interests. The "one best thing" about school in responses of junior and senior high school students was games or sports or "my friends." Goodlad feels that the energies of students are not being adequately absorbed in the business of educating themselves. Only in the schools rating high on a satisfaction index employed in the study were there some differences in the academic ambience.

The satisfaction index was derived from ratings of their schools by parents, principals, teachers, and students. It focused on the degree of congruity between goals preferred by the constituents and those perceived to be emphasized by the school, and perceptions of the intensity of problems in the school. Classification of data yielded a top quartile of most satisfying schools and a bottom quartile of least satisfying. The most satisfying schools were characterized by a higher quality of interaction among the school's participants, a positive school and classroom climate, and capabilities for renewal from within. Students admired such teacher attributes as warmth, enthusiasm, and caring about students. Such schools appeared more able to encourage educational goals. The least satisfying schools demonstrated far more frustrations: principals frequently viewed the teachers as part of the problem, and teachers felt that the principal did not support them. In some schools, noneducational matters had become so overwhelming that intellectual pursuits were bypassed, although the participants were concerned about this. Even in the most satisfying schools, however, the limited curricular and instructional patterns noted above were the mode.

Reasons for the persistence of sameness, according to Goodlad (1983c), are that teachers tend to teach the way they were taught; student teaching reinforces the model; and in-service offerings are usually random. Also, proficiency tests seem to set minimal expectations for schools as teachers attempt to meet publicized accusations of poor performance based on test scores. These habits are so ingrained in the schools that Goodlad sees change as extraordinarily difficult.

To view the problem conceptually, he contrasts the factory model, now prevalent, with the ecological model for schooling. The factory model is an input-output system; students enter at one end, are graded, tested, and come out the other end to be dispersed into jobs or colleges. The broad goals of education, proclaimed throughout the country, of complex applications of principles of logic, uses of different modes of inquiry, development of citizenship, civility, and creativity are not given high priority. Pressures for improvement come from outside, from state departments of education, distant district offices, and reform commissions.

In the ecological model, strategies for improvement come from inside the individual school, from the quality of interactions of the constituents, from rationales governing improvement. It is a self-help process, a continuing process of growth and renewal that takes cognizance of the world of today and tomorrow.

Recommendations proposed by Goodlad include the following:

1. A clear articulation by the states of the full range of goals for the schools, followed by extensive dialogue at the district and building levels of the meaning of these goals.
2. Expectations established for each school including a three-to-five year plan, a continuing planning process, and effective leadership. (New concepts of leadership are demanded, not a limited view of instructional leadership that merely works harder at narrow objectives. See Chapter Two.)
3. Continuing attention to curriculum and instruction using processes of dialogue, decision making, and evaluation.
4. New organizational arrangements to take the career flatness out of teaching: head teachers, career teachers, aides, and interns, for example.
5. New roles for students in which they become far more responsible for their own learning and that of their classmates. An example is peer teaching in which talented students help others in small groups or one-to-one. Students will learn from teaching.

High School Reform Projects. Reform proposals described above are directed toward elementary and secondary education, with suggestions for higher education. Other advocates are concentrating on the high school (Gray 1982). The following are nationally recognized.

A Study of High Schools is chaired by Theodore Sizer (1983) and sponsored by the National Association of Secondary School Principals and the National Association of Independent Schools. This group expects to issue a historical review of forces that have shaped the development of high schools, a report on intensive field studies, and concrete recommendations for improving the quality of teaching and learning. A team of fifteen researchers is visiting high schools and gathering data.

The Paideia Proposal is written by Mortimer Alder (1982) who, with a small group of educators, suggests a common core curriculum of academic learnings for all high school students to have the same objectives and course of study. Reading materials would be selected from the "great books," and instruction would be based on great ideas from the classics in ways designed to stimulate intellectual discipline and philosophical thought. Teacher preparation would be geared to this uniform approach. The proposal was developed from the Paideia group's discussions as they met several times to refine Alder's ideas about public schooling. There is no permanent organization ready at present to take up this Paideia cause.

The College Board's Educational EQuality Project (1983) is a ten-year effort of school and college educators to strengthen the academic quality of secondary education and to ensure equality of opportunity for postsecondary education of all students. Hundreds of persons served on advisory panels, all of them closely connected with schools and colleges—professors, teachers, and students. Hearings in the form of dialogues were held at many locations across the country. Recommendations are organized in levels of advancement: basic competencies considered essential for all high school students in reading, writing, speaking, listening, mathematics, reasoning, and studying; knowledge and skills essential for success in academic fields in college; and further abilities to be acquired in high school for those expecting to take advanced programs in science, mathematics, engineering, or foreign languages. Dissemination is expected to be achieved through a widespread organization of 2,500 schools, colleges, and other educational associations. Examples of recommended competencies are given in Chapter Seven.

High School: A Report on Secondary Education in America, a study sponsored by the Carnegie Foundation for the Advancement of Teaching and reported by Ernest Boyer (1983), is based on a three-year analysis of public secondary education. Twelve themes provide a detailed agenda of proposals for reforming and revitalizing the nation's high schools. These are: clear and vital goals, proficiency in language skills, a core of common learnings for all, improved transition from school to work, community service for students, renewal of the teaching profession, effective classroom instruction, links with technology, better use of time, emphasis on the principal's leadership ability, strengthened coordination with postsecondary education and business, and a public commitment of support.

Teams of twenty-five educators made an extended investigation of fifteen high schools across the nation with varying characteristics. Related studies were analyzed, including Goodlad's "Study of Schooling" and James Coleman's *High School and Beyond* (1983). The latter is a long-range study of the relationship between courses taken in high school by graduates and their occupations. To implement reforms proposed in the report, the Carnegie Foundation will make a few grants to selected schools.

Redefining General Education in the American High School, sponsored by the Association for Supervision and Curriculum Develoment and directed by Gordon Cawelti (1982), is a network of seventeen high schools organized to consult with each other in revising curricula for general education. Self-study, a futures emphasis, team meetings to confer, and sharing views on what needs to be done in the high schools are all features of the networking process. Models and plans will be developed and may differ from school to school. Implementation is expected to occur over a three to five year period.

From this array of "reform literature," it is obvious that school and college curricula are on the threshold of a new era. In the face of powerful groups that influence curriculum development (federal and state authorities, courts, the New Right, and professional reform advocates), what are the roles and responsibilities of grass roots participants: school administrators, curriculum specialists, teachers, students, parents, and other citizens?

POWERS AND ROLES OF PARTICIPANTS

School Administrators

The school board and professional educators are responsible for allocating values in formulating and administering curriculum policy. Formal channels flow from the board to the superintendent to the principals and other middle managers. As Wirt and Kirst (1982, pp. 127-62) have pointed out, voter influence can generate constraints on school authorities; thus, it behooves curriculum developers to look within the community environment as well as the school system to find major influences that can lead to stress. Resources supportive to progress in curriculum development can also be found or generated there as well. Professional leadership skills are needed to promote cooperative endeavors, the development of talents, and the willing support of constituents. Sharing power in curriculum development with teachers, experts, students, parents, and other lay citizens is difficult and involves risks. Effective communication is necessary. The administrator must be responsible for clarifying the decision-making structure right from the beginning of a task so that participants do not become disappointed with the organization, expect exclusive control, or charge that certain interests have been kept out to achieve a preconceived outcome.

Although somewhat bound by federal, state, and local regulations, school administrators still have considerable power to influence curriculum development. The principal has frequently been identified as the key to attaining quality and effectiveness in school climate. In fact, in many districts where enrollment is declining and resources are scarce, the principal has become the curriculum leader, and other supervisory resources have vanished. (The many dimensions of leadership are explored in Chapter Two.)

The Curriculum Specialist or Supervisor

If the persons designated by a local district as curriculum leaders—curriculum directors, curriculum associates, assistant superintendents for curriculum and instruction, instructional supervisors, and similar titles—see their roles as limited to that of facilitators, then it is small wonder that some of these positions have been eliminated. Curriculum leadership consists of far more than arranging the time and place, the chairs and tables, coffee, and display of materials.

One example of incompetence or irresponsibility on the part of curriculum specialists was a widespread custom of the 1950s, which helped precipitate the curriculum reform movement of that decade. As noted in Chapter One, the curriculum committees of local school systems, composed of teachers and curriculum specialists, would write numerous "curriculum guides" that were mainly outlines of content and activities lifted from several textbooks. In turn, textbook publishers collected these curriculum guides and published more textbooks, setting up a cycle of mediocrity in curriculum development that lasted for more than a generation. Public attention to curriculum content, particularly in science and mathematics, highlighted by Sputnik's first exploration of space jolted publishers, curriculum directors, and teachers into a realization that some school subjects had not kept up with new knowledge. New teaching materials, produced through federal and foundation funds, inspired adaptations by publishers and a more critical approach to the creation of local curriculum guides. Currently, at the local level, curriculum development procedures are better planned than was evident prior to the reforms of the sixties. Curriculum leaders of the new reform movements of the eighties would do well to examine past experiences in the curriculum development field and seek ways to learn from previous gains and losses.

Today curriculum leadership can be measured by the degrees of specialists' skills in acquainting the participating groups and individuals with the best that is known from related research, bringing the participants in contact with viable curriculum models, and employing a range of organizational skills including:

1. Identifying the needs and problems by using unbiased methods.
2. Defining goals and objectives at several levels of decision making.
3. Developing plans and procedures that invite the trust of the participants and elicit cooperative decision making.
4. Involving people of different as well as like interests and backgrounds in discussing issues, developing plans, and working together on effective action programs.
5. Finding ways to communicate and use feedback both inside the school and within the larger community.
6. Planning a workable time-phased implementation schedule for moving the agreed-upon curriculum into the mainstream of the school system.
7. Using evaluation processes that will produce continuing and constructive change and renewal.

Teachers

There is general agreement that curriculum change and improvement will not take place unless teachers are closely involved. The initial curriculum reforms of the 1950s and 1960s failed to a large extent because teachers were not involved in developing the innovations and did not have sufficient support and leadership from their supervisors and administrators, according to a comprehensive study by the National Science Foundation (1979, p. 47).

Becoming involved means acquiring curriculum development skills. Curriculum decision making and development are not just rights to be granted to selected groups or individuals; they are skills that require special competencies. The abilities needed for curriculum development have been set forth in Hilda Taba's classic work (1962) and are still appropriate today. In addition to face-to-face experience with students, sufficient familiarity with the content of specific subject fields is needed to guide the process of selecting valid core ideas and content. Knowledge of learners and learning processes is needed to guide the selection of learning activities and their sequences. Competence is needed in the choice of diagnostic and evaluation devices and in interpreting data. Ability is needed in diagnosing human factors and interpersonal relations, recognizing blocks to overcome, levels of perception, and attitudes of the participants.

Familiarity with group processes is also required. Teachers as curriculum developers must know how to mobilize groups, initiate them into curriculum work, diagnose their concerns, develop problems and plans from those concerns, formulate objectives, project hypotheses from local or general research, and translate these hypotheses into curriculum possibilities.

Although teacher associations have mainly concentrated on salary increases, benefits, and working conditions, more involvement in curriculum planning is seen as a next step. For example, the National Education Association (1980) issued a position statement on the desirability of a strengthened future role in curriculum decisions and curriculum development. Major points are:

1. Teachers must be centrally involved in curriculum planning. The NEA and its affiliates should negotiate and in other ways assure that teachers are meaningfully engaged in such planning. Curricula that have had active teacher involvement in their development will greatly benefit students because they will be more closely targeted to their needs and be more readily and enthusiastically implemented in the classroom.

2. Through staff development programs, teachers should be helped to acquire curriculum development skills. Teacher education programs have been especially deficient in helping teachers develop curriculum planning skills.

3. Other professional educators, community members, and students should also be involved in curriculum planning. It is reasonable to assume that the more persons meaningfully involved in the planning, the more these same persons will work to put the plans into practice and give them a fair and intensive trial.

4. Curriculum development should be a continuous process. Planners should always look for what appears to be effective and should be retained and what appears to be questionable and should be modified (pp. 23–27).

The NEA's self-assignments touch on new and continuing responsibilities. Persons working in curriculum development must reach into fields that are not usually included in the curriculum for teacher education: high technology, economics, futures research, law, and others. As is the case with each level of participant in curriculum development, teachers need links with the others. Each level of participation has its unique contribution to make and its particular set of responsibilities, but they all need to interact and communicate with one another.

Students

Although student participation in curriculum decisions can be accepted in principle, involving students on a broader scale than just choosing courses is difficult to fit into a neat recipe for procedure. Some students want to participate in planning, while others resist the extra time and effort needed.

It behooves those in leadership positions to be politically aware of students' feelings about the curriculum. The school crises that developed in many communities from approximately 1968 through 1970 were outstanding examples of student resistance to curriculum decisions in which they had had no part. Throughout the preceding academic "curriculum reform" decade, students seemed to be the participants who were least consulted in curriculum planning, and they reacted in many instances with either extreme activism (demands for black studies, student rights, and peace efforts) or extreme apathy (the hippie movement). As a result, teachers and other adults in the schools became more sensitive to students' perceptions of the curriculum, and many have found ways to involve students productively.

The most common type of student participation in curriculum planning occurs at the classroom level. Many teachers seek the opinions of students, even very young students, through classroom discussions, opportunities to vote on alternative program plans, or individual conferences. In the secondary schools, planning and carrying out oral history projects, other action-learning projects in the community, student exchange programs with other schools, independent study programs, and study tours are examples of student involvement in curriculum planning in which they assume responsibility with teachers for accomplishing joint agreements. Less frequent is the involvement of students in developing basic curriculum plans for a school or department, although secondary students are occasionally invited to participate in curriculum advisory groups, and their contributions are sincerely sought by teachers, curriculum specialists, parents, and others on the committee.

Students seem to want to determine how much or how little they will become involved in curriculum planning. Early in the 1970s, an experimental alternative school was organized in Chicago that was designed to involve students in decision making, not only about such matters as dress, grooming, and attendance rules, but also about the planning, selection, and evaluation of the curriculum. Before the opening of the alternative school, the students' underground papers and rap sessions had regularly criticized the establishment for excluding students from this type of planning and decision making. Yet a participant observer, Donald Moore, who spent two years in this alternative school (1972), reported that when the opportunities were fully provided, students made little use of them. At staff-student meetings organized for the purpose of planning, students seemed to be chiefly interested in making sure that their rights about freedom of dress and expression were fully guaranteed, that they could complain to the staff about anything they disliked, and that they had the right to omit any activity, including curriculum planning, anytime they wished. Decision making about curriculum offerings soon fell almost entirely to the staff, although staff members continued to urge students to take part.

Although results of student involvement in curriculum decision making have been uneven, schools should regard participation in decision making as a skill to be developed, not just a right to be granted. Students with no previous experience in decision making will not suddenly be converted into enthusiastic partcipants in a process that places new demands on them for acquiring skills, collecting information, weighing causes and effects, and spending time in deliberations that may seem endless, pointless, and boring.

Parents, Other Citizens, Business and Industry

Partnership is the major concept underlying involvement of parents and other lay persons in curriculum planning. Partnership implies a common effort toward common goals. The emphasis here is on the leadership of professional educators and the mutual accountability for student learning rather than on professional power and exclusiveness, according to David Seeley (1982). An immediate advantage of the partnership concept for education, he notes, is the assistance it provides in escaping the dilemma of whom to blame for educational failure.

One notable positive movement in parent involvement is the increase of parent volunteers in the schools. Volunteerism can have several different meanings. It can refer to participation on advisory and policy-making committees, helping children with special projects, sharing expertise as a resource person in a curriculum field, or serving as a tutor for children with special needs.

An example of a school advisory council is the California School Improvement Program, which is designed to improve the quality of public education by stimulating change on a school site basis. A school site council composed equally of educators, parents, community members, and, at the secondary level, students, is formed in every participating school. Qualifying schools receive a small amount per pupil in state funds to use as the planning council sees fit. The purpose of the site council is to (a) identify the strengths and weaknesses of the school's education program, (b) plan activities that build on strengths and respond to weaknesses, (c) evaluate the results of these efforts, and (d) modify things that are not working. The School Improvement Program involves thirty-five hundred schools in California (Kirst 1980, p. 104).

In checking with the California State Department of Education, we found that in 1983, after ten years of existence, the program continues to be satisfying and is considered stabilized. The original idea, to provide parent advocates for children, has largely worked well and has helped to balance some former problems of teacher advocates for teachers and administrator advocates for administrators. Schools that participate seem to have developed a school-team attitude that yields useful results. Elementary school discussions tend to center around academic questions, such as reading and mathematics, while secondary parents and student representatives seem more interested in campus conditions and student activities. Parents of secondary students who have academic questions are more likely to work directly with school department heads or individual teachers. Modest state funds, set aside to stimulate the work of the school site councils, have provided local incentives. One problem of the near future is the limited money supply for schools.

On the home front, parents are again being persuaded to help their children with homework. At the preschool age, reading aloud to very young children has long been advocated for parents because it correlates with later school ability and motivation for reading. Another positive trend is the interest in courses or study materials on "parenting." This involves educating parents about their responsibilities for the well-being of their children, including matters of health and nutrition, intellectual development, discipline, and the many other aspects of effective child rearing.

Corporations and business establishments are now forming new partnerships with schools that show a break in long-standing custom. Although this is not widespread, observers note an upswing in activity. New types of corporate involvement extend far beyond the traditional contribution to vocational education and have spread into curriculum development areas as well as financial management. The rapidly changing nature of the work place, caused primarily by the rapid evolution of computer-related technologies and the need for schools to produce students who can think, communicate, listen, and work with other people, are the reasons business has begun to take a more active role in school matters.

Illustrations of this involvement collected by Thomas Toch (1982) include "Adopt-a-School" programs or "School-Business Partnerships," in which corporations encourage employees to go into the school and give lectures, tutor, or offer career counseling; contributions of equipment or services such as alcohol-education courses or seminars on banking principles; and contributions of executives' time and expertise to study the management system of a large school system and offer advice for improvement. These and other trends in the news seem to indicate that civic and business leaders are looking at education as a focal point for the future.

CONCLUSION

The political context of curriculum decision making is complex and calls for resourceful leaders. Curriculum decisions in a pluralistic society must meet stresses produced by the differing values and philosophies of ethnic groups, classes, and sexes; conservatives and liberals; the old and the young; the rich and the poor; and urban, suburban, and rural interests.

These conclusions can be drawn:

1. Any attempts to keep potential issues and alternatives from being discussed or even recognized would be a formidable barrier to progress.

2. The concept of participation must be accepted by educators, and they must work for shared responsibility with their publics.
3. Curriculum leaders must be aware of legislation and judicial decisions affecting the curriculum.
4. Changes in what students learn will not take place through mere legal requirements unless these are integrated into a comprehensive program of teacher education, public awareness, and student engagement.
5. Supportive resources are necessary for curriculum change, but money alone is not enough as has been shown in numerous federal projects that resulted in money spent with only superficial results.
6. The increased numbers of participants in curriculum decisions today, the complexities of arranging involvement, and the necessity of being attentive to the legal aspects all require far more time for curriculum decisions to be made than in the past.
7. There are today more points in the decision-making process at which proposals can be vetoed. It is one thing to launch a new program and quite another to get it implemented successfully in the classroom.
8. The time has come for educational leaders to agree on what education is supposed to accomplish and to move assertively into the political arena with some solutions to educational problems.

REFERENCES

Adler, Mortimer J. *The Paideia Proposal: An Educational Manifesto*. New York: Macmillan Co., 1982.

Association of American Publishers. *Limiting What Students Shall Read*. Washington, D.C.: AAP, 1981.

Bacharach, Samuel B., and Mitchell, Stephen M. "Critical Variables in the Formation and Maintenance of Consensus in School Districts." *Educational Administration Quarterly* 17 (Fall 1981): 74-97.

Bendiner, Robert. *The Politics of Schools: A Crisis in Self-Government*. New York: Harper & Row, 1969.

Berman, Paul, and McLaughlin, Milbrey W. "Implementation of Educational Innovation." *The Educational Forum* 40 (1976): 345-70.

Birchall, Greg. "Standing Up to the Textbook Censors." *ERIC Keeping Up*. Newsletter. April 1981.

Blackwood, Paul E. "Science." In *Using Current Curriculum Developments*, edited by Robert S. Gilchrist, pp. 59-70. Alexandria, Va.: Association for Supervision and Curriculum Development, 1963.

Boyer, Ernest L. *High School: A Report on Secondary Education in America*. Washington, D.C.: Carnegie Foundation for the Advancement of Teaching, 1983.

Brodinsky, Ben. "The New Right: The Movement and Its Impact." *Phi Delta Kappan* 64 (October 1982): 87–94. (Responses: 94–101).

Caldwell, Peggy, and Walton, Susan. "Many States Assess Lessons of Florida 'Exit-Test' Lawsuit." *Education Week* 2 (May 25, 1983): 1, 16–17.

Cawelti, Gordon. "Redefining General Education for the American High School." *Educational Leadership* 39 (May 1982): 570–71.

Coleman, James S. *High School and Beyond.* Chicago: National Opinion Research Center, 1983.

The College Board. *Academic Preparation for College: What Students Need to Know and Be Able to Do.* New York: The College Board, 1983.

Davis, Robert B. "Mathematics." In *New Curriculum Developments,* edited by Glenys G. Unruh, pp. 46–56. Alexandria, Va.: Association for Supervision and Curriculum Development, 1965.

Dodson, Dan W. "Authority, Power, and Education." In *Education for an Open Society,* pp. 99–108. Yearbook of the Association for Supervision and Curriculum Development. Alexandria, Va.: ASCD, 1974.

Education Commission of the States. *Report of the National Task Force on Education for Economic Growth.* Denver: ECS, 1983.

Foley, Robert. "The Community's Role in Dealing With Censorship." *Educational Leadership* 40 (January 1983): 51–54.

Goodlad, John I. *A Place Called School.* New York: McGraw-Hill, 1983a.

Goodlad, John I. "A Study of Schooling: Some Findings and Hypotheses." *Phi Delta Kappan* 64 (March 1983b): 465–70.

Goodlad, John I. "A Study of Schooling: Some Implications for School Improvement." *Phi Delta Kappan* 64 (April 1983c): 552–58.

Goodlad, John I., et al. *Behind the Classroom Door.* Columbus, Ohio: Charles Jones, 1970.

Gray, Dennis. "The 1980s: Season for High School Reform." *Educational Leadership* 39 (May 1982): 564–68.

Henning, Joel F., et al. *Mandate for Change: The Impact of Law on Educational Innovation.* Chicago: The American Bar Association, 1979.

Institute for Research on Teaching. "Content Influenced by Many Factors." In *Communication Quarterly* 4 (Fall 1981): 2. Newsletter, Michigan State University, East Lansing.

Kimbrough, Ralph B. *Political Power and Educational Decision-Making.* Chicago: Rand McNally, 1964.

Kirst, Michael W. "How Should Schools be Ruled?" *Educational Leadership* 38 (November 1980): 103–4.

Klein, Barry. "Florida's Minimum Competency Test Ruled Constitutional." *Education Week* 2 (May 11, 1983): 1, 17.

Lamm, Richard. "Promoting Finitude." *The Amicus Journal* (Summer 1980): 6–8.

Masotti, Louis H. *The New Trier Experience.* Cleveland, Ohio: The Press of Western Reserve University, 1967.

Meranto, Philip. *School Politics in the Metropolis.* Columbus, Ohio: Charles E. Merrill, 1970.

Moore, Donald R., ed. "Strengthening Alternative High Schools." *Harvard Educational Review* 42 (August 1972): 313–49.

National Assessment of Educational Progress. *Reading, Thinking and Writing: Results from the 1979–80 National Assessment of Reading and Literature.* Denver, Co.: NAEP, 1981.

National Commission on Excellence in Education. *A Nation at Risk: The Imperative for Educational Reform.* (Report) Washington, D.C.: U.S. Government Printing Office, 1983.

National Education Association. *Curriculum Issues for the Eighties: Structure, Content, Context.* Washington, D.C.: NEA, 1980.

National Institute of Education. *Current Issues, Problems, and Concerns in Curriculum Development.* Washington, D.C.: NIE, January 15, 1976.

National Science Foundation. *What are the Needs in Precollege Science, Mathematics, and Social Science Education? Views from the Field.* Washington, D.C.: NSF, 1979.

Park, J. Charles. "Preachers, Politics, and Public Education: A Review of Right-Wing Pressures Against Public Schooling in America." *Phi Delta Kappan* 61 (May 1980): 608–12.

Ranbom, Sheppard. "Educators Seek Solutions to 'Crisis' in Teaching." *Education Week* 2 (March 2, 1983): 1, 13.

Rand Corporation. *Aggregate Effects on Federal Education Programs.* Santa Monica, Calif.: Rand Corp., 1981.

Scribner, Jay D., ed. *The Politics of Education,* part II. Seventy-sixth Yearbook of the National Society for the Study of Education. Chicago: University of Chicago Press, 1977.

Seeley, David S. "Education Through Partnership." *Educational Leadership* 40 (November 1982): 42–43.

Sizer, Theodore R. "High School Reform: The Need for Engineering." *Phi Delta Kappan* 64 (June 1983): 679–83.

Skoog, Gerald. "Legal Issues Involved in Evolution vs. Creationism." *Educational Leadership* 38 (November 1980): 154–56.

Smith, Cynthia. "State Chiefs Endorse New Curriculum Priorities." *Education Week* 2 (November 24, 1982): 9, 14.

Taba, Hilda. *Curriculum Development: Theory and Practice.* New York: Harcourt, Brace and World, 1962.

Toch, Thomas. "New Activism Marks Corporate Role in Schools." *Education Week* 2 (November 10, 1982): 1, 11, 14.

Turlington, Ralph D. "Good News from Florida: Our Minimum Competency Program Is Working." *Phi Delta Kappan* 60 (May 1979): 649–54.

Twentieth Century Fund. *The Report of the Task Force on Federal Elementary and Secondary Education Policy.* New York: Twentieth Century Fund, 1983.

Unruh, Glenys G., and Alexander, William M. *Innovations in Secondary Education.* New York: Holt, Rinehart, and Winston, 1970.

van Geel, Tyll. "The New Law of the Curriculum." In *Value Conflicts and Curriculum Issues,* edited by John Schaffarzick and Gary Sykes, pp. 25–72. Berkeley: McCutchan, 1979.

Walker, Decker F. "What Curriculum Research?" *Journal of Curriculum Studies* 5 (1973): 58–72.

Wirt, Frederick M., and Kirst, Michael W. *Schools in Conflict*. Berkeley: McCutchan, 1982.

Zirkel, Perry A., ed. *A Digest of Supreme Court Decisions Affecting Education*. Bloomington, Ind.: Phi Delta Kappan, 1978.

ADDITIONAL READINGS

Apple, Michael W. "Politics and National Curriculum Policy." *Curriculum Inquiry* 7 (Winter 1977): 335-61.

Brandt, Ronald S., ed. *Partners: Parents and Schools*. Alexandria, Va.: Association for Supervision and Curriculum Development, 1979.

Hulburd, David. *This Happened in Pasadena*. New York: Macmillan Co., 1951.

Lieberman, Ann, and McLaughlin, Milbrey W. *Policy Making in Education*, part I. Eighty-first Yearbook of the National Society for the Study of Education. Chicago: University of Chicago Press, 1982.

Mosher, Edith K. "Politics and Pedagogy: A New Mix." *Educational Leadership* 38 (November 1980): 110-11.

Mosteller, Frederick, and Moynihan, Daniel P., eds. *On Equality of Educational Opportunity*. New York: Vintage Books, 1972.

Newman, Fred M., and Oliver, Donald W. *Clarifying Public Controversy*. Boston: Little, Brown, & Co., 1970.

Odden, Allan, and Dougherty, Van. *State Programs of School Improvement: A 50-State Survey*. Denver: Education Commission of the States, 1982.

Orelove, Fred P. "Administering Education for the Severely Handicapped After P.L. 94-142." *Phi Delta Kappan* 59 (June 1978): 699-702.

Reid, William. "Rationalism or Humanism: The Future of Curriculum Studies." *Journal of Curriculum Theorizing* 2 (Winter 1980): 93-108.

Schaffarzick, Jon, and Sykes, Gary. *Value Conflicts and Curriculum Issues*. Berkeley: McCutchan, 1979.

Unruh, Glenys G. "Curriculum Politics." In *Fundamental Curriculum Decisions*, pp. 99-111. Yearbook of the Association for Supervision and Curriculum Development. Alexandria, Va.: ASCD, 1983.

Unruh, Glenys G. "The Future of Public Schooling in the United States." *Illinois School Research and Development* 19 (Winter 1983): 1-6.

4

Theoretical Assumptions

Without a theoretical base, curriculum development can produce piecemeal reforms, curriculum imbalance, and short-lived innovations. One must consider the interaction of the elements that comprise the total curriculum. Too little attention has been given to the theoretical assumptions underlying curriculum development and their interpretation in the everyday life of the classroom. Although there have been numerous research studies in the curriculum field, they tend to deal with relatively narrow or insignificant problems that yield little or no understanding of the curriculum as a totality.

This chapter is directed toward clarifying definitions, exploring conflicting conceptions of the curriculum, and presenting an example of theory construction for curriculum development. Alternative theories that can be tested through multiple working hypotheses directed toward substantial improvements in practice are needed.

Contextual factors affecting curriculum development are many, varied, complicated, interconnected, and constantly changing. Thus, a theory of curriculum development that can be responsive to individual and social needs in a complex, changing society cannot be built around linear or single-principle concepts. In addition to the many environmental factors involved, the participants must be considered. Also knowledge does not stand still; it is constantly being revised, extended, and interpreted from varying points of view.

Even the definitions related to curriculum vary from one source to another. George Beauchamp (1972) found that the people using different meanings of curriculum seem to fall into three groups: one group thinks of curriculum as a plan for subsequent action; another views curriculum and instruction as synonymous or unified; and a third group sees curriculum as a broad term encompassing the learner's psychological processes as he or she acquires educational experiences. Daniel Tanner and Laurel Tanner traced the history of curriculum definitions, showing changes over time. Their study found a broad range of definitions including: curriculum as cumulative tradition of organized knowledge, modes of thought, race experience, planned learning environment, cognitive-affective content and process, instructional plan, instructional ends, technological system of production, and reconstruction of knowledge and experience (1980, pp. 3–43). Robert Zais (1981), reviewing numerous definitions of curriculum, concluded that preoccupation with fine points and precise definitions was not very productive and could block progress in curriculum development.

Definitions, nevertheless, should provide direction and be guides to action. Therefore, it is important to define terms for a given discussion or theoretical base. The following statements set forth the definitions of curriculum, instruction, and curriculum development on which this book is based.

CURRICULUM

Curriculum is defined as a plan for achieving intended learning outcomes: a plan concerned with purpose, with what is to be learned, and with the results of instruction. Curriculum is comprised of several elements: learning outcomes, selection, and structure. Learning outcomes include knowledge, attitudes, and skills. Knowledge encompasses facts, information, principles, and generalizations that help an individual understand his or her world better. Attitudes include values, beliefs, interpersonal feelings, creative thinking, appreciations, self-esteem, and other aspects of affective growth. Skills are techniques, processes, and abilities that enable the individual to be versatile in using knowledge and physical resources effectively to extend the horizons of his or her world.

Selection is an inherent element of curriculum. Selection is made from many sources of curriculum, including books, other materials, people, ideas, travel, and so forth. Selection recognizes the interrelatedness of knowledge, attitudes, and skills; that concepts and generalizations do not occur singly or in isolation but form clusters; and that motivation for learning is derived from the significance of the content. Selection also recognizes that modern communication media make cultural content available in many new dimensions.

Structure identifies order or sequence, or else it notes that order is immaterial. Structure for an individual may develop from his or her interests and motivations when a range of alternatives is available.

INSTRUCTION

Instruction is the process of teaching, of providing learning environments that offer students a wide range of interactions with people, things, places, and ideas through which the curriculum is delivered. The learning environment may include books, other printed materials, films, television programs, self-instructional packages, tape recordings, and many other modern types of media. The environment for instruction includes the world both inside and outside the school. Responsibility lies with the teacher to devise strategic environments so that educational goals can be reached. The quality of teacher-student interaction is of utmost importance. It must be distinguished from a "recitation" methodology; rather it must be motivational and assist in the integration of knowledge and the generation of new ideas.

CURRICULUM DEVELOPMENT

Curriculum development is a planning process: a complex process of assessing needs, identifying desired learning outcomes, preparing for instruction to achieve the outcomes, and meeting the cultural, social, and personal needs that the curriculum is to serve. Criteria for evaluating the curriculum are provided once learning outcomes are identified. Evaluation provides a means for constant revision and improvement of the curriculum.

Curriculum development involves many kinds of decisions on several different levels—classroom, institutional, governmental—that influence a variety of educational settings and populations: early childhood, elementary, middle school, secondary, college, vocational. Curriculum development may refer to a very small unit, such as a teacher and one or ten students, or to a statewide or national group. It may pertain to a subject field or an interdisciplinary area. The clientele may have pluralistic backgrounds or a homogeneous culture. They may be oriented toward rural or urban interests. They could be handicapped, normal, or gifted.

Curriculum development is never "finished"; it is an ongoing process that constantly evolves, extending, expanding, revising, and replacing elements of the curriculum. The learning goals must change if individuals are to draw effectively on the growing realms of knowledge, to develop new skills in a rapidly changing world, and to develop insights into and constructive approaches to unresolved problems. Other chapters of this book treat the components of curriculum development in detail: needs, goals and objectives, content areas, evaluation.

Definitions are not enough in building a theoretical base for curriculum development. A search must also be made for underlying principles or conceptions of the curriculum that have developed over time. Yet major orientations have often been in conflict. Their advocates seem to rely on shoulds and oughts, with an occasional how (as in the technological conception). Few, if any, have developed a theory with testable hypotheses, although several authors cite a need for theory.

THE CONCEPTUAL MAZE

Conflicting conceptions of the curriculum can lead to controversy in the school and its community; therefore, it behooves school administrators to understand widely different orientations to the concept of curriculum. Effective leadership in curriculum development depends on the ability to explain a particular approach and to involve others in the planning process.

Elliot Eisner and Elizabeth Vallance (1974) have identified five conflicting conceptions of the curriculum: cognitive, technological, self-actualization, social reconstruction, and academic rationalism. Similar approaches were identified by Tanner and Tanner (1980) and classified generally as traditional bodies of knowledge, modes of thought, transmittal of the culture, experiential, and technological. They noted that conceptions change over time. Geneva Gay (1980) named four discernible models for conceptualizing the curriculum: academic, experiential, technical, and pragmatic, and she emphasized that curriculum practitioners do not implement one conception in a "pure" approach to the exclusion of the others but are more likely to use an eclectic approach and draw bits and pieces from different theoretical models. Harold Shane and Bernadine Tabler (1981) sketched a diagram (Figure 3) that illustrates how the various conceptions of the curriculum relate to one another or can be utilized in an eclectic approach. Other authors have classified major orientations under similar categories. The following discussion draws upon Eisner's and Vallance's headings and includes descriptive information from related literature. While these principal conceptions do not exhaust the field, they are readily identifiable in the "real world" and can be used as tools for analyzing what might otherwise be a conceptual jungle.

Cognitive Processes

Developing the student's intellectual processes is the focus of the cognitive approach to curriculum. It is concerned with how learning takes place in the classroom and developing cognitive skills that can be

Figure 3. A Taxonomy of Curriculum Options

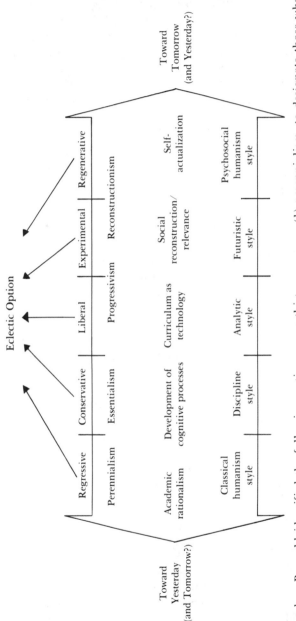

Eclectic Option

Toward
Yesterday
(and Tomorrow?)

Toward
Tomorrow
(and Yesterday?)

Regressive	Conservative	Liberal	Experimental	Regenerative
Perennialism	Essentialism	Progressivism	Reconstructionism	
Academic rationalism	Development of cognitive processes	Curriculum as technology	Social reconstruction/relevance	Self-actualization
Classical humanism style	Discipline style	Analytic style	Futuristic style	Psychosocial humanism style

Theodore Brameld identified the following options some thirty years ago: (1) perennialism, to designate those who see "perenially contemporary" values in the cultural heritage (e.g., Robert M. Hutchins, Mortimer Adler, Stringfellow Barr); (2) essentialism, which emphasizes basic education (e.g., William Bagley, Henry C. Morrison, Arthur Bestor); (3) progressivism, to label the early proponents of open education (e.g., Carleton W. Washburne); and (4) reconstructionism, which considers schooling as a means of developing a "new social order" (e.g., George S. Counts, Theodore Brameld, and more recently such prophets of reform as Ivan Illich).

Elliot Eisner and Elizabeth Vallance (1974) use the following terms to distinguish conflicting curriculum conceptions: (1) academic rationalism, (2) development of cognitive processes, (3) curriculum as technology, (4) social reconstruction/relevance, and (5) self-actualization/consummatory experience.

Donald E. Orlosky and B. Othanel Smith (1978) use the following terms: (1) the classical humanism style, (2) the discipline style, (3) the analytic style, and (4) the futuristic style, and psychosocial humanism style (associated with Abraham H. Maslow and Carl Rogers).

From Harold G. Shane and M. Bernadine Tabler, *Educating for a New Millenium* (Bloomington, Ind.: Phi Delta Kappa Educational Foundation, 1981) p. 11.

generalized, applied to learning virtually any content. The cognitive approach is frequently traced back to John Dewey (1933), who viewed curriculum as an opportunity to grow in reflective thinking; that is, to test conclusions through applications in new situations. He distinguishes reflective thinking from disciplinary thinking, which simply imposes the scholar's mode of thought in a given discipline onto the immature learner, who is then expected to replicate it. Dewey felt that learning is learning to think, an idea that is currently under attack by advocates of the New Right, who prefer control over the mind according to their precepts to any free-ranging intellectual inquiry.

Numerous curriculum reformers of the 1960s and early 1970s, taking their cue from Jerome Bruner (1960), focused on the processes of building generalizable intellectual skills. For example, the science curricula advocated by the American Association for the Advancement of Science are organized around the development of specific cognitive processes similar to those of Bloom's taxonomy (1956): observation, classification, analysis, synthesis, and inference or a similar progression of developing the power of intellect. The cognitive stages of Jean Piaget's developmental psychology (1970) have been widely applied in curriculum development, particularly in early childhood programs. In Piaget's view, intellectual growth from birth through adolescence occurs in stages beginning with sensory motor, followed by preoperational thought, intuitive thought, concrete operations, and formal logic.

Teaching thinking skills continues to be a concern of curriculum developers and educators (Brandt 1981). One illustration is a four-year pilot project in Saint Louis, which found that after only six weeks of instruction in scientific problem solving eleventh and twelfth graders raised their abilities to think scientifically by twenty points on a cognitive skills test covering major elements used by scientists as criteria for scientific thinking (Long 1981, p. 5). Another example, is a curriculum program known as "Instrumental Enrichment," created by Reuven Feuerstein for the specific purpose of teaching intellectual skills, which has received international attention. Originated in Israel, the methods and materials are used in an estimated three hundred schools in the United States (Link 1980, Hobbs 1980).

Technological Conceptions

Those who wrote approvable proposals to government agencies during the heyday of federal funding of education, roughly 1965–1980, will recognize this model. It is variously referred to as a behavioral objectives model, technocratic model, efficiency-centered approach, application of logical positivism, or curriculum as ends rather than means.

William Pinar (1981) characterizes the technological approach as the traditionalists model, and he asserts that the majority of all curricularists adhere to it. Few, in fact realize that they are traditionalists as the model saturates the fields of literature and training so thoroughly that students of curriculum hear of little else. The curriculum field's birth in the 1920s was a time when scientific techniques from business and industry shaped educational theory and practice. This has had a lasting effect on curriculum, says Pinar, who continues:

This model is characterized by its ameliorative orientation, ahistorical posture, and an allegiance to behaviorism.... The curriculum worker is dedicated to the "improvement" of schools. He honors this dedication by accepting the curriculum structure as it is. "Curriculum change" is measured by comparing resulting behaviors with original objectives.... Accepting the curriculum structure as it is and working to improve it is what is meant by the "technician's mentality." In a capsule way, it can be likened to adjusting an automobile engine part in order to make it function more effectively (p. 89).

The technological approach is often adapted to other major orientations, particularly the academic or subject-centered conceptions of curriculum. A feature of this approach is the construction of objectives that specify quantifiable outcomes. Then content and learning activities, sequenced and directed toward the specified outcomes, are designed. A time-frame is usually included, and success depends on the degree to which the desired objectives are met. Management by objectives, mastery learning, accountability, and competency testing are familiar terms within this model.

Efficiency orientations for curriculum development can be traced back at least to Franklin Bobbitt (1918), who borrowed from Frederick W. Taylor's scientific management model (1911), and applied it to the curriculum domain. Bobbitt argued for maximum efficiency through efficient management of the curriculum and precisely predicted outcomes.

This emphasis on efficiency was captured by Ralph Tyler, whose *Basic Principles of Curriculum and Instruction* (1950) has exerted a continuing influence on curriculum development. His four questions have produced an aura of rationality and the implication of a "problem-free" approach to curriculum development that permeates much of the current practice. His questions are:

1. What educational purposes should the school seek to attain?
2. How can learning experiences that are likely to be useful in attaining these objectives be selected?
3. How can learning experiences be organized for effective instruction?
4. How can the effectiveness of learning experiences be evaluated?

Although frequently referred to as theoretical, Tyler's rationale is a model, not a theory. Its impact on curriculum development cannot be underestimated, and many specialists in curriculum development have attempted to improve or extend it. Hilda Taba (1962) proposed a seven-step model involving diagnosis of needs, formulation of objectives, selection of content, organization of content, selection of learning experiences, and determination of what and how to evaluate. Variations of the Taba model for curriculum development are widely used today. Few educators will dispute the power of purpose; thus, objectives or goal-based curricula seem to have emerged as the current norm.

As noted above, the scientific management or technological approach received a tremendous boost from government funding agencies in recent years, but as federal funds decline and power in education shifts to state and local authorities, it will be interesting to see how this changes curriculum development. Will other conceptions of the curriculum shove aside the management model with its burden of paperwork or will computer and information processing technology come to the aid of the teacher in even more refinements of management of curriculum and instruction?

Self-actualization

Sometimes called the experiential model, this conception of the curriculum is a subjective, learner-centered, activity-oriented approach. It utilizes self-directed, unstructured programs and emphasizes the affective domain. Curriculum decisions are made cooperatively by teachers and students. Earlier advocates of self-actualization as the central conception for curriculum planning included Carl Rogers (1962), Abraham Maslow (1968), and William Kilpatrick (1934).

This orientation refers to schooling as a means of personal fulfillment, a context in which individuals can discover their particular talents and identities. Needed, according to Joseph Junell, are liberal-minded teachers, who are "trusting and accepting of others, however bizarre their ideas or appearance" (1974, p. 112).

In the self-actualization approach, the curriculum is seen as an end in itself, as a stage in the life process, as both content and tools for further self-discovery. Writers in this field emphasize the language of humanism and existentialism. Philip Phenix calls it a curriculum of transcendence that "provides the context of engendering, gestating, expecting, and celebrating the moments of singular awareness and inner illumination when each person comes into the consciousness of his inimitable personal being" (1971, p. 279). This orientation inspired certain aspects of the open education models of the 1960s and 1970s, specific types of alternative schools, and, earlier, some interpretations of the progressive education movement (as described in the historical treatment of curriculum development, Chapter One).

Social Reconstruction-Reconceptualism

"Should the schools develop young people to fit into present society as it is, or does the school have a revolutionary mission to develop young people who will seek to improve the society?" This question, asked by Tyler (1950, p. 35), and then ignored as a focus for his investigation, is at the heart of one of the curriculum-related issues raised by reconceptualists—the most critical of the social reconstructionists.

Social justice is the strongest theme of the reconceptualists. In their view, traditionalists fail to see the relationship of schooling to society and continue to support inequities by reproducing them in the schools. Reconceptualists have provoked reexamination of predominant patterns. They have raised questions through historical criticism to illuminate oppressive features so that educators will no longer continue to borrow technological models without being aware of their sociopolitical implications.

To James Macdonald and Esther Zaret, "Education is the activity of liberation (à la Nietzsche): liberation from ignorance, fear, want, disease, and alienation from oppression...." (1975, p. 4). Dwayne Huebner speculates that if schools could liberate the person, they could transform the world (1981, p. 132). But in this view schools are not currently "educating"—they are merely training young people to fit into society as it is. The present organization of schools seems designed to maintain a class system, assert the reconceptualists, who point to the grading system, the topics of subject matter, even the three-group reading class as means used by the schools to maintain the present socioeconomic and sociopolitical system in America. (See Giroux 1980, Giroux and Penna 1981, Anyon 1981.)

According to Paulo Friere (1970, p. 15) and others, there is no such thing as a neutral educational process; either the schools are teaching conformity to the present system or else teaching students how to transform their world. The reconceptualists' view is that current curriculum workers avoid the issue; instead they talk about development of the individual, which Macdonald says is an elitist idea—that members of society should be "like us" (1977). Although hands-on prescriptions are scarce on how to proceed toward achieving liberation, the reconceptualists are provoking new arenas of curriculum discussion.

The school as an instrument for social reform is a thread that runs throughout curriculum history. Counts's book *Dare the Schools Build a New Social Order?* (1932) teased the imagination of educators at the time, but no change can be traced to that source. Other social reformers, looking for captive audiences, have called on the schools to include curriculum segments on such issues as the Americanization of immigrants, prohibition of alcoholic drinks, advocacy of peace, consumer rights, creationism, and abolishment of racism. Futurists are presently advocating curriculum content on "education for survival" in the face of future trends. Social concerns seem to have their best access to the curriculum through the social studies, which often become an arena for controversy.

Academic Rationalism

Ask any high school student what his or her curriculum is, and you will hear a list of subjects; for example, mathematics, history, science, English, foreign languages, and so on. This response reflects a long-standing conception of curriculum as the body of subjects or subject matter to be "covered" by students. The so-called curriculum "reforms" of the 1950s and 1960s were academic in nature but brought new approaches to traditional subject matter through inquiries into the structure of knowledge (Schwab 1974).

Shaped by the history of education, the academic model encompasses the perennialist and the essentialist conceptions of curriculum. Robert Hutchins (1936) held that the curriculum should consist principally of the "permanent studies," that is, grammar, reading, rhetoric, logic, mathematics, and the greatest books of the Western world. William Bagley (1907) expressed the essentialist position when he described the curriculum as a storehouse of organized cultural experience. Arthur Bestor (1956), a widely read critic of the schools in his time, held that the curriculum should consist of disciplined study in five areas: grammar, literature, and writing; mathematics; sciences; history; and foreign languages.

Mortimer Adler (1982), a contemporary who advocates revival of the classics, has prescribed reading materials selected from the "great books" and a methodology for high school students. As described in *The Paideia Proposal*, the high school curriculum would revive and exemplify Robert Hutchins' proposals of the 1930s for instruction based on the classics in ways that would stimulate intellectual discipline and philosophical thought. (For discussion of this and other current high school reform recommendations with an academic emphasis, see Chapter Three.)

To avoid narrowness and rigidity in the development of curriculum, the scope of the total culture must be considered. Planners must look beyond such terms as *academic rationalism, essentialism, humanism, behaviorism,* and other single principles and draw insights from the depth and breadth of a comprehensive view of culture. Otherwise, curriculum planning will become very superficial.

SCOPE OF THE TOTAL CULTURE

Culture is defined as the environment of ideas, experiences, beliefs, traditions, customs, institutions, sciences, arts, technologies, humanities, and commonsense ways of doing things that are part of the shared life of the people. Culture is complex; it consists of many related modes, and it is constantly undergoing reconstruction. Thus, when curriculum development draws from the total culture and recognizes both ends and means, the process becomes more responsive and creates new culture.

The process of curriculum development...includes selection from the total culture and the creation of a pattern of encounter that will maximize the authenticity of the material and the probability of its being internalized by learners. As a system of ideas and beliefs, it includes aspects of the cognitive world isolated by disciplines and/or subjects in terms of facts, information, generalizations, principles, laws, and the like. It also includes awareness of and facility in the use of expressive symbols such as art, music, and language. Further, it includes systems of value orientations for action in the form of such things as modes of inquiry, seeking new knowledge, respecting the integrity and worth of individuals, being concerned for other peoples, using democratic procedures, and so forth. ... Cultural systems are substantive aspects of social and personality systems and evolve in a constant interaction shaped and influenced by the dynamics of structures and action in...culture, society, and personality (Macdonald 1971, pp. 97-98).

Origins of the proposition regarding culture and curriculum development can be traced back through the literature for more than a century and are found in the writings of anthropologists, philosophers, psychologists, social scientists, and others. For example, in 1837, Ralph Waldo Emerson (1966), in his address "The American Scholar," spoke of education by nature, by books, by action, and by duties. Similar thoughts appeared in the writings of Cardinal Newman and John Stuart Mill in the nineteenth century. In 1926, Harold Rugg noted that curriculum making must be continuous and carried out with a comprehensive view of the whole, that the rift between curriculum and society must be bridged for curriculum is constructed out of the very materials of American life. George Counts (1952) maintained that the responsibilities of the school included curriculum development directed toward constructive modification and development of the nation's economy, social structure, cultural institutions, and outlook on the world. Curriculum development should lead toward creating as well as transmitting culture, meeting and maintaining democratic social relationships, and increasing individual self-realization, Counts asserted.

Curriculum development can be approached through countless points of entry. Problems arise when curriculum developers rely on single or limited avenues and sources and ignore other significant dimensions of the culture. Curriculum development must recognize the importance of both process and product—of the process of developing curriculum, the curriculum plan being developed, and the instructional processes to be generated.

The scope of available culture is almost limitless. It involves societal conditions, knowledge from the academic disciplines, professional knowledge about learning and educative processes, philosophical and value bases, futures research, realities in the classroom, and the pluralistic ethnic backgrounds of the participants and their needs and desires.

Some distortions inhibit our perceptions of the total culture. Irving Buchen (1974) illustrates several such distortions from the field of curriculum development in the humanities. He notes that planners of humanities programs that officially seek interdisciplinary relationships frequently exclude the physical sciences or bewail the dehumanization of man by technology. Yet these same persons consult concordances put together by computers, cite articles reproduced by copying machines, allude to rare manuscripts made available on microfilm, and listen to chants and folk rituals on audiotape cassettes. Even more serious, in Buchen's view, is that such an attitude frequently jeopardizes communication with students who are often quite comfortable with computers and communication machines, recognizing that they as human beings have not been mechanized as a result of using the products of technology.

DISCIPLINES, INTERDISCIPLINES, AND MULTIDISCIPLINES

A major cultural source for curriculum is the academic disciplines, both individually and in combinations. The contributions of the separate disciplines, multidisciplinary approaches, and interdisciplinary approaches are all essential to quality in curriculum development.

The Disciplines

The curricular reform of the 1960s accomplished some significant successes, although it was later called into question because its proponents viewed it for a time as all the reform that was needed and therefore omitted work on societal and human problems. The academic disciplines underwent a searching analysis and received attention that they had rarely enjoyed in previous educational reform movements. Curriculum developers departed from the old concept of the discipline as a range of information to be "covered" in the classroom and entered a new era in which, to quote Herman Eschenbacher (1974, p. 507), "the academic disciplines are perceived as models or systems through which to assimilate the unknown into what we already know in order to make change comprehensible and manageable." The discipline was viewed as providing a technique for ordering data, applying them to a question of some significance, and establishing the rules by which the answer is validated. The discipline, in sum, notes Eschenbacher, is a functional analytic tool that remains when the ephemera of content have evaporated.

The desired product, continues Eschenbacher, is a quality of mind, an intellectual independence or style that expresses itself in ways of acting. It seems axiomatic that if what people learn does not change them in some way, it makes little difference what they learn. Although the disciplines have rarely functioned in this way in public education, and teachers have expected students to receive information rather than to develop independent answers, the curriculum reform movement of the 1960s brought new perceptions to curriculum developers and introduced the concept, now basic in curriculum development, that the educative process should help students learn how to learn. Each discipline promotes its own interpretations of modes of inquiry and directs applications of its techniques to real problems.

Multidisciplines and Interdisciplines

A multidisciplinary curriculum is distinguishable from an interdisciplinary curriculum. The former is a parallel approach to curriculum development in which each discipline has something to contribute about a given problem while remaining a discrete entity. Interdisciplinary approaches make use of what Winthrop (1974) terms the *convergence approach* in which each discipline methodologically complements and illuminates the other. A convergence problem is one whose solution—if one is possible—requires considerable information from a number of different but specialized fields, seeks relationships between the kinds of information, notes the intersections of relationships that apply to the problem under study, applies a method of analysis to a problem that cuts across several fields, and relates the solution to the values of the community and to the context within which the curriculum is being developed.

A critical difficulty facing curriculum developers is that some of the most pressing and complex problems—problems that the schools are expected to heed—cannot be contained within the boundaries of any one discipline or frequently even within combinations of them. Problem solvers must draw on other aspects of the total culture to approach these questions. Examples abound: studies of war and peace, the environment, the social effects of science and technology, communication, the status of women, crime and rehabilitation, meeting the needs of developing countries, racism in America, and scenarios of the future.

Eschenbacher (1974, p. 508) uses the "urban problem" of decay or decline as an example of the necessity for interdisciplinary approaches to curriculum development:

One wishes to know the dimensions of the problem, to come to understand it, to do something to alleviate it, if only out of self-interest. The schools should offer help, not through exhortation or preachment, but by enabling each child to develop a perspective that will foster analysis and make some personal sense of the problem for him. The social sciences, it is supposed, provide the means to achieve this. The urban problem is historical because it has been a long time evolving and because it breaks the surface of the historical consciousness only when certain forces intersect. These can be identified and analyzed by involving the historical method, but the analysis, although it furthers understanding, is only partial. Another part of the problem is economic, and is concerned with the apportionment of wealth, products, job opportunities, and the like. Another part is political, and still another aspect concerns social-class assignments, mobility, values, and so on. No single discipline is sufficient to encompass the problem as a totality.

Eschenbacher emphasizes that a separate discipline or multidisciplinary approach is not sufficient because the analytic process—a characteristic of interdisciplinary or convergent approaches—is the desired outcome. Curriculum development cannot be concerned with the product of a discipline only; it must be concerned with the process, and to rest on content without considering technique is to confuse ends and means. Providing students with analytic tools for drawing from the several disciplines in an interdisciplinary convergence on problems recognizes the essential factor of integrative learning. The disciplines are then used for conceptualization and as powerful referents for interpreting experience. Eschenbacher concludes that such an approach represents our best available opportunity for promoting autonomy and fostering growth. Critically applied, the disciplines support intellectual discernment and independence, the ends most coveted in a free system.

Interdisciplinary Approaches: Pro and Con

Although resistance to interdisciplinary approaches to curriculum has been strong, awareness of the advantages of these approaches is increasing. Biases against interdisciplinary work come from tradition and resistance to change. Both the public and academicians fear that the contribution of a particular discipline will be diminished, that specialists who venture outside of their subject fields will lose stature, and that no one can possibly master several fields.

In response to these objections, Winthrop (1974) notes that contributions to the solution of many of the gravest problems facing education will have to cross disciplinary boundaries, that the status feelings of a single-discipline scholar spring from a elitist outlook and that such a view cannot be taken seriously in an era when mankind is hard pressed to seek solutions to grave problems. The claim that no one can master several fields is true, but no interdisciplinary scholar claims to be a master of several fields. Such a scholar is problem oriented and acquires needed information from several areas relevant to the problem without having to become a master in each area.

Ronald Hyman and other writers collected in *Approaches to Curriculum* (1973) make a case for an interdisciplinary approach to the curriculum. They contend that the lack of vitality of the present high school curriculum is due to its failure to come to grips with many issues about which young people are highly concerned. Gordon Cawelti (1974) points out that many students have only the barest notion of the economics of private enterprise, inflation, recession, prices, and unemployment. Until there is broader public understanding of the effects of a given corrective policy when it is instituted, tedious debates over economic issues will probably continue and will resolve nothing until there is deeper comprehension based on economic facts and principles.

Other examples can be drawn from the arts. Without broad interdisciplinary programs in humanities, the arts, and aesthetic education, students in this area have only limited opportunities. Consequences of this limitation are evident today in the garish architecture and unaesthetic community design of areas in many cities. Tastes in film are at such a limited level that violence and sex seem to be the topics that draw the widest audiences.

On the issues of our deteriorating environment and scarcity of resources, most schools do offer courses. But environmental or population studies are frequently free-floating courses or units here and there in which students are helped to become aware of environmental problems but not to know what they can do about them. They are left with a feeling of hopelessness and a conviction that disaster is inevitable, if not for this generation then for future generations. However, a number of interdisciplinary programs in some schools can be cited as examples.

Lawrence Paros (1973) describes a curriculum known as "The City Game," in which high school students focused on the issue of urban decay and social and political change in Providence, Rhode Island. Through problem-solving activities that searched out information, used simulation games, provided face-to-face contacts and interaction with businessmen and city officials, and involved students on decision-making city commissions, students worked in four major areas related to environmental and population problems: (1) health and welfare, including medical care, problems of the aged, drugs, mental health, retardation, social welfare, and ecology; (2) law and justice, including civil rights and liberties, juvenile justice, contemporary issues in law enforcement, and state and local government; (3) education, including early childhood development, alternative theories of child-rearing, problems in inner-city education, and explorations of "changing the system"; and (4) communications, including journalism, radio, television, and creative writing.

This interdisciplinary example is compatible with John Dewey's advice in *Experience and Education* (1938) that schools "break loose from the cut-and-dried material which formed the staple of the old education." The field of experience is very wide, he said, and it varies in its contents from place to place and from time to time. Dewey differentiated education based on experience from traditional education in that conditions found in present experience are used as sources of problems. It is the educator's responsibility, Dewey asserted, to see that these problems arouse in the learner an active quest for information and for production of new ideas, which then become the basis for further experiences in which new problems are encountered.

Most of our modern problems, social or otherwise, require an interdisciplinary convergence approach. Unless curriculum development draws from the total culture and the total context, it will be unresponsive to changing knowledge and social and personal needs and, therefore, ineffective.

For the curriculum developer, attention to the complexities of the total culture and rapid change is still not enough. This is a country that subscribes to democracy. Therefore, the principles of democracy must apply in the planning of curriculum and the processes of instruction. In some quarters, even the word *democracy* seems old-fashioned, and critics scoff and say that the original intent of democracy has been lost somewhere. If that is so, then it is time for the schools to reexamine the concepts and relearn the behaviors that democracy should stand for.

DEMOCRACY

Democracy is defined as a state of society characterized by freedom of expression, respect for the essential dignity and worth of the human individual, and equal opportunity for each person to develop optimally and freely with emphasis on community and mutual responsibility and without discrimination on the basis of sex, race, religion, age, social or economic class, national origin, or handicap. In this definition, we are basically concerned with democratic goals, principles, and means as applied to curriculum development and the educative process.

The broad goals of democracy in the United States reflect the set of values phrased in general, abstract language as an American creed by Gunnar Myrdal (1962). They include the worth and dignity of the individual; equality; inalienable rights to life, liberty, property, and the pursuit of happiness; consent of the governed; majority rule; the rule of law and due process of law; community and national welfare; and rights to freedom of speech, press, religion, assembly, and private association. Other, less constitutionally oriented values include brotherhood, charity, mercy, nonviolence, perseverance, hard work, competence, expertise, rugged individualism, compromise, cooperation, honesty, loyalty, and integrity of personal conscience. Myrdal describes how values are proclaimed in American life (1962, p. 4):

The schools teach them, the churches preach them, the courts pronounce their judicial decisions in their terms. They permeate editorials with a pattern of idealism so ingrained that the writers can scarcely free themselves from it even if they tried. They have fixed a custom of indulging in high sounding generalities.

Myrdal makes some searching observations about different interpretations of this creed by conservatives and liberals, blacks and whites, rich and poor, the advocates of one interest, and the backers of an opposing interest. He describes the American dilemma as the widespread tension between our high-level ideals and our actual practices in which real power seems to be exercised by military, industrial, and political interests.

The problem of differing interpretations of the American creed is also examined by Fred Newmann and Donald Oliver (1970). They note that conflicting commitments are frequently manifestations of diverse interpretations and paradoxes in American culture—for example, the emphasis on competition and rugged individualism on the one hand and a profound contradictory concern for community cooperation and compromise on the other.

Both ends and means are included in the creed without categorization or order. However, a fundamental value that supersedes others is that of individual human dignity, Newmann and Oliver note. Such creed values as national security, separation of powers, property rights, and due process of law do not possess intrinsic goodness in themselves, but their implementation relates to the fulfillment of the fundamental value of individual human worth. This value emphasizes the integrity of each person because he or she is a person. Individual worth includes the ability to make choices that affect one's life (for example, in career, religion, politics, or family relations), the guarantees of physical protection of life and property, equal treatment under the law, the ability to defend oneself against prosecution by the state, and other values.

To support a proposition focused on democratic goals and means as part of an approach to a theory of curriculum development requires further clarification of terms and concepts. While definitions of American democracy are almost nonexistent in high school textbooks, as reported in a survey by Benjamin Rader (1974), two types of definitions are distinguished by Doyle Buckwalter (1973) from other sources. In one sense democracy is a moral goal, and in another it is a form of government. Confusion results if the moral goal and the governmental form are not differentiated from one another.

As Buckwalter observes, it is far easier to identify democratic moral goals than it is to describe the democratic form of government. The moral goal of democracy is to improve the general welfare of all humans, and the phase "all men are created equal" means that each individual is infinitely precious. The emphasis on the individual implies that democracy is not selective but applies to all types of people—the obedient, the lawless, the wise, the illiterate, the rich, the poor, the white, the black, the capable, and the incompetent.

Buckwalter notes that unless there is a reassertion and diligent application of democratic principles to everchanging conditions, American democracy faces a fundamental danger. Above all other approaches to governing, democracy must be continually practiced to be accepted, states Buckwalter, and he adds that no space program or foreign or domestic policy can substitute for the binding quality of faith—faith that people working together can eradicate problems.

Frederick Mayer (1973, p. 22) emphasizes the same point: "The actual process of democracy—with its party bickering, blatant advertising, crime and corruption, economic domination, fragmentation of interests, and public apathy—may cause a sense of revulsion. But democracy is an educative process capable of indefinite renewal."

Mayer asserts that democratic principles differ from concepts of aristocracy on this very point. Democracy does not concede different standards for "thinkers" and for "ordinary individuals." In ancient times, Aristotle advocated excluding merchants from active government because he asserted that they did not have time for reflection. Both thinking and acting, one transforming the other, are characteristics of a democratic process and lead to the concept of freedom, another basic principle of democracy.

Freedom is defined by Archibald MacLeish (1951) as the freedom of the individual human being to think for himself or herself and to come to the truth by the light of his or her own mind and conscience. He continues (p. 28):

Our reliance in this country is on the inquiring, individual human mind. Our strength is founded there: our resilience, our ability to face an everchanging future and to master it. We are not frozen into the backward-facing impotence of those societies fixed in the rigidness of an official dogma, to which the future is the mirror of the past. We are free to make the future for ourselves.

Similarly, Erich Fromm (1968, p. 52) observes that freedom is not just freedom from oppression of various kinds but also "freedom to create and to construct, to wonder and to venture. Such freedom requires that the individual be active and responsible, not a slave or a well-fed cog in a machine."

To be active and to be responsible require effort and commitment. Harry Broudy (1971) reminds us that the most differentiating characteristic of democratic and nondemocratic societies is the belief in the former that all those whose interests are affected should have a voice—usually an equal voice—in influencing the decision in a decidable situation that involves a diversity of interests. Having a voice implies that democracy is like a problem to be worked on and solved, not a spectator sport.

DILEMMAS OF DEMOCRACY

Apathy of the citizenry toward government and politics, confusion over the meanings of pluralism and egalitarianism in American society, and discrepancies between the principles of democracy and the actual practices in many schools are disturbing dilemmas.

Principles Not Practiced

Discrepancies between democratic principles and practices sometimes exist at governmental levels in relatively minor institutions. Mayer (1973) illustrates the point by citing a small college that at one time prided itself on having an excellent political science course on the principles of democracy, but its own structure was a living negation of democratic processes. The college was governed by a board of trustees that had no sense of responsibility toward its community. While the chief administrator of the college acted in public as a pillar of democracy, in his life as an educational leader he tyrannized his faculty and behaved toward his subordinates like a dictator. Clearly, says Mayer, there is a substantial difference between talking about democracy and actually living it.

We are reminded of Machiavelli's cynicism in *The Prince* (1963) when he advises heads of state that the *appearance* of goodness and acquiescence to conventional morality is sufficient. This model, taken seriously by countless rulers, has been disastrous in both ancient and modern times.

Democracy depends on overcoming the gap between the professed ideal and the actual practice.

Discrepancies between democratic principles and practices are also observable in vast bureaucracies, both public and private. Such organizations as the Internal Revenue Service, the Postal Services, major television networks, manufacturing corporations, and urban school systems sometimes seem quite remote and unresponsive to their constituents' needs and concerns.

Different groups have unequal effectiveness in influencing public policy. For example, wealthy and powerful industrialists can afford to employ lobbyists to pursue special interests in legislatures, while volunteer groups with conflicting interests may have much weaker influence. Well-educated parents have frequently exerted more pressure on schools for special (sometimes expensive) programs to benefit their children than the poor and uneducated could exert.

Citizen Apathy

The apathy of many citizens toward governmental affairs poses still another dilemma of American democracy. Having the right to vote brings with it responsibilities for studying the background of issues, discussing one's views with others of varying viewpoints, and applying critical thinking skills to public controversies. Unless citizens believe that they are in touch with their political and governmental institutions and that they can play a responsible role in the process of governing, a free society cannot long survive. In a huge, intricately organized society, a strong national government is needed, but strong and responsible government is also needed at the grass roots level. Access, responsiveness, accountability, and effectiveness are guiding concepts in improving our democratic form of government—concepts that require active citizenship to be meaningful. Although citizen apathy toward governmental, political, educational, and societal institutions is more prevalent than we desire, signs are cropping up of the public showing increasing interest in matters within these arenas.

Pluralism and Egalitarianism

The value of pluralism also poses a dilemma for American democracy. Stemming from the principle of individual human dignity, pluralism assumes the right of different groups (for example, a religious sect, a black organization, a women's liberation group, a sportsmen's club, a student rights group) to exist, protected from intrusion or domination by outsiders considered to have alien values. However, Newmann and Oliver (1970) emphasize that if such pluralism is to invigorate the larger society by expanding alternative paths to dignity, group members and outsiders must have enough contact to become aware of each other's options. Then the group risks destroying its distinctive nature by intermingling with other interests. Discerning the fine line between enough contact so that each segment can be aware of and possibly adopt the other's approach and enough isolation for each group to work toward its particular vision of human fulfillment presents a dilemma in modern practice, both in schools and in the larger society.

Related to the dilemma between the ideals of cultural pluralism and the actual practice are quandaries about the concept of egalitarianism. Christopher Hodgkinson (1973) discusses the dilemma of a strict interpretation of equality, in which everyone is treated in the same way. He draws from sociological findings that, without exception, human societies structure themselves according to some system of class—that two people placed on a desert island will inevitably create a social structure in which one is superior to the other. Hodgkinson notes that humans differ from each other in many ways, both as individuals and as groups, and small-group psychology has found that inequalities unavoidably emerge in decision-making groups. Excellence and meritocracy, continues Hodgkinson, tend to be limited to a few persons in any given area. Thus, while we have no difficulty with the principle of meritocracy in choosing our surgeon or airline pilot, the problem becomes a dilemma if democracy is interpreted to mean that all persons are the same in interests, energies, nature, and skills and thus must be treated exactly alike.

A broader interpretation of egalitarianism is provided by Terryl Anderson (1973) in a response to Hodgkinson. Characterizing democracy as application of a single value (everyone treated the same) is troublesome in Anderson's view. More basic to conceptions of democracy is the notion of equality as appropriate treatment for each person, with emphasis on individual differences and talents. To contend that the democratic ideal means elimination of all dissimilarity or the assumption that all persons have the same interests, energies, nature, and skills is a narrow view. Indeed, democracy seeks the cultivation of diversity, including varieties of excellence. Democracy is a complex of values, such as freedom, justice, and equality, that form a network of criteria used to judge the potential of particular social arrangements for providing all persons optimum opportunities. Democracy in the American ideal is different in very fundamental respects from a Platonic class society, in which most people are considered incapable of being full citizens, and only the intellectuals are fit to rule.

John Dewey's (1937) expression of a broader view of democracy can clarify confused thinking on these dilemmas. He believed that the participation of individuals in creating, managing, and forming the values that underlie their social institutions is an essential feature of a democratic way of life. Dewey emphasized that what a person can and will become as a human being, both individually and in association with others, is affected by the institutions of society; therefore, each individual must share in the development of those institutions. Lack of participation by the individual is detrimental not only to his or her personal growth but also to society as a whole, which is deprived of that contribution. As Dewey maintained, democratic forms are simply the best means yet devised for realizing democracy in the wider sense.

Democracy, notes Mayer (1973), can be appreciated more for its future possibilities than for its past failings. We must not abandon democracy because of its dilemmas but rather must make it a reality in our own lives and institutions, through active problem-solving participation.

DEMOCRATIC MEANS IN THE EDUCATIVE PROCESS

The philosophy of Paulo Freire (1970) offers insights in our search for democratic means in the educative process. Freire's conviction, supported by a wide background of experience, is that every human being, no matter how ignorant or submerged he or she may be, is capable of looking critically at his or her world in dialogue with others. The business of the school is to provide the proper tools for dialogue so that the individual can gradually perceive his or her personal and social reality and deal critically with it. Freire's writings have applications not only in the field of education but also in the struggle for national development. They emphasize that pedagogy—the learning experience—must be forged *with* not *for* individuals and groups. Thinking must lead to action, thus constituting an authentic praxis, which can be achieved only when the leaders believe in the ability of the people to reason. Freire says (p. 52):

Critical and liberating dialogue, which presupposes action, must be carried on with the oppressed at whatever the stage of their struggle for liberation. The content of that dialogue can and should vary in accordance with historical conditions and the level at which the oppressed perceive reality. But to substitute monologue, slogans, and communiques for dialogue is to attempt to liberate the oppressed with the instruments of domestication . . . and transform them into masses which can be manipulated.

Throughout his writings, Freire stresses the importance of "generative themes"—the dialogue of education as the practice of freedom. Dialogue, in Freire's view, affords the participants the opportunity to discover generative themes and to stimulate their personal awareness in relation to these themes. Man has the ability to create culture, to transform reality by drawing on ideas and concepts of the past, the present, and the future.

Frederick Mayer (1973) provides further philosophical insights into the construction of democratic means. He speaks of the "perennial pilgrimage of democracy." In the schools, democratic means are those that demand the most intense degree of rationality, the broadest humanity, and the most fervent participation. The school must set the climate for a democracy, asserts Mayer (pp. 24-25):

Without genuine concern and humanitarian agitation, democracy is a pretense. This implies a constant reform of institutions so that the needs of the individual are recognized and so that rules and standards do not become coercive . . . Democracy does not start when one becomes an adult; it must be embodied as much in kindergarten as in graduate school, in the home as well as in other social institutions . . . To be proficient in knowledge is not enough. A new society of genuine democracy requires active learning and autonomous motivation. It requires a missionary spirit without fanaticism. The joys of culture are to be universalized, the benefits of freedom are to be shared, the citadels of ignorance and regression are to be conquered, the deserts of physical and spiritual poverty are to be transformed.

Mayer emphasizes that democratic means in the educative process reach beyond the boundaries of the school to all ages. Learning has no limitation, and the social and political institutions have a responsibility for determining the effectiveness of learning; but, in Mayer's view, democracy requires the school, of all institutions, to be the main source of learning and social change.

Two factors emerge from the literature as critical for attaining the broad goals of American democracy through educational means that are consonant with democratic ideals: (1) the attitudes and behavior of the curriculum specialist (including the teacher and the administrator), and (2) the nature of attention given in the classroom to major social and political issues of our time and of the future.

Freire's (1970) sharp insights are again appropriate. Too many students today, he says, from kindergarten to university, view the educational system as their enemy. He attributes this attitude to the relationship between teachers and students. Education is suffering from "narration sickness," in which the teacher talks about the world as if it were motionless, static, compartmentalized, and predictable, says Freire; or else the teacher expounds on topics completely alien to the experience of the students. Coining the term *banking education,* Freire defines it as education that is an act of depositing, in which the students are the depositories and the teacher is the depositor. The scope of action allowed to the students is merely receiving, filing, and storing the deposits. Freire emphasizes that unless the mode of inquiry is present, permitting creativity, transformation, and the emergence of new knowledge through invention and reinvention, schooling falls into the structure of oppression.

Thus far in this chapter, we have presented an almost bewildering array of underlying concepts for curriculum and instruction. To provide order and given direction to the planning of curriculum in a comprehensive manner, one needs an identifiable set of assumptions to use at the local level. The illustration later in this chapter of an approach to theory development is one example. Others can be designed to suit particular situations.

NEED FOR A THEORY

The curriculum developer, to find a way through the conceptual maze, needs a theory to give coherence and rationality to decisions made concerning the curriculum. Louise Berman (1968, p. 2) contends that problems of conflicting interests cannot be resolved until the points of emphasis or priority are established. Taba (1962, p. 413) states that "any enterprise as complex as curriculum development requires some kind of theoretical or conceptual framework to guide it." Frank Steeves and Fenwick English note that without a theoretical base for curriculum development (even if it is only a list of assumptions), it would be extremely difficult to generate testable hypotheses and to construct a meaningful evaluation design to determine the adequacy of curriculum development (1978, p. 288).

Theory is based on a value position and interrelated concepts. It is a belief system that provides criteria to guide the practitioner in making rational choices among alternative courses of action and sources of knowledge, in making value decisions, and in predicting the consequences of various solutions to dilemmas. Theory provides a frame of reference against which the practitioner can raise questions and test hypotheses. Since the curriculum developer does not work in isolation, curriculum-related questions such as the following will be raised, calling for decisions that affect others:

1. What role does advanced technology in communications media play in curriculum development and instruction? How shall the curriculum cope with the power of the mass media to shape opinions and attitudes?
2. In view of the world's dwindling natural resources, its increasing population, the threat of irrevocable damage to the biosphere, and the apparent need to reverse the "growth is good" concept, what should be taught in economics, science, sociology, aesthetics, and other fields?
3. If new values are needed by the human race, what issues and dilemmas are to be faced, and what processes and content shall be used to face them? What experiences shall be made available to

students? What disciplines shall be drawn upon for knowledge? How shall the planner assist students in developing the valuing and decision-making skills they need in order to make reasoned choices?

4. Is a new work ethic arising that can give direction to curriculum development—an ethic in which job satisfaction, the feeling of contribution, cooperation, or creation takes precedence over the income earned? If so, how can individual self-realization and mutual responsibility for social problems be developed in relation to this ethic?

5. What types of learning environments and physical facilities will be needed as a support system for the curriculum? Should the curriculum developer look to the home, the school, the community, or all as the setting for the curriculum? What relationship should the curriculum developer advocate between open, action, and experiential learning on the one hand and didactics, directives, and rote on the other?

Alvin Toffler (1970) reminds us that the industrial age ushered in a form of mass education that was a perfect introduction to industrial society: its regimentation, lack of individualization, rigid systems of seating, grouping, grading, and marking, and authoritarian role of the teacher were precisely those that would make education an effective instrument for adapting the population to industrialism. The student was not expected to make decisions; they were made for him. At the other extreme, A. S. Neill's Summerhill model has been severely criticized for its permissiveness and lack of apparent direction. What theories underlie the many important and varied curriculum decisions needed today?

These are some types of questions illustrating the practitioner's need for theory. But a theory cannot be delivered to the practitioner ready made for adoption; practitioners must take part in its construction if it is to be meaningful.

George Beauchamp (1968, pp. 33–34) has synthesized other commentators on theory, and he points out that

the operational vistas opened up and explained by theories increase the possible choices for the practitioner; the theories, however, do not tell him how to act. A theory may clarify relationships among any given set of events. . . . Theory is not what is practiced. A person cannot practice a set of logically related statements; he performs an activity. Theories of instruction, for example, might account for classroom discipline, grouping practices, lesson planning, and instructional materials as components of instruction, but the theories cannot tell teachers how to behave with respect to those functions. . . . Nevertheless, it is the job of educational theory to guide educational practices. In turn, theory is modified by practice and research that emanate from it.

Clear though the need for theory may be, however, practitioners have persistent difficulties understanding what theory is and how it is developed, as the history of theory development in education and problems associated with it clearly reveal. The next section of this chapter recaps that history and then identifies the elements of theory, including definitions, concepts, steps in constructing theory, and functions of theory. Although some confusion exists about how theory making applies to education and thus to curriculum development, a consensus is emerging.

THE THEORY PROBLEM

Early leaders in the effort to call the attention of educators to the significance of theory in education were amazed and disappointed to find unexpected ignorance, indifference, and even hostility to learning more about the meaning of theory. The breakthrough in the development of theory in education came in educational administration in the 1950s, and, after a slow start, the development gained ground and spread to other areas of education, such as instruction and curriculum. In 1959 Daniel Griffiths reviewed the "theory problem," and the following historical comments are largely drawn from his observations and those of other contributors to his volume. Griffith's review pertains to educational administration, but parallel situations regarding understandings about theory also exist in curriculum development and other fields of education, and analogies can be drawn.

Griffiths traced the stimulus for theory development to the Kellogg Foundation, which provided grants to several universities between 1946 and 1959 for the study and improvement of educational administration. In 1947, several professors of educational administration and a few interested practitioners formed an organization known as the National Conference of Professors of Educational Administration (NCPEA), and from this group a significant movement emerged. Before 1950, the content of educational administration seemed to be comprised of folklore, testimonials of administrators from wealthy or innovative districts, speculations of college professors, and opinions of administrators and professors who had written or lectured widely. The content of courses in educational administration generally consisted of a description of practices, cautious recommendations of promising techniques, personal success stories, and lively anecdotes, all surrounded with the halo of common sense conferred by a professor or reportedly successful administrator. There was no well-defined and organized body of subject matter and no theoretical structure.

An important turning point occurred in 1954. At the summer conference of the NCPEA, a number of theorists of human behavior from social science fields met with professors of educational administration. Together they challenged the type of thinking that had been prevalent in educational administration. They offered suggestions for new approaches to thinking in the field and inspired a critical analysis reported by Arthur Coladarci and Jacob Getzels (1955).

One year later, the University Council for Educational Administration (UCEA) was organized. With financial assistance from the Kellogg Foundation, it worked actively toward the development of theory by stimulating seminars and research studies. Progress was slow, however, as revealed by Hollis Moore's 1957 review of research activities. A critique by Andrew Halpin (1958) of the reported research noted that a prodigious effort had been made to collect information, but it consisted of exhortations, how-to-do-it prescriptions, catalogs of opinion, or status investigations that did not permit generalization beyond the immediate data.

By the time of Griffiths's 1959 publication, it had become evident to the leaders in theory development that they had gone far beyond the general comprehension of the meaning of theory. Disappointingly they found not only lack of acquaintance with theory, but also resistance to it. A prevalent view among both practitioners and professors of education was that theory was useless.

A typical scoffer's comment was made by a professor who pointed out proudly that his course titled "Principles of School Administration" was a "practical course, none of that theory stuff." An observer knowledgeable in theory commented that the syllabus failed to reveal any "principles" and agreed that there was certainly no theory in the course!

Why were educators adverse to theory? Coladarci and Getzels identified several factors explaining the antitheory bias in the mid 1950s:

1. *Factualism.* "Get the facts" seemed to be almost a national slogan but with no regard paid to interrelationships among facts, as though education could be merely an encyclopedia of facts.
2. *Authority.* There appeared to be an unwarranted and even alarming amount of respect for prominent speakers and writers, whose chief claim to fame might be merely that they came from a well-known school district or university.
3. *Lack of definitions.* There was little consistency at that time in the use of terms to describe events, and the same words were frequently used with a wide variety of meanings in discussions of theory.
4. *Personal opinion.* A major drawback to progress in the development of theory was jealousy about ideas held by various individuals. Ideas were personalized, and it seemed that to criticize an idea was to criticize an individual.

5. *Impracticality.* A common complaint was that it was better to be practical than theoretical. For example, if an individual or group advocated the use of lay committees in a school system, it was more often because a neighboring school district or one reported in the literature had used the technique rather than because of knowledge of interaction theory. John Dewey had not fully come into his own, and little attention had been given to his contention that

theory is in the end...the most practical of all things, because the widening of the range of attention beyond merely purpose and desire eventually results in the creation of wider and farther-reaching purposes and enables us to make use of a much wider and deeper range of conditions and means than were expressed in the observation of primitive practical purposes (1929, p. 17).

WHAT THEORY IS NOT

In the early days of theory development in education it seemed expedient to explain theory by making clear what it was *not.* Griffiths (1959) unequivocally eliminated a few popular misconceptions of theory, and others have been added to this list of what theories are not.

Not a rule of thumb. Frequently a style or pattern of operation is mistakenly called a theory: "We operate on the theory that student government is necessary to build morale."

Not a brainstormed flight of fancy. Thoughts tossed around in bull sessions are sometimes labeled theories: "My theory is that schools will someday use the daily newspapers as the entire curriculum."

Not an "ought to." A personal point of view, value statement, or set of "oughts" is sometimes called a theory: "My theory is that instructional management systems can be successful in every subject field."

Not a taxonomy. A taxonomy is a classification of data according to order, natural relationships, or governing principles that can be used for description of a subject matter or for diagnosing a problem. Taxonomies both summarize and inspire descriptive studies. Descriptive and taxonomic studies have been popular in educational investigations, and the information yielded is useful in building a theory. These sources are not theory, however.

Not the literature. Theory is not a term synonymous with classical works. Neither is it synonymous with the literature of educational criticism. However, these are also useful in developing a theory.

WHAT THEORY IS

Theory is here defined as a set of propositions derived from data and creative thinking from which constructs are formed to describe interactions among variables and to generate hypotheses. Theory describes, explains, goes beyond the data; it predicts and leads to new knowledge.

Characteristics of theory are stated by several writers, and these aid in clarifying the definition. The interrelatedness of a set of statements or events is a characteristic commonly noted. Fred Kerlinger brought together several dimensions when he wrote (1965, p. 11), "a theory is a set of interrelated constructs, definitions, and propositions that presents a systematic view of phenomena by specifying relations among variables with the purpose of explaining and predicting the phenomena."

The power of theories to generate new knowledge is another characteristic that is generally accepted. For example, theories summarize and inspire not descriptive studies but rather verificational studies— studies constructed to test specific hypotheses "generated from the theory" (Zetterberg 1965, p. 28). Zetterberg explains (pp. vii-viii) that a theory may

coordinate many methodologically imperfect findings into a rather trustworthy whole in the form of a small number of information-packed sentences or equations. Moreover, some of the bits and pieces coordinated into this trustworthy whole can be the challenging insights of the classics . . . [of a field] . . . and the celebrated writers of literature; in short, far from trivial propositions.

The relationship between hypotheses and theories is explained by Deobold Van Dalen (1966, p. 172), who says that a theory may contain several logically interrelated hypotheses. Van Dalen notes that hypotheses and theories are alike in that they are both conceptual, and both seek to explain and predict phenomena; but a theory usually offers a more general or higher-level explanation than a hypothesis. Van Dalen emphasizes that a theory usually presents a comprehensive conceptual scheme that explains diverse phenomena, and considerable empirical evidence is therefore needed to support it. No matter how wide a variety of confirming data is obtained, however, the theory is not established as an absolute truth.

This point is also made by Griffiths (1959, p. 11), who comments:

The instability of theory has caused many to suspect the whole notion of theory, yet this is not a necessary deterrent. Theories are not built for eternity. Theories are developed to help in the identification and clarification of problems here and now and in the immediate future. They are also constructed so that better theories might be built in the future. Theory building might be construed as a pyramiding task. Present theories rest on those of the past. When one examines past theories, even in the physical sciences, one notes the theories which were demonstrated to be untrue.

DEFINITIONS

Model

The terms *model* and *theory* are sometimes used interchangeably; however, models are not theories. A model is a set of plans, principles, or criteria based on a stated or implied rationale and presented as a unified framework worthy of being initiated or replicated. The pattern to be followed is evident in the structure of the model, which may be a graphic figure, symbolic description, or verbal statement. The term *paradigm* is frequently used in theoretical literature as a synonym of *model*.

A theory, defined and discussed in the previous section, is similar in some respects to a model as it is a coherent set of hypothetical, conceptual, and pragmatic principles. But theory goes beyond the model as a frame of reference for a field of inquiry. In this way theories are used for deducing new generalizations, formulating hypotheses, predicting, and leading to new knowledge and to action.

Data

Information gathered as a basis for reasoning or inference is a general definition of data. Data may be expressed qualitatively; that is, using word descriptions such as verbal observations of factors that hinder or foster change in the curriculum. Data may also be expressed quantitatively in mathematical symbols, such as those used to describe the occurrence frequency of a given condition or to measure achievement on a test.

Construct

A construct is a formation developed or created by a process of mental synthesis and/or by assembling parts or elements into an abstract creation. In the illustration of theory construction following this definition section, construct takes the form of a matrix and narrative interpretation.

Hypothesis

A hypothesis is a provisional or possible explanation that implies given consequences, which the researcher then seeks to confirm by providing factual evidence. It is an if-then tentative explanation: if x, then y. This temporary working statement requires testing to determine its worth.

Propositions

A proposition is a major premise on which subsequent meaning rests. It is a formal statement proposing something for development, discussion, testing, and verification. Propositions relate variates (variables) to one another, and two variates are needed at a minimum to have one theoretical proposition (Homans 1960, Zetterberg 1965). One-variate statements are not theoretical propositions; they are descriptive statements; for example, x varies. An explicit example is, modern children spend excessive amounts of time looking at television. A two-variate statement must point out that if x varies, then y varies. A two-variate statement could be, If the time children spend looking at television increases, then their reading ability decreases. In this illustration television is designated as a *determinant* (cause or independent variable) and reading is designated as a *result* (effect or dependent variable). The cause and effect relationship indicates the direction in which the variates influence each other; that is, poor reading is said to come from excessive television viewing; excessive television viewing does not come from poor reading.

Propositions may form a chain pattern if a result in one reappears as a determinant in another. For example, knowledge of attitudes of a group may lead to prestige for a person; prestige may lead to authority; and authority may lead to centrality in the group. Studies have been cited to show that all of these variables are positively correlated (Hopkins 1964).

A matrix is another form for presenting propositions and specifying their interrelationships. The matrix is more useful than the chain pattern for searching out relationships because the chain pattern is restricted to sequential propositions.

In the illustration of theory construction that follows, theoretical propositions are arranged on two axes of a matrix. Possible interrelations between these variables, identified at points of intersection on the matrix, become the constructs from which hypotheses for testing can be derived.

ILLUSTRATIVE PROPOSITIONS

Seven propositions that can have a bearing on curriculum development are suggested.

1. *Freedom for the individual.* Associated with this proposition are the concepts of human worth and dignity, respect, peace, love, equality, justice, brotherhood, health, and prosperity. In the process of curriculum development, questions are raised about the nature of freedom and the place of social and moral values: What shall we do about apathetic students, ethnic studies, the quality of the curriculum in the inner-city schools, examining unethical practices in government, studying causes of crime, developing skills of decision making, relating world resources to starving peoples,

investigating causes and effects of environmental problems, adjusting to a high-tech society, and making studies of predictive futures? The way such questions are answered will influence the participants' growth in developing social and moral values.

2. *Expanded view of culture.* The "total" culture goes far beyond the textbook. It can include a rich environment of ideas, experiences, beliefs, traditions, customs, institutions, sciences, arts, technologies, humanities, and common sense ways of doing things that are part of the shared life of people. The total culture includes separate disciplines and interdisciplinary approaches; national and world events; dialogue with others; and the human quest for values, attitudes, knowledge, and skills that will equip us to live rightly and well in a free society, as discussed earlier in this chapter.

3. *Democratic goals and means.* Support for democracy, a lofty goal of schools and society in America, is drawn in this set of propositions from the founding principles of the nation, from philosophers, observers of democratic and undemocratic practices, and from several investigative studies. Democracy is viewed as a moral goal of the educative process and of American society that should be exemplified by the use of democratic means to reach democratic ends.

4. *Commitment to planned change.* Planned change needs emphasis in curriculum development because the alternative is to be buffeted here and there by the conflicting demands of pressure groups. Curriculum specialists need to know the dynamic technological, social, and economic developments that are forecast for the future. People are needed to do long-range planning for curriculum development, not mere spectators to be swept along by the times, reacting superficially. (Planning as a concept is explored in Chapter Two under "Effective Leadership.")

5. *Comprehensive assessment of needs.* The concept of need is a fairly recent discovery in education, particularly needs of the participants most closely affected by curriculum development. Need, as a fundamental consideration in curriculum, is defined as the difference between existing actuality and envisioned ideal circumstances. Participants' needs may be educational or psychological. Needs assessments are procedures, both structured and informal, for identifying gaps between the ideal and the real. (See Chapter Six for further discussion of this topic.)

6. *Links among participants.* Collaborative efforts, interaction, and communication among participants and referent groups can

generate power for curriculum development. Participants are those who have a direct share in curriculum development close to the classroom: boards of education, administrators, curriculum specialists, teachers, students, and parents. Referent groups are those who should be consulted about curriculum development, but they have more indirect relationships, interests, and concerns: university professors, researchers, consultants, publishers, and the general public. Links are cooperative actions or communication systems that connect the persons concerned with a given unit of curriculum development and the resultant curriculum and instruction.

The absence of adequate participation and joint efforts was viewed by Harry Broudy (1966) as the reason the scholarly proposals for reform in his day did not bring about lasting change. The scholars' approach was tinged with intellectual snobbery, he said, and schools and teacher education institutions seemed to be expected to adopt the new materials and methods although they had only been invited to give a bare minimum of consultation during the planning stages. He advocates that professional curriculum researchers and writers seek participation by parents, teachers, students, administrators, and interested citizens. Parents may decide to support or not support the school. Teachers may decide to follow an administrative directive or covertly ignore it. Students may choose to learn or not to learn. Other groups have ways of expressing satisfaction or dissatisfaction. On the other hand, Broudy emphasizes that curriculum development cannot be left to the hunches of the average person any more than it can be left to the scholars alone. Curriculum development must take into account our highly complex and interdependent society and draw on the best known sources of knowledge as well as human attitudes and values. Links are necessary. (Chapter Three provides further discussion about the influence various parties have on curriculum development).

7. *Open-systems concepts.* Curriculum development is a combination of interacting systems and subsystems. A system is a complex unit of parts related to each other in a manner that serves a common purpose. Open-systems concepts imply a constant state of self-renewal; a continuous reorganization to meet new problems, examine new complexities, and use new ideas and information as part of the planning and renewal process. Closed-systems approaches to problems are static, they analyze challenges in terms of some preestablished internal structure and ignore external environments such as sociopolitical and socioeconomic issues or new knowledge in related fields.

A MATRIX OF CONSTRUCTS

The seven propositions presented above each yields a key concept that contributes to quality in curriculum development. These are shown in Figure 4. From the propositions, a matrix of constructs is presented in Figure 5. In the matrix the propositions are arranged as determinants (causes) on the horizontal axis and as results (effects, consequences) on the vertical axis. The matrix provides an inventory of propositions, both as determinants and as results, and a schema for studying their interrelationships at each point of intersection and at combinations of intersections. Each proposition interacting with another proposition strengthens both, and one leads to effects in the other. These interrelationships form broad constructs or syntheses, derived from the points of intersection, that reach beyond the data and yield general hypotheses for testing.

Figure 4. Propositions

Concept	Statement
1. Freedom for the individual	If planning for the freedom of individuals is included, the curriculum development process will become more responsive to social, ethical, and moral valuing.
2. Expanded view of culture	If planners draw upon more of the total culture, the curriculum development process will respond to the needs and concerns of the persons served by the school.
3. Democratic goals and means	If means are used that not only exemplify but also strengthen the nation's founding goals, curriculum development will respond to and embody the purposes of American democracy.
4. Commitment to planned change	If there is a commitment to planned change, the curriculum development process will become responsive to dynamic and futuristic technological and social developments.
5. Comprehensive assessment of needs	If there is a more comprehensive assessment of needs, the curriculum development process will be more responsive to both individual and group concerns.
6. Links among participants	If the number and intensity of links among participants increase, the curriculum development process will become more responsive to their common needs.
7. Open systems concepts	If concepts of open systems are used, the curriculum development process will become more responsive to the need for interrelating its factors and participants.

Figure 5. Matrix of Constructs (C)

Results

Propositions	1. Freedom for the individual	2. Expanded view of culture	3. Democratic goals and means	4. Commitment to planned change	5. Comprehensive assessment of needs	6. Links among participants	7. Open systems concepts
1. Freedom for the individual	—	$C_{1,2}$	$C_{1,3}$	$C_{1,4}$	$C_{1,5}$	$C_{1,6}$	$C_{1,7}$
2. Expanded view of culture	$C_{2,1}$	—	$C_{2,3}$	$C_{2,4}$	$C_{2,5}$	$C_{2,6}$	$C_{2,7}$
3. Democratic goals and means	$C_{3,1}$	$C_{3,2}$	—	$C_{3,4}$	$C_{3,5}$	$C_{3,6}$	$C_{3,7}$
4. Commitment to planned change	$C_{4,1}$	$C_{4,2}$	$C_{4,3}$	—	$C_{4,5}$	$C_{4,6}$	$C_{4,7}$
5. Comprehensive assessment of needs	$C_{5,1}$	$C_{5,2}$	$C_{5,3}$	$C_{5,4}$	—	$C_{5,6}$	$C_{5,7}$
6. Links among participants	$C_{6,1}$	$C_{6,2}$	$C_{6,3}$	$C_{6,4}$	$C_{6,5}$	—	$C_{6,7}$
7. Open systems concepts	$C_{7,1}$	$C_{7,2}$	$C_{7,3}$	$C_{7,4}$	$C_{7,5}$	$C_{7,6}$	—

Determinants

In the cells of the matrix, C is used as a symbol for construct; thus, constructs are identified as $C_{1,2}$, $C_{1,3}$, and so forth. As an illustration, $C_{1,2}$ indicates that if there is humanistic planning for freedom of the individual (determinant), then there is a more expanded view of culture (result).

Types of Relationships

When two propositions interact, constructs are formed, as shown in the cells of the matrix. Each cell or construct can spin off hypotheses to be considered or tested later. In the examples that follow, each construct is analyzed in terms of its type or types of interrelationships. This is done as a means of looking for causal links. Relationships may have one or more of the following attributes (Zetterberg 1965, pp. 69-72):

1. *reversible* (if x, then y, and if y, then x) or *irreversible* (if x, then y, but if y, then no conclusion about x)
2. *deterministic* (if x, then always y) or *stochastic* (if x, then probably y)
3. *sequential* (if x, then later y) or *coextensive* (if x, then also y)
4. *sufficient* (if x, then y regardless of anything else) or *contingent* (if x, then y but only if z)
5. *necessary* (only if x, then y) or *substitutable* (if x, then y, but if z, then also y)
6. *interdependent* (a large change brought about through a series of interacting small changes)

Construct $C_{2,1}$

As a responsive curriculum development process includes an expanded view of the culture, a greater degree of planning for the freedom of the individual will result. A coextensive relationship is illustrated by this construct: as culture is included more widely, curriculum development becomes more responsive to the values of planning for freedom.

Hypotheses for Testing

If white and black curriculum developers investigate together the particular concerns of each race about the culture of the other, then their attitudes toward the opposite race, as measured by appropriate instruments, will increase positively.

If philosophical anthropology—study of the nature of man and society and of the human predicament and human development for the purpose of improving the human condition (Edel 1966)— is used by more curriculum developers as the organizing component of the social studies curriculum in the public schools (instead of history and geography), the behavior in schools of teachers, students, curriculum specialists, and administrators will change positively toward planning for the freedom of the individual.

Construct $C_{2,3}$

As the curriculum development process draws increasingly from an expanded view of culture, more influence is exerted toward designing educational means for strengthening American democratic goals. A stochastic relationship exists: that is, if x, then probably y. If curriculum developers draw from the expanded concept of culture, it is probable that more resources will be brought to bear on designing educational means for reaching democratic goals.

Hypothesis for Testing

If community and school interpenetrate (thus expanding each view of culture) by designing work experiences in the community for students and learning experiences in the schools for lay persons, then the degree of consensus will increase on those educational means that strengthen American democratic goals.

Constructs $C_{1,3}$, $C_{1,4}$, and $C_{1,6}$

In the curriculum development process, when planning for the freedom of the individual is given a value priority, increased attention will be given to educational means that strengthen democratic goals, provisions for planned change, and links among referent groups. An interdependent relationship is evident. Consideration of planning for the freedom of individuals leads to more knowledge about issues, which leads to greater consideration of principles involved, which leads to greater collaboration, and so forth. As each factor gains strength, the related factors also gain strength.

Hypothesis for Testing

If dialogue on values is increased at the state and local boards of education, increased curriculum development priority will be given to systematic instruction in decision-making skills in the public schools.

Constructs $C_{2,6}$ and $C_{6,2}$

As curriculum developers draw knowledge, attitudes, and skills from an expanded view of the available culture, links among referent groups in curriculum development will increase, generating greater responsiveness in curriculum development. This construct is the reversible type (broader inclusion of the culture leads to broader links, and vice versa) and is coextensive (an increase in either the inclusion of culture or group links leads to an increase in the other). It is also a contingent construct because the quality of curriculum development depends on links and an expanded view of culture.

Hypothesis for Testing

If interaction and collaboration in curriculum development increase among black, Hispanic, and white students, teachers, parents, and administrators representing several socioeconomic strata, then polarizations and conflicts of values will decrease, and the degree of consensus on curriculum development goals will increase.

Construct $C_{4,1}$

A commitment to planned change, which is necessary in response to dynamic futuristic developments, can exert influence toward planning for the freedom of individuals. A stochastic relationship, as contrasted to a deterministic one, is expressed. Probability is high that applications of the concepts of planned change, if fully understood, can influence the present shifting situation in societal values and beliefs toward planning for freedom—human worth and dignity, respect for the individual, and a person-centered society.

Hypotheses for Testing

If dissatisfied students who have dropped out of a traditional high school participate with adults in planning an alternative high school (including problem formulation, goal setting, finding alternative means for reaching objectives, and self-evaluation), then the students will attend regularly and exhibit observable interest in achieving the goals that were set.

If opportunities are planned for secondary school students to experience interdisciplinary and action learnings related to a major social concern for the future (for example, dwindling resources and increasing consumption of goods), then the students will be able to identify legislative decisions that either harm or benefit the goals of a person-centered society.

If young students are confronted with value dilemmas in case studies or role-playing situations, then they will be able to identify illustrations of honesty and justice.

Construct $C_{4,3}$

In the curriculum development process, a commitment to planned change will expedite educational means that exemplify American democratic goals, and the degree of attainment of the goals of planned freedom for the individual will increase. This construct shows an interdependent relationship. An increase in one variable leads to an increase in a second variable, which in turn improves the first variable, and so on. As more attention is given to planned change, which includes clarification and specification of goals and means, democratic goals become more effective in practice; and, as their effectiveness increases, planning becomes more effective.

Hypothesis for Testing

If the school administrators of a local district systematically and collaboratively increase their skills in planning change, increased attention will be given to designing specific means for reaching the goals of American democracy in education.

Construct $C_{4,5}$

When the concepts of planned change expand in scope, assessment of the needs and purposes of the various participants becomes more comprehensive; the curriculum development process is then less subject to conflicting and competing pressures and more responsive. A stochastic relationship exists: as planning skills increase, sensitivity to needs and purposes will probably increase.

Hypothesis for Testing

If a state department of education increases its staff skills in planning for change, its scope of inputs about the needs and purposes of referent groups will expand, and its contacts with schools will increase.

Constructs $C_{5,1}$, $C_{5,2}$, $C_{5,3}$, $C_{5,4}$, $C_{5,6}$, and $C_{5,7}$

In the curriculum development process, as needs assessment becomes comprehensive, strength will be gained in moral commitment to planning for the freedom of individuals, views of culture will expand, use of educational means to reach American democratic goals will increase, attention will be directed to the concept of planned change, links among referent groups will increase, and open systems concepts will be more widely used. Interdependent relationships are exemplified in this major construct; that is, the more that is known about needs, the more importance is given to other factors in the curriculum development process.

Hypotheses for Testing

If an open-ended Delphi-type survey of local district needs solicits and uses the expressed curricular concerns of random samples of students, teachers, parents, curriculum specialists, administrators, and university professors of education, then curriculum development will give higher priority to excellence.

If a needs assessment by the state department of education for curriculum development purposes provides for feedback from students, teachers, administrators, parents, and representatives of research and development centers on their concerns about societal issues, personal development, and academic knowledge (rather than excluding one or more of these areas), statewide curriculum development processes will produce curricular and instructional plans providing for emphasis in all three areas—social relations, personal development, and academic knowledge.

Constructs $C_{6,3}$ and $C_{3,6}$

When links among the referent groups increase, educational means will be implemented that exemplify and strengthen American democratic goals for education. This construct is the reversible type (links lead to means for reaching democratic goals, and democratic means lead to links). It is also coextensive (as either increases, it affects the other positively).

Hypotheses for Testing

If children in elementary schools have practice in developing their curriculum plans in collaboration with teachers and curriculum specialists, all parties will increase their understanding and application of the democratic goals of education.

If secondary school teachers and students collaborate more in planning for curriculum and instruction, the dropout rate (physical and psychological) will decrease.

Construct $C_{6,5}$

If interaction and collaboration among referent groups increase, each group will become more knowledgeable of and empathetic to the needs and purposes of other groups, thus generating more responsiveness in curriculum development. Here we have a reversible relationship in that higher frequency of interaction and collaboration leads to greater empathy for the needs and purposes of others, and greater empathy leads to higher frequency of interaction and collaboration.

Hypothesis for Testing

In resolving value-laden curriculum problems and conflicts between students and local adult referent groups, if the needs and purposes of each group can be presented in orderly discussion settings to all others involved, then a mutually acceptable curriculum plan will be developed.

Construct $C_{6,7}$

In the curriculum development process, links among referent groups are an essential factor in the use of open systems concepts. The relationship is the type Zetterberg describes as necessary. The inclusion of collaborative, interactive, and linking efforts among referent groups is a necessary factor in the success of open systems concepts in increasing quality in curriculum development.

Hypothesis for Testing

If curriculum development includes adequate links among its referent groups, then it may start from various loci (for example, the psychology of learners, subject matter interests, research and development centers, local user-based developers, societal demands, or student protest movements) and become responsive in a comprehensive manner, avoiding either-or approaches to the needs of learners, to societal conditions, or to bodies of knowledge.

Construct $C_{7,3}$

The greater the use of systems concepts, the greater will be the focus on educational means that exemplify and strengthen the spirit of American democratic goals. A stochastic relationship is expressed; that is, if systems approaches are used reliably, with adequate procedures for setting goals, assessing needs, specifying objectives and priorities, devising alternative procedures, and using evaluation as feedback for modification, then means for attainment of the broad democratic goals of American education will probably be practiced.

Hypothesis for Testing

If curriculum development provides for instruction in decision making, children will be able to differentiate practical applications of democratic values from undemocratic values.

Constructs $C_{2,7}$, $C_{3,7}$, $C_{4,7}$, $C_{5,7}$, and $C_{6,7}$

When curriculum development draws on the total culture, gives concerted attention to designing educational means to reach democratic goals, uses concepts of planned change, assesses the needs and purposes of the various participants, and establishes operational links among the referent groups, then there is greater use of systems concepts leading to responsiveness to the needs of people, societal conditions, and changing knowledge. Here is a multivariate and interdependent relationship. The large change—excellence in curriculum development—is brought about through a series of interacting interdependent factors and changes.

Hypothesis for Testing

If three high schools in three diverse settings (urban, suburban, rural) presently using grading procedures that intentionally assign students to tracks according to rank order or otherwise judge students as failures or successes each initiate links among students, teachers, and administrators to accomplish comprehensive assessment of needs, planned change, mutual goal setting, design of alternative means to reach goals, and wider use of the resources of culture, then systems concepts will be used, and the curriculum development process will produce these effects:

a. Formative evaluation will receive more emphasis than summative education.
b. Teachers will use a wider variety of instructional methods.
c. In-service plans will center around the use of formative evaluation as a diagnostic tool to assist students in finding alternative ways to achieve learning outcomes.
d. Observation analyses will reveal a decrease in negative talk by teachers and an increase in positive student participation in classroom discourse.
e. Attitudes toward school will be more positive and less negative as measured by written instruments.
f. Time spent in class discussions for problem solving will increase.
g. The student dropout rate will decrease.

Construct $C_{7,1}$

The greater use of open systems concepts in processes of curriculum development that are responsive to the needs of people, societal conditions, and changing knowledge, the more moral commitment will be generated toward reaching important goals. An interdependent relationship and an extension of the construct immediately preceding this one express the relationships of these factors. Here we have a chain pattern within the $C_{7,1}$ cell that expresses how an expanded view of the total culture, a focus on educational means to exemplify and strengthen democratic goals, a commitment to planned change, comprehensive needs assessment, and links among referent groups use systems concepts leading to values of planned freedom, which in turn lead to further chain patterns among the propositions and generate power by building on each other.

Hypothesis for Testing

If a local school district organizes to use open systems concepts in curriculum development (as defined in this theory), the school practices and attitudes as measured on appropriate observational instruments will increase in the values of democracy.

TOWARD A THEORETICAL BASE

The propositions, constructs, and hypotheses suggested here are intended to illustrate one method of theory construction. The endless relationships at points of intersection and combinations of intersections show how rich and complex the ramifications of a broad theoretical base for curriculum development can be. The matrix presentation is intended to demonstrate a way to generate new ideas and new knowledge about curriculum development. Curriculum developers should construct theoretical foundations to fit the time, place, and mission of their particular situations.

REFERENCES

Adler, Mortimer J. *The Paideia Proposal: An Educational Manifesto.* New York: Macmillan Co., 1982.

Anderson, Terryl. "A Broader View of Democracy." *Phi Delta Kappan* 54 (January 1973): 319-20.

Anyon, Jean. "Schools as Agencies of Social Legitimation." *Journal of Curriculum Theorizing* 3, 2 (Summer 1981): 86-103.

Bagley, William C. *Classroom Management.* New York: Macmillan Co., 1907, p. 2.

Beauchamp, George A. "Basic Components of a Curriculum Theory." *Curriculum Theory Network* 2 (Fall 1972): 16-22.

Beauchamp, George A. *Curriculum Theory.* 2d ed. Wilmette, Ill.: Kagg Press, 1968.

Berman, Louise. *New Priorities in the Curriculum.* Columbus, Ohio: Charles E. Merrill, 1968.

Bestor, Arthur. *The Restoration of Learning.* New York: Alfred A. Knopf, 1956, pp. 48-49.

Bloom, Benjamin S., ed. *Taxonomy of Educational Objectives, Handbook 1: Cognitive Domain.* New York: David McKay, 1956.

Bobbitt, Franklin. *The Curriculum.* Boston: Houghton Mifflin, 1918.

Brandt, Ronald S. "Teaching Thinking Skills." *Educational Leadership* 39 (October 1981): Issue.

Broudy, Harry S. "Democratic Values and Educational Goals." In *The Curriculum: Retrospect and Prospect,* part I, pp. 113-52. Seventieth Yearbook of the National Society for the Study of Education. Chicago: University of Chicago Press, 1971.

Broudy, Harry S. "Needed: A Unifying Theory of Education." In *Curriculum Change: Direction and Process,* pp. 15-26. Alexandria, Va.: Association for Supervision and Curriculum Development, 1966.

Bruner, Jerome S. *The Process of Education.* Cambridge: Harvard University Press, 1960.

Buchen, Irving H. "Humanism and Futurism: Enemies or Allies?" In *Learning for Tomorrow,* edited by Alvin Toffler, pp. 132-43. New York: Random House, 1974.

Buckwalter, Doyle W. "The American Dilemma." *Social Studies* 64 (January 1973): 3-10.

Cawelti, Gordon, ed. *Vitalizing High Schools: A Summary of Six National Proposals for Reforming Secondary Schools and a Curriculum Critique.* Alexandria, Va.: Association for Supervision and Curriculum Development, 1974.

Coladarci, Arthur P., and Getzels, Jacob W. *The Use of Theory in Educational Administration.* Stanford, Calif.: Stanford University Press, 1955.

Counts, George S. *Education and American Civilization.* New York: Bureau of Publications, Teachers College, Columbia University, 1952.

Counts, George. *Dare the Schools Build a New Social Order?* New York: John Day, 1932.

Dewey, John. *Experience and Education.* New York: Collier Books, 1938.

Dewey, John. "Democracy and Educational Administration." *School and Society* 45 (3 April 1937): 457-62.

Dewey, John. *How We Think*, rev. ed. Lexington, Mass.: Heath, 1933.

Dewey, John. *Sources of a Science Education.* New York: Liveright, 1929.

Edel, A. "The Contribution of Philosophical Anthropology to Educational Development." In *Philosophy and Educational Development*, edited by G. Barnett, pp. 69-91. Boston: Houghton Mifflin, 1966.

Eisner, Elliot W., and Vallance, Elizabeth, eds. *Conflicting Conceptions of Curriculum.* Berkeley: McCutchan, 1974.

Emerson, Ralph Waldo. "The American Scholar." In *Emerson on Education*, edited by H. M. Jones, pp. 77-101. New York: Teacher's College Press, Columbia University, 1966.

Eschenbacher, Herman F. "Social Studies, Social Science, and School Reform." *Intellect* 102 (Summer 1974): 507-9.

Friere, Paulo. *Pedagogy of the Oppressed.* New York: Seabury Press, 1970.

Fromm, Erich. *The Heart of Man.* New York: Harper & Row, 1968.

Gay, Geneva. "Conceptual Models of the Curriculum-Planning Process." In *Considered Action for Curriculum Improvement*, pp. 120-43. Yearbook for the Association for Supervision and Curriculum Development. Alexandria, Va.: ASCD, 1980.

Giroux, Henry A. "Beyond the Limits of Radical Education Reform: Toward a Critical Theory of Education." *The Journal of Curriculum Theorizing* 2:1 (Winter 1980): 20-46.

Giroux, Henry A., and Penna, Anthony N. "Social Education in the Classroom: The Dynamics of the Hidden Curriculum." In *Curriculum and Instruction*, edited by Henry A. Giroux, Anthony N. Penna, and William F. Pinar, pp. 209-30. Berkeley: McCutchan, 1981.

Griffiths, Daniel E. *Administrative Theory.* New York: Appleton-Century-Crofts, 1959.

Halpin, Andrew E., ed. *Administrative Theory in Education.* Chicago: Midwest Administration Center, 1958.

Hobbs, Nicholas. "Feuerstein's Instrumental Enrichment: Teaching Intelligence to Adolescents." *Educational Leadership* 37 (April 1980): 566-68.

Hodgkinson, Christopher. "Why Democracy Won't Work." *Phi Delta Kappan* 54 (January 1973): 316-17.

Homans, George C. *The Human Group.* New York: Harcourt, Brace and World, 1950.

Hopkins, Terence K. *The Exercise of Influence in Small Groups.* Totowa, N.J.: Bedminster Press, 1964.

Huebner, Dwayne. "Toward a Political Economy of Curriculum and Human Development." In *Curriculum and Instruction,* edited by Henry A. Giroux, Anthony Penna, and William F. Pinar, pp. 124-38. Berkeley: McCutchan, 1981.

Hutchins, Robert M. *The Higher Learning in America.* New Haven, Conn.: Yale University Press, 1936, pp. 82-85.

Hyman, Ronald J., ed. *Approaches in Curriculum.* Englewood Cliffs, N.J.: Prentice-Hall, 1973.

Junell, Joseph S. "Is Rational Man Our First Priority?" *Phi Delta Kappan* 52 (November 1970): 147-53.

Kerlinger, Fred N. *Foundations of Behavioral Research.* New York: Holt, Rinehart, and Winston, 1965.

Kilpatrick, William H. "Definition of the Activity Movement Today." In *The Activity Movement,* pp. 45-64. Thirty-third Yearbook, part II of the National Society for the Study of Education. Bloomington, Ill.: Public School Publishing Co., 1934.

Link, Frances R. "Instrumental Enrichment: The Classroom Perspective." *The Educational Forum* 44 (May 1980): 424-28.

Long, Ernestine M. "Cognitive Skills Rise, Fall, Depending on Settings, Roles." *Human Intelligence.* Newsletter, P.O. Box 1163, Birmingham, Mich. (November-December 1981) p. 5.

Macdonald, James B. "Value Bases and Issues for Curriculum." In *Curriculum Theory,* edited by Alex Molnar and John A. Zahorik, pp. 10-21. Alexandria, Va.: Association for Supervision and Curriculum Development, 1977.

Macdonald, James B. "Curriculum Development in Relation to Social and Intellectual Systems. In *The Curriculum: Retrospect and Prospect,* part I, pp. 97-112. Seventieth Yearbook of the National Society for the Study of Education. Chicago: University of Chicago Press, 1971.

Macdonald, James B., and Zaret, Esther, eds. *Schools in Search of Meaning.* Yearbook of the Association for Supervision and Curriculum Development. Alexandria, Va.: ASCD, 1975.

Machiavelli, Niccolo. *The Prince.* Edited by Lester G. Crocker. New York: Washington Square Press, 1963.

MacLeish, Archibald. "To Make Men Free." *Atlantic* 188 (November 1951): 27-30.

Maslow, Abraham H. "Some Educational Implications of the Humanistic Psychologies." *Harvard Educational Review* 38 (Fall 1968): 685-96.

Mayer, Frederick. *Education for a New Society.* Bloomington, Ind.: Phi Delta Kappan Educational Foundation, 1973.

Moore, Hollis A., Jr. *Studies in School Administration.* Arlington, Va.: American Association of School Administrators, 1957.

Myrdal, Gunnar. *An American Dilemma.* New York: Harper & Row, 1962.

Neill, A. S. *Summerhill*. New York: Hart, 1960.

Newmann, Fred M., and Oliver, Donald W. *Clarifying Public Controversy*. Boston: Little, Brown & Co., 1970.

Paros, Lawrence. "The City Game." In *Title III and Changing Educational Designs*, pp. 10-12. Washington, D.C.: George Washington University, 1973.

Phenix, Philip H. "Transcendence and the Curriculum." *Teachers College Record* 73 (December 1971): 279.

Piaget, Jean. *Science of Education and the Psychology of the Child*. New York: Orion Press, 1970.

Pinar, William F. "The Reconceptualization of Curriculum Studies." In *Curriculum and Instruction*, edited by Henry A. Giroux, Anthony N. Penna, and William F. Pinar, pp. 87-97. Berkeley: McCutchan, 1981.

Rader, Benjamin G. "Jacksonian Democracy: Myth or Reality?" *Social Studies* 65 (January 1974): 17-22.

Rogers, Carl R. "Toward Becoming a Fully Functioning Person." In *Perceiving, Behaving, Becoming: A New Focus for Education*, pp. 21-33. Yearbook of the Association for Supervision and Curriculum Development. Alexandria, Va.: ASCD, 1962.

Rugg, Harold, ed. "Curriculum-making: Points of Emphasis," and "The Foundations of Curriculum-making." In *The Foundations and Technique of Curriculum-making*, parts I and II. Twenty-sixth Yearbook of the National Society for the Study of Education. Bloomington, Ill.: Public School Publishing, 1926.

Schwab, Joseph J. "The Concept of the Structure of a Discipline." In *Conflicting Conceptions of Curriculum*, edited by Eliot W. Eisner and Elizabeth Vallance, pp. 162-75. Berkeley: McCutchan, 1974.

Shane, Harold G. and Tabler, M. Bernadine. *Educating for a New Millenium*. Bloomington, Ind.: Phi Delta Kappan, 1981.

Steeves, Frank L., and English, Fenwick W. *Secondary Curriculum for a Changing World*. Columbus, Ohio: Charles E. Merrill, 1978.

Taba, Hilda. *Curriculum Development: Theory and Practice*. New York: Harcourt, Brace and World, 1962.

Tanner, Daniel, and Tanner, Laurel N. *Curriculum Development*, 2d ed. New York: Macmillan Co., 1980.

Taylor, Frederick W. *The Principles of Scientific Management*. New York: Harper & Row, 1911.

Toffler, Alvin. *Future Shock*. New York: Bantam Books, 1970.

Tyler, Ralph. *Basic Principles of Curriculum and Instruction*. Chicago: University of Chicago Press, 1950.

Van Dalen, Deobold B. *Understanding Educational Research*. New York: McGraw-Hill, 1966.

Winthrop, Henry. "The World We Have Wrought." *Educational Forum* 38 (January 1974): 163-70.

Zais, Robert S. "Conceptions of Curriculum and the Curriculum Field." In *Curriculum and Instruction*, edited by Henry A. Giroux, Anthony N. Penna, and William F. Pinar. Berkeley: McCutchan, 1980.

Zetterberg, Hans L. *On Theory and Verification in Sociology.* Totowa, N.J.: Bedmister Press, 1965.

ADDITIONAL READINGS

Beauchamp, George A. *Curriculum Theory.* 4th ed. Itasca, Ill.: Peacock, 1981.

Block, James H. "Mastery Learning: The Current State of the Craft." *Educational Leadership* 37 (November 1979): 114–17.

Callahan, Raymond. *Education and the Cult of Efficiency.* Chicago: University of Chicago Press, 1962.

"Curriculum Theory." *Theory into Practice* 21 (Winter 1982): Issue 1–68.

Giroux, Henry, and Purpel, David, eds. *The Hidden Curriculum and Moral Education.* Berkeley: McCutchan, 1983.

Griffiths, Daniel E. "The Nature and Meaning of Theory." In *Behavioral Science and Educational Administration,* part II, pp. 95–118. Sixty-third Yearbook of the National Society for the Study of Education. Chicago: University of Chicago Press, 1964.

Kagan, Jerome. "Jean Piaget's Contributions." *Phi Delta Kappan* 62 (December 1980): 245–46.

Kliebard, Herbert M. "Bureaucracy and Curriculum Theory." In *Freedom, Bureaucracy, and Schooling,* pp. 74–93. Yearbook of the Association for Supervision and Curriculum Development. Alexandria, Va.: ASCD, 1971.

Pinar, William, ed. *Curriculum Theorizing: The Reconceptualists.* Berkeley: McCutchan, 1975.

Popham, W. James, et al. *Instructional Objectives.* Chicago: Rand McNally, 1969.

Posner, George J. "The Use of Construct Validation Procedures in Curriculum Research." *Curriculum Theory Network* 2 (Spring 1973): 34–46.

5

Goals and Objectives

Goals and objectives play a critical part in the development of curriculum and in instruction and evaluation. Preparing goals and objectives requires both care and deliberation. They provide direction for the entire educational enterprise of a school or other organizational unit and stipulate its quality. Other concepts such as scope and sequence and the criteria for content selection are ineffective unless they are based on significant goals and objectives. The best that is known about goals for education in America should be reflected in the philosophy of each school.

Determining the broad goals or mission of the school or other unit is the first step in curriculum development. The philosophy of the school usually guides goal development, which may be preceded or followed by a needs assessment. The goals must reflect policy, present and future conditions, priorities, resources available, awareness of the constituents' desires and needs. These goals must in turn serve as a guide for developing more specific objectives, learning activities, curriculum implementation, and evaluation for feedback. In this chapter the discussion includes the power of purpose, goals in perspective, the setting for goal development, and the local task.

THE POWER OF PURPOSE

The development and writing out of goals is a crucial task requiring time, energy, insights, and intelligence. John Dewey said:

The formation of purposes and the organization of means to execute them are the work of intelligence. . . . The formation of purposes is a rather complex intellectual operation involving observation of surrounding conditions, knowledge of what has happened in the past . . . and an evaluation of the significance of the past and present for action (1938, pp. 67-69).

Dewey emphasized that purpose translates into a plan for action based on estimating the consequences of that action. Purpose, therefore, provides a drive to do, to achieve something. A chosen purpose sets direction because other possible purposes, interests, and impulses are relegated to the storage bin.

The power of goals and objectives can be a potent force for curriculum improvement when Dewey's principles are applied. Dewey's "surrounding conditions" translate into the needs of the learners, knowledge of curriculum and instruction, community aspirations, and availability of physical, economic, and human resources.

GOALS IN PERSPECTIVE

American people from colonial times on have been interested in education and have, at different times, tried to state the mission of schools and education.

Classic Goals

Probably the first goal statement was a justification for the establishment of Harvard in 1636. It read, in part, ". . . to advance learning and perpetuate it to posterity, dreading to leave an illiterate ministry to the churches, when our present ministers shall lie in the dust (Kandel 1930, p. 120)." The writers here were concerned about their churches (society), and a needs assessment was hardly necessary for them.

About 1789, Benjamin Franklin—sometimes referred to as the founder of the early academy—became concerned that there was far too much to be learned in the few years allotted to education. He characterized the purpose of the academy by saying (quoted by Kandel), ". . . it would be well if they (the youth) could be taught *everything* that is useful and *everything* that is ornamental. But art is long and their time is short. It is therefore proposed that they learn those things that are likely to be *most useful* and *most ornamental;* regard being had to the several professions for which they are intended" (p. 171). This goal statement relates to content and some guidance for its selection. Nothing is said about the learner nor the community.

Herbert Spencer, writing in 1861, was concerned with preparing people to live their lives to the fullest in both an economic and social sense. He raised the question, "What knowledge is of most worth?" and answered it by saying, "Science," which for him was useful in earning a living, performing his family and social duties, and developing the aesthetic, intellectual, and religious life. Spencer continued his analysis and finally decided that the goals of education were self preservation (health); securing the necessities of life (vocational); rearing and disciplining children (worthy home membership); maintaining proper social and political relations (citizenship); and preparing for the profitable use of leisure time (Mulhern 1946, p. 414). Spencer was concerned about the needs of both the learner and the society.

Probably the first statement in America concerning the purposes of elementary education was written into the 1642 Massachusetts law, which required the selectmen of towns to see that all children were able "to read and understand the principles of religion and the capital laws of this country...." (Mulhern 1946, p. 279). In 1647, writing was added to this curriculum. By 1690, *The New England Primer* was published and a few religious treaties were in use. Toward the end of the eighteenth century, Noah Webster's "blue backed" *American Spelling Book,* a combined speller and reader, brought spelling into favor, and soon there were spelling matches everywhere. By the first half of the nineteenth century reading, ciphering, spelling, and some history were the curriculum and were controlled by the books then in existence.

By 1860, the curriculum for younger children had expanded only slightly. Elwood P. Cubberly found that the usual offerings were letters and syllables, reading, writing, spelling, numbers, elementary language, and good behavior (1919, p. 222). Curriculum development, if it could be identified as such, was confined to deciding which books to provide for the children, adding subjects from time to time that were thought to be good for them, and borrowing ideas from other schools. Pupils were taught by didactic methods: lectures, exhortations, examinations over details and isolated bits of information that required a good memory. Books were few in number or variety. The goals for education were not yet in an authoritative written form, but "everyone knew what schools were for." Attention was beginning to focus on the aims of education, however, especially for secondary schools.

Expanding the Goals for Education

Over three centuries, the American people have gradually expanded their goals for education. Beginning with narrow academic and religious goals in the 1600s, they added vocational and social goals in the 1700s and 1800s. Goals of personal development, aesthetic values, cultural awareness, and others were added in the 1900s.

Developing goals and objectives for education in an effort to define the mission of the schools and to provide direction has occupied the time and energy of numerous individuals and groups. Not all of these, certainly, can be chronicled here; nor would that be of great value. Some of these statements are referred to frequently in the literature of today and may be regarded as lineal descendants of those earlier efforts.

This constant attention to statements about the goals of education has been a way of responding to criticisms of the schools. Common criticisms of the schools over time have stated that the schools' curricula were too narrow; schools were taking on too many responsibilities and should be more selective; they were ignoring large areas of important information and knowledge; and they were preparing their charges inadequately for work or for further education.

One attempt to address these defects was the Seven Cardinal Principles statement, a forerunner of a number of such attempts to define the mission of the schools. It was set forth in 1918 by the Commission on the Reorganization of Secondary Education. The major objectives of education were to be (1) health, (2) command of the fundamental processes, (3) worthy home membership, (4) worthy use of leisure time, (5) vocation, (6) citizenship, and (7) ethical character.

Another example of goal development at the national level illustrates an attempt to define a mission. In 1947 the National Association of Secondary School Principals published the *Imperative Needs of Youth*. This was not their only publication on the subject but one that received much attention. The needs were identified as to develop (1) salable skills; (2) health and physical fitness; (3) citizenship; (4) the family and society; (5) consumer intelligence; (6) science and scientific method; (7) knowledge of literature, art, music, nature; (8) use of leisure time; (9) respect for others; (10) thinking rationally and communicating clearly.

Interest in goals for schools was not confined to the secondary levels. An endeavor to refine thinking about elementary education and to provide goals for its development was the *Report of the Mid-Century Committee on Outcomes in Elementary Education* (Kearney 1953). There is an obvious similarity between this set of goals and other sets of goals cited above. Categories of goals developed in this study were: (1) communication, (2) aesthetic development, (3) quantitative understanding, (4) health and physical education, (5) mental hygiene, (6) social relations, (7) social studies, (8) values and ethics, and (9) science and the scientific method. Elementary school students completing a curriculum developed on the basis of these goals were thought to have been reasonably well prepared to go directly to work but also prepared to go on to high school.

A footnote to this recitation of numerous goal writing projects is one instigated by President Eisenhower. He selected the President's Commission on National Goals, consisting of two college presidents, three corporation presidents, an editor of a nationally known newspaper, an ambassador, a governor, a judge, a general, and a labor official. In 1960, the commission published *Goals for Americans*. Educators at the direction of this report found support for their own efforts to maintain the democratic process and the high ideals of the American way of life.

Goals for Today's Schools

Goals for schooling have constantly expanded until today public schools are said to be attempting to do all things for all people, and they may not be doing very many of them effectively enough. Thus far, however, little evidence exists that the American people, especially parents, want the schools to drop any of the broad goals that have emerged over the past three hundred years. In preparing for the monumental Study of Schooling, John Goodlad and his associates engaged in an analysis of school goals that had been published by state and local boards of education, various special commissions, and other groups. From approximately one hundred goals, twelve major ones emerged that appeared to contain the essence of the total list. Each was further defined by subgoals and a rationale statement (1979, pp. 44–52).

In brief, the Goodlad analysis yielded these major goals for schooling in the United States:

1. Mastery of basic skills or fundamental processes: In our technological civilization, an individual's ability to participate in the activities of society depends on mastery of these fundamental processes.
2. Career or vocational education: An individual's personal satisfaction in life will be significantly related to satisfaction with her or his job. Intelligent career decisions will require knowledge of personal aptitudes and interests in relation to career possibilities.
3. Intellectual development: As civilization has become more complex, people have had to rely more heavily on their rational abilities. Full intellectual development of each member of society is necessary.
4. Enculturation: Studies that illuminate our relationship with the past yield insights into our society and its values; further, these strengthen an individual's sense of belonging, identity, and direction for his or her own life.
5. Interpersonal relations: Schools should help every child understand, appreciate, and value persons belonging to social, cultural, and ethnic groups different from one's own and to increase affiliation and decrease alienation.
6. Autonomy: Unless schools produce self-directed citizens, they have failed both society and the individual. As society becomes more

complex, demands on individuals multiply. Schools should help prepare children for a world of rapid change by developing in them the capacity to assume responsibility for their own needs.

7. Citizenship: To counteract the present human ability to destroy humanity and the environment requires citizen involvement in the political and social life of this country. A democracy can only survive by the participation of its members.

8. Creativity and aesthetic perception: Abilities for creating new and meaningful things and appreciating the creations of other human beings is essential both for personal self-realization and for the benefit of society.

9. Self-concept: The self-concept of an individual serves as a reference point and feedback mechanism for personal goals and aspirations. Facilitating factors for a healthy self-concept can be provided in the school environment.

10. Emotional and physical well-being: Emotional stability and physical fitness are perceived as necessary conditions for attaining the other goals, but they are also worthy ends in themselves.

11. Moral and ethical character: Developing the judgment needed to evaluate events and phenomena as right or wrong and a commitment to truth, moral integrity, moral conduct, and a desire to strengthen the moral fabric of society are the values manifested by this goal.

12. Self-realization: Efforts to develop a better self contribute to the development of a better society.

These twelve goals that emerged from Goodlad's Study of Schooling broadly represent the external expectations for education. They generally state what school personnel are expected to attend to and what they might be held accountable for. The above list closely resembles goal statements for education issued by the various states, although states frequently categorize their goals in four major divisions: academic, vocational, social-civic, and personal.

The Accountability Influence. In adapting "accountability" models, many states have recommended a process in which a common set of statewide goals is to be translated locally into specific objectives. This is then followed by an assessment of student needs in relation to objectives. Local efforts are to be directed toward weaknesses, followed by local self-appraisal and feedback to state authorities. Critics warn that narrow interpretations of goals can become a process of reductionism that yields a limited and piecemeal type of curriculum. Such a curriculum ignores the holistic nature of teaching and learning, the need for orchestration of complex factors, and attention to local factors.

Searching for the Mission of the Schools. The development of goals for education and subsequent subgoals and objectives for schools is no easy task. Some school officials, curriculum directors, and teachers faced with this problem collect various statements of philosophy and goals from state departments of education and other schools, usually similar in size and socioeconomic settings. The disadvantages of adopting goals from elsewhere are that there is a tendency toward the average in qualitative statements of objectives as well as a waning of creativity, and a lack of matching with local conditions, all of which could cause the objectives and curriculum content not to fit a particular school district. Examining collections of goals and objectives from elsewhere does, however, provide a sense of the normative expectations held by other educators. Moreover it could serve to generate ideas.

In the interest of generating ideas, not only for goal statements but also for applications to teaching-learning situations and suggestions for evaluative measures, the Association for Supervision and Curriculum Development sponsored a study by the ASCD Committee on Research and Theory (1980). The committee collected lists of goal statements from such educational agencies as the Educational Testing Service, the North Dakota Study Group on Evaluation, Phi Delta Kappa, the National Assessment of Educational Progress, the Learning Research and Development Center, NIE Clearinghouse on Teacher Education, Research for Better Schools, and several state departments of education. A great deal of similarity was revealed among the different lists. Pennsylvania's list served as a primary basis for summarizing the entirety.

The mission of education in the public schools can be broadly defined by the goal statements distilled from many sources by ASCD or from the Study of Schooling, reviewed above, or from a combination of both. By their breadth of coverage and comprehensiveness, these goal statements can be said to express the schools' mission in terms of today's views. Historical goals, except for that of religion in the public schools, have been incorporated and enlarged, and more goals have been added with the passing of time.

GOAL STATEMENTS

The ten goals listed by the ASCD Committee on Research and Theory are reproduced below (1980, pp. 9–12). Each goal was analyzed by the committee in terms of its relationships to the other goals to determine whether its attainment was (1) a prerequisite to the attainment of the other goals, (2) an indicator that other goals had already been attained, (3) a facilitator to the attainment of other goals, or (4) an interference with the attainment of other goals.

Goal One: Basic Skills

Subgoals
1. Acquires information and meaning through observing, listening, and reading
2. Processes the acquired information and meaning through skills of reflective thinking
3. Shares information and expresses meaning through speaking, writing, and nonverbal means
4. Acquires information and meaning through the use of mathematical symbols
5. Manipulates symbols and uses mathematical reasoning
6. Shares information and expresses meaning through the use of mathematical symbols

Goal Two: Self-Conceptualization

Subgoals
1. Recognizes that self-concept is acquired in interaction with other people
2. Distinguishes between significant and nonsignificant others and their self-evaluations
3. Takes into account significant others and disregards nonsignificant others in the self-conceptualizing process
4. Distinguishes among many concepts of self in various roles or social situations
5. Assesses own functioning in each of several different situations
6. Perceives accurately, assesses validly, and responds appropriately to others' evaluations in the context of each specific role situation rather than to generalize to all situations

Goal Three: Understanding Others

Subgoals
1. Bases actions and decisions on the knowledge that individuals differ and are similar in many ways
2. Bases actions and decisions on the knowledge that values and behaviors are learned and differ from one social group to another
3. Bases actions and decisions on the understanding of lifestyles or behaviors within the context of the value system of the societies in which they were learned
4. Acts on the belief that each individual has value as a human being and should be respected as a worthwhile person in his or her own right
5. Bases actions and decisions on the understanding that as individuals move from one society to another, they can learn new lifestyles and can learn to behave appropriately in different societal contexts
6. Acts on the behalf that human behavior is influenced by many factors and is best understood in terms of the relevant personal context in which it occurred

7. Seeks interactions and feels comfortable with others who are different in race, religion, social level, or personal attributes as well as those who are similar in these characteristics
8. Withholds judgment of another's actions until after trying to understand the personal and social context of that action

Goal Four: Using Accumulated Knowledge to Interpret the World

Subgoals
1. Applies basic principles and concepts of the sciences, arts, and humanities to interpret personal experiences
2. Applies basic principles and concepts of the sciences, arts, and humanities to analyze and act upon public issues
3. Applies basic principles and concepts of the sciences, arts, and humanities to understand natural phenomena
4. Applies basic principles and concepts of the sciences, arts, and humanities to evaluate technological progress
5. Applies basic principles and concepts of the sciences, arts, and humanities to appreciate aesthetic events

Goal Five: Continuous Learning

Subgoals
1. Seeks and values learning experiences
2. Act as a self-reliant learner, capable of autonomous learning
3. Bases actions and decisions on the knowledge that it is necessary to continue to learn throughout life because of the inevitability of change

Goal Six: Mental and Physical Well-Being

Subgoals
1. Practices appropriate personal hygiene
2. Consumes a nutritionally balanced, wholesome diet
3. Exercises sufficiently to maintain personal health
4. Avoids, to the extent possible, consuming materials harmful to health, particularly addictive ones
5. Performs daily activities in a manner to prevent injury to self and others
6. Adapts to environmental constraints while seeking to change destructive elements in the environment
7. Maintains personal integration while functioning flexibly in varied situations
8. Behaves rationally based upon reasonable perceptions of self and society
9. Perceives self positively with a generally competent sense of well-being
10. Participates in satisfying leisure-time activities

Goal Seven: Participation in the Economic World of Production and Consumption

Subgoals
1. Bases decisions on an awareness and knowledge of career options
2. Interacts with others on the basis of an understanding and valuing of the characteristics and functions of different occupations
3. Selects and pursues career opportunities consonant with social and personal needs and capabilities
4. Makes informed consumer decisions based on appropriate knowledge of products, needs, and resources

Goal Eight: Responsible Societal Membership

Subgoals
1. Acts consonant with an understanding of the basic interdependence of the biological and physical resources of the environment
2. Acts consonant with an understanding of the interrelationships among complex organizations and agencies in modern society
3. Acts in accordance with a basic ethical framework incorporating those values contributing to group living, such as honesty, fairness, compassion, and integrity
4. Assumes responsibility for own acts
5. Works in groups to achieve mutual goals
6. Invokes law and authority to protect the rights of all persons
7. Exercises duties of citizenship, such as voting
8. Bases actions and decisions on a sense of political efficacy
9. Exercises the right of dissent in accordance with personal conscience and human justice
10. Assumes responsibility for dependent persons of all ages in a manner consistent with both their growth and development needs, and the needs of society

Goal Nine: Creativity

Subgoals
1. Generates a range of imaginative alternatives to stimuli
2. Entertains and values the imaginative alternatives of others

Goal Ten: Coping with Change

Subgoals
1. Works for goals on realistic personal performance standards
2. Decides when a risk is worth taking
3. Works now for goals to be realized in the future
4. Entertains new perceptions of the world
5. Tolerates ambiguity

6. Bases actions and decisions on an understanding that change is a natural process in society and one which increases exponentially
7. Bases actions on an understanding that coping with change is a continuous process throughout life
8. Acts with an appreciation that in a changing world, flexibility and adaptability are strengths rather than weaknesses
9. Selects viable alternatives for actions in changing circumstances

The goals seemed to fall into four clusters:

I.   Goal one, basic skills, is a prerequisite to attainment of all other goals but only when basic skills are defined as a broad set of functional skills, not narrow items of content or not just the three Rs.
II. Basic understanding of self, others, and the world as expressed in goals two, three, and four.
III. Day-to-day living skills, comprised by goals five, six, and seven.
IV. Quality of life, included in goals eight, nine, and ten.

Interrelationships. The ASCD Committee on Research and Theory concluded from its analysis that this set of goals is indeed integrated and reflective of the holistic nature of the individual. Figure 6 pictures the directionality of relationships and interdependence among the ten goals (1980, p. 14).

Conclusions drawn from the study of relationships include:

1. A complementary and interactive relationship does exist among the goals and subgoals.
2. The achievement of some goals is essential to or facilitates the attainment of other goals.
3. Time limitations may dictate the relative emphasis, or lack thereof, on one or more goals at a particular educational level and thereby restrict respective attainment.
4. Basic skills, as defined in goal one, are prerequisite to all other goals.
5. Removing any one goal affects the achievement of other goals.
6. Achieving any one goal does not interfere with the achievement of any other goal.
7. The goals concerned with understanding others, self, and the world facilitate the achievement of any other subsequent goals.
8. All of the goals are characteristic of humane people in a humane society (p. 15).

Again it is obvious from the ASCD survey that goal statements are guides for the direction and expenditure of effort and resources. They also

Figure 6. Diagram of Goal Relationships

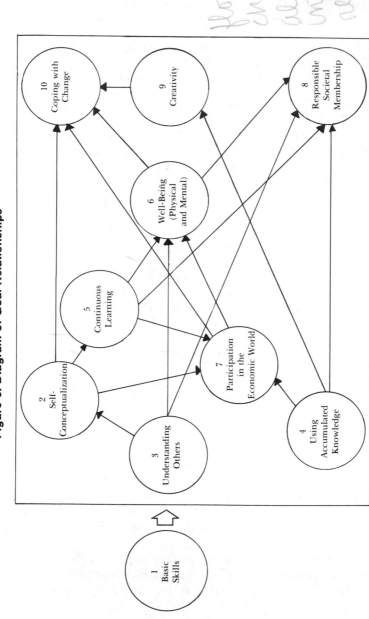

From ASCD Committee on Research and Theory, *Measuring and Attaining the Goals of Education* (Alexandria, Va.: Association for Supervision and Curriculum Development, 1980), p. 14. Reprinted with permission of the Association for Supervision and Curriculum Development. Copyright © 1980 by the Association for Supervision and Curriculum Development. All rights reserved.

represent the basic expectations people have for the educational institution. As such statements are drawn and redrawn, an element of correction is inserted either to meet current criticism or to respond to anticipated needs arising from changing social, political, or economic considerations.

THE SETTING FOR GOAL DEVELOPMENT

In order to assume the proper leadership role in establishing goals and objectives, curriculum developers should be very familiar with the local setting. Who are the people? What are their ethnic backgrounds, cultural mores, socioeconomic conditions, and political beliefs? It would be good to know the prevailing attitudes toward current social, political, and educational problems and issues, as well as the trends in the community, whether growing and progressive or deteriorating.

The morale of students and faculty and the climate in the school system should provide some clues about the problem of involving people in writing objectives and improving the curriculum. Knowing something about the faculty, staff, administration, and students and their receptivity to change or innovation is also important. Through knowing the interests, abilities, motivations, and specializations of the personnel, the curriculum developer should be able to estimate who can give appropriate assistance at critical points in the progress toward a developed curriculum.

Obviously she or he should know the curriculum development process from beginning to end and must have already decided whether to begin with a philosophy and goals or a needs assessment. An extended analysis of the philosophy and goals of education as held by the faculty, the administration, and the community could lead to inferences of needs. Some needs of youth, however, might be left out unless there is a thorough understanding of Dewey's "surrounding conditions." The students of one community may need a different set of goal priorities than another, while both communities subscribe to American ideals. Curriculum developers in Ketchikan, Alaska, Mason, Michigan, and New York City will arrive at different translations of these broad goals into classroom objectives.

Knowledge of group processes and the ability to work harmoniously with people and to initiate and direct committee action are important. Much curriculum development work is done in committees, and it is useful indeed to be able to facilitate group work as well as intergroup work. It may also be necessary to generate enthusiasm and find ways to sustain it in committee members because curriculum work can be tedious. Knowing the resources available for meeting objectives and having the ability to locate, evaluate, select, and organize learning materials are of great value; these should be shared so the process of constant renewal will be built in.

Professional sharing becomes a part of ongoing in-service education. The curriculum developer should have or develop the ability to state clearly and explain succinctly both system goals and concomitant objectives. This skill should also be passed on because every teacher needs it. All personnel should be educated to appreciate the power of purpose.

DECISIONS IN GOAL DEVELOPMENT

The educational goals of a school district, university, or other unit should be broad, comprehensive, and balanced in terms of the local interests and needs. Establishing processes for constructing the broad goals or a mission statement is the responsibility of the top management or leadership persons, such as the superintendent and board of a school district. The general goals should lead to meaningful specific objectives, developed by principals, teachers, and coordinators at the building and classroom levels. These should then lead to plans that translate into instruction.

Too often school districts have issued either vague goals for education that are meaningless in terms of guiding instruction, or else they have produced volumes of mechanistic objectives that fail to provide opportunities for teachers to stimulate growth in students' abilities to generalize, create, and explore solutions to new problems.

The history of specific and behavioral objectives goes back at least seven decades. In 1922, Edward Thorndike listed three thousand objectives for arithmetic. Franklin Bobbitt (1924) wrote specific objectives for numerous subject fields based on an analysis of the "actual activities of mankind." Bobbitt viewed this approach as necessary for controlling the curriculum, although later writers criticized it as an example of reductionism with constricting effects on instruction. Bobbitt did, however, design and execute a comprehensive plan for curriculum development.

Bobbitt and 1,500 graduate students from his classes spent twelve years observing and cataloging a broad range of human activities. Thousands of items were classified and consolidated, resulting in the following classifications of objectives: (1) language and communication, (2) health, (3) citizenship, (4) social behavior, (5) mental hygiene, (6) leisure time activities, (7) religion, (8) homemaking and parenting, (9) avocational, and (10) one's occupation or profession. The curriculum to be developed consisted of literature and reading, social studies, natural sciences, mathematics, physical education and health, practical arts for men and for women, art, speech and composition, modern languages, and Latin.

W.W. Charters, whose 1923 work was an inspiration to Bobbitt, had proposed that the curriculum should be constructed from specific competencies or, "ideals" as he called them based on job analysis. Charters viewed activity analysis as an extension of job analysis, which could be accomplished by introspection, interviewing, working on the job, and questionnaires. In job analysis, every movement can be isolated for study; sequences can be identified to evaluate the order of actions; and faulty movements or useless movements can be examined and eliminated.

This approach to instruction for acquiring specific competencies has been widely adapted in technical education. For example, the skills needed by a machine operator can be studied and described so an unskilled person can learn them. The first step is to observe the operator in action. Every movement is noted and listed; then pictures are taken for further study.

The next step in the process is to interview the operator. Certain movements can be explained, and reasons can be given for patterns of movements. Operators may describe a "feel" they have for a machine. For example, a feeling tells the operator the machine is running well, smoothly, and at the right speed. A skilled, experienced, and sensitive operator can often detect an impending malfunction before it happens and thus prevent a costly shutdown. This kind of information does not show up on a film unless a specific attempt is made by the filmmaker to do so.

Another step is to consult a known expert in the field, one who knows the machine and what it can do. This person is asked to review the actions or movements collected by the observers and to analyze them. Next, the pictures are analyzed, and the expert assists in completing the catalogue of movements and machine processes. Then the expert puts them in order. Sequences are very important; only when mastered can one be said to be skilled. When all the necessary skills have been learned, the job has been learned.

In recent years, Charters' task analysis system, which seemed to work well for technical instruction in vocational education, has been adapted to "back to basics" techniques, instructional management designs, criterion-referenced testing, and other programs for specifying performance standards for teachers and students.

John Goodlad (1979), in reflecting on these historical examples of narrowing influences on the curriculum, finds a parallel between them and the current mandates legislated by a number of states for minimum competency testing. He emphasizes that the more specific objectives should be developed within the school system, school buildings, and classrooms where they are to be used; they should not be imposed from outside because the responsibility of the state is to offer guidance in setting broad goals for education. Ralph Tyler, who has been influential in stressing the place of goals and objectives in curriculum and instruction, said, "Other things being equal, more general objectives are desirable rather than less general objectives. However, to identify appropriate learning experiences, it is helpful to differentiate rather clearly types of behavior which are quite different in their characteristics" (1950, p. 57).

Broad and Narrow Curriculum Decisions

Developing goals and objectives for curriculum and instruction is not an either-or matter of broad or narrow scope. Both are needed but at different levels of curriculum planning and implementation. In the broad general phases of curriculum development, goals and other decisions are formulated systemwide and at a high level. It is at this level that ideas are identified that are potentially powerful for determining action and distributing funds. Narrower, more concise phases, delineate specific curricula with specific objectives for separate programs, schools, classrooms, individuals, or small groups of students. This specificity, however, fits the larger goals.

Figure 7 illustrates applying the principles of generality and specificity to several functions of curriculum development. The implicit relationships to the process of setting goals and objectives are shown as well. Fenwick English and Betty Steffy (1982) have designated the broad general decisions about curriculum development "strategic" decisions, and the specific and narrower ones "tactic" decisions.

While precise predefinition can be too arbitary and restrictive, different behaviors are still to be expected in different subject areas and situations. Tyler identified these categories for attention in the preparation of objectives for curriculum and instruction: the development of work habits and study skills; effective ways of thinking; social attitudes, interests, appreciations, and sensitivities; the maintenance of physical health; and the development of a philosophy of life (1950, p. 58).

In 1981, Tyler suggested using four safeguards either for writing more specific objectives or as screens against which to test objectives. The first is the educational philosophy of the school district and of the school itself, whether secondary or elementary. The philosophy and goals or mission statement serve to include or exclude certain learning experiences. Next is a consideration of the learner, his or her ability, capacity, interests, and achievements to date. Fortunately, most schools have records on these points but the judgment of experienced teachers is also valuable.

Community mores—what is acceptable or expected in terms of objectives and student behavior—is the third criterion to be considered by writers of objectives. The cultural level of the community, the social and political attitudes and opinions of the citizens are additional variables within this criterion. Some objectives and some learning experiences are not acceptable in communities that are either conservative or liberal. At these points, Tyler writes, curriculum developers must use their good judgment. His fourth safeguard in the construction of specific objectives involves a relatively long period of time. As experience and information accumulate, these will highlight the problems created by the objectives already in use. Refining goal statements is likely to be a continuing process, and revision

Figure 7. Curriculum Development Continuum from General to Specific

	Strategy	Tactic
Scope	Systemwide, all levels	Program, school, or classroom specific
Specificity	Low level of detail	Higher level of detail
Delineation of Instruction Methods	Broad or nonexistent	Embedded and more specific, closer to the classroom
Organization, Location of Decision	Highest levels of management/policy	Much lower level, building, classroom
Risk Involved	High risk, more uncertainty	Lower risk, much less uncertainty
Assessment	Broadly indicated as a requirement upon which to make decisions and reexamine policy	Specifically delineated by objective, type, expected standards of achievement for groups of students
Consideration of Alternatives	Broad, conceptual	Narrow, operational

From Fenwick W. English and Betty E. Steffy, "Curriculum as a Strategic Management Tool," *Educational Leadership* 39 (January 1982): 278. Reprinted with permission of the Association for Supervision and Curriculum Development, Fenwick W. English, and Betty E. Steffy.

procedures should be built into the development process. Committees of varied composition should periodically evaluate the objectives in a given area by gathering all the accumulating data available and asking, "Is this what we should be doing?" Writing objectives include these processes: drafting, defining, selecting, refining, and editing. A single draft will probably never be adequate.

LEVELS OF GOALS AND OBJECTIVES

Making decisions about goals and objectives is the most important step of curriculum development because all subsequent steps are designed to generate ways of meeting these goals and objectives. It is necessary to recognize that goals and objectives must be focused toward different levels of operation. Is the statement to be addressed to the school system at large, the program or academic discipline, or a particular course at the high school, or are these to be objectives for a specific unit of instruction? All of these levels represent planning goals. At the classroom or lesson plan level, the teacher is interested in performance, and the objectives would be measurable in some specific ways. Figure 8 presents an example of objective ordering for a science curriculum prepared by the Northwest Regional Educational Laboratory of Portland, Oregon. It illustrates levels of objectives from general to specific.

When writing objectives for different grade levels, curriculum experts usually refer to some outside criterion against which to compare their work such as a well recognized publication on growth and development. An example of this process is shown in Figure 9, taken with permission from a publication of the School District of University City, Missouri. The objectives in this model are tested against stages of growth described by Jean Piaget (1955). The stages are sensory motor, ages zero to two years; preoperational thought, ages two to four years; intuitive thought, five to seven years; concrete operations, seven to eleven years; and formal logic, ages eleven to fifteen. Examples of objectives in several subject areas are shown for grades two, five, and eight tested against three Piagetian stages: intuitive thought, concrete operations, and formal logic.

Arrival at the point of distributing sets of grade level objectives, such as the example in Figure 9 comes after months, even years, of collaborative effort on the part of a large number of persons within a school district.

WORK PLANS AND TASKS

Depending upon how seriously deficient or outdated the curriculum currently is, developing goals and objectives based on trends, redefined assumptions, findings from research, experimental programs, and new

Figure 8.   Types of Goals and Objectives for Student Learning

System Goal	The student knows and is able to apply basic scientific and technological processes.	
Program Goal	The student is able to use the conventional language, instruments, and operations of science.	*Planning*
Course Goal	The student is able to classify organisms according to their conventional taxonomic categories.	
Instructional Goal	The student is able to classify correctly as needleleaf the cuttings of hemlocks, pines, spruces, firs, larches, cypresses, redwoods, and cedars.	
Behavioral Objective	Given cuttings of ten trees, several of which are needleleaf, the student is able to identify correctly which are needleleaf.	*Measurement*
Performance Objective	Given cuttings of ten trees, seven of which are needleleaf, the student is able to identify correctly at least six of the seven as belonging to the needleleaf class.	

developments could require up to three years before the introduction of a comprehensive renewal program. Plans would begin with a rigorous, objective evaluation of the current curriculum and probably a needs assessment (see Chapter Six). A representative committee, drawn from the professional staff of all grade levels, established to assist the curriculum leader in initiating the studies, should provide various kinds of help, involve people inside and outside the system, collect available materials, data, and information, and then monitor the progress. Time is needed for this kind of work.

Figure 9. Curriculum Expectations and Piaget's Stages of Growth

GRADE 2
Curriculum Expectations

COGNITIVE DEVELOPMENTAL PHASE	Reading	Language Arts	Mathematics	Social Studies	Health Education
INTUITIVE THOUGHT (5-7 years) 1. Development of concept of numbers 2. Preoccupation with parts rather than whole 3. Beginning to see relationships 4. Difficulty in maintaining more than one idea	1. Should be able to demonstrate the ability to use word recognition techniques 2. Should be able to demonstrate the ability to perceive relationships 3. Should be able to demonstrate a knowledge of word meaning 4. Should be able to demonstrate the ability to convey meaning in oral reading 5. Should be able to demonstrate	1. Should be able to make up stories 2. Should be able to describe factual events and experiences 3. Should be able to explain how to do and make things 4. Should be able to use capital letters for initials, abbreviations, holidays 5. Should be able to use correct spelling 6. Should be able to build sentences with an	1. Should be able to read and write standard numerals 2. Should be able to use symbols to compare numbers 3. Given five numerals should be able to arrange them in sequence from smallest to largest 4. Should be able to solve word problems including addition and subtraction 5. Should recognize multiplication concepts	1. Should be able to draw simple maps of the classroom and other parts of the school 2. Should be able to locate community facilities on a map of University City 3. Should be able to describe ways in which members of the community choose their leaders 4. Should be able to talk to leaders of ethnic groups represented in the community	1. Should be able to use non-scientific terminology in naming the parts of the eye and its function 2. Should be able to distinguish between noise and music 3. Should be able to use an ear model to show the parts of an ear 4. Should be able to discuss how ear infections can damage the ear 5. Should be able to name the

comprehensive skills necessary for success in reading

6. Should be able to demonstrate study skills necessary for academic success
7. Should be able to use reading to assist in personal development

awareness of the subject and predicate

7. Should begin to use cursive handwriting
8. Should begin to develop individual writing styles and expanding vocabulary

6. Should be able to multiply two factors whose product is less than twenty
7. Should be able to read, interpret and construct simple picture graphs
8. Should be able to draw and label circles, rectangles, squares and triangles
9. Should be able to read a scale and a thermometer

and the classroom about their careers

5. Should be able to participate with teachers in changing classroom procedures in a democratic manner
6. Should be able to distinguish fact from opinion
7. Should be able to distinguish between types of jobs

parts of the eye that can be seen

6. Should be able to develop an appreciation of the sense of vision through being blindfolded

Figure 9, continued

C u r r i c u l u m E x p e c t a t i o n s

COGNITIVE DEVELOPMENTAL PHASE	Reading	Language Arts	Mathematics	Social Studies	Health Education
CONCRETE OPERATIONS (7-11 years) 1. First level of logical thinking 2. Has the power of reversibility; that is, can relate back to the original idea 3. Assimilative and accommodative processes interact 4. Moves from inductive to deductive reasoning	1. Should be able to use word recognition techniques by recognizing the accents in a word 2. Should be able to increase the number of sight words committed to memory 3. Should be able to demonstrate the ability to perceive relationships by identifying the setting of a story as well as recognizing changes in mood	1. Should be able to use noun phrases and verb phrases 2. Should be able to use transitive and intransitive verbs 3. Should be able to use a dictionary for pronunciation purposes 4. Should be able to use adverbs and prepositional phrases 5. Should be able to take notes from an encyclopedia article 6. Should be able to write stories with dialogue	1. Should be able to use symbols to compare whole numbers 2. Should be able to read and write decimals to tenths and hundredths 3. Should be able to write multiples of tenths in fractions and decimals 4. Should be able to apply the laws of divisibility 5. Should be able to subtract numerals up to eight digits 6. Should be able	1. Should be able to describe the motives that drove people to explore the new world 2. Should be able to describe grievances that early colonists had against England 3. Should be able to analyze the effect of slavery on slaves and American society 4. Should be able to describe the role of blacks in developing the nation after the Civil War and name	1. Should be able to name the kinds of foods where germs grow most rapidly 2. Should be able to define digestion 3. Should be able to list the changes in living patterns that would protect the environment 4. Should be able to list several health agencies and organizations and services provided 5. Should be able to describe the need for and work

or time within a story

4. Should be able to demonstrate comprehension skills necessary for success in reading by reading with expression and recognizing the humor of exaggeration and puns

7. Should be able to write scripts for plays
8. Should be able to listen to and write poems
9. Should be able to write articles for a class magazine or newspaper
10. Should be able to expand the use of the library

to establish differences by rounding to nearest 1,000 or 10,000
7. Should be able to multiply factors up to four digits
8. Should be able to find average of a set of numbers

important black leaders
5. Should be able to evaluate the importance of religious freedom in the settling of America
6. Should be able to identify current national problems and propose some solutions
7. Should be able to state ways in which the democratic form of government allows for peaceful resolution

of law and law enforcement officers
6. Should be able to select acceptable ways of expressing emotions
7. Should be able to demonstrate knowledge of traditional and current trends in roles of family members

Figure 9, continued

Curriculum Expectations

COGNITIVE DEVELOPMENTAL PHASE	Reading	Language Arts	Mathematics	Social Studies	Health Education
FORMAL OPERATIONS (11-15 years)	1. Should be able to identify and interpret labels and symbols	1. Should be able to comprehend printed material needed to succeed in his or her educational, vocational, and social interests	1. Should be able to develop an understanding of and proficiency with operations on subsets of rational numbers	1. Should be able to recognize the political, social, and economic ways that can take different forms in various cultures	1. Should be able to match diseases and infectious agents when given lists of each
1. Engages in individualized thinking	2. Should be able to interpret labels and selection for specific purposes	2. Should be able to respond to literature in subjective, analytical, and evaluative ways	2. Should be able to extend the development of concepts of space and subsets of space	2. Should be able to investigate basic beliefs of religious and moral philosophies and their impact on cultures	2. Should be able to list factors contributing to cancer, heart disease, emphysema, arthritis, and other chronic diseases
2. Able to do hypothetical thinking	3. Should be able to provide proper responses to commonly used signs	3. Should be able to interpret literature in the humanities as a reflection of life, values, and ideas of this and other cultures	3. Should be able to extend the development of understandings and techniques of equations and inequalities	3. Should be able to examine art forms and how they reflect the attitudes and thoughts of people	3. Should be able to identify cells and observe shapes of different ones in plants and animals
3. Able to manipulate various ideas and social practices simultaneously	4. Should be able to use reference materials and sources to obtain information	4. Should be able to use language effec-	4. Should be able to extend the	4. Should be able to discover the origins of law in societies and the impact of legal systems on the society	4. Should be able to describe metabolic dis-
4. Confirms established social values and adheres to self-chosen ethical principles	5. Should be able to recognize the main idea				

orders related
to food habits

6. Should be able
to know the
purpose of
the writer
7. Should be able
to complete
forms correctly.

8. Should be able
to interpret
business corre-
spondence and
contracts

tively in inter-
action with others
5. Should be able to
recognize that ideas
are expressed in
many ways
6. Should be able to
write honestly,
creatively, and
clearly
7. Should be able to
adapt speech and
writing to different
purposes and audi-
ences as well as
communication forms

development of
precise termi-
nology and
symbolism of
mathematics
5. Should be able
to develop
abilities and
reasonings in
mathematical
situations
6. Should be able
to develop an
understanding
of structural
properties in
number systems

5. Should be able to
identify the basic
patterns of human
development
6. Should be able to
generalize about the
development, expan-
sion and/or decline
of selected cultures
7. Should be able to
develop a healthy
skepticism that will
avoid the propagan-
dist and simplistic
view of historical
events and personal-
ities

From *K-12 Guidance Model*. School District of University City, Missouri, 1981, pp. 6, 9, 19.

Here are some general ideas based on experience that are useful in planning new or renewed objectives for curriculum and instruction:

1. Involving the people who will be concerned with the curriculum and decision making is universally prescribed by educators.
2. There must be paid or released time for teachers and others involved in the work. This may be a negotiable item, but the days when teachers as volunteers remained after school or returned to the school on weekends or during summers are now only memories in most school districts.
3. There must be adequate funds for the project.
4. Several professional days should be scheduled throughout the school year for communication with the faculty. These are opportunities to identify and discuss problems as they arise, examine solutions, and share ideas. This exchange also provides reinforcement; the teacher-to-teacher discussions have been found to be important in developing objectives and following through in instruction.
5. Tryouts of ideas, materials, and teaching strategies provide opportunities to eliminate problems before the objectives are introduced throughout the system.

The leader may find a timeline useful in planning. With one, it is possible to see at a glance how long the plan will take; how much progress has been made and the discrepancy, if any, between the rate of progress and the target date for completion. Teachers find such a visualized plan less threatening than one which states that a new plan must be operational at once. It is assumed that the general goals have been established prior to use of the following plan or its adaptations.

Phase I
Fall Spring Summer

Phase I

Fall: Discussing curriculum inadequacies
                 Discussing procedures
                 Assigning committees
                 Preparing list of tasks ahead

Spring: Launching needs assessment study
                 Searching the literature
                 Discussing new curriculum materials, ideas, research, trends, and so on
                 Discussing the possibilities of adopting and adapting objectives or developing original ones

Summer: Drafting instructional objectives
Gathering materials for content
Preparing the first units for tryouts

Phase II
Fall Spring Summer

Phase II

Fall: Beginning orientation of total faculty
Beginning public meetings
Trying out the first units and evaluating the experience
Reworking the units as needed on the basis of evaluations
Continuing public meetings

Spring: Preparing for writing in the summer workshop
Gathering materials
Training additional writers
Preparing evaluative instruments
Continuing faculty and public communication

Summer: Completing the writing of the curriculum and the evaluative instruments
Continuing orientation of entire faculty and staff

Phase III
Fall Spring Summer

Phase III

Fall: Reporting to the board of education
Initiating tryouts systemwide
Continuing faculty and staff meetings on professional days
Keeping public informed
Monitoring progress and problems and preparing lists of jobs and assignments

Spring: Continuing evaluations of objectives for learning effectiveness, the content, the validity of measuring instruments, teaching strategies
Checking faculty and public opinion
Preparing the agenda for the third summer workshop

Summer: The quality of the objectives is dependent on evaluations. Revisions could be indicated in any or all of the following: the statements of objectives, learning experiences, teaching strategies, tests and evaluation instruments.

               Continuing attention should be given to public information.

SUMMARY

The task for the local schools is to set goals according to needs, keeping in mind the mission of the schools but tailoring goals to local conditions. The needs of people, of society, and of education are constantly changing. Attention to trends and forecasts, as discussed in Chapter Ten, is essential in order to make wise choices among alternative futures.

The educational goals in a given community should justify learning objectives at many levels (district, building, classroom, individual) that will bring into being the broader goals. The learning objectives in turn should justify specific teaching-learning events that will bring about the learning objectives. Evaluation processes should tell to what extent goals and objectives have been reached and provide feedback for further curriculum development and instructional improvement. Evaluation, however, should not be merely yes or no responses to questions of reaching or not reaching targets. Evaluation should go beyond, look into cause and effect relationships, side effects, the quality as well as quantity of attainment, and inspire insights into needed improvements. Curriculum evaluation is discussed in Chapter Nine, and we discuss measuring goal attainment according to the ASCD categories shown above. It remains for the professional educators in the field to orchestrate and integrate the many dimensions of learning into a holistic design for curriculum and instruction that is not only well planned but well implemented.

REFERENCES

ASCD Committee on Research and Theory. *Measuring and Attaining the Goals of Education.* Alexandria, Va.: Association for Supervision and Curriculum Development, 1980.

Bobbitt, Franklin. *How to Make a Curriculum.* Boston: Houghton Mifflin, 1924.

Charters, W.W. *Curriculum Construction.* New York: Macmillan Co., 1923.

Commission on the Reorganization of Secondary Education. *Cardinal Principles of Education.* Bulletin No. 35. Washington, D.C.: U.S. Government Printing Office, 1918.

Cubberley, Ellwood P. *Public Education in the United States.* Boston: Houghton Mifflin, 1919.

Dewey, John. *Experience and Education.* New York: Collier, 1938.

English, Fenwick W., and Steffy, Betty E. "Curriculum as a Strategic Management Tool." *Education Leadership* 39 (January 1982): 276-78.

Goodlad, John I. *What Schools Are For.* Bloomington, Ind.: Phi Delta Kappa Educational Foundation, 1979.

Kandel, I. L. *A History of Secondary Education.* Boston: Houghton Mifflin, 1930.

Kearney, Nolan C. *Elementary School Objectives.* New York: Russell Sage Foundation, 1953.

Mulhern, James. *A History of Education.* New York: Ronald Press, 1946.

National Association of Secondary School Principals. *The Imperative Needs of Youth.* NASSP Bulletin 31 (March 1947): 2, 7-144.

Piaget, Jean. *The Language and Thought of the Child.* New York: Meridian Books, 1955.

The President's Commission on National Goals. *Goals for Americans.* New York: Spectrum Press, 1960.

School District of University City. "Curriculum Expectations and Piaget's Stages of Growth." From *K-12 Guidance Model.* University City, Mo.: The District, 1981.

Thorndike, Edward L. *Psychology of Arithmetic.* New York: Macmillan Co., 1922.

Tyler, Ralph W. "Specific Approaches to Curriculum Development." In *Curriculum and Instruction,* edited by Henry O. Giroux, Anthony N. Penna, and William F. Pinar, pp. 17-30. Berkeley: McCutchan, 1981.

Tyler, Ralph W. *Basic Principles of Curriculum and Instruction.* Chicago: University of Chicago Press, 1950.

ADDITIONAL READINGS

Bloom, Benjamin S., et al. *Taxonomy of Educational Objectives, Handbook I: Cognitive Domain.* New York: David McKay, 1956.

Brandt, Ronald S., and Tyler, Ralph W. "Goals and Objectives." In *Fundamental Curriculum Decisions,* pp. 40-52. Yearbook of the Association for Supervision and Curriculum Development. Alexandria, Va.: ASCD, 1983.

Goodlad, John I. *A Place Called School.* New York: McGraw-Hill, 1983.

Gow, Doris T., and Casey, Tommye W. "Selecting Learning Activities." In *Fundamental Curriculum Decisions,* pp. 112-25. Yearbook of the Association for Supervision and Curriculum Development. Alexandria, Va.: ASCD, 1983.

Harrow, Anita J. *A Taxonomy of the Psychomotor Domain.* New York: David McKay, 1972.

Instructional Objectives Exchange. Box 24095-M. Los Angeles, California 90024-0095. Measurable Objectives Collections in the Basic Skills.

Krathwohl, David R.; Bloom, Benjamin S.; and Masia, Bertram B. *Taxonomy of Educational Objectives, Handbook II: Affective Domain.* New York: David McKay, 1956.

Mager, Robert F. *Preparing Instructional Objectives.* Palo Alto, Calif. Fearon, 1962.

McGreal, Thomas L. "Helping Teachers Set Goals." *Educational Leadership* 37 (February 1980): 414-19.

6

Assessing the Needs

Need is a fundamental consideration in curriculum planning. It is also a fairly recent consideration in the curriculum-planning process, particularly in the case of the self-perceived needs of those most directly affected by curriculum and instruction. Studies of psychological needs as sources of drive or motivation have provided the theoretical background for certain aspects of classroom life, but educational needs have historically been prescribed by our elders.

Need, in relation to curriculum and instruction, is defined as the difference between actuality and the envisioned ideal circumstances; a difference between the real and the ideal in condition, quality, or attitude. When a need is not being met, something desirable is missing; there are conditions requiring change, supply, or relief. Both educational needs and psychological needs affect the processes of curriculum development and implementation.

Needs assessments are procedures, both structured and informal, for identifying gaps between the here-and-now situation and the desired goals. Needs assessments seek to locate the places where something is wanting. Depending on the purpose, needs assessments may either precede or follow the determination of goals. Needs are also useful to know when revising, modifying, and expanding the curriculum.

The mission of the school—its philosophy and intent in broad terms—is usually the umbrella under which the curriculum development process takes place. Goals that are more specific but still expressed in general terms may be set forth by the board and superintendent after they have input from their constituents, as described in Chapter Four. The needs assessment would follow; from it would stem the objectives, written in clear and direct language, and then the learning activities. Evaluation would enter the

173

cycle, and there would be a constant recycling of all components over time. (Chaper Nine discusses the many aspects of curriculum evaluation.)

The needs assessment would precede either the mission statement or the general goals or both when there is a desire to start anew, to take a fresh look at the educational enterprise, or to begin approaching curriculum development and instructional processes more systematically. We will give an example of this later in the chapter.

Assessment of needs may deal with gaps between current and desired resources, processes, and/or results. In its deepest sense, however, a needs assessment is concerned with discrepancies between current outcomes and desired outcomes. The needs of society are generally reflected in educational needs assessments as responses to problems of education or emerging problems that anticipate the future.

Assessing psychological needs requires insight and knowledge about human emotions, growth, and development. Although necessarily concerned with the outcomes of a plan and with the processes to be used, curriculum improvement also depends on the driving forces—the needs— that determine whether a student's attention and effort are fully engaged. Curriculum development has all too frequently been concerned with educational needs as identified by "experts," who have not given sufficient attention to the students' psychological needs as motivational factors.

THE HISTORY OF NEED

The history of need in the educational literature has taken many turns. Early in American schooling, the needs of youth were defined as they appeared to adults. The adults then became preoccupied with how to get children and youths to sense these needs and adopt the goals set for them by the adults. During the progressive education era of the 1920s and later, described in Chapter One, there was an overemphasis on students' "felt needs," which were not always the best way to guide students who lacked mature judgment. Attention then moved to the identification of the needs of youth by distinguished professional associations.

In 1944, the Educational Policies Commission published the "Imperative Needs of Youth" in its statement on *Education for All American Youth*. In 1947, the National Association of Secondary School Principals reissued an almost identical list under the same title. The ten imperative needs were said to be: to develop salable skills; to maintain good health and physical fitness; to understand the rights and duties of citizens; to know how to purchase and use goods and services intelligently; to understand the significance of the family; to understand the influence of science on human life; to have an appreciation of literature, art, music, and nature; to be able to use leisure time well and to budget it wisely; to develop respect for others; and to grow in the ability to think rationally. As noted in Chapter Five, these needs became the basis for various sets of goal statements for schools.

During that period in educational history, need psychology attracted considerable attention. Taking off from Sigmund Freud's recognition of the importance of subconscious motivation, psychologist after psychologist developed lists of basic needs or drives. In drawing upon psychological principles for applications to curriculum, William Featherstone (1950) advocated a total social and material environment for schooling that "gives rise to such feeling states or affects as self-confidence, belongingness, optimism, interest, peace of mind, freedom of spirit, and a belief that one has or is acquiring reasonably adequate resources with which to meet unforeseen occasions" (p. 77). Abraham Maslow (1954), Daniel Prescott (1938), and Robert Havighurst (1953) identified numerous motivational factors that impel students in certain directions and repel them from others; success or failure, love or hate.

Later, Erik Erikson (1963) elaborated further on the positives and negatives that influence motivation and bear on psychological need. The developmental stages that he described follow.

Basic trust versus basic mistrust (infancy): The child's earliest environment should establish a sense of trust in oneself and one's environment. Mistrust arises from unpleasant physical or psychological experiences.

Autonomy versus shame and doubt (early childhood): While the child is being encouraged to be independent, the environment must protect against meaningless discouraging experiences.

Intiative versus guilt (play age): This period of vigorous learning helps the child experience her limitations, exercise will and determination without too great a sense of guilt, and develop conscience.

Industry versus inferiority (primary school age): This should be a period of steady and calm growth if the previous stages have been well worked through. Erikson warns that a chief danger of this phase could be development of feelings of inferiority and inadequacy.

Identity versus confusion (adolescence): Physiological changes make adolescence a period of storm and stress for young people as they try to work out their roles in society. This is a time when wise counseling from adults or trustworthy peers is valuable.

Intimacy versus isolation (young adulthood): Once the sense of identity is achieved, individuals can develop a sense of intimacy with their peers; otherwise they will shy away from interpersonal relations.

Generativity versus stagnation (adulthood): Erikson saw this concept as something that includes but goes beyond productivity and creativity. It refers to the responsibility for guiding the next generation. If not achieved, it can lead to stagnation and personal impoverishment.

Ego integrity versus despair (senescence): Senior citizens, looking back on their lives, should be able to feel that they have run the course well and have adapted to the successes and disappointments that came along. Without this integrity of the ego, the golden years would be spent in despair.

Each stage has implications for those who plan curriculum and instruction. If these are as important as psychologists have told us, they are indeed basic needs that the schools cannot ignore.

Despite the emphasis on psychological need during the forties and fifties, at least two of the more outstanding writers in curriculum development gave only brief attention to psychological needs; they seemed to emphasize educational need as the chief concern of curriculum developers. Ralph Tyler's *Basic Principles of Curriculum and Instruction* (1950) appeared to underestimate psychological needs. Although Tyler was cognizant of the latter and referred to two types of need, he gave psychological need no more than a nod of recognition:

It is well to keep . . . two meanings of the term "needs" distinct so that they will not be confused in our discussion. The first use of the term represents a gap between some conception of a desirable norm, that is, some standard of philosophic value and the actual status. Need in this sense is the gap between what is and what should be. The other use of the term by some psychologists represents tensions in the organism which must be brought into equilibrium for a normal healthy condition of the organism to be maintained (pp. 7-8).

The reference to tensions in the organism is not developed in succeeding pages of his text, and Tyler's discussion centers around establishing a curriculum in terms of educational needs. Consequently, the type of curriculum ordinarily developed from his rationale is compartmentalized into subject fields, and coverage of content and skills is uppermost. Recognizing the personal needs of students is left to the ingenuity of those teachers perceptive enough to recognize individual problems.

Even as distinguished an authority on curriculum development as Hilda Taba seemed to take the view that psychological needs are adequately dealt with in the various subjects of the curriculum and that social and educational needs should move to the forefront in curriculum planning. She said (1962, p. 287), "It is clear, for example, that needs representing psychological requirements are less focal to the curriculum of the public school than are the needs representing social demands and the requirements of educational objectives."

For years, interpretations of Tyler and Taba have led to the very type of either-or thinking that Taba deplores at the outset of her volume on curriculum development. Those who produce curriculum materials have continued to emphasize the "needs" of the various subjects in the curriculum and the needs of society—the need to reach grade equivalents in the basic skills of reading and mathematics; society's needs incorporated into social studies; and, in recent times, science's needs in order to meet international challenges.

Taba recognized the difficulty of adding the complex dimension of psychological needs to curriculum development. She resolved the problem in essence, by assigning this dimension elsewhere:

Many psychological needs lie outside the power of educational approach either within or outside the school. Yet, these psychological needs must be understood and taken into account in curriculum building because they are a part of the constellation of conditions under which learning takes place. While schools may not be in a position to eliminate deep-seated psychological insecurities, curricula must be adjusted to the demands of security needs, and schools need to provide learning conditions which at least do not create additional insecurities. In this sense, then, all needs are of concern to the educator, but only some of these can be provided for explicitly through the curriculum. Others may be of greater concern to the psychologist and the mental hygienist (p. 287).

Admittedly, curriculum developers face an awesome task in meeting the challenge of universal education. They bear the burden of determining essential educational needs, subject-centered, and societal needs, without opening the Pandora's box of existential, psychological, ethical, and other inner needs. Nevertheless, such needs are important considerations.

During and after World War II, needs assessments became an interest of the armed services. Delphi techniques, consisting of rounds of questionnaires, conferences, or interviews with a narrowing focus on matters meriting prior attention, were utilized to gather the opinions of experts for the purpose of estimating probable effects of enemy action and possible defense measures. Subsequently the Delphi and similar techniques have been applied to technological forecasting for purposes of predicting trends.

Needs assessments came into their full glory in educational matters, however, during and since the accountability movement of the late sixties and the seventies. Requests for grants by the federal government clearly required needs assessments and subsequent needs data prior to approval for funding. State after state began to mandate needs assessments as a part of the effort to raise standardized achievement scores through required minimum competency testing. Kits, models, sample surveys, and planning handbooks proliferated. The best of these are now recorded in ERIC and may be retrieved on request by using the descriptors and code numbers listed in ERIC's catalogues, *Resources in Education*. The accumulated literature on needs assessments is an invaluable resource for curriculum directors.

TYPES OF NEEDS ASSESSMENTS

Roger Kaufman (1977) has defined six different types of needs assessments and suggested some possible applications of each:

Alpha. This type of needs assessment is primarily concerned with policy formulation, and the types that follow primarily focus on policy execution. Alpha is the most basic and fundamental of the six proposed needs-assessment modes. It is the most direct route to identifying and achieving deep change. An example would be a needs assessment undertaken by a school district willing to find out whether its previous goals, curriculum, and procedures should be changed. The starting point would require that all parties to the needs assessment—board members, teachers, administrators, parents—put aside their current goals and opinions on what students ought to do and instead study deeply the outcomes they want; that is, the ultimate contribution the school and its students should make to society, the ways education should help students to be successful in today's and tomorrow's world, and the learnings needed for effective citizenship in our democracy. In the alpha needs assessment, the participants are concerned with what should be, with choices, rather than examining deficits in the status quo. They are willing to change the current goals and objectives. The needs assessment, based on consideration of desirable outcomes, would precede development of the mission statement. It would form the basis for a new set of goal statements and their subsequent objectives and learning activities, all geared toward fresh concepts of building a constructive, participative, changing society. "We are more likely not to forget the goals if they are set on the basis of a needs assessment," according to Daniel Stufflebeam (Brandt 1978, p. 251).

Beta. A beta type needs assessment might be implemented when a school district felt it was sure that the goals, objectives, and policies of the system were correct, but that it had become appropriate to determine the gap in current learner performance as compared to desired performance. Standardized tests and/or some standard criteria of performance might be used.

Gamma. This is a mode of needs assessment in which people are asked to sort or place in order the existing goals and objectives, both for process and outcomes, with the purpose of obtaining a ranking of goals. Based on the list of sorted priorities that results, alternative programs or materials can be emphasized in the school system. Various kits are available for the gamma variety of needs assessment such as the Phi Delta Kappa kit, described in a later section.

Delta. The fourth type is not usually seen as a needs assessment but can be considered so since it is a discrepancy-determination procedure. Its purpose is to implement selected alternatives. To do this, it is necessary to manage the process of achieving outcomes. When starting at this point, the district or organization has already decided what to do and usually how to do it. The function then of this mode is to determine gaps in prespecified performances. Management by objectives and instructional management plans are examples of this model.

Epsilon. This type of needs assessment is similar to summative evaluation. It is used to determine discrepancies between results and objectives for the end of term or of project or of program. The purpose is to make decisions on the next steps. In other words, this mode is used to determine the gaps between the goals and objectives and the actual accomplishments. Summative and formative evaluations are discussed in Chapter Nine.

Zeta. The sixth type of needs assessment is a gap analysis that provides constant and continual renewal. This mode requires the collection and use of data at any point in time in the conception, analysis, design, implementation, or evaluation for the purpose of making decisions about changing, keeping, or stopping the various parts of the effort. Corrective action could be instituted at any point and so could a decision not to change. Districts employing a regularized curriculum renewal cycle would use the Zeta type of recurring needs assessment.

NEEDS ASSESSMENTS IN A CURRICULUM DEVELOPMENT CYCLE

The place of a needs assessment in curriculum development is graphically shown in Figure 10, taken from English and Kaufman (1975, p. 50). The assumption underlying this figure is that the goals have already been determined and that there is a continuing cycle of curriculum renewal. *Reality* refers to the current outcomes as expressed through needs assessments of learner needs, educator needs, society needs, and requirements for minimum survival.

**Figure 10.   The Curriculum Development Cycle Using a Needs
Assessment Base**

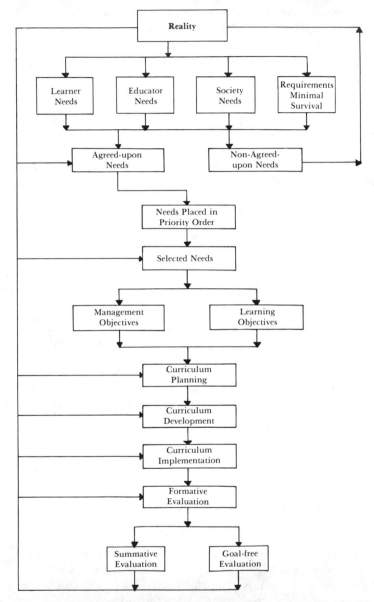

Fenwick English and Roger Kaufman would sort these needs into two categories: needs that are agreed upon by the participants and those that are not agreed upon. The non-agreed-upon needs are "cycled" back through the needs identification procedure. The agreed-upon needs are then placed in priority order. The highest priority needs are selected for acting on. From these selected needs, management objectives as well as objectives for learning are established. Next, curricula are planned and then developed before implementation. During curriculum implementation, there is a formative evaluation that can serve to feed back performance information to any or all of the previous steps as required.

After implementation and as many formative evaluation steps as deemed necessary, two types of evaluation are completed: a summative evaluation in which objectives or accomplishment is assessed, and a goal-free evaluation in which unexpected results are assessed. Both types of data are used to refine and renew that system at any point in its previous development. This curriculum development cycle thus forms a system that is both self-correcting and self-correctable.

METHODOLOGIES

Without assessing needs, curriculum developers risk constructing a "solution" for which there is no related problem. Needs assessments allow for the involvement of a broader constituency; respondents have a chance to express both their levels of expectation and their understanding of current practice. A wide variety of responses is possible that allows for more diversity of opinion and opportunity for analysis. All of this can lead to a more positive direction in using the findings of the assessments for improving the curriculum, according to English and Kaufman (1975).

Subjective and factual data are both needed for an adequate needs assessment. For example, self-perception of one's own needs is not always reliable; this was shown by a study of teacher needs for in-service education relating to the teaching of reading (Jones and Hayes 1980). In this study, the teachers' knowledge of reading and reading instruction, as assessed by a well-known inventory, was compared with their perceptions of their own needs for further knowledge in the same areas. The lack of match seemed to say that determining needs requires gathering factual data beyond perceptual information. This might include structured interviews, observations, formal testing, and other measures.

Figure 11 shows the use of both perceptual data and factual information in relating to educational goal attainment. The perceptual information collected through the interview process indicated the judgments of parents, students, staff, and other community members on the effectiveness of the existing program. The factual information included curricular analysis and profile information on the students of the district (Masinton, et al. 1981). Various methods, programs, and kits are available for assessing needs and examples follow.

The Delphi Method

Delphi techniques, named for the ancient prophetic oracle, were invented in the early 1950s for the purpose of estimating the probable effects of a massive nuclear bomb attack on the United States. Subsequently they have been applied to technological forecasting. Other applications have proliferated, particularly in educational matters. Evaluation of health care, the direction of long-range trends in science and technology with their probable effects on our lives, and allocation of research and development funds have all been areas for the use of Delphi techniques. Educational needs assessments has been another area.

Delphi methods can provide reliable subjective data for use in studies where hard data are unavailable or too costly. It is a method for gathering expert opinions from the "advice community" on which decision makers frequently rely. It systematizes the process of gathering subjective judgments, and it lends greater objectivity to the opinions of those representing conflicting viewpoints. A Delphi method can structure a group communication process so that a group of individuals as a whole can deal with a complex problem. Feedback from individual contributions of information and knowledge is provided, and there is some assessment of a group judgment, some opportunity for individuals to revise their views, and a degree of anonymity for individual opinions on needs.

Uses of the Delphi method in planning for curriculum development include: gathering data not accurately known or available; distinguishing between real and perceived needs; exposing personal values and social goals; evaluating possible budget allocations; developing cause and effect relationships; and putting together a model, a system, a set of goals, or a five-year plan.

In determining whether to use Delphi, it could be appropriate if one or more of the following conditions exist.

1. The problem can benefit from subjective judgments on a collective basis.
2. The individuals who should contribute to the examination of the problem represent diverse backgrounds with respect to experience or expertise.
3. More individuals are needed to offer advice than can effectively interact in a face-to-face exchange.
4. Time and cost make frequent group meetings unworkable.

Figure 11.   Assessing Perceptual and Factual Needs for Improving Outcomes

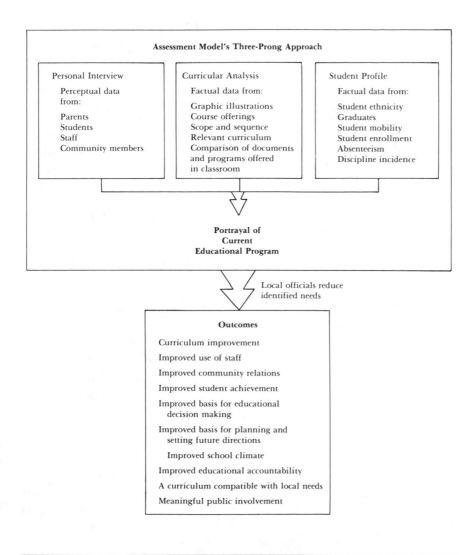

Assessment Model's Three-Prong Approach

Personal Interview

Perceptual data from:

Parents
Students
Staff
Community members

Curricular Analysis

Factual data from:

Graphic illustrations
Course offerings
Scope and sequence
Relevant curriculum
Comparison of documents
and programs offered
in classroom

Student Profile

Factual data from:

Student ethnicity
Graduates
Student mobility
Student enrollment
Absenteeism
Discipline incidence

Portrayal of
Current
Educational Program

Local officials reduce
identified needs

Outcomes

Curriculum improvement

Improved use of staff

Improved community relations

Improved student achievement

Improved basis for educational
decision making

Improved basis for planning and
setting future directions

Improved school climate

Improved educational accountability

A curriculum compatible with local needs

Meaningful public involvement

From Harry W. Masinton, Johanna Smith, and Dudley Solomon, "A Three-Prong Approach Takes Mystery Out of Needs Assessment," *NASSP Bulletin* 65 (November 1981), p. 14.

5. Disagreements among individuals are severe or politically unpalatable so that the communication process must be refereed and/or anonymity assured.
6. The heterogeneity of the participants must be preserved to assure valid results.

There are two distinct forms of Delphi: the Delphi exercise and the Delphi conference. The Delphi exercise begins with a questionnaire designed by a small team. This is sent out to a larger respondent group, which represents the various populations. After the questionnaire is returned, the monitor team summarizes the results and, based upon the results, develops a new questionnaire for the respondent group. Individuals in the respondent group are given at least one opportunity to reevaluate their original answers after the group response has been examined.

The Delphi conference has the advantage of eliminating the delay caused in summarizing each round of the Delphi exercise. It takes place by means of group conferences or discussion sessions. These are led by people competent in facilitating group processes. All disagreements should be exposed and explored while working toward a consensus. It is also possible to conduct the Delphi conference via telephone, involving persons at great distances from one another. A comprehensive review of the Delphi method is provided by Harold Linstone and Murray Turoff (1975).

Test Scores, Polls, and Surveys as Needs Assessments

No known shortcut to a high quality assessment of needs exists. Local adaptations and amplifications are always necessary even for the best of formats prepared elsewhere such as, for example, national polls or survey questions issued by a state department. Certainly, reliance on standardized test scores alone is not a needs assessment but is rather one source of data available to a much broader investigation.

Fenwick English and Roger Kaufman emphasize that "a school system which allows itself to define needs solely from standardized tests has signed away its prerogatives and options for program development and [its] responsibility" (1975, p. 21). They prefer that assessment of needs goes beyond student achievement in basic skills to identify gaps between present conditions and desirable outcomes for students as they enter society and assume adult responsibilities.

School administrators occasionally regard a national poll of public opinion such as the annual Gallup Poll (1983) as an indication of local needs, or else they may use its format and seek local opinions. While the view from the public has its lessons for school authorities, it represents only one partner in the concept of educational partners—school and community. National polls usually focus on newsworthy interests of the public such as discipline, drug abuse, crime, finances, busing, class size, and the public's perceptions of good teachers or a good curriculum. These are important areas of concern, but they are only a part of the concept of needs. Also included should be a larger vision that refers to the contribution students should be able to make to society after they leave school, according to Roger Kaufman and Robert Stakenas (1981). Such an assessment would also recognize that the good of the school is the self-sufficiency of individuals in society. It is a holistic concept that goes beyond the boundaries of the school and provides links between the curriculum and instruction and the society as a whole.

Surveys of educators, citizens, and students by state departments of education are frequently helpful to local school districts in preparing statements of the school's mission and goals, which can then form the basis for planning assessments of needs. Local interpretations and applications of suggestions from the state's headquarters are necessary if there are to be meaningful effects. Mission statements drawn from three state-sponsored studies are shown as examples.

Florida

All students shall acquire a knowledge and understanding of the opportunities open to them for preparing for a productive life and shall develop those skills and abilities that will enable them to take full advantage of those opportunities—including a positive attitude toward work and respect for the dignity of all honorable occupations.

Michigan

Michigan education must assure the development of youth as citizens who have self-respect, respect for others, and respect for law.

Texas

All students should achieve knowledge about comparative political systems with emphasis on democratic institutions, the American heritage, and the responsibilites and privileges of citzenship. (English and Kaufman 1975, p. 23.)

When a mission statement similar to these is developed prior to a needs assessment, it leads to general goals that can be used to determine discrepancies between the current status and the desired outcomes. Objectives would be set to guide action. The sequence of curriculum development and instructional activities would be as shown in this simplified diagram. Dotted lines indicate feedback and opportunities to review or revise.

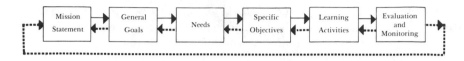

ASSIGNING PRIORITIES

A school district or educational organization might list so many needs that it would be impossible to serve all of them. Some needs will require more emphasis than others, and as resources for education are scarce, it will be necessary to establish priorities among needs. It is also important to recognize both met and unmet needs, as Daniel Stufflebeam has noted (Brandt 1978). If the focus is just on the unmet needs, the school may transfer energy and resources from needs that are currently being met, thus neglecting them. Long-range planning avoids this pitfall of needs assessment and curriculum development.

Various professionally designed kits are available to assist school districts in assigning priorities to a number of educational needs, which then lead to the development of goals, objectives, and a curriculum. One example is described next.

A Needs Assessment Instrument

A carefully prepared instrument that offers a procedure for assigning priorities to educational goals and, at the same time, assessing the needs of the local district or school unit in relation to these goals and objectives is the *Educational Planning Model* (n.d.), produced by the Program Development Center of Northern California and distributed by the Commission on Educational Planning of Phi Delta Kappa. Numerous communities and schools have used this program. It provides directions, strategies, and techniques for drawing cross-section representatives from citizens at large, adults directly involved in the educational process, and students. Both discussions and written responses are used. Several rounds of meetings are required, and specific procedures are followed. Once the district's needs have been assessed, the program provides instructions for translating them into objectives at a program level. The program also accommodates additional goals and objectives that may be contributed by the participants. This is the original list (Phi Delta Kappa EG Form 4):

EDUCATIONAL GOALS
(These are not in any order of importance.)

Learn how to be a good citizen
A. Develop an awareness of civic rights and responsibilities.
B. Develop attitudes for productive citizenship in a democracy.
C. Develop an attitude of respect for personal and public property.
D. Develop an understanding of the obligations and responsibilities of citizenship.

Learn how to respect and get along with people who think, dress, and act differently
A. Develop an appreciation for and an understanding of other people and other cultures.
B. Develop an understanding of the political, economic, and social patterns of the rest of the world.
C. Develop an awareness of the interdependence of races, creeds, nations, and cultures.
D. Develop an awareness of the processes of group relationships.

Learn about and try to understand the changes that take place in the world
A. Develop ability to adjust to the changing demands of society.
B. Develop an awareness of and the ability to adjust to a changing world and its problems.
C. Develop understanding of the past, identity with the present, and the ability to meet the future.

Develop skills in reading, writing, speaking, and listening.
A. Develop the ability to communicate ideas and feelings effectively.
B. Develop skills in oral and written English.

Understand and practice democratic ideas and ideals
A. Develop loyalty to American democratic ideals.
B. Develop patriotism and loyalty to ideas of democracy.
C. Develop knowledge and appreciation of the rights and privileges in our democracy.
D. Develop an understanding of our American heritage.

Learn how to examine and use information
A. Develop the ability to examine constructively and creatively.
B. Develop the ability to use scientific methods.
C. Develop reasoning abilities.
D. Develop skills to think and proceed logically.

Understand and practice the skills of family living
A. Develop understanding and appreciation of the principles of living in the family group.
B. Develop attitudes leading to acceptance of responsibilities as family members.
C. Develop an awareness of future family responsibilities and achievement of skills in preparing to accept them.

Learn to respect and get along with people with whom we work and live
A. Develop appreciation and respect for the worth and dignity of individuals.
B. Develop respect for individual worth and understanding of minority opinions and acceptance of majority decisions.
C. Develop a cooperative attitude toward living and working with others.

Develop skills to enter a specific field of work
A. Develop abilities and skills needed for immediate employment.
B. Develop an awareness of opportunities and requirements related to a specific field of work.
C. Develop an appreciation of good workmanship.

Learn how to be a good manager of money, property, and resources
A. Develop an understanding of economics, principles and responsibilities.
B. Develop ability and understanding in personal buying, selling, and investment.
C. Develop skills in management of natural and human resources and man's environment.

Develop a desire for learning now and in the future
A. Develop intellectual curiosity and eagerness for lifelong learning.
B. Develop a positive attitude toward learning.
C. Develop a positive attitude toward continuing independent education.

Learn how to use leisure time
A. Develop ability to use leisure time productively.
B. Develop a positive attitude toward participation in a range of leisure time activities—physical, intellectual, and creative.
C. Develop appreciation and interests which will lead to wise and enjoyable use of leisure time.

Practice and understand the ideas of health and safety
A. Establish an effective individual physical fitness program.
B. Develop an understanding of good physical health and well being.

C. Establish sound personal health habits and information.
D. Develop a concern for public health and safety.

Appreciate culture and beauty in the world
A. Develop abilities for effective expression of ideas and cultural appreciation (fine arts).
B. Cultivate appreciation for beauty in various forms.
C. Develop creative self-expression through various media (art, music, writing, and so on).
D. Develop special talents in music, art, literature, and foreign languages.

Gain information needed to make job selections
A. Promote self-understanding and self-direction in relation to the student's occupational interests.
B. Develop the ability to use information and counseling services related to the selection of a job.
C. Develop a knowledge of specific information about a particular vocation.

Develop a pride in work and a feeling of self-worth
A. Develop a feeling of student pride in achievements and progress.
B. Develop self-understanding and self-awareness.
C. Develop the student's feeling of positive self-worth, security, and self-assurance.

Develop good character and self-respect
A. Develop moral responsibility and a sound ethical and moral behavior.
B. Develop the student's capacity to discipline self for work, study, and play constructively.
C. Develop a moral and ethical sense of values, goals, and processes of free society.
D. Develop standards of personal character and ideas.

Gain a general education
A. Develop background and skills in the use of numbers, natural sciences, mathematics, and social sciences.
B. Develop a fund of information and concepts.
C. Develop special interests and abilities.

Cautions to Observe

When presented a detailed list such as the example given, citizens may come up with negative comments about the goals themselves. They may say that the goals should not be ranked in any order as they are *all* important. It should be remembered here that the public has never been exposed to much debate or discussion on educational policy, and it may be necessary to engage the public in a more sustained dialogue on educational matters. Otherwise, it will be difficult to frame questions dealing with educational priorities in terms of organizational outcomes that make sense to the general public.

Another way to assign priorities in a needs assessment is to submit a list of educational needs that have been predetermined by a representative group. Ask the constituents viewing the list to assign a place to them according to importance. If this type of needs assessment is used, it is essential to be wary of several hazards, according to Regina Paul and Henry Brickell (1982), and to avoid them.

Avoid:

1. Learning goals hopelessly scrambled together with teaching processes, school operations, and indicators of school climates in a disorganized list on which matters of different order are put in competition with each other. An example would be spelling, discipline, transportation, and ability grouping.
2. Learning goals offered at different levels of abstraction so that some items accidentally overlap or contain others. "Knows American history" would not appear on the same list with "Knows the causes of the Civil War."
3. Learning goals not representative enough to cover all school areas or subjects so that some key arenas of learning may be totally ignored. Pressure for basics may cause the arts and foreign languages to be overlooked or even science and social studies. Physical education may be left out.
4. Learning goals written only for the head and none for the heart or the hand, leading to a fact-heavy curriculum. Needed are goals that lead to appreciations of the contributions to American life made by different races, religions, and nationalities; opportunities in music, art, dancing, sports, and field and laboratory experiences.
5. Learning goals only rated but not ranked so that all goals could seem equally important, and no priorities could be set. Rating each item on a list of learning goals as number one on a one to five scale will not help in planning curriculum. Paul and Brickell suggested that the respondents allocate an imaginary thousand dollars among the areas competing for students' time on task. Usually the money doesn't go far enough!
6. Learning goals chosen because of their importance for students to learn but that are not responsibilities of the school. Much is to be

learned by students, but not all of it can be taught in school. For example, the school can hardly control home values or solve socioeconomic inequalities in the community. Schools are primarily responsible for teaching that leads to academic and citizenship goals, self-realization, and vocations.

ASSESSMENT OF NEEDS ASSESSMENT PROCEDURES

Whether the needs assessment is used for goal setting, for rating a preset list of goals, for determining current concerns and problems, or for other purposes, each procedure has its advantages and disadvantages. Belle Ruth Witkin (1977) has reviewed and compared the salient characteristics of several widely known instruments and methods, which characterize the range of choices available. Figure 12 is a condensation of that information.

Witkin also provides extensive information regarding publisher sources and offers further discussion of each procedure classification. Models and instruments are grouped according to the purposes that underlie assessments of needs. These categories are: goal-rating procedures, methods for gathering performance and other data on existing conditions, discrepancy surveys to assess current needs, complete kits for school use, futuring techniques, specialized techniques, regional and state models, community occupational needs assessments, and communication-focused methods.

According to Witkin, there is no one right way to do a needs assessment; the methodology depends on many factors, such as the point at which needs must enter the planning process, the decisions to be made, and the uses to which the data will be put.

LOCAL ADAPTATIONS

Three adaptations of needs assessment models or procedures are described in the following illustrations: staff development, use of a state department plan, and an open-end assessment.

Needs Assessment for Staff Development

An assessment of needs for knowledge and skills can lead to professional growth when participants are motivated toward self-improvement. A study conducted by Terry Ley (1981) used the *Statement on the Preparation of Teachers of English and the Language Arts* of the National Council of Teachers of English as a needs assessment instrument. It listed forty-three qualifications in these areas: knowledge that English teachers need, abilities that English teachers must have, and attitudes that English

Figure 12. Advantages and Disadvantages of Needs Assessment Procedures

Procedure	Advantages	Disadvantages
Goal Setting: Generate own goals	Encourages community involvement; partners must work out their philosophy; different groups reconcile differences on educational purposes; partners feel a commitment to the goals.	Very time consuming; impetus for needs assessment may be dissipated; partners may think that the list of goals equals "needs"; differences among client groups must be reconciled.
Use preset list	Takes much less time; goals usually at a consistent level of generality; goals less likely to be confused with solutions or problems; usually have been set by experts and likely to be stated more consistently; prevents "reinventing the wheel."	There may be too many or too few for local situation; goals may not apply; may be too narrow or too broad; may include only immediate goals, not future ones; often cover only the cognitive domain; some lists confuse learner and institutional goals; may limit the creative thinking of the group.
Goal-Rating Methods: Card sorts	Easy to use individually or in small groups; most people enjoy the process; allows for interaction, if desired.	May be too mechanical; difficult to do if the number of goals is very large; must have packaged materials or make them.
Rating sheets or goal-rating questionnaires	Easy to use; easy to duplicate materials; rater can see all goals or items at once.	Respondents may fall into a pattern due to the order of the items; not as interesting as card sorts; individual judgments only.
Paired weighting procedure	More exact than simple ratings or card sorts; people enjoy it; easy to get group ratings.	Process cumbersome if more than ten or twelve goals; forced choices sometimes difficult.

Technique	Advantages	Disadvantages
Magnitude estimation scaling	Shows *relative* rankings; greater specificity; gives better data for analyzing reasons for discrepancies between respondent groups; easy to administer; shows response patterns of subgroups.	Scoring and data analysis are more difficult than other methods—require computer; technique not widely known; take longer to analyze and graph data than simple "difference" techniques.
Determination of "What Is": Perceptual judgments of parents, teachers, and students	Can compare perceptions of different groups; perceptions are valid data of a kind; easy to compare goal importance with goal attainment on similar scales; usually easy to quantify; can be related to "hard" data.	May not reflect the actual situation; if sampling is inadequate, results will be biased; ease of quantifying may obscure invalid data; tends to oversimplify the problems; based on limited knowledge.
Standardized test (norm referenced)	Data are quantifiable; data can be easily compared over time for ongoing assessments; data can be related to goals or objectives; groups of students may be compared; provides baseline data on the level of need.	Test norms may not be appropriate for a given population; tests may be inappropriate for the goals used; if too much reliance on test, other data and values may be overlooked; usually reflects only cognitive achievement.
Criterion-referenced tests	Can be directly related to local goals; can help define "what should be" as competencies to be mastered.	Criterion levels may be arbitrary or invalid; may be difficult to interpret scores for degree of "need."
Student work	Gives evidence of creativity, divergent thinking not tapped by most tests; can be related directly to school goals.	Difficult to quantify data and to compare groups for extent of "need"; some goals might not have appropriate "products"; more time consuming than examining ratings or tests.
Discrepancy Analysis: Simple differences between two sets of ratings	Easy to do; does not require consultant help or computer; low cost and time.	Oversimplifies the decision making; if either set is invalid, the results will be invalid; may provide irrelevant information.

Figure 12, continued

Procedure	Advantages	Disadvantages
Combined analyses in qualitative statements	Takes more factors into consideration; can integrate perceptual data with test scores and input data; allows more differentiation; usually more valid than difference scores.	Harder to do; more time consuming; most models offer no guidelines for this method; not as easy to communicate results to public.
Criticality index or function	Relates goal importance and goal attainment functionally; can differentiate more critical from less critical goal areas multidimensionally; easy to graph and communicate the results.	Apparent precision may obscure invalid data on either dimension.
Setting Priorities: Take goals rated highest in importance	Easy to do; shortens time for assessment, allows more time for program planning and action on goals.	Least valid method; a *goal* is not the same as a *need*.
Use highest ranked goals which also show highest discrepancies in attainment	Fairly easy to do; takes two factors into consideration.	May oversimplify the real situation; does not take factors of feasibility or utility into account.
Decision rule (e.g., Center for the Study of Education Model)	Takes many factors into account; puts emphasis on priorities for action; results more likely to be implemented because more specific than other methods.	Takes more time; not as easy to explain to working committees; may seem too complex; may overemphasize utility at expense of innovativeness and new directions for the school.

Special Procedures:		
Critical-incident technique	Concrete; does not start with assumptions of what "should be"; uses everyday language of participants; good at assessing system needs affecting learner attainment.	Implications of the incidents not always clear; may be difficult to categorize incidents; translating incidents into goals may confuse learner and institutional goals.
Delphi technique	Prevents over influence of opinion leaders on group deliberations; provides feedback and opportunity to modify opinions; demonstrates success in reaching consensus; ensures anonymity of responses.	Time consuming; may require research assistance.
Fault Tree analysis	Needs are derived on a logical basis; traces causes of discrepancies; interrelates hundreds of events in graphic form; has qualitative and quantitative base for assigning priorities.	Requires a trained FTA analyst to construct and quantify the tree; may be too time consuming; does not follow classic discrepancy approach; participants must be trained to give inputs and assist in quantifying.

From Belle Ruth Witkin, "Needs Assessment Kits, Models, and Tools," *Educational Technology* 17 (November 1977), pp. 15-17.

teachers should demonstrate in their work with students. The instrument was administered to 150 Alabama English teachers selected at random. The findings were that, generally, teachers felt that the qualifications listed by the National Council of Teachers of English are indeed important to the successful teaching of English today. However, the teachers did not report high levels of self-confidence about possessing the listed qualifications, and they indicated that they needed improvement in approximately half of the qualifications. The instrument identified program needs for professional growth as well as for preservice preparation for English teachers. This effort at a needs assessment would have been even more meaningful if students and citizens could have been involved.

State Plans Adapted Locally

Several states have prepared handbooks for assisting local districts in curriculum planning. As mentioned earlier, information is available through ERIC. As an example, the North Carolina Department of Public Instruction (1976) issued a handbook that presents a model in which need assessment precedes the development of the mission statement.

The first step is a situational analysis. Local districts gather all possible data, which comprise a comprehensive needs assessment. Information is obtained through a written questionnaire involving the staff and hundreds of citizens, visits of administrators to classrooms; attendance at community meetings; evaluations done in previous years; accreditation reports; telephone surveys; test results; data from the state department of education; and individual conferences with students, parents, teachers, and administrators. Analysis, coherence, and interpretation are accomplished with the assistance of a citizen-staff advisory committee.

The second step is to develop a broad and comprehensive mission statement followed by development of goal statements; next is rank ordering the goals for relative importance or indicating the greatest gaps between current and desired performance. Development of instructional and support services objectives follow, and a year-to-year evaluation and revision is expected.

In a different state plan, needs are assessed after the mission statement is adopted. Inspired by the recent surge of studies to identify pertinent characteristics of "effective schools," the Connecticut State Department of Education has developed detailed written and oral instruments known as the *Connecticut School Effectiveness Interview* and *Questionnaire* (1982). This needs assessment is based on seven major categories of school effectiveness: (1) safe and orderly environment; (2) knowledge and understanding of the school's mission, goals, and priorities; (3) quality of the principal's instructional leadership; (4) climate of expectations for students; (5) student time on task and opportunity to learn; (6) monitoring of student progress; and (7) home-school relations.

This is an example of an assessment designed to ascertain the perceptions of faculty and administrators based on their experience in a given school. In Connecticut, it is expected to provide a focus on school effectiveness programs. Other state plans for assessing needs vary in purpose and frequently involve citizens and students as well as professional staff. State departments are usually willing to share materials with others on request.

An Open-End Needs Assessment

In contrast to the packaged lists of needs prepared by external agencies are open-ended versions that begin with an almost blank sheet of paper. The next example reveals the judgments of citizens, staff, and students when asked an open-ended question: "What do you consider to be the most critical problems facing our school district?"

One of the authors coordinated the participation of many persons in this needs assessment. Later, from analysis and interpretation of the data, the district developed its mission statement (philosophy), goal statements, objectives, learning activities, and evaluation and monitoring processes. The sequence in this case was:

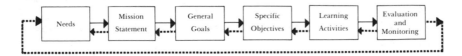

Feedback, of course, has constantly altered and updated each aspect. A new needs assessment, utilizing a computerized, locally developed instrument was conducted in 1977 as follow up.

The initial needs assessment, an open ended Delphi-type, was conducted in 1971 in the School District of University City, Missouri. It surveyed curricular and instructional needs as viewed by four participant groups. A statistical sampling method selected respondents from the professional staff, students of grades five through twelve, parents, and representatives of civic, philanthropic, and religious organizations of the community. Successive rounds of questionnaires were used to seek their opinions.

Students' perceptions included several needs relating to the immediate school environment. Adults' perceptions tended to emphasize basic skills, societal concerns, and various benefits and resources that make the teaching career more enjoyable. Despite the diversity of emphases, all groups concurred on several needs. The following needs were mentioned by all groups in the first round, although not necessarily assigned a high priority in the second round. Some were phrased in different terminology but with similar intent.

Teaching students to assume more responsibility for their own work and behavior

Orderly behavior in the schools

Improved communication among students, staff, parents, and community

Individual attention to students

More interesting courses

Racial harmony among students

More civic projects and use of community resources

Improvement of the counseling program

The top ten needs (including tie votes) identified by each group were:

Students, grades five through twelve

The school should have fair rules and apply them to all students, reduce favoritism to some students, and find ways to prevent fights.

The school building and grounds should be cleaner, with no trash lying around.

The school should teach more responsibiity to children and give more attention to children who cause problems.

The school should take some action after receiving our replies to this questionnaire.

Black and white students should work together for common goals and harmony.

Courses should be developed to include more practical experiences, such as field trips, visits to corporations, and visits to community organizations.

Students should have more involvement with the community and with community projects.

Counselors should communicate more with students, give more information, listen to students as individuals, and devote more time and effort to student problems.

Air conditioners should be provided in warm weather.

More variety and more interesting work should be provided in the various school subjects, with more choice allowed in the kinds of classes and time spent in class.

Rules of discipline should be enforced firmly for all offenders by teachers and administrators.

School buildings and the facilities within them, including lockers, drinking fountains, and heating systems, should be kept in better repair, and more attractive paint and decorations should be used.

Parents

Adequate salaries should be offered to attract and keep good teachers.

There are too many pupils per teacher, which lessens individual instruction.

Technical and vocational training is needed for both male and female students who do not care to go on to higher education.

Reading specialists are needed for all grade levels to improve reading skills.

Curriculum should be designed to teach children how to live and cope in a pluralistic society and to improve the child's acceptance of his or her elders and of minority groups. Curriculum should also stress manners and courtesy.

More effective teachers and better qualified ones are needed.

Emphasis should be placed on the causes and consequences of good and bad health habits.

Questionnaires should be sent out periodically to parents so that they can express their ideas on a continuing basis.

Black experiences should be recognized throughout the curriculum, not in a separate program.

Children should have more time with teachers; there should be more one-to-one teacher-student dialogues.

Civic, philanthropic, and religious organizations

Each child should be taught to assume responsibility for his or her acts.

Efforts should be made by the school and the community to generate faith in the board of education.

Ineffective teachers should not be retained.

There should be greater emphasis on verbal and written skills.

Tutoring programs should be expanded to meet the needs of individual students.

There should be a critical analysis and evaluation of each teacher's ability to teach in an interracial environment.

Efforts should be made to achieve greater trust among all those concerned with schools.

Counseling at the junior and senior high schools should be improved.

Parents should be given a full explanation of any increased funds (taxes, and so on.)

There should be objective evaluations of all programs.

Teachers and administrators

A more attractive salary schedule is needed.

Additional assistance in reading is needed for low achievers.

Assistance with learning disabilities is needed.

Ways to reduce vandalism should be designed.

Additional help is needed with behavior and discipline problems.

Knowledge from research should be used to teach "unreachable" children.

Control and orderliness in buildings is necessary; a laissez-faire atmosphere is undesirable.

Improved communication with staff is needed.

More materials are needed for individual prescriptions.

Basic courses are necessary for slow students.

The mission statement, or statement of philosophy, developed by the local district (1973) and still in effect as a result of the needs assessment is:

The purpose of the school system is to share with the community the responsibility to make available the highest quality integrated, individualized education. The Board is committed to providing an educational environment that will enable each student in its trust to acquire and apply basic learning skills, respect for him/herself and others, a love of learning, and to become a responsible citizen. Basic learning skills are those which enable students to prepare for a lifetime of learning and include general education, aesthetics, and physical development.

In a community which respects and affirms diversity, the Board is committed to:
   Equality in the provision of appropriate programs and services regardless of race, religion, sex, age, or national origin.

   Close cooperation with all elements of the community—students, parents, school district staff, and citizens-at-large in developing and implementing educational objectives.

   Utilization of the human and material resources available to the District in the most efficient and productive manner possible.

We believe that the success of the District in achieving these objectives is to be measured in the ability of our schools' graduates to enjoy lifelong learning and to compete successfully and participate fully as young adults living in a free society.

After input from representative constituents, broad goals have been generated annually from the statement of philosophy. The following version was adopted by the district for 1982–83.

The school district will:
   1. Recognize its commitment to excellence in curriculum and instruction in all subject areas by continuing to foster good teaching, maintain high expectations for students, improve achievement, seek effective instructional methods, and provide substantive content.

2. Seek refinement and implementation of an effective guidance and counseling program at all levels.
3. Support school personnel in their efforts to insure an orderly atmosphere conducive to learning.
4. Ensure that human and material resources are used effectively and efficiently to maximize students' learning.
5. Increase school-community and teacher-parent cooperation for the betterment of students' learning; gain support for the school system among nonparents and develop and implement plans to maintain enrollment.
6. Continue its commitment to integrate schools and staff.
7. Assure that the contracted agency fulfills its obligations for maintenance and custodial services to the district.

From the goals came objectives, work plans for administrators, curriculum planning by teachers, and learning activities for students. (Samples of grade-level objectives for curriculum from this district's processes were shown in Chapter Five.)

HUMAN POWERS

Needs assessments should only be a first step in planning and implementing solutions to problems. Dwayne Huebner said it this way: "As educators, we have been more inclined to talk of the person in terms of needs rather than powers, and we have been inclined to speak of needs assessments or deficiencies rather than how a person uses his or her power." He suggests that we begin to ask how children use their surplus energy beyond that needed for self-maintenance and to what extent they recognize the power to construct, to produce new qualities of life for themselves, and to produce new qualities of life and new environments for others (1981, p. 131). This points out the necessity to follow up needs assessments with the identification of school and community resources that can contribute to developing power in human life. For this purpose, techniques used should be those that open possibilities for discovering new ideas and new approaches to old problems.

Paul Hersey and Kenneth Blanchard (1982) asserted that needs are synonymous with motives. Motives are directed toward goals, and motives or needs are the mainsprings of action, something within the individual that prompts that person to action.

The need with the greatest strength at a particular moment leads to activity, and the motive decreases in strength when satisfied, according to Abraham Maslow (1970). Thus, to be effective, a goal must be appropriate to the need structure of the individual involved; the goal must fit the need.

As goals are reached, interest changes. Therefore, there must be a constant realignment of goals for growth and development.

According to Maslow, human needs seem to arrange themselves into a hierarchy. His framework helps to explain the strength of certain needs, which build from basic physiological needs, toward self-actualization, the highest level.

Self-actualization
Esteem, recognition
Social, affiliation
Security, safety
Physiological

In the process of assessing needs and the subsequent development of curriculum, it is important that psychological needs be considered. Referring to Maslow's hierarchy, applications to student behavior and staff development can be made when one realizes the relative place of physical and psychological needs in assessing any given local situation.

At the lower realm of Maslow's hierarchy are physiological needs. If children are hungry, for example, it will not be possible to move them along intellectually or academically until that need is satisfied. For adults, unless the basic necessities of life (shelter, food, and clothing) are provided, other motives will be weak.

At the second level are security needs. When employees of a school system overemphasize security, desired behaviors may be thwarted, according to Hersey and Blanchard. Security-minded people are satisfied with just having a job and are not competitive; others tend to expect little of them and are seldom critical of their work. Persons at the security-safety level are mainly interested in fringe benefits such as tenure, insurance, and retirement plans.

At the third level are social or affiliation needs. After the physiological and security needs are satisfied, most persons like to interact and be with others in situations where they feel they belong and are accepted. For both children and adults in a school, it seems that if there is to be productivity beyond the two lower levels, there must be opportunities to join informal work groups. The productivity of a work group will depend on how the group members see their own goals in relation to the goals of the organization.

Esteem or prestige is Maslow's fourth level. There appears to be a widespread need for people to have recognition and the respect of others.

At the highest level is self-actualization. Two motives that are related to this are competence and achievement. The feeling of competence is closely related to the concept of expectancy. Hersey and Blanchard observed that if the successes of students or teachers overshadow their failures, then their feelings of competence will tend to be high, and they will have a positive outlook. They will see almost every new situation as an interesting challenge that they can overcome. The competence motive usually reveals itself in adults as a desire for job mastery and professional growth.

Self-actualization and new concepts of human potentiality in relation to school practices is the theme of *Perceiving, Behaving, Becoming,* (Combs et al., 1962). One of its major ideas is that learning is a function of the exploration and discovery of personal meaning, that personal meanings can lead to feelings of adequacy, and that what produces greater adequacy also facilitates learning. When needs assessments can open avenues leading to the development of better and better human values, then they will have contributed to the development of human life, as Huebner suggested.

EMERGING TRENDS

The needs of our diverse student population have moved the focus of American education away from emphasis on students' conformance to a curriculum with a narrow predetermined range of offerings and goals that reflect only the past. If the schools are to provide the most appropriate educational environment for each student, additional information on needs will be required from a wide range of sources. Thus, it may be predicted that the emerging trends in needs assessments will include systematic collection of opinions from many different groups inside and outside of education. Active community involvement will probably continue and increase. Assessment models will become oriented toward projections within a longer time frame, and they will be influenced by the emergence of new technologies incorporating computer analysis. The real as opposed to the apparent needs of a system will be easier to identify, and it will be possible to assess more accurately the discrepancy between the current and the desired outcomes.

REFERENCES

Brandt, Ronald. "On Evaluation: An Interview with Daniel Stufflebeam." *Educational Leadership* 35 (January 1978): 248–54.

Combs, Arthur W.; Kelley, Earl C.; Rogers, Carl R.; and Maslow, Abraham H. *Perceiving, Behaving, Becoming.* Yearbook of the Association for Supervision and Curriculum Development. Alexandria, Va.: ASCD, 1962.

Connecticut State Department of Education. *The Connecticut School Effectiveness Interview* and *The Connecticut School Effectiveness Questionnaire.* Hartford, Conn.: State Department of Education, 1982.

Educational Policies Commission. *Education for All American Youth.* Washington, D.C.: National Educational Association, 1944.

English, Fenwick W., and Kaufman, Roger A. *Needs Assessment: A Focus for Curriculum Development.* Alexandria, Va.: Association for Supervision and Curriculum Development, 1975.

ERIC. *Resources in Education.* Catalogs. Washington, D.C.: U.S. Government Printing Office, issued regularly.

Erikson, Erik H. *Childhood and Society.* 2d ed. New York: W.W. Norton and Co., 1963.

Featherstone, William B. *A Functional Curriculum for Youth.* New York: American Book Co., 1950.

Gallup, George H. "The 15th Annual Gallup Poll of the Public's Attitude Toward the Public Schools." *Phi Delta Kappan* 65 (September 1983): 26-47.

Havighurst, Robert J. *Human Development and Education.* New York: Longmans, Green, 1953.

Hersey, Paul, and Blanchard, Kenneth. *Management of Organizational Behavior: Utilizing Human Resources.* Englewood Cliffs, N.J.: Prentice-Hall, 1982.

Huebner, Dwayne. "Toward a Political Economy of Curriculum and Human Development." In *Curriculum and Instruction,* edited by Henry A. Giroux, Anthony N. Penna, and William F. Pinar, pp. 124-38. Berkeley: McCutchan, 1981.

Jones, Linda L., and Hayes, Andrew E. "How Valid Are Surveys of Teacher Needs?" *Educational Leadership* 37 (February 1980): 390-92.

Kaufman, Roger. "A Possible Taxonomy of Needs Assessments." *Educational Technology* 17 (November 1977): 60-64.

Kaufman, Roger, and Stakenas, Robert G. "Needs Assessment and Holistic Planning." *Educational Leadership* 38 (May 1981): 612-16.

Ley, Terry C. "Using NCTE's Preparation Statement as a Needs Assessment Instrument." *English Education* 13 (October 1981): 156-64.

Linstone, Harold A., and Turoff, Murray, eds. *The Delphi Method: Techniques and Applications.* Reading, Mass.: Addison-Wesley, 1975.

Masinton, Harry W.; Smith, Johanna; and Solomon, Dudley. "A Three-Prong Approach Takes Mystery Out of Needs Assessment." *National Association of Secondary School Principals Bulletin* 65 (November 1981): 11-18.

Maslow, Abraham H. *Motivation and Personality.* New York: Harper & Row, 1954 and 1970.

National Association of Secondary School Principals. "The Imperative Needs of Youth." *National Association of Secondary School Principals Bulletin* 31 (March 1947): 2, 7-144.

North Carolina Department of Public Instruction. *Handbook for Planning in Local School Systems.* Raleigh, N.C.: State Department of Education, 1976.

Paul, Regina H., and Brickell, Henry M. "Are You Out on a Limb?" *Educational Leadership* 39 (January 1982): 260-64.

Phi Delta Kappa. *Educational Planning Model.* Bloomington, Ind.: Phi Delta Kappa, undated.

Prescott, Daniel A. *Emotions and the Educative Process.* Washington, D.C.: American Council on Education, 1938.

Taba, Hilda. *Curriculum Development: Theory and Practice.* New York: Harcourt, Brace and World, 1962.

Tyler, Ralph W. *Basic Principles of Curriculum and Instruction.* Chicago: University of Chicago, 1950.

University City School District. *Critical Needs of the Educational Program* 1971. *Statement of Philosphy* 1973-1980. *Goals* 1982. University City, Missouri.

Witkin, Belle Ruth. "Needs Assessment Kits, Models, and Tools." *Educational Technology* 17 (November 1977): 5-18.

ADDITIONAL READINGS

Alschuler, Alfred S. "Psychological Education." In *Curriculum and the Cultural Revolution*, edited by David E. Purpel and Maurice Belanger, pp. 256-71. Berkeley: McCutchan, 1972.

English, Fenwick W. "The Politics of Needs Assessment." *Educational Technology* 17 (November 1977): 18-23.

Fessler, Ralph. "Moving from Needs Assessment to Implementation: Strategies for Planning and Staff Development." *Educational Technology* 20 (June 1980): 31-33.

Haysom, John T., and Sutton, Clive R. "Motivation: A Neglected Component in Models for Curriculum Improvement." *Curriculum Theory Network* 4: 1 (1974): 23-35.

Huebner, Dwayne. "Implications of Psychological Thought for the Curriculum." In *Influences in Curriculum Change.* Alexandria, Va.: Association for Supervision and Curriculum Development, 1968.

Kaufman, Roger A. "Needs Assessment." In *Fundamental Curriculum Decisions*, pp. 53-67. Yearbook of the Association for Supervision and Curriculum Development. Alexandria, Va.: ASCD, 1983.

Macdonald, James B.; Wolfson, Bernice J.; and Zaret, Esther. *Reschooling Society: A Conceptual Model.* Alexandria, Va.: Association for Supervision and Curriculum Development, 1973.

Morris, Robert C., and Melvin, Emily A. "An Assessment of Student Perceptions of Needs Deficiencies." *Education* 102 (Fall 1981): 2-12.

Passow, A. Harry, ed. *Nurturing Individual Potential.* Yearbook of the Association for Supervision and Curriculum Development. Alexandria, Va.: ASCD, 1964.

Popham, W. James. *Educational Needs Assessment in the Cognitive, Affective, and Psychomotor Domains.* Los Angeles: Center for the Study of Evaluation, University of California at Los Angeles, 1969.

Sweigert, Ray L. "The Discovery of Need in Education: Developing A Need Inquiry System." *Journal of Secondary Education* 43 (December 1968): 345-48.

7

Examining the Content Areas

Curriculum content is commonly thought of as the information stored in printed materials, audio and visual recordings, computers, other electronic devices, or transmitted by word of mouth. John Dewey called the stored information of humankind "available capital" for the teacher, but he pointed out that it is only *potential* content for the learner. Information becomes content for the learner as it gives meaning to purposeful activities of the learner (1916, p. 216). Thus, selecting the content for curriculum and instruction is only a part of the content-related tasks of curriculum development; content must be accompanied by the planning of meaningful learning activities.

In this chapter, the discussion treats six areas of the academic curriculum: English (reading, writing, speaking, listening), mathematics, science, social studies, foreign languages, and the arts. A number of commissions and professional groups, whose proposals are discussed in Chapter Three, are seeking to strengthen the common learnings or academic areas of the curriculum in response to pervasive signs that schools are not educating young people as well as they could be or should. Bearing directly on the substance of the academic areas listed above is the ten-year effort of the College Board to strengthen the academic quality of secondary education and to ensure equality of opportunity in postsecondary education for all students. Basic academic competencies needed prior to all types of postsecondary education have been published by the College Board (1983), and this is augmented with detailed information on the knowledge and skills needed for effective work in an academic college. Hundreds of school and college educators took part in the deliberations that produced the recommendations. Examples of basic and advanced competencies, knowledge, and skills are given under their subject headings in this chapter.

The academic areas are discussed here in respect to current status, goals, trends, and problems. Although presented separately, the subject fields obviously depend on each other in many ways. The desirability of attaining a balanced and comprehensive curriculum is one of the underlying assumptions of this chapter. The curriculum should provide room for subjects not treated here, such as health and physical education and vocational subjects, which are needed by many students. Another underlying assumption is that a course is more than a textbook; for that reason, we have suggested a variety of techniques and materials.

ENGLISH

No other area of the curriculum receives as much criticism as reading, writing, and spelling when students fail to perform well. If Johnny can't read or write, he makes the headlines. Schools have been faulted in recent years for graduating functionally illiterate students, and tremendous efforts and huge sums of money have gone into projects designed to raise student achievement in reading and the other English language skills— writing, speaking, and listening. Successes are reported from several schools; and according to reports from testing and assessment agencies, some test scores on a national scale are showing improvement or at least holding steady after a long decline.

Reading

Test scores on standardized tests do not tell the whole story about reading achievement, however. The National Assessment of Educational Progress (1981) reported that American students seemed to be learning basic reading skills but not how to analyze or evaluate what they read. The Center for the Study of Reading at the University of Illinois did a five-year research study and concluded that multiple factors contributed to this problem. Commercially produced reading materials frequently emphasized word recognition at the expense of comprehension, and they usually relied on "fill-in-the-blank" formats. Students often found the materials boring, or bland and colorless at best. There seemed to be little opportunity for insight into characters' thoughts and feelings; no conflict was introduced. Skilled students soon lost interest in these materials, while beginning readers found that the simple words and short sentences with choppy or disconnected texts seldom created pleasure in reading (Walton 1981). The use of standardized tests, which follow the multiple choice computer-scored format, further diminished the emphasis on reading comprehension.

The currently traditional ways of teaching reading at all levels rely on teacher-dominated questioning with brief answers from students; this further reduces opportunities for students to develop comprehension skills. Classroom lectures may not give students a chance to develop their own interpretations, and apparently many students have not learned how to search out evidence for their judgments in a systematic fashion (National Assessment of Educational Progress 1981).

According to reports of the College Board high school students should have these basic academic competencies in reading (pp. 7–8):

1. The ability to identify and comprehend the main and subordinate ideas in a written work and to summarize the ideas in one's own words.
2. The ability to recognize different purposes and methods of writing, to identify a writer's point of view and tone, and to interpret a writer's meaning inferentially as well as literally.
3. The ability to separate one's personal opinions and assumptions from a writer's.
4. The ability to vary one's reading speed and method (survey, skim, review, question, and master) according to the type of material and one's purpose for reading.
5. The ability to use the features of books and other reference materials, such as table of contents, preface, introduction, titles and subtitles, index, glossary, appendix, bibliography.
6. The ability to define unfamiliar words by decoding, using contextual clues, or by using a dictionary.

More advanced learning outcomes listed by the College Board (1983, p. 15) in reading and literature for high schools are:

1. The ability to read critically by asking pertinent questions about what they have read, by recognizing assumptions and implications, and by evaluating ideas.
2. The ability to read a literary text analytically, seeing relationships between form and content.
3. The ability to read with understanding a range of literature, rich in quality and representative of different literary forms and various cultures.
4. Interest in and a sense of inquiry about written words.
5. The ability to respond actively and imaginatively to literature.

The arts and skills of English are essential in today's communications revolution—written, spoken, heard, and read—to communicate ideas and attitudes, expand thought, and inform. But if high school students are not competent in *basic* reading abilities, what are the curriculum needs? What makes a qualitative difference in reading skills? Emphasis on reading in the elementary grades and more substantive standards for high school English courses can make a difference. Early intervention has been found to make a difference, and various early childhood (preschool) programs are credited with stimulating intellectual development, which can lead to more success in school than would otherwise have been possible. Parent education for the preschool years can make a difference.

Children enter school with a wide range of attitudes toward reading. It is not unusual to find kindergarten children who can read. Others want to read when they come to school, and with these the problem of readiness is minimal. Then there are some children who cannot read and do not know what it means. In the inner city, children of school age have been found who had no acquaintance with books at all.

Once in school, children have been passed on from grade to grade although they read far below their grade placement. For these children, most schools provide specialized reading instruction, usually in addition to the regular class instruction.

The steps involved in assessing a child's needs in reading instruction are usually pretesting to determine the student's entry level, diagnosis of the reading problems, and prescription of remediation. A two-year study by the Institute for Research on Teaching at Michigan State University, however, found no reliable relationship between diagnosis and remediation in the cases studied. In other words, the practitioners seemed to behave inconsistently; treatments seemed to have little bearing on the diagnoses. It was observed that there was little opportunity for follow-up over several years to determine whether a given remedy "worked." Plans are to continue the study with the aim of generating information on specific treatments for specific problems (1981). This study typifies questions that arise concerning research on reading. It is obvious from the report above that diagnosis has little value when remediation is not matched to the reading problem nor careful records kept of what works best with which students, at what age, and under what conditions. Cooperation between teachers and specialists when assistance is available and an intense desire to help students learn to read are essential in overcoming difficulties. Diligent curriculum leaders and teachers can find help in the library. Much research has been funded in the field of reading, and numerous variables have been tested for cause and effect with different populations. Findings from studies and experiments can be analyzed insightfully, implications teased from the data, and new knowledge assembled about the teaching and learning of reading.

The total reading program for elementary and secondary schools could be organized around two general objectives: (1) basic skills, and (2) awareness, enjoyment, comprehension, and analysis of good literature in such forms as essays, poetry, prose, plays, biographies, novels, and reports. At each succeeding grade the objectives should require a higher degree of competence, a broader range of knowledge, and an increasing familiarity with the great storehouse of literature.

Writing

Concerns about the quality of students' writing seem second only to concerns about reading. Writing projects, usually funded by special grants, have delved into the causes and cures for poor writing. (See Nancy Olson 1981 for listing.) Many of these studies have upheld a principle frequently expressed by the National Council of Teachers of English: that if students concentrate in mechanics before they have any ideas down on paper to work with, they will learn to fear composing. (For example see Emig 1971, Haley-James 1981.) Suggestions are to encourage the student to think about the topic, then put promising ideas down on paper, reflect over them, then rearrange, clarify, and polish. At that point, punctuation and other mechanics would be checked.

One of the problems in teaching writing has been the way papers are graded. Papers may come back to the students slashed with red check marks or an X or a big question mark in the margin. Gordon Brossell has asserted that these markings have next to no instructional value. Teachers could improve instruction if they would confer with the student as well as write complete sentences in response to the student's lack of clarity or grammar problem. In some cases writing in a more appropriate word or expression or giving the reason for a different punctuation would be helpful to the student. This kind of instruction would serve both personal and social ends (1977, pp. 61–65).

Several of the writing projects have invented new ways of assessing students' papers, such as holistic scoring that uses a matrix or rubric which provides a way to identify types of competencies or errors. This is then followed by class discussion or student conference.

Some teachers have had success in teaching writing in the early grades by beginning with oral compositions. Pupils make up stories or narrate stories from their experiences, giving attention to organization, the progression of events, high points, and endings. Moving from oral presentations to written compositions reduces the tension, puts emphasis on creativity, and makes the mechanics contribute to rather than detract from the writing.

Basic academic competencies in writing that high school students ought to have include these listed by the College Board (1983, p. 8):

1. The ability to conceive ideas about a topic for the purpose of writing.
2. The ability to organize, select, and relate ideas and to outline and develop them in coherent paragraphs.
3. The ability to write standard English sentences with correct:
   sentence structure
   verbal forms
   punctuation, capitalization, possessives, plural forms, and other matters of mechanics
   word choice and spelling.
4. The ability to vary one's writing style, including vocabulary and sentence structure, for different readers and purposes.
5. The ability to improve one's own writing by restructuring, correcting errors, and rewriting.
6. The ability to gather information from primary and secondary sources; to write a report using this research; to quote, paraphrase, and summarize accurately; and to cite sources properly.

Advanced skills and knowledge of writing are also listed by the College Board (1983, p. 15):

1. The recognition that writing is a process involving a number of elements, including collecting information and formulating ideas, determining their relationships, drafting, arranging paragraphs in an appropriate order and building transitions between them, and revising what has been written.
2. The ability to write as a way of discovering and clarifying ideas.
3. The ability to write appropriately for different occasions, audiences, and purposes (persuading, explaining, describing, telling a story).
4. Skill and assurance in using the conventions of standard written English.

Writing competencies are *developed* abilities; the outcomes of learning, practice, and intellectual discussions. Writing skills are acquired when there is an encouraging learning environment. There are different levels of competency; beginning in the earliest years of schooling, opportunities to write—that is, compose—must be plentiful. Students must be encouraged (not discouraged with red ink), and as they progress through the grades they must be presented with higher expectations and increased standards as well as appropriate stimulation.

Speaking

Speaking as a field of study is one of the oldest subjects in the curriculum. The Greek philosophers studied it and used it along with dialectics. The Romans knew it as rhetoric, and Roman senators studied and practiced the art of oratory. In the latter part of the nineteenth and in the first decades of the twentieth centuries, studying oratory, declamations, and elocution was popular. For many years debates have been popular; they are currently used by candidates for public office to allow comparison of the strong and weak points in each candidate's platform.

In today's schools, however, speaking pursued as a language art to develop self-expression and to communicate effectively finds little space in the daily schedule. Drama and debate are usually relegated to extracurricular status, and "speech" is available as a special education area for those with a physical handicap in speaking.

Reasons are given for treating speaking lightly in the curriculum. One is that the school cannot teach everything; time in school is limited. In recent years one topic after another has been added to the curriculum, but seldom is one dropped. Another reason is that the preparation of elementary and secondary English teachers often leaves out training in speaking or else gives it only a nod.

Nevertheless, a balanced curriculum would provide for opportunities to conceive and develop ideas about a topic for the purpose of speaking to a group; to choose and organize ideas related to the topics; to present them in standard English; and to evaluate similar presentations by others. Students should develop the ability to take part constructively in class discussions and conferences with adults. The ability to ask and answer questions coherently and concisely is important, as is the ability to vary the use of spoken language to suit different occasions.

James Britton (1977) stresses the importance of language as a means of learning about the world. He has reviewed language acquisition studies and suggests, in the light of so much recent discovery about language and learning in infancy, that curriculum and instruction must be reorganized to provide time for talk between pupils. This would be a revolution of prevailing practice as studies have shown overwhelmingly that it is the teacher who talks most and specifies who talks when. Britton emphasizes that learning derives from performance, and speaking is one of the ways of representing experience.

Talking, listening, reading, and writing can be taught separately, but this is not advised. As these are various forms of language, any growth in one will have an effect on the others. Brossell emphasizes that the real "basics" of language usage are the need to communicate, the need to understand, the need to make meanings, and the need to interact (1977, p. 46).

As students progress through school, experiences that interweave speaking and listening are called for. Opportunities at all levels of schooling should be planned for students to exchange ideas constructively during class discussions, to answer and ask questions clearly and concisely, to develop ideas about a topic for speaking to a group, and to present ideas coherently in standard English. In the early years, an explanatory talk by a child may accompany a practical activity, such as caring for an aquarium, and be added to traditional "show and tell" presentations or story time. The beginnings of conversational or discussion skills can be developed in small groups of two, three, or four by pursuing topics chosen by the children.

Older students can profit by beginning a sequence of study with discussion of a topic or literary work and then continue with thinking, reading, reporting, and so on. Participation in discussions, panel presentations, debates, simulated press conferences, and summit meetings can entail clarifying issues, establishing meanings, probing, extending, and summarizing. Dramatic activities are valuable and can include charades, role-playing, simulations, and various kinds of interpretive work with dramatic scripts.

Listening

Although it is an integral part of the language arts, listening receives surprisingly little attention in the literature. Educators seem to assume that listening is an automatic attribute; all that is needed is for the student to "concentrate" on what is being said. Listening is a skill to be developed, however. The young child initially learns to speak by listening but soon goes beyond imitating and memorizing to seeing and learning from the effects. Unless the listening skill is consciously developed through schooling, it may be arrested on plateaus that inhibit learning.

Listening should be distinguished from merely hearing. It includes the ability to identify and comprehend the main and subordinate ideas in oral presentations and discussions, to accurately report what others have said, to detect propaganda or commercialism on television, and to participate meaningfully in class discussions. The ability to decode and translate auditory stimuli is as complex and specialized as the ability to obtain meaning from visual stimuli is. In teaching and learning, using both auditory and visual impressions is more effective than using either sense alone.

A modern curriculum depends on listening skills more than in past years because electronics have entered into instruction. Some schools and public libraries have developed and support electronic centers, including projectors, tape recorders, radios, television monitors, computers, and other types of teaching machines. Some school and college libraries have carrels in which a student may call up a single lecture or all the lectures of a course in sequence or listen to recordings of the artists. Social studies students can listen to public addresses by presidents of the United States. Important events may be recorded and preserved for future generations.

Class lessons may be recorded and used for later review by students. Students of speech or of music can learn to listen for pitch, timbre, and voice placement. Students in the natural sciences may record and study the songs of birds, the sounds of insects, the sound of waves dashing on the beach, or the sounds of other interesting phenomena. Foreign language students learn to speak and understand a new language by listening to tape recordings.

In curriculum planning for the language arts, it should be recognized that listening skills can be learned. Depending on the students' development, the curriculum should offer instruction that assists them in learning how to:

1. Determine whether posture and extraneous sounds and noises affect listening.
2. Choose the appropriate purpose for listening (information, appreciation, recreation, motivation, and analysis).
3. Find the central ideas.
4. Distinguish between the main points and details.
5. Keep a summary of the main points.
6. Distinguish between facts and opinions.
7. Detect the relevancy of statements.
8. Detect the motives of the speaker (informational, persuasive, or perhaps seeking active support by the listeners).
9. Examine what is said for its timeliness and usefulness.

The challenge in the language arts is obvious. From kindergarten through the twelfth grade, principals, curriculum directors, and teachers should create language-learning environments. Good language habits increase the ability to learn, promote mental health, and underlie constructive social interaction.

MATHEMATICS

In mathematics education it is important to look at where we have been and where it is possible to go as well as to examine critically the status of mathematics teaching today. Concerns about the mathematics skills of the young have attracted public press coverage since the 1950s. Although proposed reforms in mathematics education had been on the drawing boards at leading universities for several years before Sputnik's appearance, that event provided both impetus and funding. Commonly known as the "new math," this was later criticized for its formalized language, abstract techniques, and lack of relevance to everyday arithmetical uses. Specialists who were leaders in the creation of new teaching materials stressed the need

for a reorganization of subject matter so that students could approach the
subject through understanding the structure of the field; for example, in
terms of concepts like symbolism, number, relation, function, field,
measurement, and proof. Emphasis was on enabling the student to perceive
patterns rather than on utility. The nonutilitarian aspect helped to bring
about the "basics" backlash of the 1970s, but the problem-solving emphasis
of the new math and its encouragement of discovery methods have opened
new vistas of mathematics for students working with computers in the
1980s.

Basics

The back-to-basics movement of the early 1970s seemed to limit the
teaching of elementary mathematics to basic computation in addition,
subtraction, multiplication, and division. Alarm about declining test
scores, publicity of bad news about children's achievement, and pressure
from parents pervaded classrooms in ways that seemed to decrease
children's abilities to solve complicated problems. Drill on arithmetic facts
dominated over opportunities for perceptual leaps through mental
arithmetic, graphics and geometrical examples, or applications of set
theory. In turn, the publishing industry, which tends to play it safe, began
producing textbooks that emphasized rote learning.

In recognizing the need for computational skills, curriculum
development leaned heavily toward behavioristic models that subdivided
mathematical content into objectives or small bits of mathematical
knowledge. These were designed to be mastered in a sequential order that
would collectively produce coherence from related parts. The use of
behavioral objectives, according to researcher Donald Dessart (1981), made
a significant contribution to mathematics education because it sharpened
the focus on student behavior at the end of a learning activity. Achieving a
certain skill at a certain level made "pedagogical sense" as a means of
curriculum planning, and behavioral objectives have enjoyed considerable
popularity. Parents who were nostalgic for the good old days became
happier when their children could recite arithmetic facts.

However, it soon became evident to Dessart and other researchers that the
higher cognitive goals of instruction—critical thinking, creating, and
problem solving—were not being met by the behavioral objectives model.
While basic computation is necessary and must be learned, it can suffer
from overemphasis on rote and recipe learning. When this happens, the
child often fails to develop flexibility, the mental suppleness needed to
attack new and unfamiliar problems. With the advent of the pocket
calculator, it is no longer necessary to be a whiz kid at simple computation.
Currently, many teachers organize certain kinds of mathematical content,

such as algorithms, with a behavioristic theory, and problem solving with a holistic theory. In problem-solving processes, emphasis is on tolerance for manipulating the pieces of the problem in an orderly but not necessarily sequential manner so that the student may arrive at an insight or solution to the problem.

Society's Needs

A valid demand placed on curriculum makers is for them to recognize that some vocations and society as a whole require certain mathematical skills. Engineers, electricians, and accountants are needed. Individuals need to know how to use measuring devices, income tax tables, and figure interest. Metrics must be understood. These examples require problem-solving abilities as well as computational skills. The curriculum should be such that practical skills could be acquired as part of a more comprehensive mathematics that recognizes analytical and creative thinking as well as acquisition of facts.

Emerging Views

The importance of understanding concepts and processes and learning problem-solving skills cannot be overemphasized by curriculum planners. What many mathematics specialists suspected was confirmed in an assessment of mathematics achievement of American students by the National Assessment of Educational Progress (1982). Results showed that many skills had been learned at a superficial level, and many students had not learned basic problem-solving skills.

The emerging consensus is that problem solving and learning more advanced skills reinforce the learning of computational skills and provide meaning for their application. Problem solving should not be deferred until computational skills are "learned," according to Mary Grace Kantowski's research report (1981). Otherwise, the school will not prepare children for life in an advanced technological age. For example, the computer, probably the most important technological and cultural phenomenon of history, is insufficiently used thus far in the classroom. Even the pocket calculator is seldom seen there.

Although not the exclusive domain of one or the other, hand-held calculators in mathematics are primarily valuable for computational uses and microcomputers, for conceptual problem-solving uses. The calculator not only increases the quantity of exercises completed by students but also helps them discover decimals, negative integers, square roots, and large numbers. Providing students with calculators has the potential to open important mathematical ideas to students, including probability, statistics, functions, graphs, and coordinate geometry. At the same time they encourage positive attitudes toward mathematics. Microcomputers can permit students to work at different paces, select different paths to solutions, and provide cues or information needed. The graphics mode of a computer can allow the student to see figures as they are generated, thus aiding in the solution of complex problems.

Recommendations by Mathematics Leaders

A series of recommendations for curriculum developers of the 1980s was set forth by the National Council of Teachers of Mathematics (1981) with funding assistance from the National Science Foundation. The recommendations are that the focus of school mathematics must be on problem solving, and problem solving must be redefined to include a broad range of strategies, processes, and modes of presentation that will cover the full potential of mathematical applications. Teachers should not be limited to conventional "word problems." It was further stated that basic skills in mathematics must encompass more than computational facility. There should be increased emphasis on collecting, organizing, presenting, and interpreting data with estimation activities incorporated into all areas of the mathematics program. Estimation, a necessary tool in the use of calculators and computers, is an approximate calculation made mentally that assists the person in knowing whether the digital display or printout refers to tens, hundreds, thousands, or decimal fractions.

The National Council of Teachers of Mathematics further recommended that schools provide calculators and computers in adequate supply, that teaching time and instructional resources be apportioned to the importance of the mathematical topic to be presented, that more mathematics study be required of all students with a flexible range of options, and that the success of programs and student learning not be evaluated only by conventional testing. Minimum competencies are not to be construed as adequate; problem solving and its processes are to be evaluated as well.

The College Board (1983, pp. 9, 19-22) outlined in detail (a) basic competencies needed by all high school students prior to any avenue of postsecondary education or training, (b) skills and knowledge needed by students who expect to pursue an academic college education, and (c) more extensive proficiencies needed by those expecting to major in science or engineering or take advanced courses in mathematics or computer science. Only a few examples are given here. The levels of difficulty are lettered as shown above.

Computing

a. The ability to select and use appropriate approaches and tools in solving problems (mental calculation, trial and error, paper-and-pencil techniques, calculator, and computer).

b. Familiarity with computer programming and the use of prepared computer programs in mathematics.

   The ability to use mental computation and estimation to evaluate calculator and computer results.

   Familiarity with the methods used to solve mathematical problems when calculators or computers are the tools.

c. The ability to write computer programs to solve a variety of mathematical problems.

   Familiarity with the methodology of developing computer programs and with the considerations of design, structure, and style that are an important part of this methodology.

Statistics

a. The ability to use elementary concepts of probability and statistics.

b. The ability to gather and interpret data and to represent them graphically.

   The ability to apply techniques for summarizing data using such statistical concepts as average, median, and mode.

   Familiarity with techniques of statistical reasoning and common misuses of statistics.

c. Understanding of simulation techniques used to model experimental situations.

   Knowledge of elementary concepts of probability needed in the study and understanding of statistics.

Other content areas of mathematics in the College Board's recommendations for high schools—besides basic competencies—include algebra, geometry, and functions. This set of recommendations is consistent with that of other contemporary reform groups. All are concerned that people need, more than at any time in our past, fluency in mathematics so that they can contribute to and function well in today's and tomorrow's world.

SCIENCE

Problems facing the curriculum developer working on science education in America are enormous. These problems run the gamut of misconceptions about what is "basic" in science, overreliance on textbooks and didactic teaching methods, massive and expensive curriculum reforms that scarcely affect the classroom, to failure of most science teachers and curriculum leaders to recognize that the most important problems facing humankind today are not being considered in the schools. In an age of science, schools seem immune to its messages for curriculum and instruction (Sigda 1983).

A major study sponsored by the National Science Foundation (1980) emphasized that the role of science and technology is increasing throughout our society and that persons in a wide range of occupations other than scientific or engineering must have a greater understanding of science and technology than ever before. Yet our educational system does not now provide opportunities for most students to gain such an understanding.

Interviews with more than a hundred scholars, worldwide, by Harold Shane revealed a consensus that today's schools do not teach concepts that will help students understand the importance of a balanced man-to-nature interrelationship. These ideas are not built into the curriculum. The concepts of the interdependence of nations and peoples, evolution, population pressure, the limitations of the earth's nonrenewable resources, the unity of all living things, and the obsolescence of war as a way to resolve international conflicts are important matters for consideration by curriculum planners (Shane and Tabler 1981).

America's eminence in science is restricted to a relatively small number of elite graduates of its schools and colleges, who are unmatched anywhere in the field of scientific research. But America falls behind other highly industrialized countries in the scientific literacy of its average students, according to the NSF study. The Soviet educational mobilization in science and math is said to be far more threatening to the national security of the United States than the launching of Sputnik ever was (White 1982). Japan, an advanced technological country, is reported to be using products of the American science curriculum reforms from the sixties that were scarcely touched in this country.

Science does not seem to be a favorite subject area of high school students in the United States. Only one-fourth identified science as a preference. As a choice, they ranked it below English, mathematics, and social studies according to the third study of the National Assessment of Educational Progress (1978). In another study, Robert Stake and Jack Easley (1978) found that examples of elementary science teaching based on modern goals for science were rare, and recitation was the primary mode of teaching science in junior high, with little opportunity for experiential learning.

Happily, occasional elementary classrooms do capitalize on the eagerness and curiosity of youngsters by providing environments with scientific stimuli—terrariums, aquariums, geologic artifacts, instruments for measurement, and so on—as well as places where children can explore questions about the earth, space, living things, and ways of measuring.

Some of the skills to be learned in the elementary grades are (1) observing with increasingly powerful discrimination, (2) classifying objects into either similar or dissimilar groups, (3) describing what has been observed with increasing accuracy, (4) learning to pose appropriate questions, and (5) accumulating information. In the upper grades, science education should lead students to move from questioning to developing hypotheses to be tested followed by independent investigations in some depth. In the upper grades and high school, students should be able to find and use various resources to answer questions or solve problems. Students should appreciate the laboratory as a contrived environment (and concept) in which natural conditions may be simulated and solutions to questions tested. Thinking should become more analytical, and the fund of personal knowledge should be increasing.

In general, however, extensive surveys by the National Science Foundation and nine professional educational associations, reported by Roger Yager (1981), found that school science programs are usually characterized by textbooks. The textbooks seem to be about science but they do not discuss how to carry out scientific work. Laboratory and fieldwork are necessary for developing in students the abilities to distinguish between scientific evidence and opinion, to ask appropriate questions, to recognize the role of observation and experimentation in working toward scientific theories, and to organize and communicate the results obtained by experimentation.

Complex societal issues resulting from scientific and technological developments in the United States and other countries should be addressed intelligently in schools, according to the College Board report (1983). The benefits and risks inherent in these developments require a knowledge and understanding of science and its methods, including, for example, nuclear power, genetic engineering, fertilizers and pesticides, robotics, information and data processing, and organ transplantation.

The National Science Foundation report urges teachers to expand the science curriculum, not to be restricted to an outdated textbook and reliance on questions that are limited to the textbook's information, terminology, and definitions. The basics movement may have set back progress in science education. According to the same report (Yager 1981), science educators protest that science is basic but incorrectly conclude that the present science curriculum is adequate. A reexamination of science programs and purposes in light of new knowledge is needed.

The current status of science seems inconsistent with the huge infusions of federal funds that accompanied curriculum reform in science during the

1950s and 1960s. Since then, almost no change has taken place in the content or teaching methods in school science courses despite immense technological and social changes in the nation. The many current problems and predictable future ones that require scientific knowledge, understanding, and problem-solving skills are being neglected. Why is this? Community leaders in business and industry show an interest in science and concern about its curriculum. According to the National Assessment of Educational Progress (1978), at least one-fourth of the high school students are interested. However, according to Yager's analysis of survey findings, curriculum directors and science teachers are too comfortable with traditional courses, textbooks, methods, and out-of-date state curriculum guides to change and improve science programs and teaching. Leadership is needed, and increasing pressures for attention to quality in education will undoubtedly bring leadership forth.

The task of curriculum leaders is to initiate a major reexamination of the goals of science at all levels and in all of the disciplines of science. Norris Harms (1981), who headed Project Synthesis, a landmark study of needs in science education, recommends that decision makers examine the goals of science education to which they subscribe for consistency with these factors:

1. The needs of individuals to use science in their lives in an increasingly technological world.
2. The needs of an informed citizenry in dealing responsibly with science and technology-related issues.
3. The need to be aware of changes in emphasis within the various sciences.
4. The needs of students to make informed choices concerning their future careers and preparation for those careers.
5. The need to be cognizant of students' individual goals and potential ability.
6. The need to be aware of community resources, values, and expectations.

At all elementary and secondary levels of science education, developing the competencies associated with problem solving should be one of the major goals of curriculum development. This involves—in appropriate degrees at all levels of schooling—a science curriculum that assists students in identifying and formulating problems; proposing and evaluating ways to solve them; drawing reasonable conclusions from information found in various sources, whether written, spoken, or displayed in tables and graphs; and defending one's conclusions rationally. Problem-solving activities are those that lead to comprehension, development, and use of concepts and generalizations. In a world increasingly affected by developments in science and technology, the study of science is essential for responsible citizenship.

SOCIAL STUDIES

Contrasts and contradictions seem to characterize the current status of social studies education. Looking over the professional literature or attending a conference of the National Council for the Social Studies would imply that significant changes and innovations are underway in focus, content, and methodology. Then, sensational news reports on the activities of censors in some localities would suggest attempts by social studies teachers to introduce radical social reforms via their secondary school classrooms.

Yet the comprehensive three-part national survey sponsored by the National Science Foundation (Shaver et al., 1980) found that there had been little change, and this constituted the most ambitious and extensive study ever conducted on the status of social studies, science, and mathematics in American schools. Graduates of twenty years ago or more would generally find social studies classes today very similar to what they studied, although some schools have changed more than others. There is diversity yet sameness in the nation's social studies offerings.

There are more state-mandated courses in social studies than in any other subject area according to a survey by Joel Henning and others (1979). The most typical scope of the social studies curriculum in secondary schools is world geography and history, grade seven; American history, grade eight; civics or world cultures, grade nine; world history, grade ten; American history, grade eleven; and electives from government, sociology, psychology, economics, anthropology, or geography in grade twelve. There appears to be no justification for changing the label to *social science* instead of social studies, as systematic inquiry into social phenomena is rare in secondary schools.

The impact of the new social studies—that is, the products of the curriculum reform movement of the 1960s and 1970s—has been relatively slight. Nevertheless, important issues revolve around social studies education, and important tasks require responsible leadership for shared decision making in social studies curriculum development.

Three questions bring the social studies into focus for curriculum developers. Why did the curriculum reforms fail to capture the attention of the classroom teacher? What are the chief issues in social studies? What are the tasks facing local curriculum leaders?

Impact of Curriculum Reforms

Reasons given by teachers for their lack of interest in the projects of the curriculum reform era were: (1) the methodologies seemed to disrupt classroom control; (2) the movement to higher cognitive and open-ended objectives was uncomfortable; and (3) students' reading abilities were poor and attention to "basics" became a priority (Shaver 1980).

The greatest impact of the curriculum reforms of the 1960s and 1970s in social studies appears to have been on textbooks. Aspects of newer content have been incorporated, and the teachers' manuals suggest techniques for stimulating discussion or the decision-making processes. Sociological concepts and political behavior have been more widely accepted than anthropological themes.

Eliminating bias from history textbooks continues to be a problem. Textbooks of several years ago, as reported by Jimmie Linsin (1974), who analyzed five leading history texts, scarcely mentioned blacks. Women were portrayed as objects of weakness, and they were usually mentioned only as a relative of a notable male. Succeeding history textbooks, analyzed by Douglas Superka, Sharryl Hawke, and Irving Morrissett (1980) depicted a more racially and ethnically pluralistic society in America, with more members of minority groups and women in prominent roles, less chauvinism, less narrow nationalism, more information about people of various cultures, and more discussion of issues such as global interdependence. A newer study reported by Susan Walton (1983), titled "Ethnic Groups in History Textbooks," finds that contemporary writers seem to cast Americans into roles of oppressors and oppressed. The texts seem to stress the "victimization" of ethnic minorities in the United States and to neglect the broad perspectives of history and the contributions of various groups as well as the processes of integrating them into American society.

Contemporary textbooks in general tend to avoid controversial issues. They rely heavily on imparting information and lend themselves to lecture-recitation methods. They have been strongly influenced by the back-to-basics push, with emphasis on readability, chronology, name and place geography, and map skills, according to Irving Morrissett's survey (1983). He concluded that textbooks have inadequately treated the content of history, political science, and other social sciences (p. 46).

The curriculum reforms left elementary social studies virtually untouched, and the elementary curriculum has continued to use the expanding environment as its primary organizing theme. Current textbooks follow a pattern from kindergarten through sixth grade that moves from the home to the neighborhood and community, the state, the nation, and the world. Critics of this pattern can relate ridiculous anecdotes of its limitations, such as the first graders who asked the teacher questions about Afghanistan, inspired by television newscasts, and were told they would have to wait until sixth grade to learn about that.

The best known of the "new" social studies programs for elementary grades are Man: A Course of Study, which introduces anthropological concepts, and Our Working World, based on economic education. Both are Brunerian in principle; that is, they recognize Jerome Bruner's view (1960) that almost any concept can be taught at any grade level if presented clearly and appropriately.

The reforms did make a rich array of social studies materials available, although the National Science Foundation survey found that not more than one out of four social studies teachers used manipulative materials, and even fewer used electronic wares. Most popular among teachers was the overhead projector (Wright 1980).

Nevertheless, the reforms demonstrated that the book-lecture-paper method can be augmented with more discussion of problems and issues, skillful questions, the inquiry method, role playing, guest lecturers, projects, field studies, interviewing pioneers or political figures, student internships, and working in community projects. Textbooks can be expanded to include collateral readings, paperbacks, periodicals, pamphlets, posters, pictures, films, filmstrips, cassettes, videotapes, tapes, records, transparencies, charts, globes, atlases, simulation materials, dioramas, and artifacts brought back by friends, students, and faculty who visited foreign lands.

Issues in Social Studies

The social studies have frequently been targeted by special interest groups as the most accessible area of the school's curriculum for instructional components that work toward solutions to such major problems of society as peace, poverty, or the work ethic. These are problems that earlier generations would not have delegated to the public schools. Generally, classroom teachers have resisted the intrusions of special interests, and textbook publishers have tended to stay within traditional content boundaries. Still, basic social issues do need to be resolved, and curriculum leaders should be aware of them and their implications for curriculum improvement.

Socialization. A commonly accepted purpose of the social studies curriculum is socialization: teaching the young to observe the mores of the local community, respect group needs, conform to good behavior standards, and prepare for the next level of education. As society's priorities change, the emphasis of socialization changes; for example, from assimilation of immigrants to national patriotism under threat of war.

Critics frequently cite the socialization purpose of social studies as a weakness, and prefer social criticism, social reform, or individual rights as desirable goals.

Citizenship. Although citizenship is usually proclaimed as the major purpose of social studies education, disagreements persist regarding its interpretation. In 1916, the National Education Association's committee on social studies set forth citizenship as the foremost goal. Citizenship was defined in terms of knowledge, attitudes, and skills that would help students become citizens with positive attitudes toward the democratic process so that they would accept American core values as their own. In 1979, the National Council for the Social Studies reaffirmed this purpose and stated, "... the basic goal of social studies education is to prepare young people to be humane, rational, participating citizens in a world that is becoming increasingly interdependent" (p. 262). However, serious contradictions on what citizenship means have been pointed out by Suzanne Helburn (1977), who sees that attempts to encompass both a global view and national interests must stress the importance of recognizing the conflict between national goals and world needs and how to reconcile these two views of citizenship.

To clarify the concept of citizenship and its place in social studies, the Association for Supervision and Curriculum Development sponsored a national advisory panel that studied the components of basic citizenship in depth and identified the following basic competencies; these are suggested as guidelines for curriculum planners (Remy 1980, pp. 3-4):

1. *Acquiring and using information:* Competence in acquiring and processing information about political situations.
2. *Assessing involvement:* Competence in assessing one's involvement and stake in political situations, issues, decisions, and policies.
3. *Making decisions:* Competence in making thoughtful decisions regarding group governance and the problems of citizenship.
4. *Making judgments:* Competence in developing and using standards such as justice, ethics, morality, and practicality to make judgments about people, institutions, policies, and decisions.
5. *Communicating:* Competence in communicating ideas to other citizens, decision makers, leaders, and officials.
6. *Cooperating:* Competence in cooperating and working with others in groups and organizations to achieve mutual goals.
7. *Promoting interests:* Competence in working with bureaucratically organized institutions in order to promote and protect one's interests and values.

Basics. At the elementary levels, allocation of time to reading and writing has cut into that given to social studies, and the social studies textbook is frequently treated as another "reader." Even in secondary schools, there is considerable emphasis on reading the subject matter at the expense of developing higher cognitive skills.

Basic academic competencies suggested for high schools by the Educational EQuality Project of the College Board (1983), include an emphasis on study skills, most of which are highly pertinent to the social studies. Included are (p. 10):

1. The ability to set study goals and priorities consistent with stated course objectives and one's own progress, to establish surroundings and habits conducive to learning independently or with others, and to follow a schedule that accounts for both short- and long-term projects.
2. The ability to locate and use resources outside the classroom (for example, libraries, computers, interviews, and direct observation) and to incorporate knowledge from such sources into the learning process.
3. The ability to develop and use general and specialized vocabularies and to use them for reading, writing, speaking, listening, computing, and studying.
4. The ability to understand and follow customary instructions for academic work in order to recall, comprehend, analyze, summarize, and report the main ideas from reading, lectures, and other academic experiences; and to synthesize knowledge and apply it to new situations.
5. The ability to prepare for various types of examinations; to satisfy other assessments of learning in meeting course objectives.
6. The ability to accept constructive criticism and learn from it.

Inquiry. Teachers who were not schooled in inquiry processes in their own experience are unlikely to involve students in inquiry. There is so much content to be "covered" that most social studies teachers feel time is wasted when students are allowed to formulate problems and pursue their own investigations. However, teachers and curriculum leaders interested in changing the current mode should promote more use of investigative methods.

Student Motivation. A major problem reported in the literature of social studies courses is that of passive, unmotivated students. The implications for curriculum development seem obvious. Leadership is needed to help teachers see the relationship between a textbook-recitation focus and apathetic student reaction. Action is needed to raise the level of cognitive involvement of students.

Ideas for action are endless when creativity is encouraged. Studies of government are particularly rich in opportunities. Student governance can range from a sophisticated form in high school with development of a constitution, elections, and hearing procedures, to primary class discussions of the value of given rules related to specific incidents. High school classes can sponsor mock political conventions, United Nations meetings, or Supreme Court sessions. Middle-school students can brainstorm a question such as, "What would be missing in our community if there were no taxes?" They can follow a bill through the state legislature, keep in touch with their representative, and prepare a position statement to submit to that person after it has been thoughtfully critiqued by the class or teammates.

Older students can graph our national expenditures budgeted for a year and explore the principles on which each category is based: health, education, military, and foreign relations, for example. The latter can be better understood when the reasons for foreign allocations of food, money, and munitions are examined. In all types of activities, information must be gathered and examined analytically, and students must be expected to apply skills learned in other classes, such as English or mathematics.

Very young children can be introduced to mapping through doing their own sketches of home, school, or neighborhood. This can be followed by their explanations for designating certain services to certain areas. The concept of indexing can be livened through games of location and classification. History can be brought to life for any age group by interviewing people who have lived through historical events of the past fifty years or more.

Supervision. Curriculum assistance and leadership are seldom available for the social studies teacher. According to Zeb Wright, more than half of all districts provide no person with responsibilities for districtwide curriculum coordination. Even when employed, such supervisors have a multitude of tasks other than developing the social studies curriculum, with little time for contacts beyond bulletins and general meetings. Department chairpersons in some high schools provide a few services, but such posts are rare or nonexistent in junior, middle, or elementary schools (1980, pp. 11-12).

Central office supervisors, university professors, and state department officials are frequently viewed as too remote from the realities of today's classrooms to be of help. Enthusiasm about in-service sessions was found to be lacking by the National Science Foundation studies unless there were also opportunities to share ideas and concerns with other teachers. This suggests greater use of the influence and talents of master teachers within a district.

Controversial Topics. Students in social studies classes seem more likely to be studying about social reforms than participating actively in a reform movement led by a teacher, although the latter is not unheard of. While it may be easier to avoid controversy, it is also a responsibility of social studies teachers to provide ways for students to participate in social or political action by involvement in realistic experiences (not anarchical) that can develop skills in group leadership and decision making. Leaders can be interviewed; for example, of such causes as environmental protection, arms control, minority rights, or the work of the American Civil Liberties Union. Students can observe or volunteer for a time in agencies sponsoring controversial actions. When issues are studied, students should see that all sides are presented, and that facts are separated from opinions. Analysis of public issues can add an important dimension to citizenship education.

Tasks for Curriculum Development. Social studies is sometimes described as a stepchild, along with science, in the curriculum development activities of a school district. As such, it is long overdue for serious attention. Tasks ahead include finding ways to overcome the remoteness of supervision, curriculum assistance, and research from the day-to-day problems of the classroom. Practical assistance and solutions are needed for the realities of student apathy, sterile teaching methods, limited use of materials and resources, literacy problems, and grouping problems. The goals of social studies education are lofty; the current means to attain them seem narrow.

A vast knowledge about social studies and a wealth of ideas and resources await those who genuinely seek improvement. One natural development from the increase of information itself is the need for students to learn how to learn, how to draw on resources, how to analyze and apply information, and how to examine meaningful values. Harold Shane's interviews with distinguished social scientists from around the world pointed up the needs for young students to gain a sense of world history, of the various degrees of democracy, of efficacy in group decision making, of the nature of power in relation to national interests, and of probable sociopolitical developments likely to shape the world in the near future (1981, pp. 18-70).

Curriculum development should be geared toward teaching students that social studies encompass participation as well as just acquiring knowledge, attitudes, and skills.

FOREIGN LANGUAGES

A paradoxical situation currently exists in foreign language instruction in the United States: as a country, our need for global communication is enormous, yet very few students learn a second language. Foreign-language study recently hit an all-time low with only 15 percent of all high school students enrolled. This situation was called by a recent presidential commission a crisis that must be confronted (Simon 1980). Although the College Board lists foreign languages as one of the six important academic areas, the field has lost ground.

Concern about declining enrollments and the future of language study in the United States prompted the American Council on the Teaching of Foreign Languages to conduct a nationwide study of successful programs that can serve as models (Sims and Hammond 1981). Several common factors in superior foreign language programs were discovered, including these:

1. articulated curriculum
2. extensive co- and extracurricular activities that integrate language study into the fabric of school life
3. provision for a central organizing authority such as a coordinator
4. a high incidence of target language usage
5. special motivational techniques to promote such usage
6. good administrative support
7. an exploratory language course
8. unusually long course sequences
9. effective use of community resources
10. accommodation of a broad spectrum of students through a wide array of options for language study
11. study and travel abroad options; exchange programs
12. an especially strong, dynamic staff
13. provision for in-service training
14. a strong public relations effort
15. special recruiting techniques
16. a resolve to connect language study with the practical and concrete (pp. 1–2).

Exploratory and culture awareness courses, although controversial, are often included early in a foreign language sequence to attract and motivate students. Problems of attrition may arise later when students find that foreign language study also involves hard work requiring practice, memorization, homework, and effort in class. Some students do not expect an elective to require so much self-discipline. Caution is needed by teachers trained audiolingually as they may overdo audiolingual drill, which can be as stultifying as the now-obsolete grammar-translation drill.

Many ingenious ideas are available for holding the interest of students through a four-to-six-year sequence or longer. A few public schools are able to afford foreign language instruction in the elementary grades. This is conceded to be the best time to begin, but it is effective only if continued through several years of an articulated program. Students who tire of grammar study or are not interested in literature may find high school courses such as business Spanish or practical French more to their liking.

There is considerable, almost universal effort to approximate immersion conditions for learning a foreign language as the most important objective students have is to learn to communicate in another language. This means first listening and speaking and then, somewhat later, learning to read and write. Listening and speaking until some fluency is attained and a vocabulary developed form the first part of meeting this objective. Except for some directions and suggestions at the beginning of the course, the language may be spoken in class for the rest of the year. Grammar is taught as needed, and the formal study of grammar is postponed until the third or fourth year.

Anything depicting in some way the culture of the people whose language is being learned should be available in classrooms, including paperbacks, magazines, newspapers, posters, maps, paintings, carvings. As well there should be tapes, cassettes, phonograph records, and visits by immigrants who come to talk about the customs of their people and the economics of their countries.

Some high school classes have been able to raise enough money to send the entire class to the country they are studying during a vacation period. Meeting people and visiting with them provides an opportunity to practice speaking and listening to the language. Usually the hosts are as eager to try out their English as the students from the United States are to demonstrate their skills in the foreign language. Another and perhaps an even better program is the student exchange, which provides a school year abroad for American students, with foreign students coming to America. Students live in homes and are immersed in learning the language and the customs of that country. The host school usually finds it advantageous to invite the guest student to make presentations about his or her country and thus enrich the classroom experience.

Trends in foreign language instruction, identified by Jane Bourque, include emphasis on the ability to speak the foreign language and put it to practical use, emphasis on teaching culture for international understanding, involvement of more students by offering a variety of alternatives, and a search for better teaching techniques and more authentic materials. Interdisciplinary efforts are encouraged (1981, p. 479).

THE ARTS

Curriculum planners for the arts are almost certain to encounter special problems in local school districts. In the first place, the leadership responsibility for curriculum development may be vested in a generalist or principal who has little or no professional background in the arts, someone who may only dimly realize the potential of the arts for student growth and development. Even when leadership responsibility is assigned to an art educator, that person may not be interested in more than one branch of the arts or in the overall power of the arts to develop students' abilities to perceive and conceptualize. Too frequently, the art specialist is chiefly concerned with producing art exhibits or concerts.

The arts are too often placed off by themselves in school programs, relegated to a brief period of art or music once a week in the elementary school and regarded as nonsequential electives or extracurricular activities in the secondary schools. Only rarely does the curriculum include a full array of the arts: drawing, painting, sculpture, dance, poetry, drama, film, architecture, and so on.

Budget shortages are especially threatening to arts offerings in the public schools, probably because curriculum leaders have failed to educate boards of education, administrators, teachers, and the public on the impact that the arts can have when viewed as integral to the learning process. Parents want both reading and art in their children's curriculum, but if forced to choose, unguided, they will say that reading is a necessity and art a luxury.

Even the school environment works against curriculum planning for the arts in some localities as many classrooms are drab and sterile.

Potential

The perspective for what might be in arts education is comprehensive in nature. The curriculum plans should include a broad range of the arts and should be so designed that the arts are integrated into the education of every student, not just the few who seem to have special talents and interests. Kathryn Bloom (1980) stated she is convinced that:

...the quality of our individual lives and the quality of our society are directly related to the quality of our artistic life. We need the arts as the key to the higher order of things—our cultural heritage, our gift of expression, our creative faculty, our sense of beauty, ... We believe the arts could contribute as much to the general education of every child as science, social studies, and language arts.... We are once more searching for the substance of a viable humanism to rescue us from the excesses of our technology and we must find means to infect ourselves with the true contagion of the arts so that they cease to be something for the very few and become the experience of all (pp. 5, 7).

Curriculum planners should examine ways to capitalize on the potential of the arts for broadening and deepening the learning process. Conscious strategies can apply professional knowledge about the relationships of the arts to cognition. Extensive studies by David Olson (1978) on the cognitive functions of symbols and relevance to the arts are useful as background. Learning of all kinds relies on symbols. Schooling will be impoverished if it confines itself to the symbols of linguistics, mathematics, and cartography. The arts, which add limitless opportunities for understanding symbolic systems, provide an almost untapped dimension of learning. Symbols in the various arts can aid the student in discovery, thought, and emotional growth.

A curriculum for the arts that reaches only the sensory levels and not the perceptual would also be inadequate. It is a goal of arts education to provide instruction that allows students to become discriminating about and sensitive to the visual, aural, and kinetic data gathered or received from an arts object or event or environment and to analyze these data using aesthetic criteria. But *perceiving* implies a step beyond *sensing;* it requires experience with many kinds of stimuli and refinement through experience. Students, using symbols as the medium for communication, observed Stanley Madeja, can be taught not only to receive sense data from the arts but also to give meaning to those data, build concepts, and grow in knowing, perceiving, and expressing (1978, pp. 1–77).

The Setting

To maximize growth in intellectual development through the arts, the school and classroom should be a rich multisensory environment with changing stimuli. Anne Taylor (1977) recommends an environment that draws from many subject fields and finds relationships among them. Classrooms can be living museums, laboratories, and studios for learning. Art institutions in the community can be extended classrooms where students can become more aware of the historical and contemporary contexts of their lives.

The teacher must become an environmental manager, skillful in weaving experiences together and making the learning environment a stimulating aesthetic system for learning. Learning problems will not be solved by linear methods, but on a multilevel, multidisciplinary basis that relies on techniques from the arts for helping students interpret and internalize. For example, students in music classes will learn more than notation, counting, and how to memorize; they will understand that a piece of music is a statement about some aspect of life; that the composer is trying to communicate with the listener. At appropriate grade levels, students learn about melody, rhythm, timbre, pitch, accent, tempo, harmony, and volume. They become able to identify patterns in music and trace their development. To understand music thoroughly requires rigorous mental operations that involve quantitative as well as qualitative analyses. In its most sophisticated areas, such as composition, harmony, and counterpoint, music requires a high level of abstract thinking.

The visual arts have long been popular in successful schools, and a wide variety of media provides for a range of experiences. Drawing, painting, weaving, sculpturing can bring the creative imaginings of the students to life and can relate subject matter from many fields to the arts. An aesthetic backdrop for schooling is helpful in oral language development, in concept formation, in visual perception, and in forming critical aesthetic judgments. Film, a newcomer to the arts curriculum of many schools, provides a modern medium for expression that has unlimited possibilities.

The performing arts, especially drama, have a long history in education. Anthropologists have observed children in primitive societies acting out adult roles such as hunting, making war, stalking, preparing food, and other types of tribal behavior. Young children will willingly act out the worlds created by their imaginations and the real world that they know. The perceptive teacher will capitalize on the potential of drama in bringing life to literature and history. Insights and concepts can be learned through drama that might not otherwise be conveyed. In addition to generalized learnings, drama has its own competencies to be learned: pronunciation, enunciation, pacing, posture, movement, use of space, rhythm, and use of vocabulary. Rich possibilities can be explored through drama or even impromptu role playing in the classroom.

Dance has an important part in the educational process. It is one of the primary forms of human expression and has appeared in some form in all cultures. Primitive tribes expressed group rituals in dance. The Bible offers various Old Testament descriptions of dance in celebration of important events. The ritualistic and symbolic dances of the Japanese are known and admired in all parts of the world. Some of the most sublime and creative works of the twentieth century have been expressed in dance—ballet, classical, and modern dance. Geraldine Dimondstein (1971) observed that:

Studies from psychology and kinesiology tend to support the belief that from an activity point of view, movement is basic in children's learning. It may even be that movement is the initial way in which a child begins the creative process, and that within an appropriate setting, may be inspired to release that creative potential through dance. No one can determine the extent of children's imaginative or creative abilities.... Dance finds its image through gestures that are not real, but that are created and shaped. Thus, it is not a purely visual art like painting, it is not plastic in the same sense as sculpture, nor is the presentation of fantasy the same as that in poetry. Its similarity to other arts is that feelings and ideas are expressed in symbolic form. Its distinctive characteristic is that it is a kinesthetic-visual image made tangible by means of the body (pp. 3, 5).

Dance as a part of the educational program of the schools is not "subject matter" in the traditional sense; however, there is a mode of knowledge to be learned. Concepts include space (direction, level, path, range), time (rhythm, beat, measure, phrasing), and force (sustained, percussive, swinging). Problem solving is a part of the dance curriculum through exploration of concepts using related movement elements in various contexts. Because dance is an art form and not simply a physical activity, the perception must be aesthetic. Communication is through movement.

The value of dance as an art is to help students achieve an awareness of organizing their perceptions and feelings and expressing them through movement.

Progress

Despite the obstacles peculiar to developing a curriculum in the arts, progress is showing up in many schools. There is a new awareness that the arts, singly or in combination, can contribute to understandings in many areas of the school's curriculum. There is also a growing awareness that the arts are a universal human phenomenon, a means of expression since ancient times that can promote deeper understanding and acceptance today among persons of dissimilar cultural backgrounds.

Resources and support for the arts are continuing to appear. The College Board has included the visual and performing arts as one of the six essential areas that comprise the basic academic curriculum for high schools (1983). The JDR 3rd Fund, originated by John D. Rockefeller III, has sponsored extensive programs and disseminated information about them as sources for ideas on including the arts in the general education of all students (Fowler 1980). The Alliance for Arts Education, headquartered in the John F. Kennedy Center for the Performing Arts, Washington, D.C., has stimulated programs at state levels to incorporate community resources for the arts into school programs. The Aesthetic Education Program of Cemrel, Saint Louis, Missouri, has produced extensive arts-related interdisciplinary curriculum materials for elementary and middle schools.

Curriculum development in the arts has been "painted with a wide brush" in this chapter, as have the other major subject fields. Our intent was to provide a background for curriculum decisions that will be attentive to the many content factors necessary for providing a comprehensive curriculum.

REFERENCES

Bloom, Kathryn. "Defining the Task." In *An Arts in Education Source Book,* edited by Charles Fowler, pp. 1-7. New York: American Council for the Arts, 1980.

Bourque, Jane M. "Trends in Foreign Language Instruction." *Educational Leadership* 38 (March 1981): 478-81.

Britton, James. "Language and the Nature of Learning: An Individual Perspective." In *The Teaching of English,* part I, pp. 1-38. Seventy-sixth Yearbook of the National Society for the Study of Education. Chicago: University of Chicago Press, 1977.

Brossell, Gordon C. "Developing Power and Expressiveness in the Language Learning Process." In *The Teaching of English,* part I pp. 39-65. Seventy-sixth

Yearbook of the National Society for the Study of Education. Chicago: University of Chicago Press, 1977.

Bruner, Jerome S. *The Process of Education*. Cambridge, Mass.: Harvard University Press, 1960.

The College Board. *Academic Preparation for College: What Students Need to Know and Be Able to Do*. New York: The College Board, 1983.

Dessart, Donald J. "Curriculum." In *Mathematics Education Research: Implications for the 80s*, edited by Elizabeth Fennema, pp. 1-22. Alexandria, Va.: Association for Supervision and Curriculum Development, 1981.

Dewey, John. *Democracy and Education*. New York: Macmillan Co., 1916.

Dimonstein, Geraldine. *Children Dance in the Classroom*. New York: Macmillan Co., 1971.

Emig, Janet. *The Composing Processes of Twelfth Graders*. Urbana, Ill.: National Council of Teachers of English, 1971.

Fowler, Charles, ed. *An Arts in Education Source Book*. New York: The JDR 3rd Fund, 1980.

Haley-James, Shirley M., ed. *Perspectives on Writing in Grades 1-8*. NCTE Committee on Teaching Written Composition. Urbana, Ill.: National Council of Teachers of English, 1981.

Harms, Norris, and Yager, Robert E. *What Research Says to the Science Teacher*, vol. 3. Monograph. Washington, D.C.: National Science Foundation, 1981.

Helburn, Suzanne W. "Characteristics and Needs of Society as Sources of Curricula in Citizen Education." *Link*. Newsletter of the Social Science Education Consortium. September 1977.

Henning, Joel F., et al. *Mandate for Change: The Impact of Law on Educational Innovation*. Chicago: The American Bar Association, 1979.

Institute for Research on Teaching. "What are the Consequences of Instruction?" *Communication Quarterly* 4 (Spring 1981) 2.

Kantowski, Mary Grace. "Problem Solving." In *Mathematics Education Research: Implications for the 80s*, edited by Elizabeth Fennema, pp. 111-26. Alexandria, Va.: Association for Supervision and Curriculum Development, 1981.

Linsin, Jimmie. *An Analysis of the Treatment of Religion, the Blackman, and Women in American History Textbooks Used by the Public, Private, and Parochial High Schools of the City and County of Saint Louis, Missouri, 1972-73*. Dissertation. Saint Louis University, 1974.

Madeja, Stanley S., ed. *The Arts, Cognition, and Basic Skills*. Saint Louis, Mo.: Cemrel, 1978.

Morrissett, Irving, ed. *Social Studies in the 1980s*. Alexandria, Va.: Association for Supervision and Curriculum Development, 1983.

National Assessment of Educational Progress. "Analyzing Literature Difficult for Many." *National Assessment of Educational Progress Newletter* 15 (Fall 1981): 1-2.

National Assessment of Educational Progress. *Changes in Mathematical Achievement, 1978-82; Mathematical Applications; Mathematical Skills and Knowledge; and Mathematical Understandings*. Denver: National Assessment of Educational Progress, 1982.

National Assessment of Educational Progress. *Science: Third Assessment*. Denver: National Assessment of Educational Progress, 1978.

National Council for the Social Studies. "Revisions of the NCSS Social Studies Guidelines." *Social Education* 43 (April 1979): 261–78.

National Council of Teachers of Mathematics. *An Agenda for Action and Priorities in School Mathematics*. Reston, Va.: National Council of Teachers of Mathematics, 1981.

National Education Association. *Social Studies in Secondary Education*. A report of the Committee on Social Studies on the Reorganization of Secondary Education of the National Education Association. Bulletin No. 28. Washington, D.C.: Bureau of Education, 1916.

National Science Foundation. *Science and Engineering Education for the 1980s and Beyond*. Washington, D.C.: U.S. Government Printing Office, October 1980.

Olson, David R. "The Arts as Basic Skills: Three Cognitive Functions of Symbols." In *The Arts, Cognition, and Basic Skills*, edited by Stanley S. Madeja, pp. 59–81. Saint Louis, Mo.: Cemrel, 1978.

Olson, Nancy S. "Writing Instruction." *ASCD Curriculum Update*. Newsletter. Alexandria, Va.: Association for Supervision and Curriculum Development, June 1981.

Remy, Richard C. *Handbook of Basic Citizenship Competencies*. Alexandria, Va.: Association for Supervision and Curriculum Development, 1980.

Shane, Harold G., and Tabler, M. Bernadine. *Educating for a New Millenium*. Bloomington, Ind.: Phi Delta Kappa Educational Foundation, 1981.

Shaver, James P.; Davis, O. L.; and Helburn, Suzanne M. "An Interpretive Report on the Status of Precollege Social Studies Education Based on Three NSF-Funded Studies." In *What Are the Needs in PreCollege Science, Mathematics, and Social Science Education? Views from the Field*, pp. 3–18. Washington, D.C.: U.S. Government Printing Office, 1980.

Sigda, Robert B. "The Crisis in Science Education and the Realities of Science Teaching in the Classroom." *Phi Delta Kappan* 64 (May 1983): 624–27.

Simon, Paul. *The Tongue-Tied American: Confronting the Foreign Language Crisis*. New York: Continuum, 1980.

Sims, William D., and Hammond, Sandra B. *Award Winning Foreign Language Programs: Prescription for Success*. Skokie, Illinois: National Textbook Co., 1981.

Stake, Robert E., and Easley, Jack A., Jr. *Case Studies in Science Education*. Washington, D.C.: U.S. Government Printing Office, 1978.

Superka, Douglas P.; Hawke, Sharryl; and Morrissett, Irving. "The Current and Future Status of the Social Studies." *Social Education* 44 (May 1980): 362–69.

Taylor, Anne. "Needed: Aesthetic Learning Environments." In *Arts and Aesthetics: An Agenda for the Future*, edited by Stanley S. Madeja, pp. 331–351. Saint Louis, Mo.: Cemrel, 1977.

Walton, Susan. "Revised History Textbooks Creating 'New Myths' about Minorities." *Education Week* 2, May 18, 1983, p. 6.

Walton, Susan. "Lack of Comprehension Skills Traced to Oversimplified Texts." *Education Week* 1, November 23, 1981, p. 7.

White, Eileen. "Sputnik at 25." *Education Week* 2, October 13, 1982, pp. 11, 18.
Wright, J. Zeb. "The Status of Precollege Social Studies Educational Practices in U.S. Schools." In *What Are the Needs in Precollege Science, Mathematics, and Social Science Education? Views from the Field*, pp. 147-57. Washington, D.C.: U.S. Government Printing Office, 1980.
Yager, Robert E. "Science Education." *ASCD Curriculum Update*. Newsletter. Alexandria, Va.: Association for Supervision and Curriculum Development, September 1981, 1-6.

ADDITIONAL READINGS

Adler, Mortimer J. *How to Speak / How to Listen*. New York: Macmillan Co., 1983.
Bellack, Arno, et al. *The Language of the Classroom*. New York: Teachers College Press, 1966.
Brinckerhoff, Richard F., "The Current Crisis in Secondary Schools Science Education—and One Response." *National Association of Secondary School Principals Bulletin* 66 (January 1982): 40-49.
Glatthorn, Allan. *Writing in the Schools: Improvement Through Effective Leadership*. Reston, Va.: National Association of Secondary School Principals, 1982.
Hill, Shirley A., et al. *Changing School Mathematics: A Responsive Process*. Arlington, Va.: American Association of School Administrators, 1982.
Smith, B. Othanel. "Curriculum Content." In *Fundamental Curriculum Decisions*, pp. 30-39. Yearbook of the Association for Supervision and Curriculum Development. Alexandria, Va.: ASCD, 1983.
Stake, Robert E., ed. *Evaluating the Arts in Education*. Columbus, Ohio: Charles E. Merrill, 1975.
Wallace, Daisy G., ed. *Developing Basic Skills Programs in Secondary Schools*. Alexandria, Va.: Association for Supervision and Curriculum Development, 1982.
Weinland, Thomas P. "On Revitalizing the Social Studies Curriculum." *Phi Delta Kappan* 63 (March 1982): 442-43.

8

Implementing Curriculum Plans

Concerns at all levels have appeared about costly new curriculum plans and products that were never implemented—never actually used in schools and classrooms. The funds poured into curriculum improvement at the national level by the federal government and private foundations during the "decade of reform"—roughly 1955–1965—was unprecedented in history. But many of those innovative curriculum programs died on the vine, even though they were said to have been initiated and adopted by local school districts.

The Rand Corporation made a comprehensive nationwide study of the implementation of twenty-nine federal programs. Interviews, classroom observations, surveys, and studies of documents were all used to gather the data (Berman and McLaughlin 1975, 1976). The researchers found that federal efforts to promote innovations had resulted in little consistent or stable improvement in student outcomes and that innovative practices had frequently not been implemented as planned.

Similar findings were reported by John Goodlad and Frances Klein, who made observations in many classrooms of varying socioeconomic backgrounds. They concluded that "many of the changes we have believed to be taking place in schooling have not been getting into classrooms; changes widely recommended for the schools over the past 15 years were blunted on the school and classroom door" (1970, p. 97).

Apparently problems with curriculum implementation are not unique to programs developed outside the school system and then imposed on the school. Curriculum guides and new programs developed within school systems in response to self-identified needs are frequently not actually implemented, according to Fenwick English (1980). The guide often reposes unused on a shelf behind the teacher's desk, although at the same time the superintendent may be announcing the virtues of this new program in public relations bulletins to the community.

It is probable that approaches to curriculum implementation are often too shallow or simplistic. Implementing curriculum is a developmental phenomenon; a highly complex process of establishing mutual goals, applying knowledge, and using collaborative, systematic procedures for reaching those goals. Curriculum implementation does not lend itself to generalized how-to-do-it prescriptions. Decker Walker emphasizes that point:

... I doubt whether we shall ever see useful wide generalizations about curriculum change because so much depends on the particulars—the particular subject involved and the particular reforms being pursued, the particular climate of the times, what else happens to be going on at the same time, the particular locale with its unique actors. This situation is not cause for despair, but rather for caution and modest expectations... The image of the technician at the control panel directing the entire operation needs to be replaced with a more realizable one, perhaps that of the mountaineer using all of the tricks of modern science, together with personal skill and courage and an intimate study of the particular terrain, to scale a peak (1976, pp. 51–52).

Although a universal prescription for implementation has not emerged, studies have provided insights into factors affecting implementation, levels of implementation, and components of successful examples of implementation.

FACTORS AFFECTING IMPLEMENTATION

The Rand studies revealed several factors that affected the implementation of federal programs. Motive played an important part. Projects generated in essence by opportunism, that is, availability of funds, seemed to be characterized by a lack of interest and commitment on the part of local participants from the top down, administrators to classroom teachers. As a result, very little improvement took place. On the other hand, much more favorable results occurred when a problem-solving motive for projects arose in response to locally identified needs and was combined with a strong local commitment to address those needs.

Participants' receptivity was an essential factor but not sufficient by itself. Associated with the problem-solving motive, strong attitudes, and commitment was a necessary process termed *mutual adaptation* by the Rand investigators. This involved a variety of adjustments, which may not have led to a full achievement of the project's goals but typically increased the likelihood of changes in teacher behavior and organizational practices. Flexibility in coping with unanticipated implementation problems was found by the Rand studies to be an essential factor (Berman and McLaughlin 1975, 1976).

Other observers of the change process point out that questionable assumptions about implementation are illustrated by linear models with step-by-step recipes for sequence. Seymour Sarason (1971) questions the linear approach as an assumption and cites the unique differences among settings and the complicated network of human beings that make up a school. Variations in organizational structure, styles of leadership, cultural backgrounds, historical circumstances, vested interests, and interpersonal norms among school districts tell us that those who seek curriculum leadership must understand the complexity and uniqueness of each school. There is no single change strategy that will be unfailingly effective in a variety of schools. The school's culture must be respected and accepted for what it is; local resources must be adapted as necessary for effective curriculum implementation.

Another inadvisable approach, in addition to using one change strategy to fit all, is to issue orders from the top and expect them to be transmitted unchanged through channels until they are ultimately carried out by the classroom teacher. Teachers are jealous of their autonomy in curriculum matters, Allan Glatthorn (1981) has observed, and they may strongly resist attempts by district supervisors to control what they do day-by-day in the classroom. Theodore Czajkowski and Jerry Patterson deplore any curriculum implementation that smacks of manipulation or reflects lack of respect for the users. They suggest that derogatory terms which appeared in the "reform" literature set back implementing of new programs: for example, "teacher-proof curriculum," "clients," and "change agents." Communications about "installing packages," "transmitting" or "disseminating" curriculum products were also demeaning, in their view (1980, pp. 158–59).

Michael Fullan and Alan Pomfret did an extensive review of the research on curriculum and instruction implementation that is a valuable resource in that field. They found that there is no substitute for personal contact. Among other things they concluded:

If there is one finding that stands out in our review, it is that effective implementation of social innovations (those that require role changes) requires time, personal interaction and contacts, in-service training, and other forms of people-based support. Research has shown time and again that there is no substitute for primacy of personal contact among implementers, and between implementers and planners/consultants, if the difficult process of unlearning old roles and learning new ones is to occur. Equally clear is the absence of such opportunities on a regular basis during the planning and implementation of most innovations. All this means is that new approaches to educational change should include longer perspectives, more small-scale intensive projects, more resources, time and mechanisms for contact among would-be implementers at both the initiation and adoption stages, and especially during implementation. Providing these resources may not be politically and financially feasible in many situations, but there is no question that effective implementation will not occur without them (1977, pp. 391-92).

Still another factor that can determine whether the proposed plan will be implemented is that of clarity versus ambiguity as to what behaviors teachers will be expected to perform. Fullan and Pomfret found that lack of thorough exploration of the proposed program at the outset invariably led to confusion and frustration later and a low degree of implementation (1977, pp. 368-69). Teachers want to know in advance what the essential features of the curriculum change will be and what it will mean in terms of their roles.

Realities

Bruce Joyce (1981), who has made extensive studies of in-service and preservice practices, training, and research findings, outlined several realities that affect the quality of staff development in today's schools. These can be summarized as follows:

Privatism: Most teachers are isolated from one another. Few teachers have opportunities to observe other teachers at work and have little idea of what is done well and what is done poorly.

Cynicism: It seems to be in vogue for teachers to view in-service offerings as not very helpful. Thus, well-planned and effective staff development programs must struggle against this preconception. Also, teachers are often negatively critical of the training leader. University professors, local supervisors, and building administrators must establish credibility—often against strong odds.

Lack of experience with powerful training options: Many educators have never experienced really effective and powerful training. To learn new teaching strategies, teachers need to study theory, see demonstrations, have opportunities for practice with analytic feedback, and receive coaching on site. Trainers need professional expertise that combines all of these elements.

Developing problem-solving modalities: A social climate is needed in which faculties can work comfortably together in attacking problems. The reality of privatism works against this factor, but it is quite possible to overcome and establish an energetic commitment to cooperative problem solving.

Initial training: There are several gaps between preservice and in-service education. In the first place, the preservice training period is extremely short considering the immensity of the task to be done. Frequently the theory learned in the university does not match the practice that the new teacher sees in the schools. Very few teachers are familiar with alternative styles of teaching or how to use them.

Pressures toward normative teaching: Once the teacher arrives at the teaching post, pressures toward the recitation style dominate. Trying alternatives is risky in several ways. Students may question a new technique and show a lack of cooperation; other teachers and community members may be suspicious of the performance and see it as ineffective by their standards; and the initiating teacher may be uncomfortable with an uncommon methodology. A social climate that encourages risk taking and provides protection for the teacher to experiment is necessary if there is to be progress beyond the normative mode.

Self-concept: Unless teachers have reached a state of self-actualization and have acquired substantial competencies, the realities of the classroom, described above, will inhibit professional growth.

To overcome these and other negative factors, every teacher and school administrator should be a student of teaching. They should constantly study the profession, polishing their skills, developing new ones, rethinking the curriculum of the school, and making the learning environment more challenging and effective.

The primary task of staff development, according to Bruce Joyce (1981, p. 118) is threefold: to enrich the lives of educators, to generate uninterrupted efforts to improve schools, and to create conditions that enable continuous professional skill development. A storehouse of information and ideas is available to make this a reality. That is the theme of this chapter and its focus on curriculum implementation.

Levels of Maturity

Participants in in-service programs will perform at different levels of maturity unrelated to their actual ages or years of service. Paul Hersey and Kenneth Blanchard (1982) describe four degrees of maturity, and they recommend variations in situational leadership styles to match the maturity levels of the participants for more effective task outcomes (pp. 152–55).

Maturity Level One represents people who are both unable and unwilling to take responsibility for a task because they are insecure about their competence and lack confidence. These persons need a directive "telling" style that provides clear, specific instructions and close supervision.

Maturity Level Two includes people who lack skills but are willing to learn. They are confident and enthusiastic. The appropriate leadership style here is a "selling" style that provides most of the direction and offers support. Through two-way communication and explanation, this approach gradually helps the participants become more self-directed.

Maturity Level Three describes people who are able and competent but unwilling to move ahead, often because of a lack of confidence or feelings of insecurity. Hersey and Blanchard recommend a facilitating, nondirective style of leadership at this level. By two-way communication and active listening, the leader opens the door to support the participants' abilities and confidence.

Maturity Level Four includes those who are able, willing, and confident to take responsibility. A delegating style of leadership that provides little direction or support has a high probability of effectiveness with individuals at this maturity level. While the leader may identify the problem, responsibility for carrying out plans is given to these participants.

Involving persons at all levels of maturity should lead to their professional growth through carefully planned in-service programs. As teachers become reasonably competent in one kind of technique, they can begin to learn another with the help of leaders or peers. As this type of learning continues, teachers accumulate knowledge and proficiency; their feelings and attitudes change, and they become more open to new approaches and less fearful of risks. Motivation to continue self-improvement on their own initiative is more likely. Certainly the principal must be involved as a participant if not as leader. The principal's support is critical for success of the enterprise and essential in an advocate role.

The in-service program should be rich in instructional methodology, acquiring a variety of teaching styles to match the variety of students' learning styles. More than a few classroom observers have noted that most teachers rely almost exclusively on one or two methods: textbook-workbook, lecture-recitation, or reports on reading materials. By bringing together interactive groups of teachers, a wealth of exciting ideas and techniques can be shared: inquiry methods, simulations, projects, independent creative investigations, contracts, problem solving with computers, debates, panels, role playing, use of electronic resources, and field studies. Choices like these and others can add interest for students and teachers alike, providing a break from otherwise dull routines.

LEVELS OF IMPLEMENTATION

Implementation is not a clear-cut yes or no division into either using or not using an innovation; it is developmental and occurs in different levels or degrees. The study of implementation is one of the research thrusts of the Research and Development Center for Teacher Education at the University of Texas at Austin. Researchers Gene Hall and Susan Loucks (1977) have studied classrooms directly to obtain data on implementation. They noted that the only way to know for sure whether and how an innovation was being used is to assess each individual's use directly. Assumptions that the new curriculum program is being used because materials have been purchased, classrooms rearranged, or in-service training conducted are unreliable. These may indicate implementation is on the way but still at a very low level.

From dozens of classroom observations, focused interviews, follow-up probes, clinical experiences, and case notes, the center's research verified that there are eight levels indicating degrees of curriculum implementation. The focus was not on how the users felt about the innovation but on what they were actually doing about it. Figure 13 illustrates the levels of use and the decision point at each development level (1977, pp. 266-67).

DIMENSIONS OF IMPLEMENTATION

Implementation occurs not only in developmental stages, but it also consists of five dimensions, all pertaining to any given innovative curriculum program as shown by Fullan's and Pomfret's studies (1977, pp. 361-65). These dimensions are (1) subject matter or materials, (2) organizational structure, (3) role or behavior, (4) knowledge and understanding, and (5) value internalization.

Subject matter refers to content and is most often identified by an area, such as mathematics, science, history, English, and so on. In this context, subject matter refers to the order in which the content is to be conveyed, media to be used (written materials, spoken word, audiovisual materials and demonstrations), and may include tests or student assessment forms. *Organizational structure* involves changes in formal arrangements and physical conditions: allocation of time, allocation of space, and assignment or grouping of students.

Role relationship change is an essential dimension of implementing new curriculum plans, which implies more than changing a single role. Such change involves all the roles within a given relationship. Implementation may concern new teaching styles, new tasks (such as new requirements for planning and interaction), new relationships between teachers and supervisors or teachers and students, and new learning process skills to be acquired by students.

Knowledge and understanding are needed about the innovation's philosophy, values, assumptions, objectives, subject matter, implementation strategies, and other organizational components, especially role

Figure 13. Levels of Use of the Innovation

Levels of Use	Definition of Use
0 Nonuse	State in which the user has little or no knowledge of the innovation, no involvement with the innovation, and is doing nothing toward becoming involved.
Decision Point A	*Takes action to learn more detailed information about the innovation.*
I Orientation	State in which the user has recently acquired or is acquiring information about the innovation and/or has recently explored or is exploring its value orientation and its demands upon user and user system
Decision Point B	*Makes a decision to use the innovation by establishing a time to begin.*
II Preparation	State in which the user is preparing for first use of the innovation.
Decision Point C	*Changes, if any, and use are dominated by user needs*
III Mechanical Use	State in which the user focuses most effort on the short-term, day-to-day use of the innovation with little time for reflection. Changes in use are made more to meet user needs than client needs. The user is primarily engaged in a stepwise attempt to master the tasks required to use the innovation, often resulting in disjointed and superficial use.
Decision Point D	*A routine pattern of use is established.*
IV Routine	Use of the innovation is stabilized. Few, if any, changes are being made in ongoing use. Little preparation or thought is being given to improving innovation use or its consequences.

	Decision Point E	*Changes use of the innovation based on formal or informal evaluation in order to increase client outcomes.*
V	Refinement	State in which the user varies the use of the innovation to increase the impact on clients within the immediate sphere of influence. Variations are based on knowledge of both short- and long-term consequences for clients.
	Decision Point F	*Initiates changes in use of innovation based on input of and in coordination with what colleagues are doing.*
VI	Integration	State in which the user is combining own efforts to use the innovation with related activities of colleagues to achieve a collective impact on clients within their common sphere of influence.
	Decision Point G	*Begins exploring alternatives to or major modifications of the innovation presently in use.*
VII	Renewal	State in which the user reevaluates the quality of use of the innovation, seeks major modifications of or alternatives to present innovation to achieve increased impact on clients, examines new developments in the field, and explores new goals for self and the system.

From Gene E. Hall and Susan F. Loucks. "A Developmental Model for Determining Whether the Treatment Is Actually Implemented," *American Educational Research Journal* 14 (Summer 1977), pp. 266–67. Copyright 1977, American Educational Research Association, Washington, D.C.

relationships. *Value internalization* is the fifth dimension and must be linked to the specific aspects of the other four. Valuing an innovation at a global level is not sufficient in itself for implementing it; the various dimensions must be valued as well.

COMPONENTS OF SUCCESS

Adequate planning, effective use of strategies, and the capacity of the adopting unit for implementation are all characteristics of the successful examples reviewed in the literature.

Planning

Planning for implementation is critical in the process of curriculum improvement. Frequently, the planning process extends only as far as creating new ideas or adopting them from elsewhere, initiating a process, and developing the new or revised curriculum plan, but then it stops short of planning out the actual implementation process. Essential strategies for implementation, which may require two years or more for development, include: acquiring sufficient resources, involving the implementers on a continuing basis, and arranging for planned channels or two-way communication among the participants.

Strategies

Plans for the strategies of the implementation process should be explicit about such things as in-service training, resource support, feedback mechanisms, and participation. These elements are interactive and mutually reinforcing. The presence of any one without the others would limit if not eliminate its effectiveness.

In-service. Intensive in-service training as opposed to single workshops or preservice education is important for implementing any new curriculum and instruction plans. Bruce Joyce and Beverly Showers (1981) concluded from a lengthy examination of research that the major essentials for in-service training are: presenting the underlying theory or philosophy of the innovation, demonstrating skills or models of teaching the new approach, practicing in simulated or classroom settings, providing feedback information about performance and hands-on, in-classroom assistance with the new modes of teaching. These elements have seldom all been present in local in-service programs, yet their inclusion may determine whether curriculum implementation will succeed or fail.

Other studies have examined contrasts between successful and unsuccessful in-service programs. An extensive study of in-service programs was part of the series of surveys organized by the Rand Corporation (Berman and McLaughlin 1975, Berman and Pauly 1975) in local school districts across the country, which included more concentrated field work in thirty districts, Rand researchers discovered that no single conceptual model seemed to form the basis of most staff development programs. Rather there appeared to be a hodgepodge of miscellaneous workshops and courses. The study distinguished between successful and unsuccessful staff development programs. The unsuccessful programs relied on a deficit model, which assumed that teachers were not very competent and that the administration knew what teachers' deficits were and what would be best for them to do. These unsuccessful examples relied on required workshops, teacher-proof packages imported from various development centers, and outside consultants used in a lecturer mode. The general rule of these programs was to use time outside of school hours with some use of summer work in advance of the school year but little or no released time during the school term.

The more successful models studied by Rand were developmental models in which the teachers participated in solving problems. These models were more a point of view rather than a program, and teachers were viewed as professionals. Learning-by-doing was the theme with local leaders in charge. Local materials were developed by the teachers, and this stage was followed by planning that started before and continued throughout implementation of the program. Regular staff meetings provided for constant revision based on changing needs and the growing experience of the staff. A large enough number of people was involved to provide stimulation and encouragement; however, there were few large-group workshops. Usually small groups of four to eight people worked together close to the scene. Released time was provided as often as possible. Although a standardized district in-service program did not exist, there was general agreement throughout the district on the direction of instructional and curriculum improvement.

One successful in-service program for reading improvement was described by Fred Wood and Steven Thompson as a model (1981). The training began with a broad presentation of the entire implementation sequence including theory, goals, objectives, skills to be developed, and time frame. Over several months, participants were occasionally released from classroom responsibilities by a team of master substitutes who had previously been trained in a similar sequence. Participants worked in small groups, which promoted learning from one another and getting feedback about performance as they practiced new skills. Participants also observed in demonstration classrooms where the new skills were already being used, and they had access to a workroom for producing materials that were needed. Backup assistance was available to the participants in their own classrooms in the form of coaching by workshop leaders.

The value of teacher interaction to accompany hands-on activities cannot be underestimated. In 1956, Peter Blau wrote, "When one consults another there is an exchange of values; both gain something, but it also costs both something" (p. 50). The inquiring teacher acknowledges difficulties but can gain assistance without taking small concerns to the supervisor. The person consulted may lose time from a busy schedule and use energy and resources that would have been directed elsewhere but gains prestige from being consulted and learns by teaching another as well.

Resource Support. Implementing curriculum effectively requires time, materials, adequate facilities and equipment as well as human support. Planning not only for a long-term process of implementation but also for training during normal work hours can be critical to success. Implementation is not cheap; it requires released time for teachers and time scheduled for the leaders to come to the classrooms for coaching. Facilities and equipment must include work space, meeting rooms, electronic aids, and access to printing and production services. New materials for students are usually needed. These may be locally created, commercially produced, or developed by a research and development center or educational laboratory.

The wholesale inclusion of magazines, books, and other materials that merely appear to be attractive is a sure way to court trouble. Carefully selected curriculum materials often become the chief substance of the curriculum. Louise Tyler and Frances Klein (1976), whose work constitutes a thorough examination of the considerations involved in evaluating and choosing curriculum and instructional materials, recommend that clearly established criteria be applied in selecting instructional materials. Although criteria may vary from one locale to another, some general guidelines can be set forth:

1. Philosophy and goals: Are the materials compatible with the underlying philosophy and purpose of the new program?
2. Appropriateness: Are the materials appropriate for community mores and the students' age and maturity? Do the materials belong in a school rather than some other institution?
3. Range: Have difficulty and interest of the materials been considered? Will the materials reach the range of student abilities in the class at the most productive level of challenge for each one?
4. Articulation: Will a unit pick up where the last one left off? Will one grade level move the student to the next? There should be no gaps between levels to cause confusion or remedial work and no unnecessary repetition.

5. Bias: Are the persons making the choices sensitive to bias in curriculum materials; for example, omission of black history and minority representation in society, implicit suggestions that women or other groups are somehow inferior?
6. Cost: Can the district afford the chosen materials? Is there a way to share materials that will keep costs down?

After materials (print, film, graphics) have been selected according to local criteria, they must be classified and catalogued for efficient use. The organization of materials should recognize basic (high interest, low difficulty) and advanced or enriched resources (high interest, high difficulty) and sequence of presentation. There should be more materials than any one student can cover so that time is not wasted waiting for others to catch up.

Feedback Mechanism. An interactive feedback network is essential to successful implementation, as noted above, but it cannot be left to casual exchanges nor become a threatening form of evaluation. Constructive criticism is needed throughout the implementation process, and this involves several constituencies: teachers, administrators, consultants, aides, and, ideally, students and parents. Feedback mechanisms should identify problems encountered in order to provide support for addressing the problems. Absence of feedback networks during the implementation process was found to be a critical problem by Fullan and Pomfret (p. 374).

However, in the same study the authors warn that there are conditions under which feedback would not be effective. If the teacher feels that the implementation process is a test of his or her merit, feedback may be inaccurate; there may be a pretense without either genuine commitment or internalization. Teachers may have anxieties about their abilities to perform new roles, about power relationships within the group, whether the decision to participate is irreversible, and whether others in the group are really committed, as well as any concerns about performance evaluation.

Peer feedback has often proved vital to making successful progress through the problems of implementation. The Rand researchers found that regular and frequent staff meetings were an important determinant of successful implementation outcomes for all levels of schools and all types of change in programs (Berman and Pauly 1975, p. 61). Staff meetings can be nonthreatening growth experiences that stimulate group involvement in a new program and provide necessary feedback.

Participation. It is widely assumed that participation in the entire process of curriculum development by those who are to implement the new program is of paramount importance. Research in this area is inconclusive, however, according to Fullan and Pomfret, as different dimensions of participation have not been related directly to *implementation;* that is, those who participated least have not necessarily implemented least, nor those who participated most implemented most. Variations of all degrees have occurred (pp. 375–82).

James Shaver et al. (1980) reviewed the National Science Foundation studies on the fate of curriculum projects of the sixties and seventies. They observed that critics seemed to believe teachers rejected the new reform curricula because they had not been involved in the development aspects nor, except for relatively few, in the training institutes. But in fact, according to Shaver, it was more probable that teachers simply preferred to continue doing what they had done before (p. 12). Also, it was common knowledge that local districts seldom had implementation plans and failed to provide adequate in-service programs or resource support. Additionally the occasional teachers who did go away for a National Science Foundation institute were frequently regarded as mavericks when they returned to their local faculties.

Research does provide insights into the various dimensions of participation. Ideally, teachers would be fully involved at every stage of the curriculum development-implementation-evaluation process. One of the few case studies of relatively full participation by teachers at different stages of the process involved three teachers and ninety-five students from grades four to six (Hestand 1973). The subject matter was reading and mathematics, and the new organizational structure was differentiated staffing; that is, a combination of teachers, aides, and consultants, each having specific responsibilities for instruction and support services. The teachers made the initial decision to introduce differentiated staffing, formed a study committee with the principal and superintendent, and carried out a detailed study of differentiated staffing models used in other situations. They identified particular skills and strategies that they felt were lacking and selected a consultant to provide them with in-service training. The committee made all the planning and executing decisions, and then they submitted a proposal to the school board for funds to support implementation (the use of aides). Concerning evaluation, the teachers selected pretesting and posttesting instruments with their consultant's help. Implementation was judged to be successful.

This ideal a situation seldom takes place, however. In addition, the case study involved only a small unit of users, which increased its chances of success.

Other studies have revealed that successful implementation may hinge more on active involvement in the development process than on decisions per se. Several studies reviewed by Fullan and Pomfret show that having the right to decide whether to launch an innovation may lead to confusion, frustration, role overload, and eventually rejection before the process has even begun (p. 380).

A distinction can be made between participation at the managerial level and participation at the user level. If a person in authority is interested in standardizing implementation of an innovation that has a high degree of a priori description, it can be argued that a directive approach by the manager(s) will be more successful and that the users can best participate by working through the outline. An example is the widespread implementation of the individual educational programs (IEPs) for handicapped children under the mandate of Public Law 94-142.

The trend in recent successful curriculum reforms, however, supports the user perspective, which seems to have greater potential for effective implementation in local districts. The user perspective assumes that teachers (or users at any level) should decide or codecide what changes to implement in order to resolve identified problems, and they should also decide how to implement these changes. Accepting and volunteering to participate have a strong positive influence on commitment to a new program. How the proposed changes are presented to potential volunteers is also important. Teachers need opportunities to raise and discuss questions and problems before initiating the change process.

Capacity and Context. Organizational climate plays a critical role in whether or how implementation occurs. The Rand studies found that high teacher morale, active principal support, and the general support of superintendents all increased the chances of successful implementation (Berman and Pauly 1975, pp. 54–59). Findings from Fullan's and Pomfret's review indicate that age and level of education per se did not appear to relate to effective implementation. More important were value orientations regarding the innovation, the relevance of previous training, and the individual teacher's ability to use the innovation.

The political context of the program can also seriously affect its success. For example, there can be problems with voluntarism: Did teachers volunteer for the new program because of commitment to its values or because they wanted to appear progressive and get an assist up the ladder of mobility in the system?

The role of motivations can be questioned as well. If the authority in power is determined to obtain adoption in order to procure funding or enhance his or her or the district's image, and so bypasses adequate planning or provision of resources with an urgency to get the programs into the field, the impact will probably be negative. The role of evaluation, mentioned earlier, can sometimes inhibit implementation if teachers feel that they are on trial.

To avoid these political negatives, central policy makers should emphasize problem-solving approaches in which needs are addressed as mutual concerns of the participants. Variants and local adaptations should be encouraged during the implementation process. Evaluation should be directed toward facilitating implementation through feedback and other means of support rather than making judgments about personal successes or failures. Effective implementation requires time, personal interaction and contacts, in-service training, and other forms of people support. It is a complex process involving a multitude of relationships; as such it is often subject to conflict and unexpected problems. Nevertheless, without implementation of new developments there would be no progress toward curriculum improvement and gains in students' learning.

THE PLACE OF IMPLEMENTATION IN CURRICULUM DEVELOPMENT

Implementation is the process that brings all the professional tasks in curriculum development together. It integrates the philosophy, goals and objectives, subject matter, teaching strategies and learning activities, and, finally, evaluation and feedback. Implementation is the vehicle for integrating these professional challenges and tasks. The following chart illustrates these concepts.

Professional Tasks and Concerns	Dimensions of These Tasks and Concerns	Staff Development Needs
The philosophy, the mission statement	General philosophy, district and school philosophy	Studying the literature, values, and assumptions; refining the mission statement
Goals and objectives	District goals, instructional objectives	Examining goals critically, revising instructional objectives, observing learning styles
Subject matter content	Knowledge, information, concepts, structure of knowledge	Studying, absorbing new knowledge, working on sequence, scope, organization, classification, and evaluating materials
Teaching strategies, learning activities	Teaching styles, different methods, tactics, pacing	Hands-on practice for new methods, linking methods and content; one-to-one staff relationship
Evaluation and feedback	Observations, measurements, and studies	Methods of assessment, feedback for curriculum development—need for change or reinforcement; other uses for feedback, in-house studies

THE SUPERVISORY ROLE IN CURRICULUM IMPLEMENTATION

Supervision is a critical function in curriculum implementation. Three types of supervision bear on implementation, ranging from distant but necessary support to daily close-at-hand assistance. These types are:

1. Administration of supervision. This role may be performed by an assistant superintendent or principal of a large school. In curriculum implementation, the person works with the superintendent of schools in preparing recommendations to the board of education for changes in curriculum, usually as a result of committee work. Once approved, support for implementation is the responsibility of the designated administrator, including gathering the financial resources, employing new staff or consultants, overseeing supervisory operations at the school sites, and evaluating the quality of site supervision in the implementation of the new program.

2. General supervision. Principals, assistant principals, curriculum specialists or coordinators perform this role. In the implementation of new programs, this area of supervision is centrally concerned with preparing new curriculum guides, selecting materials, developing in-service programs, and coordinating auxiliary services, such as hiring substitute teachers to release teachers for training, or hiring secretaries to type and distribute outlines, guides, and so on.

3. Clinical supervision. Direct assistance in the classroom is the focus of clinical supervision. The term may be a misnomer, as it describes a team effort to implement a new program, skill, or curriculum content rather than any type of evaluative function. The clinical domain is the interaction between a specialist, consultant, or coordinator and a specific teacher; or it may be peer interaction within a team of teachers. It involves a process of planning, observing, and analyzing what the teacher and students are doing during the instructional period in which the new curriculum is being presented. Clinical supervision assumes a sincere effort by all parties, with openness of communication.

The potential of clinical supervision and its importance in curriculum implementation are beginning to be realized, but it is also recognized that supervisory persons need special training to work effectively in that area. As recently as 1976, Don Nasca found that "observation with feedback" was the least likely role a supervisor performed; more often attention was given to the general supervisory functions of identifying materials for teachers, writing reports, developing guides, and maintaining resource centers.

An Illustration of Clinical Supervision

A modest illustration of clinical supervisory services took place in a sixth grade team-teaching situation under the administrative supervision of one of the authors. Over a period of several days two teachers had been working to create an instructional unit on symbolism, using Japanese art and writing as background with reference to symbolism in our own lives today.

The two teachers planned each lesson carefully including what would be presented and how, questions to raise, and other considerations. Each one took turns teaching a lesson with the other observing and they made audiotapes of these sessions. Following each lesson, usually on their lunch hour or after school time, the two teachers listened to the tape and critiqued the presentation in regard to the criteria they had previously determined. For example, they would ask, were the teacher's questions such that students' responses would be those of observing factual characteristics or just recalling specific items of information? Were the students led from the activities and materials of the lesson to make inferences that would lead to new generalizations and extend ideas presented in the lesson to other situations? Were the students able to explain their reasons for arriving at their generalizations?

Not only did the critiquing sessions include an analysis of the teaching performance itself and the students' behavior and learning, but they also focused strongly on the curriculum content. Questions such as these were raised: Were the documents and materials motivational for the students? Were they suitable for the intellectual ability of the students? Did the content support the objectives of the lesson; that is, objectives related to the importance of symbolism as a concept?

As a result of the critiquing sessions, constant revision and rewriting took place as the unit of study progressed. It is conceivable that without this type of analysis, which is a feature of clinical supervision, a teacher might be satisfied to present a unit on Japanese art and writing in which all of the instructional time was spent on identifying the unique characteristics of the markings, with little or no transfer of learning to the larger concept of symbolism in the lives of all peoples and societies.

This example illustrates the three main stages of clinical supervision: first, preparing the plan including objectives, content, and methodology; second, carrying out instruction proper; and third, performing an after-the-fact analysis of the lesson's effects.

Phases in the Cycle of Clinical Supervision. Eight phases in the cycle of clinical supervision are described by Morris Cogan (1973). These phases would apply to peer supervision, as illustrated above or to a supervisor-teacher relationship: (1) establishing the relationship; (2) outlining the plan; (3) planning the observation; (4) observing instruction; (5) analyzing the teaching-learning process; (6) planning the post conference; (7) holding the conference; (8) renewing the planning process.

Problem Situations in Supervision

To effect change in a teacher's instruction, the supervisor must have a specific plan of action, particularly when severe problems develop. Insightfulness must come into play as the supervisor must assess the developmental level of the person supervised, that is, the degree of maturity, person's feelings of security, and the context of the occasion. It would be irresponsible of the supervisor either to brush off an emotionally charged situation by saying to the teacher, "go back in there and try harder" or merely making some sounds of empathy.

Several purposeful behaviors a supervisor might employ in crisis situations are suggested by Carl Glickman (1981, pp. 1-10):

1. Listening, indicating attention and inviting the person to describe the problem.
2. Clarifying, replying with questions intended to explore the problem and give it fuller understanding.
3. Encouraging, having the person elaborate on other factors that may have a bearing on the problem.
4. Presenting, offering the supervisor's perceptions and thoughts about the difficulties.
5. Problem solving, initiating steps aimed at exploring solutions.
6. Negotiating, attempting to resolve the matter, getting at specifics.
7. Demonstrating, showing the person how to act in a similar situation. The supervisor might take over the class and have the teacher observe, or have the teacher observe another teacher who is effective in a similar problem situation.
8. Directing, simply detailing to the person what must be done.
9. Reinforcing, delineating a plan of action for improvement in writing.
10. Monitoring, continuing to assist the person until he or she has become more competent.

The supervisor's plan for action in problem situations or in proactive situations should provide insights to all parties concerned with the complex processes of curriculum implementation and instruction. The supervisor's purpose in constructing such a plan is to search constantly for specific workable improvements.

Supervising or Evaluating Staff?

When supervision (staff development) and evaluation (staff appraisal) are responsibilities of the same person, problems of rapport can arise unless both functions are performed with professional competence. Supervision for curriculum implementation is a process of helping teachers with instruction; it is a process for development, learning, and growth. Such supervision refers to analyzing and appraising the particular instructional strategies that are being introduced and observed along with the teacher. In this context, supervision refers to value judgments about the effectiveness of the strategies, methods, and materials used in the instructional process. It is *not* synonymous with value judgments about the worth of an individual. Supervision is based on the varied needs of each teacher, and its effectiveness relies on professional, collegial relationships between teacher and administrator or supervisor.

Evaluation of teachers or other staff members is an appraisal process to determine contract renewal and conditions of continued employment. It should be based on a written evaluation plan containing criteria and expectations for teaching performance. This plan should have been issued to teachers and administrators at the beginning of employment or before the opening of the school term. Preferably, a committee that included teacher representatives would have participated in defining standards for performance.

Information relevant to the evaluation of teachers includes classroom management, teacher-student and teacher-parent relationships, interpersonal skills, preparation of teaching plans, effective use of training programs, observance of accepted principles of good teaching, support of district goals, and attention to legal and policy requirements.

Evaluation of the individual teacher should be clearly separated in the teacher's perception from supervision for purposes of staff development and curriculum implementation. To make the distinction, visits to the classroom for teacher evaluation should be scheduled in advance so that the teacher knows the purpose of that observation. The criteria in the evaluation plan would form the basis for the evaluation report, and school district policies and procedures for staff evaluation would apply.

In many schools, the double role of supervisor as instructional leader and evaluator is the responsibility of the principal—one more indication of the need for effectiveness in school administration. As an instructional leader, the principal or other administrator must establish a helping, supportive, and analysis-based relationship with teachers that is considerate of the individual's unique needs. As evaluator, legal requirements and regulations must apply, and the best interests of the organization must be considered.

TESTING THE QUALITY OF SUPERVISION

Implementation of changes in curriculum and instruction can severely test the quality of the supervisory services in a school. Instructional leadership, necessary even on a routine basis, is a critical factor when new programs are to be introduced and implemented. The ability to work harmoniously and productively with teachers and others during a process of change is a first requirement. Tasks needing cooperative effort include identifying the need for the new program, collecting relevant data, outlining goals and implementation procedures, conveying a sense of unified purpose, and following through with plans. Characteristics needed by the leader include abilities to motivate people for participation, stimulate discussion, accept others' ideas, work toward decisions, and, throughout, exemplify integrity, tolerance, purposeful behavior, self-discipline, and good judgment.

Other qualities applicable to supervision during implementation are the capacity to work with adversity, criticism, and frustration (as the course of change is never entirely smooth), the perception of others' potential and the ability to assist them in reaching their potential, competency in anticipating future events and making adequate preparation to avoid needless difficulties while at the same time guiding the participants through a constructive plan of action. Although it is difficult to delineate precisely the qualities needed for all conditions of curriculum implementation, these special and essential attributes can be identified.

REFERENCES

Berman, Paul, and McLaughlin, Milbrey W. "Implementation of Educational Innovation." *The Educational Forum* 40 (March 1976): 345-70.

Berman, Paul, and McLaughlin, Milbrey W. *Federal Programs Supporting Educational Change, Vol. IV: The Findings in Review.* Santa Monica, Calif.: The Rand Corp., 1975.

Berman, Paul, and Pauly, E. *Federal Programs Supporting Educational Change, Vol. II: Factors Affecting Change Agent Projects.* Santa Monica, Calif.: Rand Corp. 1975.

Blau, Peter M. *Bureaucracy in Modern Society.* New York: Random House, 1956.

Cogan, Morris L. *Clinical Supervision.* Boston: Houghton Mifflin, 1973.

Czajkowski, Theodore J., and Patterson, Jerry L. "Curriculum Change and the School." In *Considered Action for Curriculum Improvement*, pp. 158-75. Yearbook of the Association for Supervision and Curriculum Development. Alexandria, Va.: ASCD, 1980.

English, Fenwick W. "Curriculum Development Within the School System." In *Considered Action for Curriculum Improvement*, pp. 145-57. Yearbook of the

Association for Supervision and Curriculum Development. Alexandria, Va. ASCD, 1980.

Fullan, Michael, and Pomfret, Alan. "Research on Curriculum and Instruction Implementation." *Review of Educational Research* 47 (Winter 1977): 335-97.

Glatthorn, Allan A. "Curriculum Change in Loosely Coupled Systems." *Educational Leadership* 39 (November 1981): 110-13.

Glickman, Carl D. *Developmental Supervision*. Alexandria, Va.: Association for Supervision and Curriculum Development, 1981.

Goodlad, John I., and Klein, M. Frances. *Behind the Classroom Door* Worthington, Ohio: Charles A. Jones, 1970.

Hall, Gene E., and Loucks, Susan F. "A Developmental Model for Determining Whether the Treatment Is Actually Implemented." *American Educational Research Journal* 14 (Summer 1977): 263-76.

Hersey, Paul, and Blanchard, Kenneth H. *Management of Organizational Behavior: Utilizing Human Resources*. Englewood Cliffs, N.J.: Prentice-Hall, 1982.

Hestand, D. *Strategies and Procedures Used, and Problems Encountered in Implementing Differentiated Staffing: A Case Study*. Dissertation. Houston, Texas: University of Houston, 1973.

Joyce, Bruce. "A Memorandum for the Future." In *Staff Development/Organization Development*, pp. 113-27. Yearbook of the Association for Supervision and Curriculum Development. Alexandria, Va.: ASCD, 1981.

Joyce, Bruce, and Showers, Beverly. "Improving Inservice Training: The Messages of Research," pp. 43-48. In *Readings on Curriculum Implementation*. Alexandria, Va.: Association for Supervision and Curriculum Development, 1981.

Nasca, Don. "How Do Teachers and Supervisors Value the Role of Elementary Supervision?" *Educational Leadership* 33 (April 1976): 513-18.

Sarason, Seymour B. *The Culture of the School and the Problem of Change*. Boston: Allyn and Bacon, 1971.

Shaver, James P.; Davis, O. L.; and Helburn, Suzanne M. "An Interpretive Report on the Status of Precollege Social Studies Education Based on Three National Science Foundation-Funded Studies." In *What Are the Needs in Precollege Science, Mathematics, and Social Science Education? Views from the Field*, pp. 3-18. Washington, D.C.: U.S. Government Printing Office, 1980.

Tyler, Louise L.; Klein, M. Frances; and Associates. *Evaluating and Choosing Curriculum and Instructional Materials*. Los Angeles: Educational Resource Assoc., 1976.

Walker, Decker F. "Toward Comprehension of Curricular Realities." In *Review of Research in Education*, edited by Lee S. Shulman, pp. 51-52. Itasca, Ill.: Peacock Publishers, 1976.

Wood, Fred H., and Thompson, Steven R. "Guidelines for Better Staff Development," pp. 38-42. In *Readings on Curriculum Implementation*. Alexandria, Va.: Association for Supervision and Curriculum Development, 1981.

ADDITIONAL READINGS

Dillon-Peterson, Betty, ed. *Staff Development/Organization Development.* Yearbook of the Association for Supervision and Curriculum Development. Alexandria, Va.: ASCD, 1981.

Enochs, James C. "Up From Management." *Phi Delta Kappan* 63 (November 1981): 175-78.

Gephart, William J.; Strother, Deborah B.; Duckett, Willard R. "Instructional Clarity." *Practical Applications of Research* 3 (March 1981): 1-4.

Goodlad, John I. *The Dynamics of Educational Change.* New York: McGraw-Hill, 1975.

Griffin, Gary A. *Staff Development.* Eighty-second Yearbook of the National Society for the Study of Education. Chicago: University of Chicago Press, 1983.

Loucks, Susan F., and Lieberman, Ann. "Curriculum Implementation." In *Fundamental Curriculum Decisions,* pp. 126-41. Yearbook of the Association for Supervision and Curriculum Development. Alexandria, Va.: ASCD, 1983.

Loucks, Susan, and Pratt, Harold. "A Concerns-Based Approach To Curriculum Change." *Educational Leadership* 37 (December 1979): 212-15.

Mann, Dale. "The Politics of Training Teachers in Schools." *Teachers College Record* 77 (February 1976): 323-38.

McDonald, Frederick. "Effective Staff Development: Its Impact on Educational Improvement." *Inservice* (September 1981): 3-8. Newsletter of the National Council of States on Inservice Education.

Sullivan, Cheryl Granade. *Clinical Supervision: A State of the Art Review.* Alexandria, Va.: Association for Supervision and Curriculum Development, 1980.

Walberg, Herbert J., ed. *Improving Educational Standards and Productivity.* Berkeley: McCutchan, 1982.

Ward, Beatrice. "The Relationship Between Inservice Training, Organizational Structure and School Climate." *Inservice* (September 1981): 7-8. Newsletter of the National Council of States on Inservice Education.

Wolcott, Harry. *Teachers vs Technocrats.* Eugene, Ore.: Center for Educational Policy and Management, University of Oregon, 1977.

9

Curriculum Evaluation

Evaluation is an interactive process of description and judgment that discovers the nature and worth of something. Evaluators always attempt first to describe something and then to indicate or judge its perceived merits and shortcomings (Stake 1967, Stake and Denny, 1969). Curriculum evaluation is the process used in judging the appropriateness of curriculum choices, according to Saylor, Alexander, and Lewis (1981). They pose the following questions as significant for curriculum evaluation: Is the curriculum fulfilling the purposes for which it was designed? Are these purposes themselves valid? Is the curriculum appropriate to the particular students involved? Are the selected activities the best choices considering the goals that are sought? Is the content the best possible? Are the materials used for instructional purposes appropriate and the best available for the envisioned goals? (p. 317).

Curriculum evaluation is a process for searching out ways to improve the substance of the curriculum, the implementation procedures, the instructional methods, and the effects on student learning and behavior.

Ralph Tyler (1981) sees evaluation as a checking process that should be applied at four different stages in curriculum development. The first stage is when choosing between goals or ideas that are proposed for developing a curriculum program, a set of materials, or an instructional device. At this point he recommends reviewing evidence from others' experience and experiments that may indicate the probable effectiveness of the idea before energy is wasted on an approach that did not work elsewhere.

The second stage for evaluation is in the process of implementation. Once the plan is thought to be in operation, a check of the entire situation should be made to see whether it actually is in operation or whether certain conditions essential to success of the program are missing. At the point of implementation, alternative procedures could be discovered that would be more effective than those outlined in the original plan.

A third stage at which evaluation can contribute to the effectiveness of the curriculum is during actual operation; that is, following the early trials, it will be necessary to monitor the ongoing curriculum. Various evaluative procedures can keep students and teachers in touch with the necessary elements of the curriculum implementation process and can furnish information to guide them.

The fourth stage occurs when a program has been carried out, and it is desirable to determine whether the results are good enough to continue with it, undertake modifications, or drop the program (1981, pp. 28-29).

According to Tyler, then, evaluation becomes a process for finding out how far the learning experiences as organized and developed are actually producing the desired results; and this evaluation process would include identifying the strengths and weaknesses of the plans. In turn this approach helps to check the validity of the basic premises from which the instructional program was developed. As a result of evaluation, it should be possible to pinpoint in what respects the curriculum is effective and/or needs improvement.

Tyler's four stages of evaluation are similar to the major activities outlined by William Gephart. "Evaluation, done systematically, should provide data about the relative worth of all the program alternatives on all the criteria to be used in the decision" (1978, p. 257). Gephart sees four important activities that make up the curriculum evaluation process: (1) specifying the alternatives that are going to be considered at each stage of choice making; (2) determining the variables the decision makers will use in making their choices; (3) collecting and analyzing data; and (4) reporting the relative worth of the alternatives to the decision makers.

Evaluation implies decision making, either in the form of judgments made by the evaluators or by providing sufficient information so that the audience(s) may form value judgments. The purposes of the audiences are all important. The classroom teacher, the principal, the superintendent, the school board, the parents, the state department of education each probably has a somewhat different set of interests in evaluating the curriculum. Because of that, their needs for different types of information and reports will vary. There may be political pressures to slant the evaluation one way or another to suit the particular interests of a given audience. For example, a report may be intercepted at one or another level before it reaches the board of education, and participants may insist on loading the information one way or another at these points. Problems like these get into the ethics of evaluation.

Evaluation should be viewed as a routine practice carried out to help educators keep curriculum programs operating at their maximum effectiveness and efficiency, not as a technique only brought in during crisis situations. Evaluation in education should be an instrument for improving educational programs, not for determining whose guilt or innocence prevails (see Worthen and Rogers 1980). Evaluation should be a normal part of the continuum of setting goals, assessing needs, establishing objectives, devising learning activities, evaluating the process and the outcomes, and recycling. John McNeil (1981) has concluded that evaluation results can form the base for revising instructional objectives to meet needs revealed during the evaluation process. Results can also serve as a guide to the need for new learning opportunities and arrangements that might close gaps. Evaluation should not only pinpoint the needs but also guide educators in selecting new materials, procedures, and organizational patterns.

The many ramifications of evaluation as feedback were noted by Fred Wilhelms and his committee in 1967. They pointed out that when evaluation reaches into any step of curriculum development, its feedback affects other steps. For example, if the goals are found to be weak or too abstract, then needs may not have been assessed adequately. In turn, instructional objectives would require an overhaul and so would learning activities. Curriculum decisions in education are conditioned by our perceptions of how we are doing—the evaluation—in terms of what we had hoped to do—the goals. Therefore, systems of evaluation are needed that will feed back information to every level concerned with the educational process the kinds of data needed to improve these perceptions and consequently to improve educational decisions.

CHANGING CONCEPTS OF EDUCATIONAL EVALUATION

Interest in educational evaluation in America dates back to the scientific movement of the early 1900s, according to Jack Merwin (1969). Educational tests and measurements were in their infancy then but enjoying rapid growth, and the effects of these evaluations were noted in the school organization, courses of study, and methods of instruction.

The dominant educational psychology of the early 1900s was based on the theory of formal discipline expressed in terms of "faculty psychology." Edward Thorndike (1903, p. 45) commented that "we cannot create intellect, but we can prevent such lamentable waste of it as was caused by scholasticism." Charles Judd (1918, p. 159-60) noted that "the superintendent who reports to his board on the basis of mere opinion is rapidly becoming a relic of an earlier and unscientific age...even the principals are beginning to study their schools by exact methods and are basing their supervision on the results of their measurements of what teachers accomplish."

The years 1918 to 1925, however, brought some disenchantment with faculty psychology and increasing interest in behavioral psychology. This was identified by Ralph Tyler (1957) as a period when educational objectives were perceived for the first time in very specific terms with testing to match. The behavioral objectives evaluation model, identified historically with persons such as Bobbitt (1924) and Charters (1923) and later Mager (1962) and Popham (1969), emphasized outcome evaluation and the behavioral objectives model, which has recently been championed by advocates of teacher accountability. Another result of this approach is that current applications for federal grant funds have requirements for a statement of objectives to be achieved and procedures for measuring this achievement as a method of evaluating project effectiveness.

The impact of the scientific movement of the early 1900s continued, and in 1938 William Reavis commented, "the development of the measuring movement and the perfection of tests for the measurement of achievement and mental capacity have made possible great advances in educational administration" (p. 27). Relying on tests to evaluate the attainment of curriculum goals continues to this day. This approach is illustrated by the use of standardized tests, teacher-made objective tests, college entrance examinations, minimum competency testing, and tests for admittance to various career fields.

Despite the lingering influence of linear testing models for evaluation, a contemporary trend leans toward more qualitative evaluation of curriculum and instruction. For a variety of reasons, interest in studying the quality of classroom life has grown. John Goodlad (1979) sees this trend as a reaction to the view of the school as a factory based on the "production" model of schooling. In this linear input-output model, money and other resources are put into the schools and produce returns in the form of students' achievement gains as measured by standardized test scores. No observation of process would be needed as part of evaluation in this model, which continues to flourish in many quarters.

In noting the changing views of curriculum evaluation, Henry Brickell said, "Back in 1970, evaluators worried about whether programs achieved their objectives. More recently, in 1975, they worried about whether there was a better program for achieving the same objectives. Today, they worry about whether there are better objectives that could be brought into the classrooms and achieved instead" (1981, p. 93).

Differences Between Evaluation and Research

The concept of testing as curriculum evaluation led to an assumption that curriculum evaluation and curriculum research were the same thing. This perception, James Raths (1978) suggested, can be traced back to

Joseph Rice, whose test-based research on spelling, in 1897, shaped the field of curriculum research for decades. The underlying logic was that if students under Method A scored higher on tests than students under Method B, then Method A was presumably better than Method B and therefore merits adoption and implementation. However, students and much less teachers can rarely be randomly assigned to different curricular treatments. With such a basic element of the experimental research paradigm missing, the results of this type of a curriculum evaluation were especially vulnerable to ridicule. Also many curriculum research studies were criticized for the narrow focus of their investigation. Then, even though significant findings were frequently produced in a research effort, the report of the findings was directed to peers through the medium of very technical research journals. As a result, practitioners were rarely aware of the findings that were of significance to them.

These problems and others made it clear that curriculum evaluation should be seen as a process distinct from research in its narrowest sense, that curriculum evaluation is a much more complicated undertaking than the simple experiment. John Hemphill (1969) made the following distinctions between research and evaluation studies. Questions of value and the importance of utility involved in evaluation studies are relatively unimportant in research studies, he noted.

The research study is one in which:

1. Problem selection and definition is the responsibility of the individual doing the research.
2. Tentative answers (hypotheses) to the problem may be derived by deduction from theories or by induction from an organized body of knowledge.
3. Value judgments by the researcher are limited to those implicit in the selection of the problem.
4. Given the statement of the problem and the hypothesis, the research can be replicated.
5. The data to be collected are determined largely by the problem and the hypothesis.
6. Relevant variables can be controlled or manipulated, and systematic effects of other variables can be eliminated by randomization.

The evaluation study may be described in terms of characteristics almost the reverse of those outlined above:

1. The problem is almost completely determined by the situation in which the study is conducted. Many people may be involved in its definition and, because of its complexity, the problem initially is difficult to define.
2. Precise hypotheses usually cannot be generated; rather the task becomes one of testing generalizations from a variety of research studies, some of which are

basically contradictory. There are many gaps which in the absence of verified knowledge must be filled by reliance on judgment and experience.

3. Value judgments are made explicit in the selection and the definition of the problem as well as in the development and implementation of the procedures of the study.

4. The study is unique to a situation and seldom can be replicated, even approximately.

5. The data to be collected are heavily influenced if not determined by feasibility. Choices, when possible, reflect value judgments of decision makers or of those who set policy. There are often large differences between data for which the collection is feasible and data which are of most value to the decision makers.

6. Only superficial control of a multitude of variables important to interpretation of results is possible. Randomization to eliminate the systematic effects of these variables is extremely difficult or impractical to accomplish (pp. 190–91).

Although evaluation studies may lack the precision of research studies, their purpose is to provide information for making choices among alternatives.

Newer Evaluation Methods

Several scholars in the curriculum field have taken the lead in attempting to construct new ways of perceiving the evaluation process, and they offer new expectations for those participating in it. Multiple methodologies are needed for curriculum evaluation, and attention must be given to the audiences that the evaluations are addressing. For example, during the curriculum reform era, when many new packages and programs were appearing on the market and schools were being urged to use them, teachers began to raise questions about program evaluation. Evaluators then began attending more closely to the judgments of teachers in assessing the worth of various curriculum materials. They became increasingly interested in learning how a particular curriculum program works rather than solely "proving" various claims to be true.

In a similar vein, evaluators presently seem to be more aware that few programs, materials, or curricula work equally well with all segments of the student population. Inquiries into a curriculum's effectiveness include examining instructional variables, such as the extent to which teachers emphasize one area of content over another, the degree to which students are given the opportunity to practice what they are learning, and the quality of the feedback that students receive about their work. New perspectives of curriculum evaluation, both conceptual and methodological, are bringing fresh insights and new knowledge to curriculum development and implementation.

CONTEXTUAL DOMAINS OF CURRICULUM EVALUATION

Contextual domains are generic parts of the educative process, and therefore they are integral to curriculum evaluation. Studying the contextual variables prior to launching an extensive curriculum evaluation study—information before action—is recommended by John Goodlad (1979), Kenneth Sirotnik and Jeannie Oakes (1981), and others who participated as team members in the Study of Schooling. They perceived this study to be the most critical preliminary step in planning for curriculum improvement. Although Goodlad and associates have not proposed a ready-made contextual appraisal system, they did identify variables within the contextual domains that should be considered in an adequate evaluation of the curriculum and the instructional processes.

Contextual variables are defined by Sirotnik and Oakes (p. 166) as "those elements that contribute to the environment of the classroom, school, and community within which school-based learning takes place." The authors have identified four contextual domains: personal, instructional, institutional, and societal. In each of these domains, information can be gathered concerning the individual, the classroom, the school, and schooling in general. Data collection devices include: surveys, interviews, observation schedules, curriculum materials samplings, document reviews, and naturalistic or descriptive methods. A contextual appraisal system would include periodic assessment of student achievement. Depending on the purpose of assessing achievement, these measures could be classified in any of the four domains. Achievement testing, however, is only one of many variables in this view of curriculum evaluation.

The Personal Domain

The personal characteristics of students, parents, and teachers are likely to influence their participation in and their attitudes toward school. Students' self-concepts and educational aspirations; teachers' beliefs about education, teaching experience, reasons for entering the education profession; and parents' political beliefs, special interests, and years lived in the community are all variables related to the personal domain. Cultural patterns such as communication styles, learning modes, and belief systems have been shown to differ substantially among population subgroups, and these factors appear to have considerable influence on students' behavior and the ways schools respond to students.

The Instructional Domain

Time on task and the educational climate are among the important variables of the instructional domain. The following types of information are needed to assess the classroom context, according to Kenneth Sirotnik and Jeannie Oakes (1981):

1. Basic class descriptions including the physical environment; size, time of day, length of class periods, and subject areas; sex, age, and ethnicity of students.
2. Events in the classroom including the content of instruction, learning activities, materials, grouping patterns, teaching strategies, level of student involvement, evaluation methods used by the teacher, teacher-student interactions and their affective tone.
3. Participant responses to classroom characteristics, involving their judgments about various relationships and the quality of the school climate.

Fenwick English has provided a process known as "curriculum mapping," which is useful in describing the realities of the classroom and the curriculum that teachers have actually taught (1980). Mapping formats include content taught and time spent. Content here includes not only conventional subject matter but also the processes, activities, or methods of the classroom. One intent of curriculum mapping is to help the curriculum developer use the results to bring the written curriculum and the real curriculum into congruence with one another. Relative amounts of time spent on instruction, behavior control, and routine administrative functions all influence the quality of the instructional domain.

It is important to gather the perceptions of teachers and participant observers in evaluating the instructional domain, but it is also important to gather students' perceptions of classroom processes. Joseph Farley (1981) noted that a clearer picture of instructional quality emerges when the student's perspective is combined with other evaluation information. Interviews should follow a few simple guidelines such as establishing rapport, using neutral and open-ended but uncomplicated questions, and checking with the student for clarification.

The Institutional Domain

How satisfying is the school to its participants? William Gephart (1978) has suggested that evaluation of the curriculum setting may vary from participant to participant. Different assessments might be made by the student, the teacher, the administrator, the parent, the teachers union, and the state or federal official. Because of that, their reports may differ in emphasis.

Basic descriptive elements of the institutional domain include student population statistics, class size and teacher-pupil ratio data, student absentee and transiency rates, fiscal resources, percentage of teachers in various secondary subject areas or the amount of time spent in instruction in various subjects at elementary schools, the type of grouping procedures used at the schools, and judgments of the relative value placed on intellectual, social, vocational, and personal functions of schooling. It would also be useful to observe how the staff works together as a group, what kind of leadership the principal provides, and how parents participate in the school. Students can be asked about extracurricular activities, the helpfulness of the counselors, and the accessibility of the principal. Students will have perceptions of the student culture; that is, the friendliness of other students and which types of students seem to be most popular at school. All participants can give information about the problems the school faces.

The Societal Domain

Michael Apple (1978) has criticized evaluators who subscribe to qualitative case studies as a means of assessing the environment of the classroom if they fail to look beyond the school to its broader political and economic environment and to make that a part of the explanatory framework. The external context, he noted, has considerable influence on the allocation of teacher time, energies, and curriculum resources available to the teacher. Although the curriculum evaluation process is intended to help practitioners improve the curriculum, there may be limitations on what decision makers have the power to improve. Their attention must be directed to options that are possible within societal constraints. Community views about schooling are important; particularly, views on issues such as desegregation, financial support of public education, the role of teachers unions, minimum competency testing, global education, job experience for students, public versus private education, and similar matters.

A Framework

The definition of context in program evaluation is meaningful only when it is tailored to the needs and interests of the local school, district, and community. The entire process of identifying factors for consideration must include dialogue, decision, and action. An orderly approach to collecting data is necessary as is a coherent presentation of information at the conclusion of the study. The framework shown in Figure 14 may be useful for identifying and organizing contextual variables. Local sources of data would be filled in the matrix as needed.

It must be recognized that schools do not always function in a rational, goal-based fashion. However, feedback from a contextual appraisal is information that must be used in the evaluation report if the effort is to be worth a serious commitment of resources.

Figure 14.   A Framework for Identifying and Organizing Contextual Variables

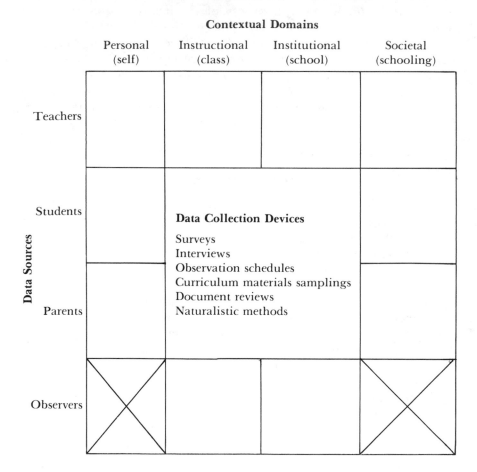

FORMATIVE AND SUMMATIVE EVALUATIONS

The distinction between formative and summative evaluations is another consideration for curriculum evaluators. James Popham described this succinctly: "If the decisions were focused on program improvement (formative evaluation), then I'd gather plenty of information about the way the program was being implemented . . . if, on the other hand, the decisions were focused on continuing versus terminating a program (summative evaluation), I'd give more attention to evidence suggesting the program's effects" (1981, p. 3). Both formative and summative evaluations are essential for curriculum development and implementation, according to Michael Scriven (1967). Scriven is credited with introducing the terms *summative* and *formative evaluation.*

Formative Evaluation

In relation to curriculum development, formative evaluation refers to the collection of appropriate evidence during the construction and trial of a new curriculum so that revisions of the curriculum can be based on this evidence. Formative evaluation is almost exclusively aimed at improving the educational experiences or product during its developmental phases. Benjamin Bloom et al. (1971) have noted that formative evaluation is using systematic evaluation of curriculum and instruction, of teaching and learning, for the purpose of improving any of these processes.

This means that in formative evaluation one must strive to develop the kind of evidence that will be most useful in the process, seek the most useful method of reporting the evidence, and search for ways of reducing the negative effect associated with evaluation—perhaps by reducing the judgmental aspects of evaluation, or, at the least, by having the users of the formative evaluation (teacher, students, curriculum makers) make the judgments. The hope is that the users of the formative evaluation will find ways of relating the results of the evaluation to the learning and instructional goals they regard as important and worthwhile (pp. 117–18).

Formative evaluation can be used at each of three stages of curriculum development: planning-designing, implementing, and disseminating to other users. At the planning-designing stage, formative evaluation can assist in gathering information about alternative approaches to achieve the goal. At the implementation stage, formative evaluation can discover factors or processes that influence the ultimate success of the program. At the time for dissemination, formative evaluation can provide data regarding the actual use of the program as a basis for adaptations and strategies for implementation.

Summative Evaluation

Summative evaluation implies that a judgment has been made about the effectiveness resulting from the curriculum after the instruction has taken place. It is the type of evaluation used at the end of a term, course, or program for making an overall decision. Summative evaluation may employ either absolute or comparative standards and judgments, and it is often based on tests of all sorts. It may also use surveys of student reaction to the instruction, teachers' views concerning the effectiveness of the curriculum and the instructional methods, follow-up studies of students who have participated in the program, parents' reactions, employers' ratings of graduates, reports from college examination bureaus, and other similar types of evidence. Summative evaluation can also contribute highly significant data for revising curriculum plans, formulating new ones, adding or dropping courses of instruction, selecting new content, revising goals and objectives, and reaching similar decisions that are made at an end point in a particular curriculum program.

MODELS AND PROCEDURES

Both formative and summative evaluations are used in many of the models and procedures described next. Models will be described under the following classifications: goal attainment, judgmental, decision facilitative, descriptive, and status assessment. Models and procedures have been categorized in these classifications somewhat subjectively, and a given model or procedure could readily be drawn from one of the others. Seldom can a program be adequately evaluated using only one model, and often the evaluator chooses an eclectic approach.

Goal-Attainment Models

Measuring the attainment of mission statements and general goals and subgoals of education presents a number of difficulties. Many goal statements refer to abstractions such as "understanding others," "basic principles and concepts of science," and "responsible societal membership." While these are common terms in education, few published instruments are available on the market for evaluating progress toward reaching these elusive aspirations.

Evaluating the Attainment of General Goals. At least one ambitious search has been made to discover instruments and procedures for measuring goal attainment. The task focused on the ten major goals of education extracted by the ASCD Committee on Research and Theory from lists of goal statements of leading educational agencies and state departments of education. (See Chapter Five.) The ASCD committee found that many of the goal statements were unsuited to measurement by paper and pencil tests and that structured or informal observations would sometimes be necessary to gather evaluative data. Thus, the committee looked into references on published and unpublished tests and observational instruments, and provided detailed information on titles, addresses, and suitability for measuring goal attainment in its report *Measuring and Attaining the Goals of Education* (1980).

For goal one, basic skills, tests are widely available. Goal two, self-conceptualization, proved difficult to measure as the goal is concerned with the process of achieving the dynamic of self-actualization, and available instruments, as listed, are intended to measure one's current concepts about self, a more static evaluation.

In searching for instruments to measure attainment of goal three, understanding others, the ASCD committee found examples that dealt with students' ability to behave in school or their tolerance of others. But they found nothing that evaluated their awareness of others' lifestyles and values. However, three instruments were identified as partially appropriate.

The search for measurement instruments was unfruitful for goal four, using accumulating knowledge to understand the world, and goal seven, participation in the economic world of production and consumption. Available tests measure the amount of student knowledge on various subjects but not how to use accumulated knowledge appropriately as stated in goal four. Definitions and research would be needed before measuring economic participation, as stated in seven.

Goal five, continuous learning, focuses on students' interests in and capacity for continuous learning. Because attention to examining this aspect of learning is relatively new, few available tests measure its subgoals. The listing does provide titles of instruments to measure motivation for learning or current self-initiated learning activities, but no titles deal with the capability or value of lifelong learning.

The search for instruments to measure goal six, mental and physical well-being, was more productive. A number of tests are available to measure mental well-being, although they tend to focus on students' problems rather than strengths. Ways to measure physical well-being were uncommon in the educational testing references, possibly because this is an area considered more appropriate for the medical profession.

Responsible societal membership, goal eight, posed special problems in measurement. While some instruments listed purport to measure how well students get along with others or else scale the degree to which students value socialization, none has been established as a reliable predictor of desirable adult behaviors as specified in the subgoals. Also, the long-range nature of the citizenship goals—participation as an adult citizen in society—poses impossible measurement problems while the student is still in school.

Creativity, the essence of goal nine, has been of interest to researchers for years. Yet available tests so far lack norms and do not claim the reliability and validity needed for comparison with standards. However, the Association for Supervision and Curriculum Development reference includes a considerable list of "creativity" tests.

Coping with change, goal ten, a necessity in today's turbulent world, marks one of the first attempts to specify "survival" subgoals. Testing instruments are not yet available, although one listed index reflects a student's motivation for achievement and provides items that indicate an ability to cope with change.

The goals and goal attainment measures listed above are not intended to be prescriptive; goal-determination is a local responsibility. These examples are provided as a guide and cue to the complexities of selecting and setting goals and then measuring their attainment.

Are the Goals Appropriate? Unless goal evaluations include a continuing study of the appropriateness of the selected goals to the local needs, schools may find themselves overloaded with more and more responsibilities. Some goals have been added by state mandates, and other responsibilities seem to fall to the lot of the schools when concerns are promoted as needs by newspapers or televised public service programs. Schools often seem unable to refuse more and more assigned tasks.

Saylor, Alexander, and Lewis (1981) stressed the importance of regularized procedures for evaluating goals from time to time to be sure that the school's program is developing out of educational goals that reflect expected changes in society as well as existing values and forces. Both formative and summative evaluations are necessary, according to the authors, at each stage of curriculum planning.

Judging the appropriateness of the mission statement is the first step. An open-ended needs assessment may discover that the overall goals of the institution should be revised. The second stage is determining the goals for the program of education of the schools—for its curriculum and instructional processes. Next, decisions are needed on specific segments of the educational program; that is, the subject areas and various focuses to meet discovered needs. Formative evaluation at all stages includes the views of experts or students on cultural trends and the judgments of competent teachers, other professional educators, parents, other citizens, and students. Summative evaluation at each stage would provide feedback on the outcomes of students' learning, growth, and development. Figure 15 shows the scope and nature of evaluation of goals.

Figure 15. The Scope and Nature of Curriculum Evaluation

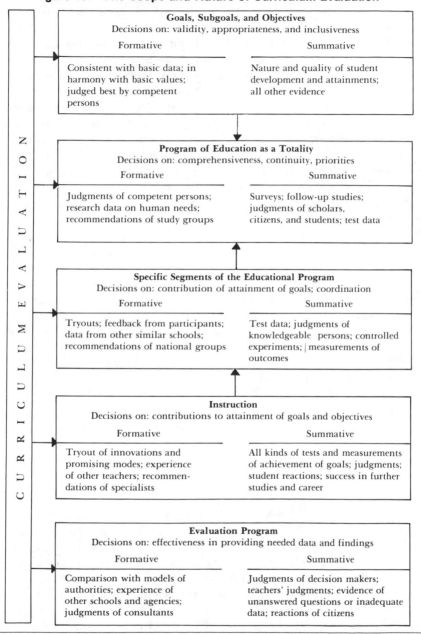

Goals, Subgoals, and Objectives
Decisions on: validity, appropriateness, and inclusiveness

Formative	Summative
Consistent with basic data; in harmony with basic values; judged best by competent persons	Nature and quality of student development and attainments; all other evidence

Program of Education as a Totality
Decisions on: comprehensiveness, continuity, priorities

Formative	Summative
Judgments of competent persons; research data on human needs; recommendations of study groups	Surveys; follow-up studies; judgments of scholars, citizens, and students; test data

Specific Segments of the Educational Program
Decisions on: contribution of attainment of goals; coordination

Formative	Summative
Tryouts; feedback from participants; data from other similar schools; recommendations of national groups	Test data; judgments of knowledgeable persons; controlled experiments; measurements of outcomes

Instruction
Decisions on: contributions to attainment of goals and objectives

Formative	Summative
Tryout of innovations and promising modes; experience of other teachers; recommendations of specialists	All kinds of tests and measurements of achievement of goals; judgments; student reactions; success in further studies and career

Evaluation Program
Decisions on: effectiveness in providing needed data and findings

Formative	Summative
Comparison with models of authorities; experience of other schools and agencies; judgments of consultants	Judgments of decision makers; teachers' judgments; evidence of unanswered questions or inadequate data; reactions of citizens

CURRICULUM EVALUATION

From Galen J. Saylor, William M. Alexander, and Arthur J. Lewis, *Curriculum Planning for Better Teaching and Learning* (New York: Holt, Rinehart, and Winston, 1981), p. 334. Copyright © 1981 by Holt, Rinehart and Winston. Reprinted by permission of Holt, Rinehart and Winston, CBS College Publishing.

Next we will examine a type of goal evaluation which focuses on the specific objectives that make up the details of day-to-day life in the classroom.

Behavioral Objectives Model. Preceding portions of this book have spoken to the history of behavioral objectives and their measurement by criterion-referenced testing. Dissatisfactions with standardized testing stimulated the widespread use of this model, although many practitioners object to the narrowness of objectives that are often assessed in this way or to minimal levels of "mastery" required in some instances. Still other objections center around the competency tests mandated by many states. A particular focus for criticism is the custom of publishing test scores which are at best an embarrassment to low-achieving schools and, at worst, a tool for demoting or dismissing administrators and teachers. These are *misuses* of the behavioral model. It has a place in curriculum evaluation, however, when properly applied. Evaluation, based on behavioral objectives is the process of weighing the outcome of instruction against each objective that was set forth and delivered via preplanned learning activities. The evaluation instrument must closely match objectives that have been provided for the desired learning to take place. An example of a behavioral objective that specifies its measure is: The student will be able to distinguish factual from normative statements in nine out of ten examples. Since the data are used mainly to make judgments at the conclusion of a course or unit of learning, evaluation of this type is summative in nature.

In a critique of the behavioral objectives model by Bloom, et al. (1971), it is noted that, unfortunately, the summative aspect is the emphasis that has been widely replicated. That is, the emphasis has been on *whether* the curriculum and instruction worked, not *why* it did or didn't. For exploring the whys in curriculum evaluation, many other models and procedures are available.

Judgmental Evaluation Models

In judgmental models, the evaluators come to conclusions about the data that have been gathered. The report usually sets forth the successes and/or failures of the program, and thus is summative in nature. In some of the other and more descriptive models, the evaluators present data and information, but the clients or the persons to be affected by the evaluation are left to draw their own conclusions.

The Eight Year Study. An early example of a judgmental model was the Eight Year Study sponsored by the Progressive Education Association in the 1930s and early 1940s, described in Chapter One. It became clear early in the study that a critical factor in the success of the innovative program would be clear statements about the objectives of the new curricula so that appropriate evaluation instruments and techniques could be developed.

Students from "progressive" high schools were matched with those who had attended "traditional" high schools; these students were followed longitudinally through college. The evaluation aspects are described by Eugene Smith and Ralph Tyler in the volume *Appraising and Recording Student Progress* (1942). Example after example is given in that report of educational objectives made operational in terms of content areas and overt student behaviors; that is, given a certain content area, how the student should think, feel, or act. Conclusions were that in some matters the traditional students excelled and in others the progressive students excelled. The report appeared right at America's entry into World War II, so the significant contribution of the Eight-Year Study to evaluation of curriculum and instruction did not receive the attention that it warranted.

Accountability. Evaluation for accountability is essentially based on a judgmental model; it uses the summative type of evaluation and also employs behavioral objectives. As noted in another section of this book, there are instances in the United States where accountability testing is credited with raising student achievement and improving the effectiveness of schools. Others complain that it can be a procrustean bed that ignores local needs and inhibits local initiative and expressions of talents for curriculum improvement. The commonsense view is to look upon mandated testing as a minimum and to go as far beyond as possible by offering a curriculum that is rich in breadth and depth.

Adversary Evaluation. This novel approach has attracted considerable publicity in program evaluation circles, particularly through reports presented as papers at the annual meetings of the American Educational Research Association, dating back to 1971. Adversary evaluation is undoubtedly a judgmental evaluation. It may not be a model in the technical sense, as it has not yet developed a unified set of principles, but it is a familiar term used to describe practices for program evaluation that resemble a courtroom trial.

In adversary evaluation the pros and cons of a program are presented by different evaluators or evaluation teams for decisions by a judge, a panel of judges, or a jury. It is a planned effort to generate opposing points of view within an overall evaluation.

Blaine Worthen and Todd Rogers, who reviewed several examples, traced the idea to Egon Guba's suggestion (1965) that educational evaluation might use aspects of the legal paradigm. Several applications of the model followed. One of the best known is the Hawaii 3 on 2 program (three teachers for two classrooms). The Northwest Regional Educational Laboratory (NWREL) organized an adversary evaluation of the large statewide and controversial team teaching program in the primary grades during the school year of 1976–1977. Two teams of notable evaluators were invited to participate, and each team was assigned either for or against the 3 on 2 program. For the better part of a year, each team gathered information on its side of the question. Then all this culminated in a courtroom scene that had high spectator attraction and generated much interest.

A complete report of the evaluation effort is available from NWREL (1977b). The advantages and disadvantages of the adversary evaluation are explored by Worthen and Rogers (1980) and by Popham and Carlson (1981). In brief, the gain is likely to be an increase in the spectrum of data and interpretations provided to decision makers, but the loss could come from unnecessary polarization that shifts attention away from the middle ground that is so often essential to rational decision making.

Decision Facilitative Evaluation Models

Models grouped in the decision-facilitative category are those in which the client or decision maker, not the evaluator, assigns value to the data that have been collected, analyzed, and reported. It is the evaluator's responsibility to meet with the client or clients to generate a list of critical decisions to be made regarding the program, to determine the types of information necessary to make those decisions, and to plan the informational sources in such a way that critical decisions are precipitated by timely and objective information.

CIPP. One of the best known of this type is the CIPP model—context, input, process, and product—developed by Daniel Stufflebeam and associates (1971). *Context* refers to information about the environment in which a program occurs and from which its goals are derived. The information should be supplied by the community, teachers, administrators, parents, and students. *Input* is drawn from information about available and/or desirable resources for obtaining the objectives. *Process* refers to the efficacy of the procedure used to implement the program. *Product* is a report of the measures and interpretations made of the program effects during and at conclusion of its existence. William Webster applied the CIPP model to a humanities program (1981) and illustrated how it could be carried out in a local school setting with options available to the decision makers as to whether to continue the program in its current setting, discontinue it, expand it, or revise it. The same humanities program was also evaluated using a different model and is described later in this chapter as the Radnor illustration.

CSE. A second example of decision facilitative models for evaluation is the CSE model named for its origin at the Center for the Study of Evaluation of the University of California at Los Angeles. As described by Marvin Alkin (1975), this model has five stages, each related to a particular kind of decision to be made. In the first stage, related to problem selection, procedures similar to needs assessment models are used for determining educational needs and identifying the goals for the program. The second stage of the CSE model is related to selecting programs that could be used to close the identified gaps as shown in the needs assessments. Included are tasks such as appraising available instructional materials that might be used in this program and selecting learning opportunities. The third stage notes departures from the original plan and provides information about modification of the program. The next stage is similar to the third stage except that the evaluator looks at the relative success of different parts of the program as it is progressing. The final stage of the CSE model concerns adoption, and this stage provides information on the achievement of goals stated in the first stage. The purpose is to help the decision makers determine the next steps for the program.

Discrepancy Models. Somewhat related to the CIPP and CSE models is the discrepancy evaluation model developed by Malcolm Provus (1971). He has described program evaluation as a process of (1) defining program standards, (2) determining whether a discrepancy exists between some aspect of program performance and the standards governing that aspect of the program, and (3) using discrepancy information either to change performance or to change program standards. The evaluator starts with an ongoing program in which standards have been established as part of the process of initiating the program. Appropriate evidence is then obtained on performance and compared with the standard, thus revealing any discrepancy. Discrepancy information always leads to a decision either to go on to the next stage, recycle the stage after there has been a change in standards or operations, or terminate the project. Provus maintained that this model necessitates an evaluation of the goals and objectives themselves. With its many points of looking at discrepancy information, it lends itself well to curriculum development.

Accreditation. Accreditation models also help form decisions. Based on discrepancy types of evaluation, standards prepared by each accrediting association usually cover the four areas listed in Stufflebeam's decision-making model: context, input, process, and product—without using his terminology, however. The institution seeking accreditation conducts a self-evaluation using the association's standards or criteria such as the Evaluative Criteria for the Evaluation of Secondary Schools, prepared by the National Study of School Evaluation (1978). The local committee prepares a report that includes comments and recommendations concerning each particular subject field or aspect of the curriculum of the school. Then a visiting committee spends up to three days in the institution to make its judgments about the program, presents a report that comments on the evaluations prepared by the institution's committee, and makes its recommendations, if any, for improving each area of the program.

If there is a discrepancy between any standard and actual practice, as reflected in the report, time is granted by the accrediting institution for correcting any deficiencies by making modifications and improvements in the program. In a sense, the accreditation model could be considered a judgmental model because the accrediting association has the power to award and withhold accreditation. Usually, however, time is allowed so that every effort can be made to bring the institution up to "standard." An inherent flaw in the accreditation model is the arbitrary set of standards. Unless these standards can be demonstrated to lead to valued goals, evaluation under this model will not enhance the quality of an educational program.

Descriptive Evaluation Models

Several less conventional approaches to program evaluation are included in this section. Terms applied to various models or types classified by the authors as *descriptive* are: naturalistic, responsive, goal-free, artistic, and educational connoisseurship and criticism. While these are not duplications of one another, all emphasize qualitative evaluation, and all study the processes in operation as well as other factors. Egon Guba described these types of program evaluation as "naturalistic inquiry," and he suggested that although less conventional in method, program evaluation can become a component of the evolving program itself rather than a disinterested monitoring undertaken to support one side or another in a political struggle. Formal evaluation reports to outsiders would be reduced in significance, and the findings would not become conclusions; rather they would provide the system with a picture of itself (1978, pp. 31–32).

Case Studies. Case studies frequently exemplify the descriptive approaches. An example is the evaluation of the humanities curriculum at Radnor Middle School (fictional name). The board of education had raised some critical questions about the program, which had become a local issue, and it sought the views of six prominent program evaluators (Brandt 1981). Each expert was asked to apply his or her evaluation model to the case and offer advice. All agreed at the outset that the evaluation of a humanities program is challenging. James Popham put it this way:

Evaluating a humanities program holds challenges akin to those involved in evaluating a formal religion. Architects of both enterprises really don't believe their efforts can possibly be evaluated here on earth. Whereas the religionist contends that genuine payoffs to the devout occur only in an afterlife, proponents of the humanities often garb their programs in such effusive rhetoric that evaluators dare approach their appraisal task only with well-warranted trembling (1981, p. 1).

The goals of the humanities curriculum were indeed lofty. As a consequence of two classes a week, students were expected to increase their aesthetic sensibilities, critical thinking skills, appreciation of human achievement in the arts, appreciation of their own and others' cultural heritages, understanding of the interrelatedness of disciplines, and communication skills. The collection of responses from the evaluators, edited by Ronald Brandt, offers an array of interesting possibilities for consideration by local evaluators. Some of the experts applied descriptive models, one person used the CIPP model, and another resorted to an eclectic approach that drew from several models. The responsive model, originated by Robert Stake and applied by himself and James Pearsol (1981) to the Radnor humanities curriculum will be described next.

Responsive Evaluation. Robert Stake (1975a) defines responsive evaluation as an educational evaluation oriented more directly to program activities than to program intent. It responds to audience requirements for information, and the different perspectives on values are included in recording the success or failure of the program. He contrasts responsive evaluation to preordinate evaluation. Preordinate evaluation emphasizes statements of goals, use of objective tests, standards held by program personnel, and research-type reports. Responsive evaluation is less reliant on formal communication than on natural communication.

Responsive evaluations require planning and structure, but they rely little on formal statements and abstract representations such as flow charts and displays of test scores. Statements of objectives, hypotheses, tests given, and teaching syllabi receive attention if they are components of the instructional program. But they are evaluated along with other program components and not as the basis for the evaluation plan. The proper amount of structure for responsive evaluation depends on the program and the persons involved.

To do a responsive evaluation, according to Stake, the evaluator conceives of a plan of observations and negotiations. The evaluator arranges for various persons to observe the program, and with their help prepares brief narratives, portrayals, product displays, and so forth. Because points of view differ, it is necessary to find out what the various audiences value and to gather expressions of worth from various individuals. The quality of this information must be checked, and participants are asked to react to the accuracy of the portrayals. Authority figures are asked to react to the importance of various findings, and audience members are asked to react to the relevance of the findings. As teachers vary according to personal beliefs and values in presenting the same outline for a lesson, and as students are capable of using different kinds of tasks to gain skills and knowledge from the same lesson outline, the evaluator, in a responsive context, may ask questions that seem presumptuous at times. When asking *why* a certain procedure was used or certain materials or examples presented, it is not unlikely that some persons will become defensive or seek to avoid confronting an educational issue. However, important questions and issues should be examined and resolved.

Responsive evaluation can be particularly useful during formative evaluation when the staff needs help in monitoring the program and when no one is sure what problems will arise. It can also be useful in summative evaluation when audiences want an understanding of a program's activity, its strengths and shortcomings, and when the evaluator can provide a vicarious experience for the client.

Which data to collect is one decision area of responsive evaluation, but how to do the evaluation is another, according to Stake. He has identified twelve prominent events as shown in Figure 16. These are placed as if on the face of a clock to illustrate that any event can follow any other event, and many events occur simultaneously. The evaluator may return to each event many times before the evaluation is finished. The point at twelve o'clock is an indicator of the numerous times that the evaluator will want to check ideas about program scope, activities, purposes, and issues against those of the clients and participants. The evaluator will want to show them the materials that have been gathered and to discuss information received on questions of value, activities in progress, curricular content, and products. These discussions will help the evaluator learn how to communicate in the particular local setting.

In the mythical Radnor humanities curriculum evaluation project, Stake and Pearsol followed the plan of a responsive evaluation model. Design was negotiated with the board and principal, and a few days a month were allocated across four months. Students, faculty, and others were involved in observations, interviews, preparing logs, and in contributions of written documents. The activities and the setting were carefully observed; observations were recorded, questioned, and interpreted; predominant issues were reported, and all of this was presented in the language of the people involved. The steps of responsive evaluation as applied to the humanities curriculum were:

1. Negotiating a framework for the evaluation study with the sponsors.
2. Eliciting topics or questions of concern from the sponsors.
3. Formulating foreshadowing questions for initial guidance.
4. Entering the scene of the evaluation and observing it.
5. Paring down information, questioning it, identifying themes and issues.
6. Presenting these initial findings in an interim report.

Figure 16. Prominent Events in a Responsive Evaluation

Talk
with clients,
program staff,
audiences

Format for
audience use

Identify
program
scope

Winnow,
match issues
to audiences

Overview
program
activities

Validate, confirm
attempt to
discomfirm

Discover
purposes,
concerns

Thematize;
prepare portrayals,
case studies

Conceptualize
issues,
problems

Observe
designated
antecedents,
transactions,
and outcomes

Select
observers,
judges,
instruments
if any

Identify,
data needs,
regarding issues

From Robert E. Stake, *Program Evaluation, Particularly Responsive Evaluation.* Occasional paper #5. Kalamazoo: Evaluation Center of Western Michigan University, 1975b, p. 19.

7. Investigating the predominant issues and concerns more fully.
8. Looking for conflicting evidence that would invalidate findings.
9. Reporting the results in narrative style for the readers (1975, p. 32-33).

Goal-Free Evaluation Model. What are the effects and side effects of a given program and what needs does it meet? These are questions pertinent to goal-free evaluation, originated by Michael Scriven (1974), who was concerned about bias in evaluation. Goal-free evaluation does not assess a program in terms of prespecified goals and objectives. It is an evaluation of actual effects and side effects against a profile of demonstrated needs. In goal-free evaluation, the evaluator is expected to be an unbiased observer not influenced by the goals and objectives set forth by the program developers. The evaluator is free to collect whatever data appear to be pertinent in considering the total consequence of a program, and these consequences are then evaluated against demonstrated needs. The demonstrated needs would be those perceived by the evaluator in the context of the situation.

An example of goal-free evaluation might be a reading program based on goal statements focusing on knowledge of phonics and syntax. Presumably, if the evaluator also discovers in assessing the total effects that several children have developed a dislike for reading in the course of the program, although they may have learned much about phonics and syntax, the reported effects of the program should bring that problem to light. Goal-free evaluation is essentially oriented to the consumers (in this case, the students), and is concerned with desirable and undesirable behaviors and attitudes that may occur because of participation in a particular curriculum project or program, although these would not have been given attention if the evaluation had been confined to reporting the results from specified goals and objectives; for example, test scores or other quantitative data. As with responsive evaluation models, the evaluator must be aware of personal sensitivities to questioning.

Artistic Evaluation. An artistic model of educational evaluation views the curriculum as a work of art, and the curriculum evaluator functions much like a literary critic or art critic. Robert Donmoyer (1981) contrasts artistic models to adversary models that cast the evaluators in the roles of prosecution and defense attorneys, goal-free models that transform the evaluator into a philosopher, and responsive models that call for the evaluator to become a journalist with occasional editorial privileges. John Mann (1968) was said to be the first to conceptualize curriculum evaluation in artistic metaphors, and his idea has been expanded by others.

Elliot Eisner (1977) has proposed a version of the artistic model of curriculum evaluation in his discussion of connoisseurship and educational criticism. The connoisseur's approach requires that classrooms be intensively observed. The difficulties that may arise in this type of evaluation could be time constraints, personal descriptions that are unsatisfactory to the persons being observed, misinterpretations between the theoretician and the practitioner, and problems of logistics, such as proper release of the report to its audiences. Nevertheless, the evaluator as artist offers educational practitioners an opportunity to step outside of themselves and view the curriculum and instruction through the eyes of another human being.

Status Assessments

Status assessments include studies that provide information on comparative achievement of given populations in relation to certain curriculum programs, such as international evaluations; longitudinal studies, such as Project Talent (Flanagan 1975); periodic status reports such as the National Assessment of Educational Progress; and local status assessments that are designed to evaluate the quality or quantity of a program or to discover missing elements, such as the evaluation of a school's multicultural educational program. The information brought forth by status reports frequently stimulates action towards improvement, even though that may not have been a declared purpose of the evaluative study.

International Evaluations. For more than twenty years, a network of educational researchers has cooperated on a number of international studies of school achievement, sponsored by the International Association for the Evaluation of Educational Achievement. Studies have been conducted in mathematics, reading, science, literature, English, French, and civics. At one time or another, twenty-eight countries have participated. The purposes of the international evaluation are to look at educational systems from an international perspective through which to explore major issues of educational policy, to train educational researchers, and to raise the standards of educational research and evaluation.

Thus far, the international studies, in providing status information, have pointed out the obvious. Findings were that clear discrepancies in achievement exist between the more and the less technologically developed nations as well as within groups of nations. The assessors suggested that their findings have implications for policy planners and for curriculum in terms of the degree of selectivity of students imposed by a nation's educational system and the financial support given to education. Most countries admit only the more able students to academic secondary schools, while the United States admits all who want to enter. Financing of education varies widely from country to country. Thus, international comparisons of test results can become skewed in favor of some countries over others (Purves and Levine 1975).

The second international mathematics study, in process, is expected to provide an analysis of the mathematics curricula of various countries and to reveal emphases on various aspects of mathematics and ways in which the subject matter is organized. It is also expected to provide information about how teachers around the world teach mathematics (Purves and Travers, 1982).

Project Talent. The long-term value of curriculum offerings can be an important purpose of evaluation, although such studies are rare. One of the better known longitudinal studies was conducted on a national level in Project Talent, which was initiated in 1960 with the testing of 400,000 secondary school students. Data were collected regarding student interests, ability test scores, and characteristics of the schools including courses offered. Fifteen years later, a representative sample of these persons was interviewed. The former students reported on their satisfaction or dissatisfaction with their current status in life activities and their reflections about secondary school courses. One overall generalization from the findings was that educational programs should be improved and modified to enable persons to achieve greater satisfaction in intellectual development and personal understandings (Flanagan 1975).

National Assessment of Educational Progress. The National Assessment of Educational Progress is an assessment plan designed to furnish information about the educational achievement of children, youths, and young adults and to indicate progress and problems in the educational programs offered by the schools of the United States. Ten study areas are assessed on four- or five-year cycles: reading, literature, music, social studies, science, writing, citizenship, mathematics, art, and career and occupational development. Test results are reported by age group, sex, region, type of community, racial group, and level of parental education. The reports are widely distributed, and they come out in newsletter form at frequent intervals as the subject areas are rotated as well as the time cycles. The impact of the assessments on the nation's curriculum is not known, but it is likely that the earlier reports stimulated the basics push and that later reports are stimulating efforts to develop thinking skills.

Local Assessments. Attention to multicultural education is an example of a local school assessment. Such an assessment could determine whether attention is being given to attitudes, feelings, and applications of learnings to real situations as well as to acquiring information. Geneva Gay (1981) has listed forty-five criteria for assessing a school's multicultural education quotient grouped by the functions of curriculum and instruction, staffing, support services, student activities, and school climate. The status report should discover whether a multicultural program is in operation that addresses many different ethnic groups.

Assessing school climate and its effectiveness is another type of status report that should be useful to instructional leaders. Richard Sagor (1981) recommends the technique of shadowing for assessing school climate. In this technique, an observer accompanies a student all day and attempts to experience everything that was experienced by that student. The purpose is to report the perceptions and findings of the students and the observers to the local school community. A similar study was reported by Lounsbury and Marani (1964) in a study of a junior high school. The shadowing technique will not provide a valid and reliable assessment of the totality of the school climate or an absolute measure of the effectiveness of its programs, but it is enlightening; and it may raise important issues about the school's program and climate.

Status assessments are useful in developing sensitivity to the ancillary consequences of teaching, commonly referred to as the "hidden curriculum." To assess whether there is a hidden curriculum in schoolwork related to the social class of the students was the focus of an assessment made by Jean Anyon (1981). Her design included five schools, and each was given a social-class designation. Fifth-grade classes were involved. From the study, it appeared that working-class students were being prepared through their school experience for jobs that are routine and mechanical in nature; whereas students from the upper classes were given schoolwork and experiences that prepared them for jobs demanding the creativity and skills necessary for a self-managed life.

In the working-class schools, it was found that the educational procedure was usually mechanical, involving rote behavior and very little decision making or choice. Emphasis was on following the right steps and following directions. Among the children there seemed to be an undercurrent of struggle against the work and indirect resistance to the flow of assignments. The investigators thought this might parallel the slowdown reaction to unsatisfactory labor conditions in later life. In the middle-class schools, the emphasis was on getting the right answers and getting a good grade; competition was encouraged. The tasks did not usually request creativity.

In affluent professional school settings, much of the work was creative activity carried out independently. The students were continually asked to express and apply ideas and concepts. In the executive elite school, emphasis was on developing one's intellectual powers, conceptualizing rules by which elements could fit together in systems, and applying the rules to solving problems.

The methods of evaluation used to gather data were classroom observations; interviews of students, teachers, principals, and district administrative staff; and assessment of curriculum and other materials in each classroom and school.

Selecting Evaluation Models

Numerous models, types, and procedures have been discussed in this chapter. Curriculum planners should not confine themselves to a single model but should choose models to suit various contexts for evaluation. Consideration should be given to the purpose of the evaluation, the audiences to be served, the size and scope of the curriculum area to be evaluated, and the constraints of time, cost, and human resources. Standards for evaluation and guidelines for judging the adequacy of an evaluation plan must also be considered.

STANDARDS FOR PROGRAM EVALUATION

In response to a widely recognized need for a comprehensive, carefully developed objective and useful way of judging evaluation plans, processes, and results, the Joint Committee on Standards for Educational Evaluation published in 1981 *Standards for Evaluation of Educational Programs, Projects, and Materials.* This useful reference reflects the experience and insights of both specialists and users of educational evaluations. Chaired by Daniel Stufflebeam and representing twelve professional educational associations, the joint committee involved dozens of persons and educational institutions in the preparation of the standards.

Although there is a wealth of knowledge about program evaluation, it became evident during federal funding of curriculum improvement programs that Congress was becoming impatient with evaluators' apparent inability to determine whether costly programs were in fact helping solve educational problems in reading, compensatory education, and other curriculum fields. This stimulated interest in the goal of developing evaluation standards, and further impetus came from leading specialists in the field of curriculum evaluation.

The benefits that are expected to be derived from use of the *Standards* include: a common language to facilitate communication and collaboration in evaluation, a set of general rules for dealing with a variety of evaluation problems, a set of working definitions to guide research and development on the evaluation process, a basis for self-regulation and accountability by professional evaluators, and an aid for developing public credibility for the evaluation field.

Thirty separate standards are each presented in detail, including an overview, guidelines, pitfalls, caveats, an illustrative case, and an analysis of the case. Categories of standards include audience identification; evaluator credibility; information scope and selection; valuation interpretation; report clarity; dissemination and timeliness; and evaluation impact. The *Standards* encourage the sound use of a variety of evaluation methods, and they contain advice for dealing with vital issues inherent in program evaluation.

To emphasize the importance of standards and guidelines for

curriculum evaluation and to summarize the chapter, we present a series of
questions that could be used as a checklist. These are drawn from criteria
published by the Northwest Regional Educational Laboratory (1977a, pp.
45–49) as an adaptation of a checklist prepared earlier by J. R. Sanders and
D. H. Nafziger (1975).

Checklist for Judging the Adequacy of an Evaluation Design

I. Criteria regarding the adequacy of the evaluation conceptualization
   A. Conceptual clarity and adequacy
      1. Is an adequate description of the whole program presented?
      2. Is a clear description given of the part of the program being
         evaluated?
      3. Is a clear description of the evaluation approach given (for
         example, comparison group study, single group study,
         goal-free evaluation, formative, summative, and so on)?
      4. Is the evaluation approach adequate and appropriate for
         evaluating the program?

   B. Scope
      1. Are the intended outcomes or goals of the program clearly
         specified?
      2. Is the scope of the evaluation broad enough to gather
         information concerning all specified program outcomes?
      3. Are any likely unintended effects from the program
         described?
      4. Is the approach of the evaluation broad enough to include
         measuring these unintended effects?
      5. Is adequate cost information about the program included in
         the scope of the evaluation?

   C. Relevance
      1. Are the audiences for the evaluation identified?
      2. Are the objectives of the evaluation explained?
      3. Are the objectives of the evaluation congruent with the
         information needs of the intended audiences?
      4. Does the information to be provided allow necessary
         decisions about the program or product to be made?

   D. Flexibility
      1. Can the design be adapted easily to accommodate changes
         in plans?

2. Are known constraints or parameters on the evaluation discussed thoroughly?
3. Can useful information be obtained in the face of unforeseen constraints, for example, noncooperation of control groups?

E. Feasibility
1. Are the evaluation resources (time, money, and personnel) adequate to carry out the projected activities?
2. Are management plans specified for conducting the evaluation?
3. Has adequate planning been done to support the feasibility of conducting complex activities?

II. Criteria concerning the adequacy of the collection and processing of information
A. Reliability
1. Are data collection procedures described well and was care taken to assure minimal error?
2. Are scoring or coding procedures objective?
3. Are the evaluation instruments reliable (that is, is reliability information included)?

B. Objectivity
1. Have attempts to control for bias in data collection and processing been described?
2. Are sources of information clearly specified?
3. Do the biases of the evaluators preclude an objective evaluation?

C. Representativeness
1. Are the data collection instruments valid?
2. Are the data collection instruments appropriate for the purposes of this evaluation?
3. Does the evaluation adequately address the questions it was intended to answer?

D. Generalizability
1. Are sampling techniques adequate to permit generalizations to the population of interest?
2. Does the cultural context of data collection techniques affect generalization?

3. Are the inferential statistics employed appropriate for the sample, data, and the questions to be answered?

III. Criteria concerning the adequacy of the presentation and reporting of information
   A. Timeliness
      1. Have efficient reporting techniques been used to meet the needs of the clients?
      2. Does the time schedule for reporting meet the needs of the audience?

   B. Pervasiveness
      1. Is information disseminated to all intended audiences?
      2. Are contractual constraints on dissemination of evaluation information observed?
      3. Are attempts being made to make the evaluation information available to relevant audiences beyond those specified in the contract?

IV. General criteria
   A. Ethical consideration
      1. Do test administration procedures follow professional standards of ethics?
      2. Have protection of human subjects guidelines been followed?
      3. Has confidentiality of data been guaranteed?

   B. Protocol
      1. Are appropriate persons contacted in the appropriate sequence?
      2. Have the client's policies and procedures been followed?

REFERENCES

Alkin, Marvin, and Fitzgibbon, G.T. "Methods and Theories of Evaluating Programs." *Journal of Research and Development in Education* 8 (September 1975): 2–15.

Anyon, Jean. "Social Class and the Hidden Curriculum of Work." In *Curriculum and Instruction*, edited by Henry A. Giroux, Anthony N. Penna, and William E. Pinar, pp. 317–41. Berkeley: McCutchan, 1981.

Apple, Michael. "Ideology and Form." In *Qualitative Evaluation*, edited by George Willis, pp. 492–521. Berkeley: McCutchan, 1978.

ASCD Committee on Research and Theory. *Measuring and Attaining the Goals of Education.* Alexandria, Va.: Association for Supervision and Curriculum Development, 1980.

Bloom, Benjamin S.; Hastings, J. Thomas; and Madaus, George F. *Handbook on Formative and Summative Evaluation of Student Learning.* New York: McGraw-Hill, 1971.

Bobbitt, Franklin. *How to Make a Curriculum.* Boston: Houghton Mifflin, 1924.

Brandt, Ronald S. *Applied Strategies for Curriculum Evaluation.* Alexandria, Va.: Association for Supervision and Curriculum Development, 1981.

Brickell, Henry M. "Groping for the Elephant." In *Applied Strategies for Curriculum Evaluation,* edited by Ronald S. Brandt, pp. 91-103. Alexandria, Va.: Association for Supervision and Curriculum Development, 1981.

Charters, W.W. *Curriculum Construction.* New York: Macmillan Co., 1923.

Donmoyer, Robert. "The Evaluator as Artist." In *Curriculum and Instruction,* edited by Henry A. Giroux, Anthony N. Penna, and William E. Pinar, pp. 342-63. Berkeley: McCutchan, 1981.

Eisner, Elliot W. "On the Uses of Educational Connoisseurship and Criticism for Evaluating Classroom Life." *Teachers College Record* (February 1977): 375-88.

English, Fenwick W. "Curriculum Mapping." *Educational Leadership* 37 (April 1980): 558-59.

Farley, Joseph M. "Student Interviews as an Evaluation Tool." *Educational Leadership* 39 (December 1981): 185-86.

Flanagan, John C. "Education's Contribution to the Quality of Life of a Sample of 30-Year-Olds." *Educational Researcher* 4 (June 1975): 13-16.

Gay, Geneva. "What Is Your School's MEQ?" *Educational Leadership* 39 (December 1981): 187-89.

Gephart, William J. "Who Will Engage in Curriculum Evaluation?" *Educational Leadership* 35 (January 1978): 255-58.

Goodlad, John I. "An Overview of 'A Study of Schooling.'" *Phi Delta Kappan* 61 (November 1979): 174-78.

Guba, Egon G. *Toward a Methodology of Naturalistic Inquiry in Educational Evaluation.* CSE Monograph Series in Education, No. III. Los Angeles: Center for the Study of Evaluation, University of California, Los Angeles, 1978.

Guba, Egon G. "Evaluation in Field Studies." Address at evaluation conference sponsored by the Ohio State Department of Education, Columbus, Ohio, 1965.

Hemphill, John K. "The Relationships Between Research and Evaluation Studies." In *Educational Evaluation: New Roles, New Means,* part II, pp. 189-220. Sixty-eighth Yearbook of the National Society for the Study of Education. Chicago: University of Chicago Press, 1969.

Joint Committee on Standards for Educational Evaluation. *Standards for Evaluations of Educational Programs, Projects, and Materials.* New York: McGraw-Hill, 1981.

Judd, Charles H. "A Look Forward." In *The Measurement of Educational Products,* part II, pp. 159-60. Seventeenth Yearbook of the National Society for the Study of Education. Bloomington, Ill.: Public School Publishing Co., 1918.

Lounsbury, John H., and Marani, Jean V. *The Junior High School We Saw.*

Alexandria, Va.: Association for Supervision and Curriculum Development, 1964.

Mager, Robert F. *Preparing Instructional Objectives.* Palo Alto, Calif.: Fearon, 1962.

Mann, John. "Curriculum Criticism." *Curriculum Theory Network* 1 (Winter 1968): 2-14.

McNeil, John D. "Evaluating the Curriculum." In *Curriculum and Instruction*, edited by Henry A. Giroux, Anthony N. Penna, and William E. Pinar, pp. 252-69. Berkeley: McCutchan, 1981.

Merwin, Jack C. "Historical Review of Changing Concepts of Education." In *Educational Evaluation: New Roles, New Means*, part II, pp. 6-25. Sixty-eighth Yearbook of the National Society for the Study of Education. Chicago: University of Chicago Press, 1969.

National Assessment of Educational Progress, 1860 Lincoln Street, Denver, Co. 80302. (Continuing series of newsletters and other publications.)

National Study of School Evaluation. *Evaluative Criteria for the Evaluation of High Schools,* 5th ed. Arlington, Va.: National Study of School Evaluation, 1978.

Northwest Regional Educational Laboratory. *Program Evaluation Skills for Busy Administrators*, prepared by Thomas R. Owens and Warren D. Evans. Portland, Ore.: Northwest Regional Educational Laboratory, 1977a.

Northwest Regional Educational Laboratory. *3 on 2 Evaluation Report, 1976-77.* Vol. I, technical report. Portland, Ore.: Northwest Regional Educational Laboratory, 1977b.

Popham, W. James. "The Evaluator's Curse." In *Applied Strategies for Curriculum Evaluation*, edited by Ronald S. Brandt, pp. 1-8. Alexander, Va.: Association for Supervision and Curriculum Development, 1981.

Popham, W. James, and Carlson, Dale. "Deep Dark Deficits of the Adversary Evaluation Model." In *Curriculum and Instruction*, edited by Henry A. Giroux, Anthony N. Penna, and William E. Pinar, pp. 271-80. Berkeley: McCutchan, 1981.

Popham, W. James, et al. *Instructional Objectives: An Analysis of Emerging Issues.* Chicago: Rand McNally, 1969.

Provus, Malcolm. *Discrepancy Evaluation for Educational Program Improvement and Assessment.* Berkeley: McCutchan, 1971.

Purves, Alan C., and Levine, Daniel U., eds. *Educational Policy and International Assessment.* Berkeley, McCutchan, 1975.

Purves, Alan C., and Travers, Kenneth J. "International Evaluation and American Curriculum." *Educational Leadership* 39 (March 1982): 440-46.

Raths, James D. "Encouraging Trends in Curriculum Evaluation." *Educational Leadership* 35 (January 1978): 243-46.

Reavis, William C. "Contributions of Research to Educational Administration." In *The Scientific Movement in Education*, part II, p. 27. Thirty-seventh Yearbook of the National Society for the Study of Education. Bloomington, Ill.: Public School Publishing Co., 1938.

Rice, Joseph M. "The Futility of the Spelling Grind." *Forum* 24 (1897): 163-72, 409-19.

Sagor, Richard. " 'Day in the Life'—A Technique for Assessing School Climate and Effectiveness." *Educational Leadership* 39 (December 1981): 190-93.

Sanders, J.R., and Nafziger, D.H. "Checklist for Judging the Adequacy of an Evaluation Design." In *Program Evaluation Skills for Busy Administrators*, prepared by Thomas R. Owens and Warren D. Evans, pp. 45-49. Portland, Ore.: Northwest Regional Educational Laboratory, 1977.

Saylor, J. Galen; Alexander, William M.; and Lewis, Arthur J. *Curriculum Planning for Better Teaching and Learning*. New York: Holt, Rinehart, and Winston, 1981.

Scriven, Michael. "Pros and Cons about Goal-free Evaluation." *Evaluation Comment* 3 (December 1974): 1-4.

Scriven, Michael. *The Methodology of Evaluation*. American Educational Research Association Monograph Series on Curriculum Evaluation. Chicago: Rand McNally, 1967.

Sirotnik, Kenneth A., and Oakes, Jeannie. "A Contextual Appraisal System for Schools: Medicine or Madness?" *Educational Leadership* 39 (December 1981): 164-79.

Smith, Eugene R., and Tyler, Ralph W. *Appraising and Recording Student Progress*. New York: Harper and Bros., 1942.

Stake, Robert E. *Evaluating the Arts in Education: A Responsive Approach*. Columbus, Ohio: Charles E. Merrill, 1975a.

Stake, Robert E. *Program Evaluation, Particularly Responsive Evaluation*. Occasional Paper No. 5. Kalamazoo: Evaluation Center of Western Michigan University, 1975b.

Stake, Robert E. "The Countenance of Educational Evaluation." *Teachers College Record* 68 (April 1967): 523-40.

Stake, Robert E., and Denny, Terry. "Needed Concepts and Techniques for Utilizing More Fully the Potential of Evaluation." In *Educational Evaluation: New Roles, New Means*, part II, pp. 370-90. Sixty-eighth Yearbook of the National Society for the Study of Education. Chicago: University of Chicago Press, 1969.

Stake, Robert E., and Pearsol, James A. "Evaluating Responsively." In *Applied Strategies for Curriculum Evaluation*, edited by Ronald S. Brandt, Alexandria, Va.: Association for Supervision and Curriculum Development, 1981.

Stufflebeam, Daniel L., et al. *Educational Evaluation and Decision Making*. Itaska, Ill.: Peacock, 1971.

Thorndike, Edward L. *Educational Psychology*. New York: Lenche and Buechner, 1903.

Tyler, Ralph W. "Specific Approaches to Curriculum Development." In *Curriculum and Instruction*, edited by Henry A. Giroux, Anthony N. Penna, and William E. Pinar, pp. 17-30. Berkeley: McCutchan, 1981.

Tyler, Ralph W. "The Curriculum—Then and Now." In *Proceedings, 1956 Invitational Conference on Testing Problems*, p. 81. Princeton, N.J.: Educational Testing Service, 1957.

Webster, William J. "CIPP in Local Evaluation." In *Applied Strategies for*

Curriculum Evaluation, edited by Ronald S. Brandt, pp. 48–57. Alexandria, Va.: Association for Supervision and Curriculum Development, 1981.

Wilhelms, Fred T., ed. *Evaluation as Feedback and Guide.* Yearbook of the Association for Supervision and Curriculum Development. Alexandria, Va.: ASCD, 1967.

Worthen, Blaine R., and Rogers, W. Todd. "Pitfalls and Potential of Adversary Evaluation." *Educational Leadership* 37 (April 1980): 536–43.

10

Future Awareness

Visions of the future have always led people on toward greater and greater challenges. Today's challenges seem immense because the prospects seem immense. Some view the forecasts with dismay; others view them with zest and approach the future with enthusiasm. In any event, trends for the future have major importance for curriculum development and instruction.

The rapid changes in social, economic, and technological conditions and world events are forcing us to be concerned about where the trends may lead. Researchers and futures analysts declare that choices can be made, that there are alternatives to choose between if those in positions of power act wisely. Analysts speak of "futures," not just *the* future, in reference to alternative forecasts, both desirable and undesirable.

One projection is gloomy; the future seems filled with serious problems that may overwhelm the citizens of the world. The other is an exciting, adventurous prospect of a future in which there will be many changes that should bring better, more productive and satisfying occupations and lifestyles. We know for certain only that our children will be living in the future. For this reason the school has a serious obligation to plan programs that make it possible for students to learn to assess trends and to gain new knowledge and skills. These programs must enable students not only to adapt, but also to gain self-sufficiency as contributing members of society who will work with others for the benefit of humanity.

Do today's elementary and secondary curriculums provide an adequate orientation to the coming changes and the ways of looking into the future? Are schools so obsessed with the ideas and habits of the past that there is neither time nor inclination to study probable futures or introduce new ways of learnings or opportunities to recognize relationships and discover clues to the solutions for perplexing societal problems?

Forecasters visualize drastic new forms of instruction and changing emphases in curriculum as results of changes in technology. Factories and offices are already undergoing transformations. Robots are replacing human workers on the assembly lines, and many office workers have had to yield their jobs to computers. New types of work will be needed, and persons now unemployed have felt the impact of the need to learn new skills.

TECHNOLOGICAL CHANGE

Abundant ideas are available to acquaint students with technological advancements. When curriculum and instruction planning can meet the challenge and when resources are at hand, students can become facile with technology at an early age and in ways that lead to critical thinking and creative problem solving. Eventually some of the traditional skills of schooling may be replaced with startling new ways.

Arthur Shostak (1981) wrote: "In any scenario of the future, keyboard skills, knowledge and accompanying technology, and machines that take dictation may downgrade the importance of teaching handwriting" (p. 357). A school that has computerized scheduling (individualized programs) and has both courses and libraries "on line" will no longer group children by age or grade. In the "world of telematique," students can carry on a dialogue with the lecturer or program producer via television. Even preschoolers can learn some of the basic skills useful in managing microelectronic media.

When the contents of libraries, magazines, and newspapers have been put into computers, and when the use of micrographics begins to mature, the teaching of reading will change drastically according to George Harmon (1981). To begin with, the vocabulary will have many new words. Also, children will learn more words per grade level, where grade levels still exist, or more words per age level compared to current norms. Many children do have more extensive oral vocabularies than they presently use in written school work; with future access to electronic aids, such children will be able to develop more fluency and higher mental processes.

In referring to the reponsibilities of the educational system of the United States, Samuel Halperin (1981) asserted, "Society's demands for educated workers will increase, most likely beyond anything our planet has ever experienced" (p. 81). He went on to point out that the continuing revolution in telecommunications, computers, and other newer technologies will put a premium on those workers with complex technological knowledge and skills. At the same time, such rapidly obsolescent technologies means that none of these technical workers and managers will ever be completely competent; training and retraining will be "in" as never before, while a sound general education on which to base this retraining will be more essential than ever.

"Education will increasingly be defined as learning how to get information; how to work at solving problems, how to recreate, self-renew, and self-direct toward that which never was before...."* (p. 81), Halperin continued. In this context, computer literacy and technological sophistication will become essential, not merely a nice extra. Home computer terminals, two-way (interactive) phone-video consoles, laser and satellite communication, and so on will become economically within the reach of many Americans. Not experiencing some level of competence with computers will soon be equated with denial of access to information and, therefore, to equal educational opportunity. Obviously, drastic changes and exciting opportunities are ahead for the schools.

Alvin Toffler (1980) suggests that elementary school children of the future will talk and read more insightfully about energy, ecology, conversation, and the sources of raw materials. They will learn to ask questions, learn how to find information, how to classify it, and how to use it to draw conclusions.

For secondary school students, studying computer languages will be required as will a knowledge of certain electronic machines. New skills and concepts will also be required. The vocabulary used in Toffler's electronic cottage—where children of all ages will be learning and participating in the work—would sound foreign to teachers of today.

The electronic cottage would be an updated revival of the cottage industries idea. Many kinds of electronic equipment can easily be installed in a home, and this equipment can perform much of the office work previously done elsewhere in a fraction of the usual time. Computers, word processors, micrographic equipment, teleprinters, optical scanners will all be available. Skills will be needed in computer graphics used by engineers, meteorologists, and architects and business graphics used to print bargraphs, charts, and to study trends and forecasting. These machines are now found in thousands of offices, but many claim advantages for transferring the machines and the work they do into the home.

Toffler's idea of an electronic cottage would cut down on commuting, the consumption of gasoline, and hence pollution. Long traffic lines would be reduced as would traffic accidents. Some of the space used for offices and sprawling headquarters could be eliminated or greatly reduced by decentralizing the work. Most of the usual paperwork of business will be eliminated by almost instantaneous electronic transmission of information that is currently found on memos, letters, bills, orders, and inventories. Such information will either be filed by computers or used to set other processes in motion. Hundreds of companies now permit some personnel to work at home, and they plan to increase the number.

What might be a very important result of this movement of business to homes is that the electronic cottage might help hold the nuclear family together. Both father and mother could do their work at home and thus provide better supervision for their offspring. As the children grew older, they could also learn to manage some of the electronic equipment so the entire family would be drawn into the work as it was in the early days of farming. Also, the community might become more stable as families became less mobile. Parents would be more likely to join service clubs, civic groups, and sponsor children's organizations or seek other ways to stimulate social growth and development as supplements to their containment at home.

Disadvantages center around the feelings of isolation that can develop in persons working alone within their electronic cottages. People need human warmth that comes from interaction with coworkers. Multiple options, used by some employers, offer alternating periods of home and office work.

People will become more self-reliant and resourceful in the technological era. For example, major appliance companies are developing plans to provide expert repair service from headquarters rendered via telephone. Consumers will make their own repairs. They will simply dial a code number, and an expert will provide directions on how to remove a part, which part, what to do about it, how to replace it, how to rewire the appliance step-by-step.

On assembly lines that are not completely automated workers will wear small two-way button mikes to receive instructions. Instruction like this is now available on farm equipment where the worker can receive complete directions for operating the machine from a built-in tape recorder.

New forms of communication will simplify reporting and record keeping. When workers make reports, they can talk into microphones that will transmit to the office transcribers and printers. No need for written reports, and sketches and diagrams can be computerized. There will be new views of literacy. In school, compositions would be placed on tapes, and the teacher's comments, corrections, and finally grades, would also come back to the student on tape. A different kind of literacy would be in use, but the movement would be in the direction of electronic information processing. According to Toffler, the old criteria of reading, especially, but also writing as indices of literacy will yield to electronics. Without being able to read people will be able to talk intelligently about art, drama, history, current events, and important ideas. There will be many changes that should bring better, faster means of communicating, collecting, storing, and retrieving information.

The advent of the electronic age should also initiate scores of new occupations and different but interesting lifestyles. There will be more opportunity to achieve self-actualization because there will be more time for social and political activity, more time for reading and reflection, and more time for travel.

Later in the chapter, applications to curriculum development will be discussed in more detail but a closer examination of trends and turbulences is in order first. Changes in family structure and in society will affect the school of the future in addition to environmental and technological changes.

SOCIAL CHANGE

Change is a constant companion of people in all societies. Change is almost imperceptible in some societies and almost too fast to be absorbed in others. The culture of the United States was for generations based on agriculture, long days of back-breaking work. Before the advent of reapers, combines, and multipurpose machines that till the soil, fertilize, apply herbicide, and plant in one operation, manpower was in demand. Many hands were needed to tend the crops, grow food, maintain the buildings and the fences. This often led to large numbers of people living in the same house. Families might consist of grandparents, parents, children—some grown and married—grandchildren, and frequently other relatives and orphans. This was the extended family.

In some cases ethnic groups brought the extended family to the Americas. Through the years these families underwent changes in structure and even living styles because conditions of work changed with the advent of power-driven machinery. Young couples on farms or in the work force sought to make it on their own and found their own housing. They lived with their children but not with other relatives, and the nuclear family came to be the norm and existed for several generations as the model for family life. Within this model, the husband and the wife managed the home and raised the family.

But changes keep moving across the human landscape. Science and research, sponsored by both industry and government, are affecting people in nearly everything they do. Technology—especially the part that deals with information, such as television and computers—is making changes in the sociology of the family. The fact that many women, married or single, have joined the work force has brought changes to the nuclear family. Toffler (1980) writes that 93 percent of the population no longer fits the previous tradition of the husband as breadwinner, and wife as homemaker and mother.

Toffler describes a number of nonnuclear family lifestyles and structures.

One of these is the growing number of single-parent families, which result from divorces, deaths, and single people having or adopting children. Other family forms are a man and woman living together without marrying, child-free couples who wish to stay that way, and a divorced man and divorced woman, both with children, marrying and merging two families. Toffler writes of "a bewildering array of family forms: homosexual marriages, communes, groups of elderly people banding together to share expenses (and lifestyles)...contract marriages, serial marriages, family clusters, and a variety of intimate networks..." In Chicago, in a single poor black neighborhood, psychiatrists found "no less than 86 different combinations of adults including numerous forms of 'mother-grandmother' families, 'mother-aunt' families, mother-stepfather families, and 'mother-other' families" (p. 215).

Today's lifestyles and family structures are not going to revert to the ways of the past; if anything, even more change can be predicted. The ways in which this influences the schools is seen in an American Association of School Administrators' report on the understandings that school personnel must have in working effectively with children from a diversity of home backgrounds (1982). Some children from single-parent families were said to have severe emotional problems, and some are from the low socioeconomic levels. Many of their learning problems have been attributed by school personnel to the fact that they are being reared by one parent; it is said that the children lack a sex role model in their lives. These are examples of the gross generalizations and myths surrounding the 11.5 million children in America from single-parent families. Care must be taken not to project all of these problems onto all such children. Teachers should be expected to give children from nontraditional homes the same caring attention that all children need.

Admittedly, divorce or separation is a very serious event, especially for the student who experiences emotional trauma and an adjustment period similar to when there is a death in the family. Counselors report that 40 percent or more of the students in some schools today come from single-parent families. But how this situation affects the children and their performance in school depends on much more than the generalizations usually attributed to these youngsters. Each family, single parent or otherwise, probably represents a different set of emotional-social circumstances and should receive individual consideration by the school.

Many family structures will seem atypical to teachers and administrators; it is possible that in an entire class not one student comes from a "normal" nuclear family. Values may be different, and children from nontraditional families may be used to more freedom and independence, may earn their own spending money, and may be precocious in the ways of their world. There are extremes; children as just described represent one end of a continuum while at the other end are children on whom parents bestow abundant financial resources and protect from as many hardships as possible. The interest children show in school and their motivation vary greatly as well.

In creating new forms of curriculum and instruction to meet the challenges of the future, schools have another problem that arises from such a meld of family forms. Curriculum development plans should be launched with the cooperation of parents and interested citizens, but many parents are not interested in curriculum projects. Some work seven days per week; some will not give up their evenings; others are content to have the school take charge—so long as there is no serious trouble. But contact must still be attempted to avoid misunderstandings. This means the school will need to spend great amounts of time on public relations—educating the community—about trends and alternatives for the future.

CONCERNS ABOUT THE FUTURE

The inevitable problems that will impinge on this country and the world have been vividly described by numerous analysts; many concerns have been highlighted, and each concern has some relevance for curriculum and instruction. Each can be frightening to students unless presented in the context of human creativity and problem-solving abilities. Studies of trends, global and national factors affecting the future, and measures presently being taken to solve problems provide unique opportunities for students to search information sources for facts and examples, develop critical-thinking skills, and apply creativity and productivity to new modes of learning. Suggestions for student involvement in their own learning made throughout this book are apropos here, as are the discussions of curriculum development and implementation. Information and assistance for teaching about the future are widely available to curriculum planners and teachers. The Global Futures Network of Toronto offers well-considered information. Useful annotated bibliographies on this subject are kept up to date by Don Glines (1983) through the California State Department of Education. Newspapers and other types of media are essential sources of information about relevant events, and they provide a context for teaching the difference between facts and propaganda or contrasting liberal and conservative viewpoints or looking for signs of the "great transition," discussed later in this chapter.

Concerns identified in the *Global 2000* and *Global Future* reports from the Council on Environmental Quality and Department of State (1980, 1981), the study made by Harold Shane and reported in collaboration with Bernadine Tabler (1981), and Carter Henderson's analysis (1982) have been combined into six major problem areas. Examples of progress being made toward solving these problems are presented with the expectation that attention will be directed to the constant flow of new knowledge in the field, that proposed solutions are not *faits accomplis* but clues to be pursued in curriculum planning.

The *Global 2000* reports, sponsored by one national administration and criticized by the next as too pessimistic, have nevertheless focused on problems needing attention. The rationale for the three-year study, made with the assistance of several hundred experts in the fields under investigation, was that public discussion would alert citizens of the United States to their responsibilities and opportunities for developing a sane and sensible future. A different approach to estimating what the future may hold was taken by Harold Shane, who traveled around the world and interviewed 132 internationally recognized scholars. Carter Henderson identified "primal forces" affecting the future, particularly the economic future. Concerns listed in each report are consistent with the others, with a few appearing singly. These follow.

Population and Food Supply

Analysts have justified concerns about overpopulation with statistics. The world population is expected to increase from 4.3 billion to an estimated 6.2 billion by 2000 and eventually stabilize at 10.5 billion in the year 2110. Although smaller than some estimates, it is still two and one-half times the number presently living on this globe. Population increase will place greater stress on the world's food supply. Food production may expand as much as 90 percent under the most optimistic assumptions, but by the year 2000 the increase will be less than 15 percent on a per capita basis, and it is the poor people who have the least ability to expand food production. There are thousands of starving people in the world, agricultural land is widely mismanaged, distribution of food to the hungry has low national and international priority, and weapons often seem to be more important. Keeping thousands of people hungry and in poverty appears to be a national policy in some areas of the world (*Global 2000*, Shane).

However, progress is being made in controlling population growth and increasing food production, particularly in Third World countries where the problem is most critical, as well as in many of the more developed countries. Incentives and disincentives related to birth control are government-sponsored in China, India, Egypt, Singapore, and Sri Lanka as well as other countries. Judith Jacobsen (1983) compares efforts elsewhere with the reluctance of the United States government to come to grips with the problem. China employs a system of bonuses and benefits that reward the small family and penalize the larger one as well as educational programs and social and political persuasion. As early as 1957, a nationwide movement began in China against early marriages. Ways have been developed to keep young people apart longer by means of employment, housing, and so on (Guillain 1966). Information and contraceptives are readily available, and the official position of the government for population control is having an effect.

As Jacobsen pointed out, it is extremely complicated to control population, improve the world's food supply, and end hunger and starvation. An example pertaining to the complex nature of those problems, and enlightening for curriculum planners who might treat the matter on a single-concept basis, is described by Henry Winthrop (1974). A team of outstanding agricultural experts, sent to India in 1959 to study the food situation and make recommendations for averting or reducing impending starvation reported that the problem involved relationships among seventy factors, including capital, research, soil surveys, fertilizers, water facilities, educational services, program coordinators, and publications. Other factors to be considered were religious beliefs, forestry problems, markets for materials, and revision of the land-tenure system. Then there were problems to be solved in population control, political disunity, communication across languages, soil conservation, and plant breeding. Reports from India today are that progress is being made on many of these problems.

A major effort to improve the world's food supply and end hunger and starvation is coordinated by the World Food Council, established after the World Food Conference in Rome in 1974. Eugene Whelan (1982) describes its purpose as providing coordination for a hodgepodge of food-aid organizations that have often duplicated one another, distributed food so unevenly that there were scarcities and wasteful surpluses that could have been avoided, or used food for empire building. The World Food Council is also heading a study of the twenty-odd agencies of the United Nations involved in food aid.

Pollution

The earth's life-support systems are threatened by pollution of air, land, and water. By-products of economic development and industrial growth have caused contamination from hazardous substances and nuclear waste, buildup of carbon dioxide in the stratospheric ozone layer, and acid rain. Virtually every aspect of the earth's ecosystem and resource base has suffered damage, which has already affected people's lives. Pollutants washed from the land, dumped into the ocean, or deposited from the atmosphere have affected the world's fisheries, thus reducing a major component of the world's food supply. Pollution of oceans, seacoasts, and inland waterways have not only destroyed essential marine habitats but have made ugly what was once beautiful. The current concern is no longer letting people of the world know what the problem is; they know. Now it is a matter of doing something about it. Barry Commoner (1972) speaks vigorously of the "closing circle" and advocates a new territory of ecological thinking. Disposal of waste is a worldwide problem awaiting significant measures for control (*Global 2000,* Henderson, 1982, Shane 1981).

Progress in this area of concern has been irregular. The dilemma of pollution control versus economic growth and development is frustrating. Cities, states, and nations need the jobs and income that new industries bring, but industries also bring emissions, waste for disposal, urban density, and blight to scenic tourist attractions. At the national level, study after study has been made and legislation proposed. Examples are recent reports by the National Academy of Sciences and a panel of scientists appointed by the White House Office of Science and Technology Policy. Both emphasized that a reduction in pollution from industrial sources would reduce acid rain and that action must be taken to prevent irreversible damage. A syndicated analysis by Philip Shabecoff (1983) predicts action by the Environmental Protection Agency, at least to some extent.

On the international level, the United Nations issued a Declaration of the Human Environment more than a decade ago that has influenced action in many countries to curtail emissions, anticipate and avoid urban density by dispersal of factories, stress exchange of information for decision making, protect and manage common resources, and emphasize opportunities for developing nations to be assisted in the location of industries in ways that could profit from lessons learned elsewhere about uncontrolled emissions (Lineberry 1973). Another effort on an international basis is the continuing attempt to determine the extent of national jurisdiction over the continental shelves for the purpose of controlling ocean pollution as well as fishing rights and national security.

Much of the effort to control pollution has been on a metropolitan basis; for example, Mexico City has launched a major program to reduce pollution from motor vehicles and industry; provide improved treatment of sewage and garbage; restore river basins, parks, and forests; and improve the quality and conservation of water.

Individuals can have an impact on severe societal problems such as pollution. Lineberry speaks of Ray Grob, a shop owner, who began a campaign to clean up the river that runs through his town and eventually involved dozens of volunteers who concentrated on a seventy-mile stretch and developed parks and scenic areas. Because of these actions the State of Ohio legislated a scenic rivers law to encourage such efforts (pp. 193–94). Helen Caldicott, an Australian pediatrician who has become internationally known for her crusade against nuclear buildup, was single handedly instrumental in stopping the testing of nuclear bombs by France in the South Pacific with its consequent atmospheric pollution and fallout on Australia and nearby islands (Jennes 1981).

Local, regional, and national environmental interest groups provide information and are within easy reach of every United States educator and student. The point to be stressed in using their materials as teaching resources is that the problem is complex and provides opportunities to delve into its spectrum of legal, economic, health, ecological, political, and communications issues.

Nonrenewable Resources

Depletion of oil reserves, tropical forests and other forested land, fertile soil, and water resources are among the most alarming of the earth's diminishing natural resources. While most of the world, rich and poor, is quite cognizant of the tie between prices and oil shortages, developing countries without their own oil resources are hardest hit. *Global 2000* reported that they are spending $50 billion per year to buy oil—almost twice the total of assistance they receive for development. In extremely poor areas, people depend on firewood and animal waste for fuel and have picked clean thousands of acres with the result that native birds and animals, too, are gone. In such areas people with no other choice for subsistence but to plant crops on poor erodible soil, graze their stock on marginal land that turns to desert from overuse, and then burn dung for fuel that is needed for fertilizing and reconditioning the land. In the more developed countries, urban sprawl, concrete surfaces and highways, and poor agricultural management in some regions have consumed huge land masses.

Although data on water availability and quality are incomplete, it is evident that problems of water supply will soon be serious in many regions of the world. Population growth alone will cause demands for water to double. Concerted efforts are needed to manage water resources better and decrease contamination from industrial wastes or disease.

Reportedly, the world's forests are being depleted as much as 400,000,000 acres annually, an area larger than some of our smaller states. Most of the loss is in the tropical regions, where at the reported rate, 40 percent of the remaining forests may disappear by 2000. Medicinal products presently depend heavily on plants from tropical forests, and forest products of all kinds are essential. In America, the controversy over saving wilderness areas is well publicized (*Global 2000*, Henderson 1982, Shane, 1981).

The picture has a brighter side, however. When faced with critical needs, human intelligence and abilities usually come to the fore, and the problem of nonrenewable resources is no exception. Much has been done; much more is needed. The sharp increase in the price of oil since 1973 has provided money for expanding our energy base. Oil and other energy sources are being developed that were not previously affordable. Alaska's Prudhoe Bay, the biggest oil field ever discovered in the United States, was made operational. Heavy crude and tar sands are being developed in Canada, the Soviet Union, China, and a number of other countries. Oil shale deposits are being developed in Australia and the United States. New types of gas are being produced, and coal production has been stepped up.

Nations abroad are forging ahead with nuclear power programs. France intends to supply 55 percent of its electric power from nuclear plants by 1985, and other European countries are not far behind (Burchell and Listokin, 1982, pp. 366–76). Israel, already a leading developer of solar energy, is experimenting with an integrated approach that would combine wave, wind, and solar energy. Other interesting studies are in progress for extracting energy from the force of ocean waves and from the mix of fresh- and saltwater when rivers meet the sea (Goldin 1980). Wind power machines and uses of solar energy are becoming commonplace in the United States.

Herculean solutions to the water shortage problem are underway around the earth as described by Bruce Stokes (1983) and Bruce Ferguson (1983). As with other shortages, more needs to be done, but some governments are supporting the process, and human imagination is at work. Rivers are being diverted to bring water to arid lands in parts of India, China, and the Soviet Union. In the United States, the Army Corps of Engineers has plans for bringing more river water to the high plains area. Some cities of the United States import water from distant reservoirs but shunt away the volumes of fresh rainwater that fall on roofs, parking lots, and other hard surfaces. To capture some of this resource, Long Island's county governments now require developers to build recharge basins to catch storm water from streets, driveways, and downspouts and direct it through a sand aquifer. Waste of water used for sewage disposal is another problem under study. At University Park, Pennsylvania, sewage is treated, processed, and used as fertilizer, with recycled water passing through an aquifer on the way to the underground water level.

Energy conservation efforts have been noteworthy, and energy consumption in the United States has been reduced in recent years through attention to insulation of houses and other buildings, mass transportation, car pooling, more efficient traffic flow, bicycling, walking, and reducing household uses of energy. Teleconferencing and other uses of technology have reduced business travel. For curriculum planners, exceptional opportunities are available to inspire students with the realization of their potential in working toward solutions to this multifaceted and global area of concern. To quote Harold Shane (1981):

It is important for everyone to understand, at an early age as possible that the earth places limitations on us.... We can [not] manipulate our way to wealth merely by political and economic tinkering (p. 353).

Loss of Species

Closely related to the problems of nonrenewable resources and problems of pollution is the decrease in biological diversity because of the disappearance or threatened extinction of certain species. By the end of the twentieth century, some researchers believe that as much as 15 to 20 percent of all species on earth could be lost because of habitat degradation. Over one thousand birds and mammals are considered to be in jeopardy now, as well as twenty thousand to thirty thousand plants. Many of these are needed for scientific advancement in genetics and medicinal drugs *(Global 2000)*.

Rachel Carson (1962) alerted the public to a difficult and critical problem by pointing out the facts that link modern pesticides and other contaminants to all parts of the environment and insisted that there are no separate environmental problems. *Silent Spring* stirred immense controversy. It was stated that the use of pesticides had resulted in an alarming decline of bird and fish species. Manufacturers of pesticides and others said it was a choice between having food production or insect pests, while environmentalists crusaded for controls. The United States government has since restricted DDT, but other chemicals are being used. However, safer and more practical methods of insect control are being developed. One example is electronic signaling devices that discourage the mating process of destructive insects.

Frank Caras (1966) and other writers have emphasized the scope of human intervention in nature's ways for wildlife. In response, numerous local, regional, and national organizations have sprung up to protect endangered species. Illustrations abound of individuals or small groups who, using the processes of our democratic system of government, were able to save a particular species and provide an example for others. Lineberry (1973, p. 149-95) recounts the story of Buela Edmiston and a small group of supporters who saved the dwarf Tule elk of California through legislation and established their habitat as a national wildlife refuge. Part of the problem faced by the government is to maintain balance: prevent extinction of species but also prevent overpopulation of any type of wildlife that would have harmful effects on other plants or animals.

One program, taking place in the Amazon jungle in Brazil, illustrates careful development of tropical forest plant and animal life. The Amazon's mammals, reptiles, amphibians, fish, birds, insects, trees, herbs, swamps, climate, diseases, and human population are all under study to determine their interdependencies. The intent is not to make a vast park but to develop the jungle intelligently, according to Paul Raeburn (1983). Following a destructive project in which 250,000 acres of forest land were cleared for production of crops that eventually failed, Brazil's National Institute for Amazonian Research is trying to see that such failures do not occur again. Thought to be the last great wilderness on earth, the Amazon region is a storehouse of natural resources. Intelligent efforts are being made to assemble information so that the government can eventually make intelligent decisions.

Nuclear or Technological Disasters

The threat of nuclear war is particularly frightening. Also alarming are reports of the vulnerability of our technological infrastructure—computers, space laboratories, science fiction weaponry, hunter-killer satellites, and push-button worldwide destructive capability. Ways have been found to tap into computers illegally and cause them to malfunction or be misdirected. Other worries are that suitcase-sized nuclear bombs in the hands of terrorists may be used. An overriding public concern is the potential for a nuclear plant catastrophe—an explosion or melt down of the reactor core (Henderson 1982, Shane 1981).

To be prepared for the most "teachable moments" whenever anxieties emerge as well as for planned units of instruction, educators should be well-informed and ready to present objective facts about potential disasters. These should be presented, however, in the context of human capacity to anticipate and keep them from happening. At the international level, arms control talks among world powers and other nations are almost continuous. No nation wants a nuclear war let loose on the planet. Seen from space, our astronauts tell us, the earth has no boundaries between nations; thus, nuclear war would not be contained within a nation—the aggressor as well as the victim would suffer. Because the problems of nuclear attack are global, the solutions must be as well. If dialogue can continue and become even more sincere, there is hope for humanity.

In regard to nuclear reactors, Burchell and Listokin (1982) point out that an explosion, such as with a nuclear bomb, is not possible. The reactor's fuel is a material containing only 3 to 5 percent fissionable material, whereas a nuclear bomb requires a solid mass of nearly pure U-235 or plutonium. A melt down is possible, but in over 200 reactor years of commercial operation, no reactor core has melted down. The widely publicized Three Mile Island accident was not a melt down in the true sense but rather a loss of cooling water on the fuel for a period. The damage to the plant was serious, but a Presidential Commission has concluded that most of the radioactivity was contained, and that the actual release will have a negligible effect on the physical health of persons in the area. The chances of a melt down disaster are very small; however, accidents can happen (p. 371).

Social responsibility for technology sometimes means *not* applying one's skills and knowledge. For example, if there are students who are tapping into computers illegally in the first flush of a feeling of power as they conquer the computer's mysteries, that is most reprehensible. No student should be allowed to approach a major computer without first realizing his or her responsibility to society, much as a young driver would never be irresponsibly turned loose at the wheel to speed dangerously along a busy highway.

Political and Economic Turbulence

On the world scene, stress between the political ideologies of the superpowers and the demands of the Third World to share in a better life have spawned many varied confrontations. A major problem is the great disparity between rich and poor countries. Poverty generates unrest and unrest generates disturbances, some violent in nature. Within the United States turbulence often stems from governmental decisions that many citizens consider to be erroneous, confused, or protective of self-serving interests. The declining industrial supremacy of the United States and the ensuing battles of tariffs and quotas has had worldwide effects as have the interrelated problems of inflation, mounting deficits, and unemployment. Other turbulences relate to values in collision. Such terms as human rights, democracy, freedom, and ownership mean different things to different people. Viewpoints also differ on growth versus conservation.

The responsibility rests with all of us to try understanding the forces producing disagreements and the resistances to change. Clues can be found in the relationships between government and markets, and ecology, knowledge, technology, and sustainable growth. Coping with these problems will test human capacity for innovation; they are symptomatic of the difficulty of accommodating the world's economic and political systems to declining industrialism.

As the world's people move from an industrial society to a postindustrial society, they will enter what Herman Kahn (1982) calls the "great transition." Jonas Salk (1973) and others have described the transition and predicted that it will be a lengthy period, possibly more than a century and, at least for a time, will be characterized by fits and starts, turmoil, thrusts forward, regressions. For several years now signs of the transition have appeared. Salk emphasizes "survival of the wisest," that is, the wisdom needed to recognize trends, commit ourselves to promoting progress, and help others understand the transition. A positive outlook and belief that a better future is possible are much more likely to bring it about. Otherwise, malaise brought on by feelings of futility will undermine morale. The great transition must be disseminated, taught, understood, and believed, says Kahn.

Industrialism is usually expressed in material terms and expectations that well-being will increase with each succeeding generation. It is a frontier ethic—there are always more resources to be found and used. Postindustrialism emphasizes knowledge as the primary resource and thus opens new options for occupations, innovations—more cultural and artistic activities, more interaction and dialogue. Herman Kahn predicts that the concept of superpowers will erode; power will become divided among more nations or alliances, thus reducing the threat of nuclear confrontations as conflict would be too disadvantageous to all. As for the gap between rich and poor nations, Kahn has pointed out that in reality the gap has spurred economic growth in the developing world, and the gap is decreasing, although slowly.

New technologies can solve problems as well as cause them, and the challenge found in the great transition is to move from a problem-prone society to a problem-controlled society, to identify problems early and devise solutions before they get out of control. This calls for efforts by individuals, groups, and society as a whole to deal with difficulties through innovation and design.

Signs of the great transition that are already evident are young people seeking new occupations that are often far different from those modeled by their parents, new options for women and minorities, new freedom in lifestyles, new technologies. Maurice Strong (1982) has identified illustrative characteristics of the postindustrial era: increased productivity in the fields of energy and technology, emphasis on conservation, more cooperation within societies and internationally, a new economics to avoid problems such as inflation, new concepts of management to meet the complex demands of societal decision making, a new global system of governance to replace the nation-state orientation of the United Nations and deal with global issues, more people participating in all processes of governance, and more regard for the intellectual, cultural, philosophical, and spiritual dimensions of human experience. More attention to equity and security will be a priority.

The curriculum should provide circumstances so that students can explore the concepts of industrialism and postindustrialism in ways leading to problem solving rather than problem avoidance or problem proneness.

IMPLICATIONS OF FORECASTS AND TRENDS FOR
CURRICULUM PLANNING

Predictions for the future may vary from forecaster to forecaster in respect to emphasis on given concerns, but general agreement exists on the direction of recognizable trends, and these have implications for curriculum planning. Capturing significant trends from the jumble of forecasts put forward by various analysts is a first step. Shane (1981) and Shane and Tabler (1981) have identified several overarching concepts that seem essential for the content of the curriculum. In the social sciences, they say, the curriculum must be more world oriented; it should include the various interpretations of democracy around the world but also the political beliefs of authoritarian governments. A global consciousness is needed to acknowledge the problems of access to minerals, food, and other products by the various peoples of the world. The concepts of social and economic justice should be understood by all students.

Anthropologists recommend that young students develop appreciation for diverse cultures, cultural pluralism, and cultural compromise. Attitudes and modes of thought are learned behaviors, and new, more humane behaviors can be developed. The importance of knowing at least one language other than one's mother tongue for cross-cultural communication is advocated. The need to appreciate the holistic quality of the basic laws of nature is emphasized by Shane. Many important properties of matter are consequences of the way in which the parts are arranged in relation to one another. Thus, grave consequences could result from carelessness in experimenting with natural fluxes of energy, which could alter climate, for example.

Learners need to understand trade-offs: to get something of value one must give something of value. For example, if we want more automobiles, we will have more pollution. This is the reality of cause and effect. Students can learn to understand that people have various options open to them throughout their lives, and each option has its inherent consequences. They can appreciate and learn from specific examples of cause and effect and generalize this knowledge to understand new situations. Until recently, students were not exposed to many of the connections and interrelationships of the human world and the natural world. Complex concepts can be introduced in some form to students of all ages, Shane reminds us. Examples include conservation (voluntary versus enforced), the unity and interdependence of nature, ecocide, entropy, systems analysis, population studies, global interdependence, and the overall concept of alternative futures.

John Naisbitt's *Megatrends* (1982) is another example of an analysis of social, political, economic, and technological movements. Each trend mentioned has significance for the future of education. We have used Naisbitt's ten megatrends as an organizer and have suggested implications for curriculum planning related to each.

MEGATRENDS...............EDUCATIONAL IMPLICATIONS

1. *Shift from an industrial to an information society.* The majority of all workers will soon be in an information occupation and involved with computers in some way.

1. It is more than ever urgent for students to master fundamentals: learn to read and write well, know English, computer language, science, mathematics, gain the analytic skills and abilities needed for constantly adapting to new knowledge and using knowledge in new combinations.

2. *Shift from forced technology to high-tech, high-touch.* The material wonders of technology must be balanced with the need to develop human potential.

2. Technology must not crowd out opportunities for personal development, group activities, the human touch. Quality circles are expressions of the need for human interaction and shared responsibilities.

3. *Shift from a national economy to a world economy.* The jet airplane and the communications satellite have transformed the planet into a global economic village.

3. Global education is necessary: learning about world trade, shifting priorities for production, world economics, global interdependence. Students should be able to realize that world trade may be the vehicle for world peace.

4. *Shift from short-term to long-term planning.* Slowly, America's business leaders are realizing the necessity for long-term strategic planning.

4. Education should help students develop vision and planning skills so that major problems such as waste of nonrenewable resources and damage to the environment and the problems of an economy based on declining industries could be circumvented before they reach the crisis stage.

5. *Shift from centralization to decentralization.* Top-down ap-

5. Curriculum leaders can capitalize on the trend to decentraliza-

proaches are out of tune with the times. State and local centers are gaining political power.

6. *Shift from institutional to self-help.* The Great Depression of the 1930s taught people that the government or other institutions would solve our problems. Now there is a reclamation of the American spirit of self-reliance.

7. *Shift from representative democracy to participatory democracy.* People whose lives are affected by a decision are more and more demanding to be a part of arriving at the decision.

8. *Shift from hierarchies to networking.* As more and more technology was introduced into society, the impersonal nature of pyramid hierarchies annoyed people more and more; also, society's problems were not being solved—and that was the beginning of networking.

9. *Shift in restructuring of population, wealth, and economic activity from north-northeast to south-southwest.* Former urban symbols of progress are declining; others are rising.

10. *Shift from either-or to multiple options.* In this nation of diversity, people have far more choices than ever before: new life styles, new options as women and men, new art forms, religions, and so on.

tion by tackling problems and creating change at the local and state levels.

6. To attain excellence in public schools, leaders should make an all-out effort to involve parents in as many phases of their children's education as possible. Parent activism, public alternative schools, small private schools, and home education may increase further in the spirit of self-help.

7. Effectiveness in educational leadership will be contingent on developing the skills of facilitating people's involvement in decision making.

8. The lesson for educators is that networks are people talking to each other, sharing ideas, information, and resources. Networking can foster self-reliance, improve productivity, and enhance work life. Rewards come from empowering oneself and others.

9. The shifting loci of growth and employment imply that education for the future should help people learn how to adapt, how to acquire new skills as conditions change.

10. School leaders will recognize that the basic unit of society is no longer the family but the individual; that ethnic and cultural diversity is to be celebrated in the schools.

Policy makers move slowly. As Naisbitt comments, "We are living in the time between eras. It is as though we have bracketed off the present from the past and the future, for we are neither here nor there. We have not quite left behind the America of the past.... but we have not embraced the future either" (p. 249). Meanwhile, social institutions, including schools, must try to move ahead and anticipate the future. Diane Ravitch (1983) notes that education by its very nature is a forecast, for in deciding what children or adults should learn now, we are making a statement about the future. Not only changing concepts about curriculum and new understandings of instruction but also new uses of technology have essential places in schools of the future.

TECHNOLOGY IN SCHOOLS

Two current and contrasting positions must be considered in predicting the effects of technology on schools by the year 2000, says Neil Postman (1983). One is that of the "technological determinist," who foresees the school of the future deriving its curriculum from the demands of computers, television, satellites, and other technologies; such schools endeavor to prepare students for the ways in which technologies will use them. Postman's perception of the opposite extreme is the position of the "technological somnambulist," who believes that the new technologies are vastly overrated and is entirely occupied with perfecting old practices and reviewing topics that deal with the technical aspects of teaching.

While either extreme is ridiculous, says Postman, neither is entirely devoid of merit. It is conceivable that some students will learn more effectively through technological inventions than they could from print and talk. On the other hand, the skills and values of literacy *are* important; they are the most enduring function of the schools, and some students will learn best through traditional procedures. The place of technology in the schools of the future will be a consequence of what educators decide now in response to the problems ahead and their understandings of how people can use technology, not how technology uses people.

Television

Television in the classroom, used as a passive medium, does not encourage the development of analytical abilities. It requires few skills, and its "curriculum" is often fragmented. More of the same is not advocated for schools. Advances in technology encourage ways in which instructional television can be used as an interactive medium, supplementary to other ways of learning. Teletext systems, videodiscs, and combinations with microcomputers or mainframe computers are being used for teaching, testing, and reinforcement or remediation, particularly in developing new skills. Students can also revise, rearrange, and annotate conceptual material using built-in editing systems. The videodisc can provide the student with individualized and interactive access to learning possibilities that would not be otherwise available.

Innovations in the uses of television are presently more common outside of schools. Television has been used to monitor takeoffs and landings at airports, monitor work on assembly lines, and monitor human behavior in various situations. Television can monitor traffic signals and change the timing when needed to keep traffic flowing. John Jenkins (1982) describes these and other examples. A two-way cable system called Qube is being tested in several locations including Columbus, Ohio. By means of a response system linked to a main computer, Qube viewers may participate in group discussions of selected programs and provide feedback to the program originators and other viewers. Program choices and conversations are stored and may be recalled. A wide variety of programs makes individual selection possible.

"Learn/Alaska" is a different program that illustrates school uses of new forms of television. The Alaska State Department of Education and the University of Alaska have collaborated to build a statewide television network and program. A satellite, SATCOM II, 23,000 miles above the earth, receives programs from four stations in Fairbanks, Juneau, Anchorage, and Kotzebue. The signals are rebroadcast to dish antennas where they are changed to television broadcast frequencies and transmitted into schools and homes (Neuman and Ball 1982). Through a statewide instructional television channel, materials are distributed to all parts of the state almost instantaneously and with relatively little cost. Lessons by specialized teachers can be beamed to the remotest areas where the school population is so sparse it would be impossible to provide the program with teachers-in-residence. The far-flung state educational system is interconnected by means of this system, which makes courses, programs, and unusual resources available for students of all ages, including college credit work. Statewide conferences and committee meetings are held by use of electronic bridging that can connect as many as eighty lines.

Telematique is a word coined by Arthur Shostak (1981) to embrace the synergistic linkage of communications and computer capabilities. He foresees student explorations of advanced capabilities that will make the resources of the world's libraries and museums available. Interaction with superstar teachers, students, and experts at distant locations will be possible. Bookless libraries (teletexts), teleconferences, electronic language translators, and campusless and professorless schools and universities are other potentials, and prototypes are already available.

Figure 17 illustrates the campusless university in operation at

Northwestern University, Chicago. Learning has moved out of the classroom and into the home and the field by means of computers, television circuits, action research, independent study and *ORACLE*. Students report to centers known as ORACLEs for testing and feedback. An ORACLE is a part of the computer-based learning utility; it is a computer program that connects students' data terminals to each other and to the teacher through the computer. Robert Johansen and James Schuyler have described this and similar examples of telematique in detail (1975).

The ORACLE network is frequently used for committee planning, board meetings, and various types of conferences that involve persons at great distances from one another. The Learn/Alaska network has similar capability.

Figure 17. A Computer-Based TV College

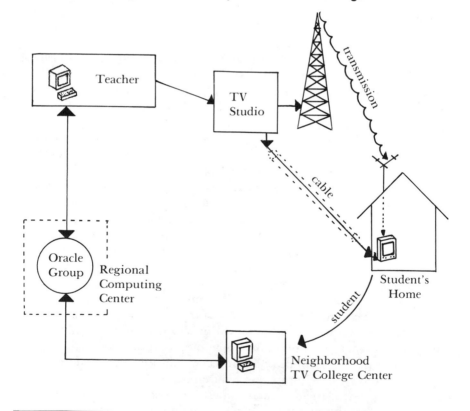

From Robert Johansen and James A. Schuyler, "Computerized Conferencing in an Educational System: A Short-Range Scenario," in *The Delphi Method*, ed. Harold A. Linstone and Murray Linoff (Reading, Mass.: Addison-Wesley, 1975), p. 556.

Computers

Advances in combined technologies, as illustrated, are made possible by advances in computers. Just ahead are fifth generation computers, knowledge-manipulating machines rather than number-manipulators. Sometimes called "smart computers," they are many times faster than before. Each of the first four generations—those based on the vacuum tube, the transister, the early integrated circuit, and the current densely packed computer chips—advanced computing power by hundreds of thousands of times. Fifth generation computers will concentrate on arrays of hundreds of chips, each computing independently, to multiply the speed of the machine. The machines will gear their fundamental way of operating to knowledge processing that uses language and other symbols. New expert systems are expected to be generated. A medical example would be expert professional advice to doctors on diagnosis in specialized cases; in chemistry, analysis of the molecular structure of substances.

Polestar of a new era for computers is the chip, a complex of electronic switches controlling electric current and fabricated on a fleck of silicon no larger than an infant's thumbnail. The chip has advanced technological capacity in quantum jumps. Allen Boraiko (1982) describes it this way (p. 421):

The chip would be extraordinary enough if it were only low-cost, compact electronics, but its ability to embody logic and memory also gives it the essence of human intellect. So, like the mind, the chip has virtually infinite application—and much the same potential to alter life fundamentally. A microprocessor, for example, can endow a machine with decision-making ability, memory for instructions, and self-adjusting controls.... Robots (made possible by the chip) that see, feel, and make simple judgments are entering factories, where less capable robots have been "reproducing" themselves for some time.

Will students stimulated by computers mature into thinkers and doers who will find effective solutions to global problems of poverty, hunger, and war? Will schools meet the challenge of computers?

Schools and Computers

There are three stages of technological development according to John Naisbitt (1982, p. 27). The first stage is following the line of least resistance, or nonthreatening innovations. Examples are video games for entertainment or robots for dangerous tasks. The second stage is using technology to improve previous technologies. Here we have an example from computers used in schools today. Many schools are using these electronic devices for computer-assisted instruction, a replacement for workbooks and flash cards previously used to drill children on facts.

Another example is computer-managed instruction, a replacement for former types of record keeping by teachers. The third stage is new directions, uses, and creations that grow out of the technology itself. This is rare in schools although some are introducing students to original programming. A review of the status of computers in schools is available from the Association for Supervision and Curriculum Development (Grady and Gawronski 1983).

Students are ready to learn more about the electronic age if signs of the times are an accurate indication. Interest has been high in electronic toys and video games. Students have tried the microcomputer, investigated the electronic library, exhausted the possibilities of television in the home. They are familiar with phone-answering devices, photocopiers, computerized checkout counters at the supermarket. Students are knowledgeable about chips and robots. They understand the processes of graphic animation. Students are ready to pursue advanced technology, but schools lack equipment and teacher training. With new interest by business and industry in schooling, perhaps corporations will make their facilities available to students and teachers as off-campus classrooms.

SCENARIOS IN CURRICULUM DEVELOPMENT

Scenarios can be productive vehicles for using creativity in strategic planning for education. Christopher Dede and Dwight Allen (1981) see scenario building as a tool with vital potential for approaching the complex tasks of future-oriented curriculum development. Scenario building can lead to understanding interconnections among economic concerns, national security, global problems, environmental depletions, and resources. Appreciating the holistic nature of the world today can lead to positive action.

Scenario building originated in the field of futures research, and it is a way to mesh envisioned and practical concerns into a planning process. The purpose is to create proposed policies for an organizational unit. The technique has been widely applied by scientists and social scientists in proposing government policies to meet problems of dwindling resources, expanding population, and others. A scenario is more than just a set of forecasts about some future time. It is a picture of an internally consistent situation. As John Sutherland has noted (1975), a succession of Delphi processes (described in Chapter Six) would provide for feedback, conferencing, and getting more information. Emphasis is on similarities and points where different views mesh so that consensus can lead to proposals for policies and action. These proposals in turn support a cluster of possibilities for positive action. Roy Amara (1975) recommends that a variety of methods be used for seeking background information: interviews, conferences, polls, questionnaires, simulations and other modeling techniques, and various computerized resources, including library searches.

Several steps take place in using scenario building as a tool in curriculum development. First, the participants would imagine as many different alternatives for future curriculum and instruction as possible. They would take into account potential community developments: population movements, employment, industry, business, the educational opportunities needed, the nature of city government, the attitude and educational level of parents and other citizens, resources available, transportation, and other pertinent factors about the community. Next, input would be sought from other faculty members, school board members, community experts, consultants, and others so that all potential problems and issues could be identified.

Assessing the future needs of the community would be the third step. A clear assessment of available and potential resources would be needed, as well as types of action that would be required by governmental or political infuences to fulfill these needs. Local data could then be appraised and organized in light of trends. Careful study and observation of future economic, social, political, and national trends must be fed into the scenario to make corrections in its course and to prepare a meaningful document as a plan for action. A part of the work would be to educate citizens about alternative futures.

Scenarios are just one way for curriculum developers to become effective problem solvers, able to face unfamiliar situations and unforeseen conditions. Learning to assess values on which choices will be made is an essential ingredient of curriculum planning for the future. The future of curriculum development and of the educational enterprise promises to be exciting and challenging.

REFERENCES

Amara, Roy. *Some Methods of Future Research,* Menlo Park, Calif: Institute for the Future, 1975.

American Association of School Administrators. *AASA Convention Reporter.* Arlington, Va.: American Association of School Administrators, 1982.

Boraiko, Allen A. "The Chip." *National Geographic* 162 (October 1982): 421–56.

Burchell, Robert W., and Listokin, David. *Energy and Land Use.* Piscataway, N.J.: Center for Urban Policy Research of Rutgers, the State University of New Jersey, 1982.

Caras, Roger A. *Last Chance on Earth: A Requiem for Wildlife.* Philadelphia: Chilton Books, 1966.

Carson, Rachel L. *Silent Spring*. Boston: Houghton Mifflin, 1962.

Commoner, Barry. *The Closing Circle*. New York: Albert A. Knopf, 1972.

Council on Environmental Quality and the Department of State. *Global Future: Time to Act*. Report to the President on Global Resources, Environment, and Population. Washington, D.C.: U.S. Government Printing Office, 1981.

Council on Environmental Quality and Department of State. *The Global 2000 Report to the President: Entering the Twenty-First Century*. Three volumes. Washington, D.C.: U.S. Government Printing Office, 1980.

Dede, Christopher, and Allen, Dwight. "Education in the 21st Century: Scenarios as a Tool for Strategic Planning." *Phi Delta Kappan* 62 (January 1981): 262–366.

Ferguson, Bruce K. "Whither Water?" *The Futurist* 17 (April 1983): 29–36.

Glines, Don. *Annotated Bibliographies on Societal and Educational Futures, Educational Alternatives and Change*, and *Resources: Educational and Societal*. Also Non-Annotated Bibliographies. Sacramento: California State Department of Education, 1983.

Global Futures Network, Inc., 26 McGill Street, Toronto, Canada M5B 1H2.

Goldin, Augusta. *Oceans of Energy*. New York: Harcourt Brace Jovanovich, 1980.

Grady, M. Tim, and Gawronski, Jane D., eds. *Computers in Curriculum and Instruction*. Alexandria, Va.: Association for Supervision and Curriculum Development, 1983.

Guillain, Robert. *When China Wakes*. New York: Walker and Co., 1966.

Halperin, Samuel. "The Future of Educational Governance: Prospects and Possibilities." In *How Can the U.S. Elementary and Secondary Education Systems Best Be Improved?* Compiled by the Congressional Research Service, Library of Congress. Washington, D.C.: U.S. Government Printing Office, 1981, pp. 75–84.

Harmon, George H. "Micrographics: Return of the 25-Cent Book?" *The Futurist* 15 (October 1981): 61–62.

Henderson, Carter. "The Darkening Outlook for the U.S. Economy." *The Futurist* 16 (February 1982): 23–27.

Jacobsen, Judith. *Promoting Population Stabilization: Incentives for Small Families*. Washington, D.C.: Worldwatch Institute, 1983.

Jenkins, John A. "The Conscience of Cable." *TWA Ambassador* 15 (March 1982): 51–54, 56, 59, 62.

Jennes, Gail. "Sequel." *People* 16 (November 30, 1981): 89–93.

Johansen, Robert, and Schuyler, James A. "Computerized Conferencing in an Educational System: A Short-Range Scenario." In *The Delphi Method*, edited by Harold A. Linstone and Murray Turoff, pp. 550–62. Reading, Mass.: Addison-Wesley, 1975.

Kahn, Herman. "The Great Transition." In *Optimistic Outlooks*, edited by Frank Feather and Rashmi Mayur, pp. 57–70. Toronto, Canada: Global Futures Network, 1982.

Lineberry, William P., ed. *Priorities for Survival*. New York: H.W. Wilson Co., 1973.

Naisbitt, John. *Megatrends: Ten New Directions Transforming Our Lives*. New York: Warner Books, Inc., 1982.

Neuman, Robert, and Ball, John. "The Space Age Comes to Alaska's Classrooms." *Electronic Learning* 1 (January/February, 1982): 53–54, 66.

Postman, Neil. "Engaging Students in the Great Conversation." *Phi Delta Kappan* 64 (January 1983): 310–16.

Raeburn, Paul. "The Amazon: Key to the Future of the Planet?" *Boulder Camera, Focus* 93 (July 3, 1983): 15–16.

Ravitch, Diane. "On Thinking about the Future." *Phi Delta Kappan* 64 (January 1983): 317–20.

Salk, Jonas. *The Survival of the Wisest*. New York: Harper and Row, 1973.

Shabecoff, Philip. "EPA Not Expected to Make Big Effort to Curtail Acid Rain." *Boulder Camera* 93 (July 6, 1983): 5A.

Shane, Harold G. "A Curriculum for the New Century." *Phi Delta Kappan* 62 (January 1981): 351–56.

Shane, Harold G. and Tabler, M. Bernadine. *Education for a New Millennium.* Bloomington: The Phi Delta Kappa Educational Foundation, 1981.

Shostak, Arthur B. "The Coming Systems Break: Technology and Schools of the Future." *Phi Delta Kappan* 62 (January 1981): 356–59.

Stokes, Bruce. "Water Shortages." *The Futurist* 17 (April 1983): 37–47.

Strong, Maurice F. "Where Do We Go from Here?" In *Optimistic Outlooks,* edited by Frank Feather and Rasmi Mayur, pp. 175–85. Toronto, Canada: Global Futures Network, 1982.

Sutherland, John W. "Architecting the Future: A Delphi-Based Paradigm for Normative System-Building." In *The Delphi Method,* edited by Harold A. Linstone and Murray Turoff, pp. 463–86. Reading, Mass.: Addison-Wesley, 1975.

Toffler, Alvin. *The Third Wave.* New York: Bantam Books, 1980.

Whelan, Eugene. "Putting Food on Tomorrow's Table." In *Optimistic Outlooks,* edited by Frank Feather and Rashmi Mayur, pp. 31–37. Toronto, Canada: Global Futures Network, 1982.

Winthrop, Henry. "The World We Have Wrought." *Educational Forum* 38 (January 1974): 163–70.

ADDITIONAL READINGS

Apple, Michael W. "Curriculum in the Year 2000: Tensions and Possibilities." *Phi Delta Kappan* 64 (January 1983): 321–26.

Botkin, James, et al. *No Limits to Learning: Bridging the Human Gap.* Club of Rome Report. Elmsford, New York: Pergamon Press, 1979.

Brown, Lester R. *Population Policies for a New Economic Era.* Washington, D.C.: Worldwatch Institute, 1983.

Combs, Arthur W. "What the Future Demands of Education." *Phi Delta Kappan.* 62 (January 1981): 369–72.

Cornish, Edward. "The Coming of an Information Society." *The Futurist* 15 (April 1981): 14–21.

Didsbury, Howard. *Student Handbook for the Study of the Future.* Washington, D.C.: World Future Society, 1981.

Duderstadt, James J., and Kikuchi, Chihiro. *Nuclear Power: Technology on Trial.* Ann Arbor: University of Michigan Press, 1979.

Feather, Frank, ed. *Through the 80s: Thinking Globally, Acting Locally.* Washington, D.C.: World Future Society, 1980.

Friedman, Wolfgang. *The Future of the Oceans.* New York: George Braziller, 1971.

Fuller, Buckminster. *Critical Path.* New York: Saint Martin's Press, 1981.

Glines, Don. "From Schooling to Learning: Rethinking Preschool Through University Education." *National Association of Secondary School Principals Bulletin* 66 (January 1982): 85–93.

Graham, Frank. *Since Silent Spring.* Boston: Houghton Mifflin, 1970.

Hamrin, Robert D. "The Information Economy: Exploiting an Infinite Resource." *The Futurist* 15 (August 1981): 25–30.

Heilbroner, Robert L. *An Inquiry into the Human Prospect.* New York: W.W. Norton and Co., 1974.

Malitor, Graham T.T. "The Information Society: The Path to Post-Industrial Growth." *The Futurist* 15 (April 1981): 23–37.

Martin, Daniel. *Three Mile Island: Prologue or Epilogue?* Cambridge, Mass.: Ballinger Publishing Co., 1980.

Martin, Marie. *Films on the Future.* Washington, D.C.: World Future Society, 1977.

National School Boards Association. *The Global Connection.* NSBA report. Washington, D.C.: National School Boards Association, 1981.

Ornstein, Allan C. "Change and Innovation in Curriculum." *Journal of Research and Development in Education* 15 (Winter 1982): 27–33.

Rubin, Louis. *Educational Reform for a Changing Society Anticipating Tomorrow's School.* Boston: Allyn and Bacon, 1978.

Theobald, Robert. *Beyond Despair.* Washington, D.C.: New Republic Book Company, 1976.

Tydeman, John. "Videotex: Ushering in the Electronic Household." *The Futurist* 16 (February 1982): 54–62.

Author Index

Subject Index

for college admission, 76-77
for evaluation, 290-293
for high school graduation, 71, 72, 77, 83
State departments of education, 53, 76, 81, 185, 196, 305, 319
State legislatures, 70-72
Strategies
  for change in curriculum development, 51-54
  for consensus, 61
  for implementation, 248-254
Students
  apathy, activism, 18-19, 21, 80, 227
  behavior, 23, 47-48
  discipline of, 3, 185
  elite graduates, 220
  expectations of, 46-48
  illiterate, 4, 79, 208
  needs, self-identified, 198
  new roles for, 82
  participation in planning, 80, 83, 87-88
  philosophy of life, 158
  responsibility, 313
  rights, 87
  satisfaction index of, 81
  work habits, study skills, 158
Study of High Schools, 82
Study of Schooling, 79-82, 147-148
Subject matter (see Academic areas; Curriculum content)
Superintendents, 40, 60-61, 156, 173, 240, 252 (see also Administrators; Leaders; Principals)
Supervision, 44, 228, 255-259
  administration of, 255
  clinical, 255-257
  and evaluation of staff, 258
  problem situations in, 257
Supreme Court (see Court decisions)

Task Force of the Twentieth Century Fund, 78-79, 93
Taxonomy, 99, 100, 122

Teachers
  career ladder, 82
  collective bargaining, 78
  expectations for, 46-48
  involvement in reforms, 68, 75-83, 240
  levels of maturity, 243-244
  needs, self-identified, 199-200
  preparation of, 75-77 (see also In-service)
  roles, responsibilities, 86-87, 156, 178, 245, 255, 264 (see also Powers and roles)
Teacher talk, 80
Technological
  change, problems, progress, 300-302, 312-313
  conception of curriculum, 4, 101
Technology
  in homes, 300-303
  and the humanities, 106
  and mathematics, 217
  in schools, 20, 83, 300-301, 318-323
  and science, 222
Telematique, 300, 319-320
Television, 300, 318-320
Testing, tests, 2, 4-5, 10, 70-72, 75-76, 81, 184, 208, 266, 274-275, 278-279
Textbooks, 74-75, 80, 208, 216, 221, 224-225, 244, 318-319 (see also Curriculum materials)
Theoretical base, 95, 98
Theory development, 118-123
Theory X, Y, Z, 37-38
Thinking skills (see Cognitive processes; Intelligence)
Time in school, on task, 77, 79, 213, 269-270
Traditionalists, 101
Transition, the great, 305, 313-314
Tuition tax credits, vouchers, 69, 78
Turbulence, economic, political, 313-314

Understanding others, 150, 153
United States Office of Education, 15, 26